DOING HEALING

*How to Minister God's Kingdom
in the Power of the Spirit*

ALEXANDER F. VENTER

ALEXANDER F. VENTER – KINGDOM TREASURES
Website: www.alexanderventer.com
Email: Shop@alexanderventer.com

Text © Alexander Venter 2009

First edition 2009, Vineyard Internatioal Publishing, South Africa
Second impression 2009, Vineyard Internatioal Publishing, South Africa
Third impression 2012, Vineyard Internatioal Publishing, South Africa
Fourth Impression 2017, Kingdom Treasures, South Africa

The Scripture quotations in this publication are taken from:

NIV – THE HOLY BIBLE, NEW INTERNATIONAL VERSION
© 1973, 1978, 1984, International Bible Society. Used by permission.
King James Version (KJV) © 1984, 1977 by Thomas Nelson, Inc.
The New Living Translation (NLT) © 1996, Tyndale Publishing House.
Used by permission.
New American Standard Bible (NASB) © The Lockman Foundation
1960, 1962, 1963, 1971, 1973. Creation House, Inc. Carol Stream, Illinois.
The Message: The Bible in Contemporary Language © 2002 Eugene H.
Peterson. All rights reserved.
New Revised Standard Version (NRSV) © 1989, Division of Christian
Education of the National Council of the Churches of Christ in the USA,
Zondervan Publishing House, Grand Rapids. Used by permission.

All rights reserved. No part of this publication may be reproduced, stored
in a retrieval system, or transmitted, in any form or by any means, electronic,
mechanical, photocopying, recording or otherwise, without the prior
permission of the author.

Cover by Mercy Arts Studios, USA

ISBN-13: 978-1983601255

ISBN-10: 198360125X

Dedication and Acknowledgements

Over the years God has used people to contribute to my own healing and teach me how to work with God to bring healing to others. A few have been formative in this regard: John Wimber (and his colleagues), Derek Prince, Francis McNutt and Leanne Payne.

I dedicate this book to them, but also to all those followers of Jesus, both individual Christians and local churches, who practise, and are seeking to practise, a ministry of healing.

Thanks to my family for their love and patience in putting up with my long hours at the computer – and to Gilli for your diligent help with the manuscript.

Thanks to The Field community and Valley Vineyard for giving me the time to write.

I owe Bruce, Vic and Robin, and especially Derek, Stephan, Rhonda and Kim (the Vineyard International Publishing team) a debt of gratitude. All of you made helpful suggestions and corrections to the manuscript, although I take final responsibility for what is written!

Contents

Preface	6

Part One: Introduction
1	Story: *My journey of healing*	16
2	Worldview: *The power of how we see things*	34
3	Definitions: *A position on disease and healing*	51

Part Two: Theology
4	Theology: *Understanding the kingdom of God*	66
5	Modelling 1: *Receiving and ministering the kingdom*	83
6	Modelling 2: *The secret of success in Jesus' ministry*	99
7	Modelling 3: *Principles and patterns in Jesus' healing ministry*	114
8	Impartation: *Transfer of kingdom ministry to the church*	125
9	Continuation: *Healing ministry in the early church and church history*	137

Part Three: Praxis
10	Practitioners 1: *The key factors in the practice of healing*	157
11	Practitioners 2: *Working with the Spirit in the grace gifts*	173
12	Practitioners 3: *Spirit intimacy, sensitivity and exercises*	187
13	Models: *Healing models and a five-step ordinary believer model*	201
14	Method 1: *Ministering healing to the spirit*	215
15	Method 2: *Ministering healing to the emotions*	227
16	Method 3: *Ministering deliverance from demonisation*	241
17	Method 4: *Ministering healing to the body*	257
18	Method 5: *Ministering healing to relationships*	269
19	Method 6: *Ministering healing to the dying and the dead*	282
20	Discernment: *Evaluating spiritual phenomena in healing*	298
21	Commission: *The church's healing ministry: "Go …"*	314

Appendices
Appendix 1: *Understanding Gnosticism*	323
Appendix 2: *Healing in the Old Testament*	331
Appendix 3: *The healing ministry of Jesus: Overview*	333
Appendix 4: *The book of Acts: Signs and wonders and the results*	337

Bibliography 341

Preface

*"If you are willing, you can heal me."
Filled with compassion, Jesus reached out his hand and touched
the man. "I am willing, be healed!" Immediately the leprosy
left him and he was healed.*
– Mark 1:40–42 RAP[1]

This book is written for those who need healing; for those who want to understand the biblical approach to healing and, more importantly, for those who practise – or want to learn how to practise – a ministry of healing.

The man in the above quote suffered from a skin disease, probably putrefying leprosy. It had alienated and destroyed him in a physical, social, emotional and spiritual sense. He was cut off from God and people, considered "ceremonially" unclean. Desperate, he came to Rabbi Jesus, knelt down and begged Jesus to heal him. He believed Jesus *could* heal him, but he was not sure if Jesus was *willing*. The Rabbi did something rare and radical. Going against the religious conventions and social mindset, he defied the prohibitions that Torah laid on the leprous and the community (Leviticus 13–14). For no reason, other than mercy, Jesus reached out his hand and tenderly touched him: "Yes, I am willing, be healed." And he was immediately healed!

You may not have leprosy, or the modern equivalent (HIV/AIDS),[2]

---

[1] Revised Alexander Paraphrase. See explanation on page 13.
[2] HIV is an acronym for human immunodeficiency virus; AIDS is acquired immune deficiency syndrome. Presently it is medically incurable and carries a social stigma similar to leprosy in Jesus' day – besides other comparisons with leprosy, which should only be made with sensitivity, as Philip Yancey and Paul Brand have shown in *The Gift*

but the need for healing is equally real. If Jesus came to reveal who God is (we believe this as Christians), we can confidently say: God is both able and willing to heal us of our diseases, *because he is a God of compassion and mercy.*

How desperate are we for healing? How in touch are we with our needs, our brokenness and pain? The outward physical and social sufferings we endure are the tip of the iceberg of the greater inner pain – the spiritual and psycho-emotional dead weight we all carry. We go through life with a crippled inner reality, unseen and unattended. Yet it wreaks havoc in our own lives and on those around us. Our suffering can be very evil and destructive. Yet God comes to us in it, working for our healing and wholeness.

The purpose of this book is to help you take responsibility for your own brokenness, to show how you can receive healing through Jesus Christ. A greater joy is learning to work with God in bringing healing to others. God is willing to heal, but he works through us as he did with Jesus. We can heal others in Jesus' name, but are we *willing*? The real reward is not only being used by God and seeing others healed, but also equipping others to minister healing effectively.

My vision is precisely that: to equip you to practise Jesus' ministry of healing, so that you in turn can train others to do the same. It was Jesus' vision: "I am telling you the truth, if you trust me, the miracles that I have been doing, you too will do; and you'll do even greater miracles than these, because I am going to my Father – thereby sending my Spirit to enable you" (John 14:12 RAP).

Healing is war, mystery and mercy

When I started this project, I asked: How do I summarise healing, and the healing ministry? Three words came to mind: War, mystery and mercy. I have touched on mercy (compassion) with reference to the healing of the leper. *Healing is first and foremost a mercy from God* in this broken world.

We are in a life-and-death war, within and without. As Christians, we are engaged in the "war of the Lamb" against sin, sickness, demons and death. It is real to the extent that we struggle with serious illness

---

of Pain (Grand Rapids: Eerdmans, 1993), pp. 311–331.

and/or take seriously the call to heal others. *Healing, and the healing ministry, is all-out war against evil.* Seeing people in need, hearing their cries for help, can fill us with compassion, compelling us to reach out, to touch the untouchables, to impart God's healing presence. Yet our own inner brokenness may cause us not to see, hear or feel for others – our need for healing predominates. Most of the time it is a bit of both – working on our own healing, while trying to help others in their healing. To one degree or another, we are all wounded healers.

Healing is also a mystery. Jesus said the kingdom of God is a mystery. When I think I have healing worked out, I find that what happens – and what doesn't happen – confuses me. I think I know, but I realise only God knows. The God of surprises heals when you least expect it. At times of little or no faith, we may merely "go through the motions", and healing happens. I have seen people miraculously healed who did not even ask God for healing. Then, after intense prayer and fasting, when you think healing is taking place, *apparently* nothing happens. I know godly people who have suffered and faithfully prayed for decades without receiving healing. These, and other contradictions, raise many questions, some of which can be answered, while others remain unanswered. We must be humble about the limits of our knowledge and respectful of the mystery of God's kingdom and its war against evil.

John Wimber said he had a file in his mind marked "Unknown" – he would ask Jesus to explain when he got to heaven! Frequently he would file away an incident, a question, a mystery, with a wry smile of unknowing. At other times he would file things away with great agony of spirit, not letting it go, but wrestling with God over the matter, determined to find answers.[3]

Even this contradiction is part of the mystery of healing. I am accepting of some situations while resisting and fighting others. I feel weak and doubtful, then assertive and persevering. I have come to realise that God is God – he will not lower himself to become a god for us to manipulate and control through our needs, desires, theological presuppositions and spiritual gymnastics. God is not a

---
[3] See John's wrestling with healing in his chapter called "The Long Struggle" in John Wimber, *Power Healing* (London: Hodder & Stoughton, 1986), pp. 23–41.

gambling machine: put in the right prayer and out jumps the healing jackpot. Sickness and healing is a mystery precisely because behind it is a sovereign God, who seeks us for himself, beyond what he can give or do for us. As David Bosch says: "A god who provides all the answers becomes an explicable and comprehensible god, but also ceases to be God."[4]

In summary, I approach this subject with faith and warfare, and with trembling respect and dependence on God. We are treading on holy ground. We should take our shoes off as the Almighty calls us to work with him in this merciful ministry to set his people free. Because we are dealing with people's pain, we cannot come with easy answers, glib pseudo-theological explanations, and the magical hope of instant prayer relief. We cannot, like the false prophets, "heal the wounds of our people lightly, as though they were not serious" (Jeremiah 6:14 RAP). A theology of relationship, suffering and mystery must go hand in hand with a theology of healing, lest we become presumptuous and arrogant, superficial and demanding, causing all sorts of damage.

The origin and title of this book

The seeds of this book go back to 1969 when, as a teenager, I began praying for sick people after I was baptized with the Holy Spirit. In 1975 I became an Assembly of God minister and continued to pray for the sick. In 1981 I met John Wimber, who had founded the Vineyard with a significant ministry of healing. Its practice was accessible for all Christians. So I joined up to learn from him!

I worked on staff with John for eight months in 1982, writing training materials to articulate the Vineyard philosophy of ministry. One of those is now reflected in *Doing Church*.[5] The major part of my research and writing – with another colleague – was taken

---

[4]David Bosch, *A Spirituality of the Road* (Scottdale: Herald Press, 1979), p. 33. Bosch quotes Augustine who said: "For it is better for them to find you (O God) and leave the question unanswered than to find the answer without finding you," p. 34. In this vein, Japanese theologian, Kosuke Koyama, speaks of "Answer Theology" versus "Relationship Theology" and the West's bankruptcy because of the former, in *No Handle on the Cross* (Maryknoll: Orbis, 1977), p. 71.
[5]Alexander Venter, *Doing Church: Building from the Bottom up*, (Cape Town: Vineyard International Publishing, 2000).

up with the theme of healing, signs and wonders. We wrote John's lecture notes for MC510: *Signs and Wonders and Church Growth,* a class he taught at Fuller Seminary. This was the first theologising on healing and the supernatural from an Evangelical kingdom of God framework.[6] The course had a great impact on Fuller and its students, but was controversially discontinued after only a few years. We also produced four teaching booklets on healing, which John used to equip the church in a ministry of healing. (I not only had the privilege of researching and writing about healing, but I practised it regularly in an experimental learning environment.) The audio cassettes and booklets were packaged as *Healing 1 – An Introduction; Healing 2 – A Biblical and Historical Perspective; Healing 3 – Categories and Operatives; Healing 4 – Models and Methodology.* These materials were taught in various nations via John's many Equipping the Saints conferences.

This seminal research and writing, with ground-breaking courses and conferences, forms the basis of this book. My years of pastoring and equipping congregations towards healing environments and ministries have also made a contribution. Jesus entrusted his healing ministry to *the (local) church* (God's healing agent in society), not primarily to individual believers. We have seen enough heroic individual "healing ministries" that take the glory from God. They are not as effective as local churches transforming their communities by a wholistic[7] practice of Jesus' healing ministry. Since 1982 I have

---

[6]In contrast to the way Pentecostals and Charismatics theologise, although Vineyard shares their Spirit practice. Thus the Vineyard sees itself as "*Empowered* Evangelical" (also called "Third Wave", *Doing Church,* pp. 43–45). See Rich Nathan and Ken Wilson, *Empowered Evangelicals* (Columbus: Vineyard Church of Columbus, 1995).

[7]I use "wholistic" to differentiate from the New Age usage of "holistic", although popularly they mean the same thing: the whole or entire person in all interdependent aspects (from Greek *holos*). However, they are as different from each other in their assumptions and usage as New Age is from biblical thinking. In New Age, holistic integration ultimately means the reconciliation and transcendence of good and evil in a higher synthesis in The Self – the worship of "the god in you". In biblical thinking, wholistic means overcoming evil in all its alienating and disintegrating affects through the worship of God – union with *God*. This union or wholistic healing is *not* assimilation without differentiation – we do *not* become God, we are *not* God – we are indwelt by and taken up into the life of the Trinitarian God revealed in Jesus Christ by the Holy Spirit. This is what Leanne Payne calls "incarnational reality" in

modelled and taught these materials in churches, from Catholic to traditional churches, Evangelicals and Charismatics. Over the years I have contextualised, updated and expanded the materials, ending up with the contents of this book.[8]

In keeping with the "doing" theme, I have called this *Doing Healing*. There is a natural progression from how we "do church" and "do reconciliation and social transformation"[9] to how we "do healing".

In *Doing Reconciliation* I explain that "doing" ideally implies "being". The tension between the two is important. Biblically, doing flows from our being in Christ. If we find our identity and significance (our being) in our ministries (our doing), we are in trouble. Many people fall into this trap because of their brokenness and need for recognition. We then use others as *a means of ministry* to meet our own ego needs (out of a messianic complex to save them).

Doing Healing emphasises the *practice* – not just talking about healing, analysing and studying it. It begins with our own healing. We learn by doing it with others; then we reflect on it, learning from our experience, and do it again. In this way, our "doing healing" contributes in a healthy way to our "being and becoming" healers. The basis of ministry is our identity in Christ (being) as sons and daughters of God, authorised to minister healing in his name. The more we practise healing ministry as *an overflow of our being in Christ*, we become healers – "being" and "living" healing, not just "doing healing". This corrects the opposite extreme in the being-doing tension: the wrong idea of "being and becoming" as *an inactive withdrawal into a private spirituality*, an isolated mystical contemplation of "mere being".[10]

The subtitle of *Doing Healing: How to Minister God's Kingdom*

---

her study of C.S. Lewis's worldview in *Real Presence* (Grand Rapids: Baker Books, 1995).
[8]In places I follow some of the original notes that I wrote for MC510 and the healing courses. As the original author, I regard such sections as my intellectual property.
[9]The second in this trilogy of "doing" books is *Doing Reconciliation: Racism, Reconciliation and Transformation in Church and World* (Cape Town: VIP, 2004). I will refer to my books as *Doing Church* and *Doing Reconciliation*.
[10]As John MacMurray has shown in *The Self as Agent* (London: Faber & Faber, 1957), personhood is discovered and defined in relational action and doing, not in isolated or inactive being.

in the Power of the Spirit, focuses on the practical applicability of this book. It places healing ministry in its correct context: bringing the kingdom of God to people by the enabling power of the Holy Spirit – neither our power, nor our kingdom. "How to minister *God's kingdom*" broadens healing beyond physical and emotional healing in people's minds. We are as utterly dependent on the presence and power of God's Spirit to heal, as the leper was on Jesus for his healing. The Spirit of Jesus *is more than willing* to heal, to empower us to do healing. Therefore: Come Holy Spirit!

The flow of thought and content

The three parts (Introduction, Theology and Praxis) make for a clear structure and developmental journey: from story to basic definitions and understandings, to the biblical theology, the practical implications and methodology of receiving and exercising healing ministry.

I begin with my story in the hope that you can identify with and learn from it. Mine is a journey in learning how to receive healing personally and to equip followers of Jesus to practise his healing ministry. We all have our stories. They are important as they bring concrete reality and integrity to our life and teaching. Authentic theology is by nature autobiographical and incarnational – not in the sense of vain sentimentality or subjective spirituality, but in showing "how grace transcends and reshapes personal identity",[11] Christian living and kingdom ministry. The Bible and church history are full of such stories.

As the chapters build logically to the end of the book, I recommend a systematic reading for the sake of the flow and development. I examine the assumed ideas and beliefs that determine how we view reality, the supernatural, God and evil ("worldview" and definitions of sickness and healing). Then I discuss the biblical view of reality

---

[11] Thomas C. Oden, *The Rebirth of Orthodoxy: Signs of New Life in Christianity* (San Francisco: Harper, 2003), p. 83. That is why writing or telling your own story is the most difficult of all tasks, at least in terms of personal integrity and the glory of God. Oden says: "Although Orthodoxy typically resists focusing inordinately upon personal narrative, it permits autobiography in order to show how ecumenical consensus transcends and reshapes personal existence … of God's own coming within personal life, as in Augustine's *Confessions*," p. 83.

– the kingdom of God – embodied in Jesus' life and healing practice. It is *the* model for healing ministry that we learn from and seek to emulate (seen in the stories of Jesus' kingdom ministry). Jesus' intention was that we, the church, should "catch it" and "do the stuff of the kingdom" (Wimber's expression). I examine this transfer of Jesus' healing ministry to the church in the context of our calling to be practitioners of healing in the name of Jesus – both local congregations and individual believers in the marketplace. It involves learning to work with God in exercising compassion, authority, power and the supernatural gifts of the Holy Spirit, and to hear his voice.

This leads to a simple five-step ordinary believer model of ministry, followed by a step-by-step method of ministry for each of the six key areas of healing: spiritual, past hurts, deliverance from demons, physical healing, relational, and healing in terms of death and dying. Lastly, I look at the supernatural and how to discern spiritual phenomena, both in the person receiving healing and the one ministering. I conclude with Jesus' commission to go and "do the stuff" of the kingdom to the ends of the earth.

Appendix 1 is an introduction to Gnosticism as applied to the practice of healing, because of its broad influence in contemporary Christianity. The remaining appendices give references to an overview of healing in the Old Testament, in Jesus' ministry, and that of the early church.

Each chapter is a study section with questions for reflection and application, for both personal and group work. Your small group could work through the book together.

In terms of my writing style, I use gender-inclusive language as far as grammar permits. I use *italics* to emphasize certain phrases or points. My RAP (Revised Alexander Paraphrase) on various Scripture passages needs explanation. I have taken to writing my own *paraphrase* (not a strict translation) of verses and passages by a comparative study of various translations of the Bible. Doing this gives me a fresh reading of the text, seeking to capture the spirit and intent of what was written. When I quote Scriptures directly, they are from the NIV, unless otherwise indicated.

Finally, a disclaimer: I write in a personal, self-disclosing and provocative manner. Here and there I comment on the Vineyard, my own Pentecostal background and other models of ministry. Hopefully we don't take ourselves too seriously as we see our stereotypical practices. G.K. Chesterton said the reason why angels can fly is because they take themselves so lightly. I aim for ease of language, storytelling and practical application, while stretching the reader in biblical understanding and theological thinking.

My prayer is that Jesus will come to you through these pages, that your heart will be strangely warmed and "burn within you", like the disciples on the road to Emmaus (Luke 24:32). May Jesus interpret the Scriptures in a way that transforms your mind, quickens your faith and motivates you to action. May the risen Lord open your eyes to see his wounds as he breaks the bread of his Word, so that you may be healed.

Alexander F. Venter
May 2008

Part One
Introduction

My goal in this section is to:

- Draw you into a story, a journey of healing, both mine and yours. My story will help you uncover some of your own pain, and will enable you in your own journey of healing.
- Establish basic assumptions, definitions and understandings, with regard to how you (ought to) see reality and how to think about disease and healing.
- Clear the ground of various kinds of incorrect thinking, false ideas and mis-beliefs about healing and disease.
- Prepare you for a comprehensive discussion on the biblical theology and practice of healing.

1

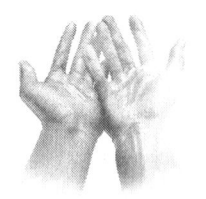

STORY: MY JOURNEY OF HEALING

Rabbi Yoshua ben Levi came upon Elijah the prophet while he was standing at the entrance of Rabbi Simeron ben Yohai's cave. He asked Elijah, "When will the Messiah come?" Elijah replied, "Go and ask him yourself."
"Where is he?"
"Sitting at the gates of the city."
"How shall I know him?"
"He is sitting among the poor covered with wounds. The others unbind all their wounds at the same time and then bind them up again. But he unbinds only one at a time and then binds it up again, saying to himself, 'Perhaps I shall be needed to help someone else bind up their wounds, and if so, I must always be ready so as not to delay for a moment.'
He is the Messiah, the wounded healer."

The wounded healer

This amazing story comes from the Jewish Talmud, written between 250 and 500 CE. Henri Nouwen has popularised it in Christian circles. He shows how its meaning is fulfilled in Jesus of Nazareth and "the ministers of the Church of Jesus Christ".[1] The message is that Messiah Jesus made his broken body the source of healing for the world. His followers are called to care not only for their own wounds, but for the wounds of others. How? By making their wounds *a source of compassion* in bringing *Christ's* healing to the world (distinct from the wrong idea that our wounds – or taking on other people's suffering – can bring them healing).

Jesus is not only the *Jewish* Messiah; he is the Liberator and Saviour of *the whole world* precisely because he is the Wounded Healer. Jesus was "a man of sorrows ... familiar with suffering ... he took up our sicknesses and carried our pain ... by his wounds we are healed" (Isaiah 53:3–5 RAP). Matthew quoted Isaiah's Messianic prophecy when he observed Jesus' compassion as he patiently "healed all the sick" late into the night (Matthew 8:14–17). Jesus felt their suffering in his body, compelling him to reach out in mercy, to heal them by the power of God's love. *This kind* of Messiah saves Israel and the world.

Our Western success ethic says the strong and popular, the powerful and prosperous are the leaders and saviours of the world. The weak and wounded are losers. They suffer because they are failures (so says the dominant mindset); *they* need to be saved – how can *they* save others? But Isaiah 53, as fulfilled in Jesus of Nazareth, turns these values on their head. Jesus had no beauty or charisma that attracted us to him. He was despised and rejected, a man marked by weakness and pain. So we turned from him in disgust, believing God was punishing

---

[1] The story and meditation is recorded in Nouwen's wonderful book, *The Wounded Healer* (New York: Image Books, 1979). I have added the last phrase in the story as a summary statement. Henri Nouwen embodied the wounded healer reality, see Christopher de Vinck (ed.), *Nouwen Then: Personal Reflections on Henri* (Grand Rapids: Zondervan, 1999). For other wounded healer stories, see Vera Philips and Edwin Robertson, *The Wounded Healer: J.B. Philips* (London: Triangle SPCK, 1984); John Wimber, *Living with Uncertainty: My Bout with Inoperable Cancer* (Anaheim: Vineyard Ministries International, 1996); Mike Endicott, *Healing at the Well* (Great Britain: Terra Nova Publications, 2000).

Part One: Introduction

him. Little did we realise he was doing it for us! Our pride blinded us to the fact that he carried *our* suffering and sickness, *our* sin and death. *Indeed, "by his wounds we are healed"*.

God uses the weak, the lowly and despised, to "shame the wise ... the strong ... to nullify ..." the proud and powerful (1 Corinthians 1:18–31). Paul says the message of *Christ's cross* is "the foolishness ... and the weakness of God" that saves the world (proving to be God's wisdom and power!). We must remember, says David Bosch, that *the cross* is the hallmark of the church. When the resurrected Messiah appeared to his disciples, it was his scars that were proof of his identity; because of *them* the disciples believed (John 20:20). Bosch asks: Will it be any different with us, his followers? Will the world believe, and allow us to touch them, unless they recognise the marks of the cross on *us*?[2]

The followers of Jesus enter into, and continue his ministry as wounded healers; not in the ultimate sense of accomplishing salvation (only he can, and did, do that); *nor* in the triumphalistic sense of wealthy world healers or high-powered motivational gurus; but in the immediate and humble sense of *being instruments of his compassion and healing*. By being in touch with our own wounds, we learn to receive healing from Jesus. Then we have mercy on others who suffer from their wounds, and touch them in Jesus' name. We feel the pain and suffering of the world in our own bodies, *for we too are broken by sin*.

The lesson we learn from the Jewish parable is this: *While we attend to our own healing, we must always be ready to help heal others*. We must avoid the extremes of a preoccupation with a culture of self ("me, myself and I"), or an obsession with healing others, as if we are their saviour (in denial of our own brokenness). My story is about this parable – my journey in becoming a wounded healer. Due to the waywardness of my own heart, it has been a slow and reluctant learning from Jesus. He has come to me repeatedly in my sin and brokenness,

---

[2] *A Spirituality of the Road*, p. 82. Koyama calls this "stigmatised theology", which is true "Apostolic theology" (i.e. the lives and teachings of the apostles were marked by Christ's suffering, being sent into the world as Jesus was) in *No Handle on the Cross*, p. 37. See Yancey and Brand for an insightful discussion on the importance of stigmata (markings on the body), and its outworking in social stigma in helping us to recognise disease or healing, and attitudes of rejection or mercy, with regard to leprosy and now HIV/AIDS, in *The Gift of Pain*, pp. 313–316.

patiently and passionately ravishing my heart with his love.[3]

Childhood woundedness

Since I was a tiny tot, I stuttered badly. I can't remember ever talking easily and freely as my older sister and brother did. What was wrong with me? Years later I asked my dad. Apparently we were in a movie theatre (I was three or four years old) when a man was shot, dragged into a room and left do die. I became highly agitated and cried, telling my dad about the man. I couldn't get my words out. Since then I stuttered.

A personal sensitivity and shame grew around this problem. My family showed signs of embarrassment and frustration, even anger, when I stuttered in front of others. My worst nightmare was answering the teacher or speaking in front of the class. When I spoke, my eyes watered, my face flushed, my heart pounded and my breathing strained. I hooked, stammered, spluttered and stuttered on every word.

Part of the problem was the angst in our home. I was afraid of my dad losing his temper whenever I did something wrong. At times he disciplined me in rage, using physical violence. My mom and dad had brutal arguments, and in later years, he became violent towards her. So I grew up with the need to keep the peace, to please and appease – with the subconscious motivation to be accepted and liked. There were many scary incidents. We coped with the trauma by turning fear into fun. For years my brother and I would fall about laughing when we did something naughty, saying, "Beware the milk bottle!" This "joke" came from my dad threatening to bash me over the head with a milk bottle when he lost his temper with me.

My parents were good and well-meaning. They loved us. But it is the traumatic childhood experiences that form the unconscious. Abuse enters the emotions and incarnates itself in the body as memories, postures of pain and fear, that affect relationships and hold us to ransom in later life – unless there has been enough love and healing to wash away the damaging memories. I grew up a highly-strung, ner-

---

[3]See other autobiographical chapters on my life journey in *Doing Church* and *Doing Reconciliation*.

vous, intense and insecure little boy. Well, not so little! I was always the tallest in my class, which made it worse for me as a stutterer. At junior school, a pretty missy came to me with her friends and asked why I was so big and strong and yet I could not stop stuttering. I was utterly humiliated, unable to answer. The teasing at school was merciless and deeply damaging.

As I entered puberty, I developed serious acne, which further compounded my poor self-image and sense of rejection. It was exaggerated in my teenage mind, but it was no less real, making me feel ugly and hideous. God is good, because he gives healthy ways of coping (there are unhealthy and destructive ways too). My athletic ability offset my self-consciousness and bolstered my self-image, winning me acceptance among my peers. I also had a sharp mind and achieved well academically, making me feel better about myself.

Teenage turning points – and more pain

The first major turning point was when I became a Christian on 7 June 1968. (I was thirteen.) It brought a tremendous sense of "homecoming". But my parents were concerned as they couldn't relate to the change in me. My friends nicknamed me Bushy, because my hair was longer than the school code allowed. Bushy became a controversial identity: This young, stuttering, radical Christian, who pushed the boundaries and stirred controversy. It was also linked to my parents' rejection and opposition to my faith. At one stage my dad stopped me attending church for eight months as he overheard me "speaking in tongues" in my room. He thought I had gone mad and wanted me to see a psychologist. Speaking in tongues gave me an amazing freedom to speak without tension in my mouth (deeply therapeutic). So I spoke in tongues as often and as loudly as I could! I learnt that this "power of the Spirit" was for personal prayer, evangelism, healing the sick and casting out demons. I began to do just that.

On my way to and from school, I did street evangelism and prayed for people. This increased my parents' opposition, driving me to prayer, Bible meditation and memorisation. These practices were a means of survival and growth in faith. Those years were profoundly foundational, largely forming the person I have become. But they were also an escape into a subjective "spirituality" that masked my real brokenness and rejection. The intense "spiritual" means of coping opened me to Gnostic influences, such as pride and elitism, legalism and guilt, and a despising of the material world. I took on elements of "toxic faith" that shielded me from facing my "toxic shame".[4] Over the years I have had to work this out of my system. My experience has taught me that toxic faith and Gnosticism are common in Pentecostal, Charismatic and Evangelical circles.

After becoming a Christian, and maybe due to my tongues speaking, I found that when I prayed *aloud* in English, I would rarely stutter. But when I spoke to people, I continued to stutter, sometimes worse than ever. It got so bad that my parents sent me to a speech therapist. She tried all the exercises: breathing, relaxation, visualization, confidence-building, mind-word control techniques – even the "stone under the tongue" – all to no avail. Then an evangelist came to town and laid hands on me in healing prayer. I did not feel any physical sensation, but I opened my mouth and spoke with the same freedom as when I prayed aloud. I knew I was healed. I went around talking with no tension in my mouth, words flowing freely. My parents were astonished!

Later a school friend confronted me with critical questions as to my healing. I became upset, questioning and doubting the healing in my mind. Suddenly my mouth was filled with tension and I began to stutter again. I was crushed! I wept and prayed, begging God to forgive me for doubting. I laboured under the belief that I now deserved to stutter as I had doubted God – it was a form of punishment. So I accepted stuttering as the will of God.

Some time later I had a profound encounter with God in my morning devotions (11 November 1970). The words in the text that I was reading came alive. I felt God calling me to speak for him to the nations. Sobbing with overwhelming awe and personal affirmation, I

---

[4]John Bradshaw's phrase in *Healing the Shame That Binds You* (Deerfield Beach: Health Communications Inc., 1988). Toxic shame goes beyond feelings of guilt to your identity, poisoning – making toxic – all dimensions of personality and relationships. Toxic faith uses God, church and ministry to escape dealing with your own brokenness – legitimising faith with little or no change. It is "having a form of godliness but denying its power" (2 Timothy 3:5).

wondered: Dare I believe what God was saying? Why would God call a person who stutters so badly to speak for him? My stuttering was a major obstacle to my calling, but I found comfort in the callings of Moses and Jeremiah. They complained to God about their inability to speak properly, and God reassured them (Exodus 4:10–12; Jeremiah 1:6–9). Dare I believe *again* that God would heal me? I prayed and prayed (*again*) for healing. I got others to lay hands on me. Nothing changed. I decided just to get on with the job of speaking for God to all who would listen to me, stuttering and all! It was agonising for me and my listeners – more so when I became the leader of the Scripture Union student ministry and began to preach.

Adult growth – The fight for healing

I entered "full-time ministry" in 1975 and got married in 1977. Passionate about God, preaching and pastoring, I persisted with sermons and Bibles studies despite my stuttering. At times I was so embarrassed that I vowed never to preach again – using Jeremiah's words: "I'll not talk about God or speak any more in his name." *But* I found that "his word was in my heart like a fire, burning in my bones, and I could not keep quiet" (20:9 RAP). God was using me, but people still asked why he did not heal me. I developed an answer (a belief) that God sent stuttering as "a thorn in the flesh" to keep me humble and dependent on him. It is amazing how the mind rationalises what the devil suggests, and what the ego allows and legitimises! If I had read 2 Corinthians 12 correctly, I would not have claimed that stuttering was my thorn in the flesh. What "great revelations" had I received (like Paul), that I should have such a thorn? I accepted stuttering as a friendly cross to carry for the rest of my life.

Another challenge emerged. Our marriage was struggling. Among the issues causing conflict, my wife became increasingly embarrassed by my stuttering. "It's your enemy, not your friend. You *can* stop stuttering *if you really want to*," she would say. In my self-pity, I felt she was disrespectful and cruel. When a young man, Lonnie Frisbee, came to our church and ministered in power, it confirmed my belief that God *could* heal me. But dare I believe again that he *would* heal me?

Then I was exposed to Derek Prince's ministry of healing and deliverance at a Renewal Conference. I went to him for ministry, but there were too many people waiting for prayer. I managed to talk briefly with him after one session as he walked to his transport. I told him about my problem and what my wife was saying. He replied, "She's right! You've got to fight this thing through God's Word and prayer. Get it out of you!"

I decided to go for it. I made stuttering my enemy, declaring war! I studied healing in the Bible, especially the theology of the kingdom of God by George Ladd. Faith grew as I read the promise that when the kingdom comes "the stammering tongue will be fluent and clear" (Isaiah 32:4). I quoted this and other verses daily over my body, working at changing my mindset, rebuking, resisting, and even hating stuttering. I wrote out cards and stuck them on my mirror: "He sent his Word to them and healed them"; "By his stripes you are healed"; "In the name of Jesus I break the power of stuttering"; "Stuttering, go! I do not want you anymore!" (Even as I quoted them, I stuttered!)

Initially it got worse as I was more conscious of stuttering. But I pushed through. This continued for about a year before I experienced a growing freedom in my speech. Then I realised that I seldom had tension when I spoke. I believed I was healed. It was "relative", because when I got nervous, tired or overexcited, the tension would return and I would hook on words. However, I knew I was healed. I am eternally grateful to God! Unless you have been bound in the way I was, you will not know the miracle and joy of speaking freely.

How do I understand or interpret this healing? It was no instant miracle as before, rather a long and intense battle, but a genuine miracle nevertheless. I know that *God* healed me *through persevering faith and cooperation.* I know it was a psychological, not a physical healing – the protracted battle undermined my subconscious conditioning to stuttering, overcoming my fear and insecurity. It broke the "hysteria" (in medical terms) or fixation of angst that held me in a habit of stuttering. In biblical terms, I was delivered from a demonisation.

A deeper healing journey – Peeling the onion

My stuttering was the tip of the iceberg. (I have alluded to my underlying mass of inner mess, my psycho-emotional brokenness that needed healing.) The visible and physical receives attention, but is seldom healed unless the spiritual and psycho-emotional woundedness is addressed. Changing the metaphor, God peels the onion to get to the core of our personal dilemma. Many people grow old without ever growing up, because they do not take responsibility for their inner brokenness. They grow old bitter and twisted, often literally so, because they do not deal with the root causes of their personal struggles.

Our unresolved stuff festers and poisons our system. It cripples the emotions, oppresses the mind and inhabits the body in postures of pain, crying out for attention until it is heard and healed. It takes courage to face our stuff, to embark on a deeper journey of healing and growth. The mystery is that some have faithfully done this without receiving the healing they expected. They have had to rely on God's sustaining grace. Carl Jung rightly said that, unless we begin a "religious" journey of healing in the second half of our lives, to address the accumulated unresolved hurt from the first half of our lives, those hurts will demonise and destroy us as we grow old. Often a midlife crisis invites us into this healing journey. It is never too late to start.

I entered my midlife crisis before midlife, when God began peeling back the onion through John Wimber and the break-up of my marriage. While working with John in 1982, he leaned forward one day and said, "Your problem is that you want to please people all the time. You've got to learn to say no!" Then he lifted his hand over me and rebuked "Rejection" in the name of Jesus Christ. The words pierced the core of my being. I felt something shift. I knew Rejection was my core brokenness and struggle.

My response to this insight was to walk around the office and say "no" to people, as a means of self-healing. It was a little extreme, but it felt so good to say, "No!" I was in a healing environment where I was loved and accepted for who I was. I had to learn how to receive from others, to be real and open, vulnerable and self-disclosing, by

Story: *My journey of healing*

unlearning my "pastor self" with its professional persona, ego needs, public posture and performance. (Pastors are notoriously the most difficult people to minister to as they are the ones doing the ministry, often in avoidance of their own brokenness and psychological games play.)

On returning to South Africa, I decided to investigate my rejection by asking my parents about my childhood. But I had to deal with their traumatic divorce. My mom came to live with us for a while and I used the time to talk through her pain, and to explore my childhood. I was not prepared for what I heard. She had become a Christian, so we spoke as fellow believers. She tearfully related how she tried to abort me on discovering she was pregnant. She had two children, was in an unhappy marriage, and did not want another child. She had managed to abort a pregnancy between my older sister and brother. (I have another sister or brother that I'll meet in God's presence one day!) My mom tried to abort me by jumping off cupboards, bathing in really hot water and drinking lots of castor oil. Then she made an appointment with a doctor who performed illegal abortions. On a Tuesday night there was a knock at our door. The police asked my mom if she knew this doctor. Was she the Helga Venter that was on his Thursday night abortion list? I was saved from death by two days!

My mom struggled for hours and hours to give birth to me – I weighed 11 pounds (just short of 5 kg). Apparently she did not hold me, leaving me at the foot of her bed after every feed. The other mothers in her hospital ward chided her. She ignored them, excusing her actions through her self-pity.

These revelations hit me hard, but they brought understanding and reconciliation between my mom and I. I could not process my rejection because my own marriage needed attention. In 1985 my wife left me and then divorced me. These were the most depressing and demonic days of my life. The pain, rejection and loneliness that I experienced were truly dark and evil. I came close to falling over the edge of a deadly and hellish precipice, from which I knew I would never recover. John Wimber sent a senior pastor from Anaheim who, together with my local colleagues, pastorally and ethically sorted through my situation. I stepped out of leadership for an extended period until there was consensus that it was time, in terms of public credibility and personal restoration, for me to resume ministry.

The divorce made me feel a total failure as a pastor. I was utterly broken and rejected in my masculinity. I had failed in the most important of all human relationships. And worse, I felt cut off from God. I cried out again and again with David: "Create in me a clean heart, O God, renew a right spirit within me. *Cast me not away from your presence, and take not your Holy Spirit from me.* Restore to me the joy of your salvation, and sustain me with a willing spirit" (Psalm 51:10–11 RAP). Would God ever forgive and restore me? The original calling of 1970 was over, in my mind. I compounded my guilt and shame by engaging in some unhealthy and sinful ways of coping, from which I have had to repent. To repeatedly reject wrong ways of coping *by turning to God in our pain, rejection and loneliness*, is not easy – everything fights against it. To do so is a tenacious act of trust, a persevering act of worship, which leads to healing and freedom.

Key healing elements in my journey

Where would I find healing for my rejection and related brokenness? That year, 1985 was the worst of years and the best of years. My divorce led me into a deeper repentance and healing journey, which has become a reservoir of acceptance and affirmation, joy and strength, growth and transformation. Repentance and healing is always a process, an incremental journey. We are rarely healed by a single event or one miraculous element. Looking back, certain key elements worked together for my healing and growth. Some became regular practices, while others were utilised when needed.

1. *Colleagues and friends* gave me a safe place of acceptance and love, where I could pour out my heart and find perspective and healing.
2. *Kinship, worship and prayer ministry.* Being part of an authentic Christian community that gathered regularly for worship, sharing and prayer was a key healing element. (People commonly withdraw from community when hurt.) I continued in my home group (no longer the leader), allowing my brokenness to

be seen – especially in intimate worship. It is the greatest healing power, putting us in touch with God's love and our pain, and connecting the two.

3. *Specific healing prayer.* From time to time I went forward in meetings for the laying on of hands. I still do that to this day.
4. *Course work.* I went through a Divorce and Recovery course. Course work can be catalytic, opening up areas of our lives to healing and growth.
5. *Formal counselling.* Formal counselling with a trained therapist had a similar, if not a more powerful catalytic effect. It can unlock long-standing areas of woundedness for restoration and healing.
6. *Key books and healing mentors.* When my ex-wife moved out of home, I was given Morton Kelsey's book on journalling.[5] I will be eternally grateful to God and Morton for his book. It was a life-saver. It brought me into a world of discovery – the "spiritual writings" of the Church Fathers, modern healers and spiritual leaders. Second to community, books have been the greatest source of healing and mentoring for me.
7. *Devotions, journalling and writing poems.* I used to write quiet time notes, but Kelsey taught me to journal. My devotional life became intimate and healing as I practised silence, praying the Scriptures and journalling. I began to write spontaneous psalms (prayer poems) in which I poured out my emotions and thoughts to God.
8. *Listening to my dreams.* Kelsey's books taught me to record and interpret my dreams – an amazing source of healing, instruction, self-knowledge and growth. My rejection, pain, guilt and fear of authority came up in recurring symbols through my dreams. They have been places of self-confrontation, open battle with evil, and numinous encounters with God.
9. *Spiritual direction and companionship.* In seeking healing, I connected with pastor friends outside my church tradition. Two gave me spiritual direction for a time and two became mutual spiritual companions, exposing me to contrasting thinking and

---

[5] *Inward Adventure* (Minneapolis: Augsburg, 1980).

introducing me to a wide range of resources.
10. *Regular retreats.* From Kelsey and other mentors, I learnt the value of taking regular retreats (both alone and with groups, both informal and led retreats). Retreats are about solitude and silence, meditation and prayer, rest and reflection. This has been crucial in my healing journey.
11. *Healthy marriage and family.* A loving marriage and healthy family is God's primary means of healing and growth this side of heaven. A dysfunctional marriage and family can be the greatest source of damage this side of hell! With the blessing of my pastoral colleagues and friends, I married Gilli in November 1987. Our marriage and our lovely children, Zander and Misha-Joy, have been the best years of my life. I cannot begin to describe God's grace and goodness in the wholistic healing and restoration that I have experienced through them. The husband-wife and parent-child relationship are the most intense and intimate relationships we will ever experience outside of the Trinity, exposing and (potentially) healing our brokenness.

The accident that reclaimed my name

I was in the flow of healing and restoration, enjoying my family and ministry, when I had a near-death experience (October 1993). Returning from a pastors' conference one night, my colleague fell asleep while driving the car. It left the road and cartwheeled back over front. The G-force pulled me out through the back window, cartwheeling me with the car. On regaining consciousness, I found myself lying under the car from my waist down. My body throbbed with excruciating pain. Instantly I thought of my wife and children. Peace came over me as I knew that God had set parameters on the accident: I would not die, but I would live to proclaim the works of the Lord. My colleague miraculously sustained no injury at all.

My right hip was shattered, my left leg was fractured in two places, a rib was broken, and blood covered my head and body from lacerations. After reconstructive surgery, I spent six weeks in hospital on my back in traction, then six weeks recuperating at home. This was an intensely spiritual time. Initially I experienced dark figures

Story: *My journey of healing*

and strange faces hovering over me and recurring nightmares of the accident. I relived the sensation of my body folding in two and I smelt Death. It dawned on me that God had saved me from death for the second time. I was overcome with gratitude. He saved me in order to fulfil all that he had planned for me in this world. I knew it was not about me; it was all about him and his salvation for his world. This near-death experience caused me to re-evaluate my life, to be fully focused on what was of ultimate importance.

After the second week in hospital, the dark figures and nightmares left. What followed was intensive care from my heavenly Father. I began meditating and memorising the psalms. For hours a day I listened to worship songs and soaked in God's presence. I learnt from Derek Prince to use God's Word as medicine, taking it three times a day after meals (Proverbs 4:20–22). So I spoke God's word of healing over my bones. Physical sensations of the Father's love flowed through me. I have seldom experienced such sensations of union with God.

First my dad and later my mom spent time with us as I recuperated at home. I again asked about the attempted abortion, my birth, and their choice of my names. Names are important. They embody identity. Probably for the first time I understood why my parents named me Alexander Ferdinand. I understood the origin and meaning of my names as part of God's sovereign purpose for my life.

Because I had been saved from death in the womb and again through the accident, I realised I needed to embrace my life and identity from conception and birth, not just from the age of thirteen. Bushy was an imposed identity, embodying the pain of my teenage years and divorce. Although Alexander is long and formal, the change in name is important. When I discovered after the accident that I had broken my hip, I thought of the story of Jacob. His wrestling with God, his hip injury and consequent limp, and his *change of name* to Israel, was profoundly significant. My name change goes to the heart of my healing journey and the reason for my existence. Every time I hear my name being called, it symbolises God's amazing grace in saving me *from* rejection and death, *for* God's unique life and purpose for me.

Part One: Introduction

Learning to practise healing

This book is not only about receiving healing, but about learning how to minister healing. Here is a brief overview of my journey in this regard.

When I first became a follower of Jesus, I learnt that healings and miracles were a thing of the past – they happened with Jesus and the early church to confirm the truth of their message. There was no visible practice of healing ministry in the church that I attended. They said that if healing happened in our day, it was the sovereign will of God. I later understood this was the standard conservative evangelical view called cessationism (healing miracles ceased with the formation of the New Testament canon in the fourth century).

Then I was baptised in the Spirit and spoke in tongues, which led me to join the Assembly of God. I learnt that God performs healing miracles in our day through the atonement of Christ and the gifts of the Spirit. The cross of Christ not only saves us, but also heals our bodies ("by his stripes we are healed"). The church elders prayed for the sick in services, anointing them with oil. Visiting evangelists prayed for the sick one-by-one in long prayer lines. This inspired me to copy them. I prayed for the sick whenever I evangelised people after school. I would pray intensely and then ask, "Are you healed?" Many said yes. Occasionally there was visible evidence of healing. Once I prayed for a man who had a cataract completely covering his eye. After I laid hands on his eye, he opened it and the opaque film had gone. He shouted his praise to God!

As a young Pentecostal pastor, I was exposed to the Word of Faith movement, attending Faith Conferences where American preachers prayed for people in long lines. Everyone watched and applauded every encounter between "the man of God" and the recipient of ministry – similar to the Pentecostal model I was practising, except they had greater emphasis on faith and the crisis moment of healing. It went like this: "Take God at his word and claim healing here and now by faith. To receive healing *in faith* means you *are* healed, no matter what the symptoms tell you. They are lies from the devil. You *are* healed! Deny the symptoms and wait for the manifestation of healing." If nothing happens, then your faith is faulty or some sin is preventing the healing. Although I saw some miracles, I became disillusioned with the showmanship and hype – their practice of prayer ministry was manipulative and their teachings were questionable.

At the same time I was exposed to the Charismatic Renewal – from liturgical and sacramental "inner healing" with Francis MacNutt, to neo-Pentecostal models majoring on deliverance from demonisation with Derek Prince. These teachings and models of healing ministry were a helpful contrast.

I became aware that my practice of healing revolved around me. *I* was the one up front performing for the people. *I* was hearing from God, dispensing healing and doing "the magic". The people enjoyed it and wanted more. Something in me wanted the power and glory that went with it. People really do want a (visible) Saviour-King – they will take you by force to make you one. Healers who are not in touch with their ego needs play to the crowd to be popular and spectacular. In so doing, they fall into Satan's trap.[6] We are naïve about the public and group dynamics of spiritual and psychological power; how it sparks and interacts between the ego needs of leaders and the salvation needs of attendees.

The pressure to be "the man of God", to "make something happen", became increasingly unbearable. I understood why some high-profile healing evangelists had serious moral failures (the "big three": money, sex and power). I realised that a "professionalisation and de-personalisation" of healing ministry was taking place. In my teens, when I "gossiped the gospel" and prayed for the sick on the streets, it was much more natural.

My grappling with these things began to be answered when I met John Wimber. Not that John and the Vineyard were, or are, God's answer to healing ministry. I can assure you he was a "recovering sinner" battling with his stuff like all of us. A pastor addressed John from the floor at a Vineyard conference in the mid-1980s: "You're an Apostle

---

[6]Every leader should read Henry Nouwen, *In the Name of Jesus: Reflections on Christian Leadership* (New York: Crossroad, 1989). He applies the desert temptations of Jesus to contemporary leadership: From the temptation to be Relevant to Prayerfulness (not turning stones to bread); from being Popular and Spectacular to authentic Ministry (not throwing yourself from the pinnacle of the Temple); from Leading to being Led (not bowing down to Satan to get all the world).

with biblical signs authenticating your Apostolic Office. We should recognise this and call you as such." With a bemused smile John said, "I haven't even been an *epistle* of Christ. Now you want to make me an *Apostle* of Christ! People ask if I'm taking America for Christ. I can't even take my own body for Christ! I'm not anyone special – just a fat man trying to get to heaven. We're *all* just servants of Jesus. It is all about *him*! We are here to do *his* ministry – not *our* ministry. In the Vineyard we *all* get to play because we are *all* called to do the stuff that Jesus did – the works of the kingdom." John repeated these sentiments as a Vineyard mantra throughout his ministry.

What I saw in John and other leaders who worked with him in the early 1980s was a hunger for the real deal. They were transparent, vulnerable and humble, with an attitude of "wanting to learn" that was impressive and inspiring. They were willing to take risks for Jesus in an honest and teachable way. I saw in their teachings on the kingdom of God (the basis for healing) and in their model of ministry (the healing practice), a shift away from "the man of God" where everything happened up front. The focus was on the people, on "equipping the saints to do the ministry" (Ephesians 4:12), a favourite Wimber phrase.

This was radical and revolutionary. It meant a way of doing healing that was easily accessible for ordinary followers of Jesus in everyday life. It meant no hype, no ministry gymnastics, no superspiritual stuff, no manipulation and crowd control, and no mystique around the man of God. I began functioning in this model of ministry.

Personal reflection, application and group discussion

1. *The wounded healer:* What is the essential meaning of the parable for you?
2. *My story:*
    - Subjectively, what spoke to you from my journey? How can you apply it in your own journey of healing?
    - Objectively, reflect on *how* I told my story. List the strengths and weaknesses in the telling of my story.
3. *Your story:* Plan a morning or a day to write your story (preferably at a retreat centre). Enter into silence and ask God for insight and help. Begin by listing three or four main themes of woundedness in your life, and list some key turning points towards healing. Use this skeletal structure to write your story. Get in touch with feelings, the moments of wounding, words, people's faces, and healing. Find God's grace in each incident, in each step of the way. (You can also record a few incidents of how you have learnt to reach out to others, to practise healing in Jesus' name.)
4. *Small group sharing:* Plan for your home group to have a season of storytelling and healing. Let one person per meeting share their life story (having done the above exercise). The person should read their story, rather than spontaneously share it. Others should listen empathically, not interrupting. At the end, people can ask questions for clarity if necessary. Then the group should do prayer ministry with the person to love and affirm them.

2

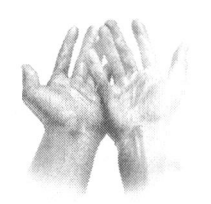

WORLDVIEW: THE POWER OF HOW WE SEE THINGS

*Thomas was not with the disciples when Jesus
appeared to them after his resurrection.
So the other disciples told him, "We've seen the Lord!"
But he replied, "Unless I see the nail marks in his hands and put my
finger where the nails were, and put my hand into his side,
I will not believe it."
A week later Thomas was with the disciples in the house.
Though the doors were locked,
Jesus came and stood among them and said,
"Shalom!" Then he said to Thomas,
"Put your finger here; see my hands. Reach out your hand
and put it into my side. Stop doubting and believe."
Thomas responded, "My Lord and my God!"
Then Jesus told him, "Because you have seen me, you have believed; but
happy and blessed are those who have not seen and yet have believed."*
– John 20:24–29 RAP

The power of how we see things

Many people, Christians included, struggle to accommodate *the spiritual and supernatural dimensions of reality* as normal and natural. It is difficult to relate to – let alone experience and practise – supernatural healings and miracles. Most of us are Doubting Thomases in this regard. Why? Because of how we see things, how we view reality in terms of our material consciousness. Let me illustrate what I am saying.

My family lives with seven other families and a couple of single people exploring kingdom community together. One Friday night at community evening, I saw a pair of spectacles on the table. I put them on. Wow! The world changed! Everything was blurred and my eyes battled to focus. When my eyes adjusted, everything seemed smaller and further away. I felt a little unbalanced. "Whose glasses are these?" I asked. They all laughed because the spectacles were way too small for my face (they belonged to one of the little boys).

I then tried the spectacles of other members of our community. I noticed that there were as many relatively different worlds out there as there were spectacles. My eyes had to focus and interpret what I was seeing with each set of lenses. After my fun, everything slowly came back to normality. That is, normality for *me*, because I realized that the "other worlds" I saw were normality for those whose spectacles I looked through.

Different lenses mean different ways of seeing the world, and consequently we could say that there are different worlds out there. We all know it is really one and the same world – it is only the lenses and the way we perceive reality that is different. There is ultimately only one reality, God's Reality (capital "R" – how God sees and knows things to be); and our perceptions of that Reality make up our own reality (small "r" – how we see and know things to be). *In this present age, both objective Reality and subjective reality exist side by side.* On his return, Jesus will consummate reality into the one Reality of the kingdom of God.

In the quote we see Doubting Thomas meeting Reality. It is a classic clash of two (R)realities, two worlds. Thomas did not have space in his reality, his frame of reference, for Jesus of Nazareth – the Messianic hope – to die on a cross and then be physically resurrected from the grave. His reasonable doubt was the conditioning of his Jewish culture and life context, the inner lenses through which he saw reality. Jesus dramatically interrupted Thomas's reality with ultimate Reality, radically rearranging his world and his view of the world. Jesus loves to do this – he refuses to be put in a tomb or a box! God is not limited in any way. He is bigger than our concept of him, our theology or worldview. Now and again he does things that remind us of this Reality. What is certain is that most things are uncertain – what we do not know is way more than what we do know or think we know!

The way we see the world, through our various cultural and contextual lenses is what we call "worldview". Or simply, *worldview is a perspective on (R)reality.* There are various worldviews, for example a European versus an African view of the world. Would the world map not look strange if it were turned upside down with Africa at the top and Europe at the bottom? It should be clear that seeing – our perspective – *involves interpretation and evaluation* because of our inner lenses. Like Thomas, we all know at times that things are not what they appear, or things are not what we see them to be, until we "verify" or experience it for ourselves. Then we often change our minds! Paul says we "see in part" and "know in part", like seeing puzzling reflections in a mirror or looking through an unfocused lens (1 Corinthians 13:12). This is how we see in this age. When we see Jesus "face to face", we will see and know as God sees and knows. Until then, we need to be aware of our lenses, the power of how we see things.

We must examine worldview and how it determines our beliefs and behaviour – especially with regard to divine healing – as our worldview conditioning is against the supernatural and miraculous.

Understanding worldview[1]

A worldview is a vision *of* life and a vision *for* life – it is both conceptual *and* behavioural. The essential characteristic is that it integrates and explains reality with an internal and external coherence that makes sense to us, giving us identity, meaning and purpose in life. If this integration and coherence is not reasonably credible, we become disconnected, fragmented or paranoid.

Worldview originates at a pre-thinking stage, formed subconsciously by *basic ideas or assumptions* about reality. This leads to both conscious and unconscious choices of what is real or not, what to trust or disregard. Underlying presuppositions give us our *beliefs and values* through which we interpret and evaluate reality. That in turn leads – as we grow into self-consciousness – to a sense of *identity, meaning and purpose*, giving us our *norms* and *goals* in life. The result is seen in our daily *attitudes and actions*, in our behavioural choices and the way we live our lives.

As noted, our *culture and context* give us our inner lenses, our basic ideas and life assumptions. They come to us through our environment, our parents, educators and significant others; through our God concept and religious faith; our ethnicity and nationality; our socio-economic position in society, and our life experiences – both good and bad. All these factors – and more – form and interact with our worldview. Our worldview in turn influences our culture and context as it makes its presence felt in us and through us. So our sense of *meaning and purpose* not only stems from our worldview, but actually affects it, affecting our culture and context. See Figure 1.

---

[1] The study of worldviews, from cultural to philosophic and scientific, is a fascinating one. *I focus on a few contrasting worldviews as they relate to healing and the supernatural.* The most comprehensive study on worldview(s) is by David Naugle, *Worldview: The History of a Concept* (Grand Rapids: Eerdmans, 2002). I have drawn on this and the following sources for this chapter: Harry Blamires, *The Christian Mind: How Should a Christian Think?* (London: SPCK, 1963); Colin Brown, *Miracles and the Critical Mind* (Grand Rapids: Eerdmans, 1984); Francis Schaeffer, *How Then Shall We Live?* (Old Tappen: Revell, 1976); James Sire, *The Universe Next Door: A Basic Worldview Catalog* (Downers Grove: IVP, 1976); Brian Walsh and Richard Middleton, *The Transforming Vision: Shaping a Christian Worldview* (Downers Grove: IVP, 1984). I have drawn especially on Charles Kraft, *Christianity with Power: Your Worldview and Your Experience of the Supernatural* (Ann Arbor: Servant Publications, 1989).

The nature of worldview

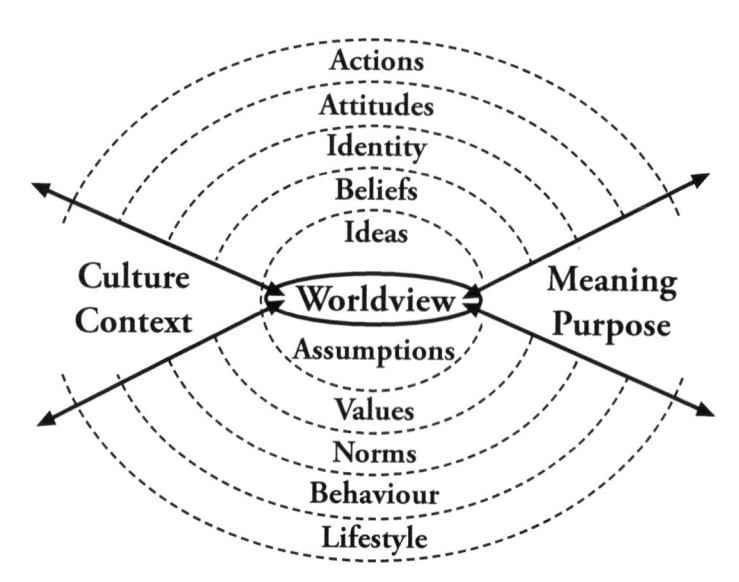

```
            Actions
           Attitudes
           Identity
            Beliefs
             Ideas
  Culture  ⟨Worldview⟩  Meaning
  Context   Assumptions  Purpose
            Values
            Norms
           Behaviour
           Lifestyle
```

Sociological studies provide an alternative approach to worldview. Many of their insights have been utilised in theological studies.[2] There are four constituent parts of a worldview: *Firstly*, it provides – and is made up of – the *characteristic stories* through which we view reality. Narrative, or storytelling, is the most common expression of worldview in any culture or context.

Secondly, the stories attempt to answer the most *basic life questions* facing human beings:

- ❧ Who are we? Gives a sense of identity (self).
- ❧ Where are we? Gives a sense of environment (context).

---

[2] Peter Berger and Thomas Luckmann, *The Social Construction of Reality: A Treatise in the Sociology of Knowledge* (Garden City: Doubleday, 1966); Paul Marshall, Sander Griffioen, and Richard Mouw (eds.), *Stained Glass: Worldviews and Social Science* (Lanham: University Press of America, 1989). In a theological context, Walsh and Middleton, *The Transforming Vision*, and N.T. Wright, *The New Testament and the People of God* (Minneapolis: Fortress Press, 1992). Wright frames his study of the historical Jesus on the four interacting parts of worldview, analysing the clash between the worldview of Jesus and first-century Judaism, in *Jesus and the Victory of God* (Minneapolis: Fortress Press, 1996). His popular version of this scholarly work is *The Challenge of Jesus* (London: SPCK, 2000).

Worldview: *The power of how we see things*

- What went wrong? Gives a sense of history and the problem with the world (evil).
- What is the solution? Gives a sense of salvation, the way out of the problem (God and purpose, or eschatology, which is the study of the end).

There are added questions, or variations of the above questions, depending on whom you read on the subject.

Thirdly, the stories and life meanings are embodied and communicated through *fundamental symbols*, such as artefacts, events, rituals, festivals and flags. Symbols are deeply cultural and national, powerful and emotional expressions of worldview. Tell a fundamentalist Muslim girl she cannot wear her head scarf to school, or burn an American flag outside the White House and see what happens.

Fourthly, the stories, life answers and symbols are incarnated and seen in *habitual praxis*, normal practices and daily lifestyles. Otherwise the symbols, stories and explanations would make no sense. Praxis reveals the person's, and the society's, intentions, motivations and aims in life, in keeping with their worldview.

The four elements or functions interact, creating the essence of a worldview – represented in the following diagram:[3]

Worldview functions

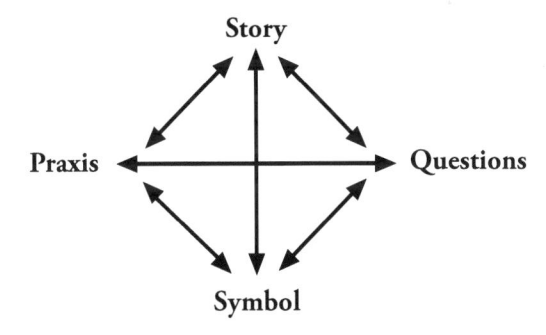

```
           Story
             ↑
             ↕
  Praxis ←――――→ Questions
             ↕
             ↓
          Symbol
```

We can see that worldview – especially from the life questions – determines our view of ourself, sickness and healing, God and evil and the supernatural. Although I do not structure the remaining

---
[3]From N.T. Wright, *The New Testament and the People of God,* p. 124.

chapters around these four interacting worldview functions, they will be worked out in various ways in how we do healing through the power of God's Spirit. We will explore the story (and stories) of Jesus; the teachings of Jesus in answer to the life questions; the symbols of Jesus, and the praxis or practices of Jesus and his early followers.

To summarise: Worldview is an assumed frame of reference, a mindset that operates at both personal and group consciousness levels. It is an explanation of (R)reality which provides a basis for evaluating and engaging (R)reality. Different assumptions lead to different conclusions. When Paul and Barnabas healed the crippled man at Lystra (Acts 14:8–15), the people assumed that only their gods could do such a miracle, so they concluded that Paul and Barnabas were gods and offered sacrifices to them. In contrast, Paul and Barnabas assumed that they were ordinary human beings used by God to heal, so they concluded: "Do not treat us like gods!"

Worldview assumptions operate mostly at a subconscious level. They surface through incidents such as I have just described. Most people do not stop to ask why they see the world – and live – the way they do. It is not easy to examine our psychological and cultural spectacles. They tend to surface when we have supernatural or cross-cultural experiences. We call it a clash of worldviews, or worldview challenge, because it questions our underlying assumptions and beliefs as it exposes our *different practices.* Although often traumatic, it is healthy to be open to other perspectives. This raises the question as to the nature of change, of personal and group transformation, and whether worldviews themselves can change.

Changing worldviews and paradigm shifts

"Paradigm" helps us to speak of worldview change and is often used synonymously with worldview.[4] Technically *paradigm is a subset of*

---

[4] "Paradigm" comes from the field of science. Thomas Kuhn says scientific changes take place as revolutions – whole paradigms shift – in *The Structure of Scientific Revolutions* (Chicago: University of Chicago Press, 1970). Paradigm is now being used in theology, business and other disciplines, see David Bosch, *Transforming Missions: Paradigm Shifts in Theology of Mission* (New York: Orbis Books, 1991); Johan Janse van Rensburg, *The Paradigm Shift: An Introduction to Postmodern Thought and Its Implications for Theology* (Pretoria: Van Schaik, 2000); Joel Barker, *Future Edge: Discov-*

worldview, a perspective on a larger segment of (R)reality. Hundreds of such semi-independent perspectives of (R)reality are organised into a worldview. *A "model" is a further subset of paradigm.* Each working model gives us thousands of applicable understandings of reality, how things hang together and operate. Thus models change relatively easily and frequently. Not so with paradigms and worldviews.

Can we change a worldview? Yes and no. We are born and raised within a worldview. To totally change or replace it with another is near impossible. Some say that can happen with a Christian worldview. Technically there is no pure Christian worldview, as our view of Reality and our interpretation of Scripture will always be conditioned by our particular cultural lenses (worldview) until Jesus comes. The Christian faith is not in competition with cultures per se. Rather, it comes into cultures and transforms them from within, as Jesus incarnated himself in the Jewish worldview and transformed Judaism from within. Changes *within* a worldview, in keeping with biblical *paradigms,* more accurately describe what happens. This is the idea of *paradigm shifts* – changes in significant segments of how we view (R)reality in keeping with the biblical view. As ideas and beliefs about (R)reality are exposed and challenged, and then changed, the worldview is adjusted.

Worldviews are dynamic, not static – *if* we are committed to growth. It takes courage to keep growing. Worldviews evolve as paradigm shifts ("quantum leaps" in perception) take place. A paradigm shift can be traumatic, but liberating, as it involves power encounter: God's Reality breaks into our reality, challenging our control of the segment being confronted. Paradigm shifts and growth can also be a gradual process of realisation and change. This is how transformation of paradigms, worldviews, individuals and groups takes place. *A change in perspective means a change in practice,* or it is no change at all.

Although Jesus shared the Jewish worldview of his followers and critics, he radically shook and shifted their paradigms with his interpretation and Messianic fulfilment of their worldview. Wright shows how Jesus challenged their power-control by his reinterpretation

---

ering the New Paradigms of Success (New York: William Morrow and Company, Inc., 1992). I follow Kraft's understanding of paradigms and how they shift (pp. 82–87).

of the classic *stories* and *symbols* of Israel. His *teachings* answered Israel's *questions*. His *life praxis* of feasting with sinners and healing the sick modelled what Israel was called to be and do.[5] Jesus stretched their worldview and shifted their paradigms in the way he touched and healed the lepers, and in the way he authoritatively drove out demons – unique in Old Testament *and* first-century Judaism (Mark 1:27). More stretching still was his use of God's power to calm the storm and raise Lazarus to life. Jesus shattered his disciples' paradigms through *his death on the cross* (his ultimate "miraculous sign", Matthew 12:38–40). Their expectation of a conquering Messiah did not allow for such a devastating event. When he died, they died, their world(view) died. But when he rose again, they came to life in a whole new way. They and their world(view) were transformed through Christ's physical resurrection. In postmodern theological terms: Jesus *deconstructed* their (old) paradigm and then *reconstructed* their (new) paradigm in his death and resurrection, in his Messianic fulfilment of the kingdom of God.

The two disciples on the road to Emmaus experienced this (Luke 24:13–35). The death of Jesus shattered them *because of* their paradigm. Their interpretation of the Hebrew Scriptures was incorrect, otherwise they *would have known* that the Messiah *must* suffer and die to enter his glory (v. 25). That night, as he reached out and broke bread with them, their eyes were opened and they saw differently: "The marks in his hands! It is Jesus! It is *really* Jesus! He's alive! He's risen from the dead! Our hearts burned within us as he unfolded God's truth about his suffering and death, and now his resurrection. *Now* we understand what he was teaching and practising all along. It is all true! It is a new (R)reality. The kingdom of God has come! A new world has begun!"[6] Crucial aspects in their lenses (their theology and life assumptions) changed. They themselves were changed, and would keep on being changed forever.

Thomas believed that his view of reality was Reality – he did not have spectacles. Many Christians naïvely and/or arrogantly believe

---
[5] See Wright in footnote 2.
[6] The RAP I imagine they shouted out all the way back to Jerusalem, and then to the ends of the earth! See N.T. Wright's definitive work on Jesus' resurrection, *The Resurrection of the Son of God* (London: SPCK, 2003).

this. He did not believe Jesus had been resurrected: "I must see it for myself!" He had seen Jesus raise Lazarus to life. This was different. Lazarus would die again, but Jesus not – so his friends told him – the Resurrection had happened! "I don't believe it! Can a ghost have physical imprints in his hands and side?"

Suddenly Jesus "entered" the room – though the doors were locked – a detail that John highlights. Thomas was traumatised. When last did you see a dead friend *physically* materialise before you, out of thin air or from a wall? "I cannot believe what I'm seeing! Is this (R)real?" Jesus greeted them in his customary way and then said: "Thomas, don't doubt – it's me. I'm not a ghost. See my hands and my side. Put your fingers and hand into these wounds." Thomas was aghast, as pale as a ghost. He saw Reality for what, or for Who, it really was. Not only his paradigm, but his whole world shifted. He spontaneously responded: "My Lord and my God," an act of worship and confession of ultimate Reality, enabled by that Reality. He was face to face with God and kingdom come, transforming him and the world around him.

Thomas believed because he saw and touched. Happy are those who believe without the hard evidence; who trust (God's) Reality beyond their (own) reality and their ability to define and control it; who open themselves to God's kingdom beyond their own frame of reference. *They* are the ones who are blessed because they experience God's kind of life. The story illustrates Dallas Willard's saying: Reality is something you run into when you are wrong. Jesus' followers experienced it regularly! Is it any different for us? Jesus still comes to us by his Spirit (the God of surprises). Our encounter with him is a participation in the shattering death of the cross and the transforming power of the resurrection.

The problem of the will and what we think we know

We are not trapped in our worldview *if* we *want* to change. Some do *not* want to see things differently, let alone change or grow. *Prejudice*, *presumption* and *power* prevent paradigm shifts and personal transformation. *Prejudice* is "do not confuse me with the facts, my mind is made up". Similarly, *presumption* is what we think we know when we do not actually know. And *power* is about the will, about pride and control. We have seen these obstacles to change in Thomas.

Harvard theologian Krister Stendahl said: "It is not so much what we do not know, but *what we think we know*, that obstructs our vision" and eventually cripples us.[7] If we were honest and teachable about what we *do not* know, tentative and explorative about what we *think* we know, and humble and responsible with what we *do* know, the world would be a different place. What Jesus did and taught provoked the prejudice, presumption and pride of the Pharisees and Jewish leaders. They opposed him at every turn on the basis of what they thought they knew about what God could or could not do. This blinded them to "the time of God's visitation", causing them to reject and oppose the salvation God offered in Messiah (Luke 19:41–44). They thought they knew it all, but their "knowledge" destroyed them. Jesus predicted it – the Temple and Jerusalem were destroyed in 70 CE, killing more than a million Jews.

We easily screen out what we think we already know, but do not really know. Seeing can be selective for various reasons, blinding ourselves and others to what we desperately need – a visitation of God. *An example of this blindness* is Jesus' encounter with the man born blind (John 9). The disciples "knew" he was blind due to his sin, or his parents' sin (v. 2). Jesus said it was neither; but rather that God's glory should be revealed in his healing. The Pharisees "knew" that the healer could not be from God because he healed on the Sabbath and therefore was "a sinner" (v. 16). Because of this "knowledge", they were not willing "to believe that he had been blind and could now see" (v. 18); nor were they willing to believe that Jesus was the Messiah because "we know this man is a sinner" (vs 22, 24). By contrast, the man born blind was honest, gaining true knowledge in his experience: "*I do not know* if he's a sinner or not. One thing I *do know*, I was blind, and now I can see!" (v. 25). Jesus then commented on how blind the Pharisees were in their supposed "knowing" – either they must repent and be healed, or remain in their knowing blindness and suffer their guilt.[8]

---
[7] In *Paul among Jews and Gentiles and Other Essays* (Philadelphia: Fortress Press, 1976), p. 7; cited in Charles Kraft, p. 65.
[8] These insights on John 9 are from Kraft, pp. 66–67.

Was their "knowing" a matter of worldview conditioning or wilful rejection of Jesus and the truth, new information and experience? The evidence suggests it was a power confrontation: they were not willing to see differently. There are none as blind as those who *will* not see. *Biblically speaking, to believe is to see; to know is to obey.* We cannot want to know without being willing to obey. Jesus said that "whoever is willing to do what God wants will know whether what I teach comes from God (or not)" (John 7:17 RAP). He accused the Pharisees of wilfully becoming "calloused, hardly hearing with their ears, and ... closing their eyes" to God's truth (Matthew 13:13–15). When we will both to see and to do what God wants of us – beyond our own understanding if necessary – we encounter Reality. Our paradigm shifts and we change. Jesus says: "If you're *really* my followers, you *will* follow and obey my teachings, and *then* you will *know* the truth, and the truth will set you free" (John 8:31–32 RAP).

Truth and freedom are critical. Is there truth? How can we know it? Christians believe that God has revealed *the* truth about life and ultimate Reality in Messiah Jesus and his Word (John 14:6). The fact that Jesus and the Bible involve *interpretation* through our worldview lenses does not mean that there is no "knowing the truth", as postmodernism claims. Being critically aware of our understanding of truth does not necessarily make it any less the truth.[9] The Bible is simply the best information available to human beings on how to live life as God lives it (modelled in Jesus and his first followers). By following Jesus and his teachings, our lenses are (re)focused, we see differently, we know (glimpses of) truth about Reality as God sees it. By trusting and obeying that truth, we are increasingly freed from

---

[9] This is a technical philosophic debate in epistemology and hermeneutics – how we know reality and how we interpret it. Simply stated, there are three approaches: Modernism or "naïve realism" says there is objective knowledge, "the truth" (assumes naturalism and empirical scientific "proof"); postmodernism or "reduced realism" says there is only subjective knowledge, "their truth" (assumes the social construction and deconstruction of reality and knowledge); and thirdly, "critical realism" says there is critical or qualified knowledge, "our truth" (assumes a storied and dialogical view of reality). With Wright and Van Huyssteen, I believe critical realism is consistent with the biblical view of truth and knowledge, see N.T. Wright *The New Testament and the People of God*, pp. 31–144; Wenzel van Huyssteen, *Theology and the Justification of Faith: Constructing Theories in Systematic Theology* (Grand Rapids: Eerdmans, 1989).

false ideas, fears, sin, damaging attitudes and actions. It is not only freedom *from*, but freedom *for* God and his world, increasingly seeing and acting as God would in any situation.

In short, our will can help or hinder the transformation of our worldview conditioning. We can trust or resist biblical paradigm shifts and power encounters. As Paul says, we need to *commit intentionally to a transformational process* by offering our bodies as living sacrifices to God and by the renewing of our minds so that we can live God's "good, pleasing and perfect will", living it on earth as it is done in heaven (Romans 12:1–2 cf. Matthew 6:10).

Contrasting worldviews and spiritual power

Beginning with Jesus, Messianic Judaism (later called Christianity) was characterised by supernatural power. It spread throughout the Mediterranean world through power encounter.[10] As Yahweh defeated the Egyptian gods through Moses' miracles freeing Israel from slavery, so Jesus and his early followers defeated sin, sickness, demons and death. In this (Messianic) Jewish worldview, it was natural for the supernatural to interact with daily human reality. The Bible and other classic literature records the normality of extrasensory phenomena and spiritual experiences such as dreams and visions, prophecies and oracles, angelic and demonic visitations, healings and miracles.

The Two-Thirds World (Latin America, Africa, the Middle East and Asia) easily relates to this experience of (R)reality. They share a spiritual worldview, each with its own variation. Most First World people struggle to relate to the biblical and Two-Thirds worldview because of their *rational and material mindset.* They have to prove, categorise, explain and harmonise "the other" in their frame of reference to remain in control of their world(view). This is being challenged as East and South invade North and West via mass people movement, ethnic practices, spiritual experiences, New Age thinking and Gnostic literature, resulting in growing social tension and conflict.

---

[10] Morton Kelsey researches the spread of Christianity through the power of healing and miracles in *Healing and Christianity* (San Francisco: Harper & Row, 1973), expanded in *Psychology, Medicine and Christian Healing* (San Francisco: Harper & Row, 1988).

The West is ripe for *spiritual* revolution because it is mystically, mythically and morally bankrupt – the scientific and materialistic worldview has not met the deepest human needs. We are technologically overdeveloped but spiritually and emotionally underdeveloped, giving rise to an indiscriminate spiritual hunger for alternative experience and power, with the possible deception that may follow.[11] From God's perspective the West is ripe for the gospel of Jesus Christ that is demonstrated in acts of sacrificial love and raw power.

Is the church of Jesus Christ ready to meet this challenge? Through the centuries, the church's Hebraic spiritual worldview and practice of God's power was challenged and undermined by contrary philosophies.[12] Western Christianity (Roman Catholics and Protestants, in contrast to the Eastern Orthodox Church) became captive to a modernist worldview, in which the human being – the rational mind – was crowned god of this world. The world was seen as natural and material, with scientific enquiry, cause and effect explaining everything. The spiritual frame of reference was abandoned, and God and spirituality were consigned to the realm of religion, faith or superstition.

Western dualistic faith separated the secular and sacred, the objective and subjective, devaluing emotions and spiritual experience, resulting in a rational Christianity with minimal power. To know was to have the right information; to believe was to give mental assent, regardless of personal experience (which was always suspect). Consequently our *minds struggle with spiritual phenomena: It is not "normal"*

---

[11] For example, over 300 million *Harry Potter* books and 40 million *Da Vinci Code* books have been eagerly consumed by millions of readers – especially young people. We are yet to see the full destructive effects of *the subconscious resymbolisation of the Western mind* that is taking place – away from the Judaeo-Christian worldview to a resurgent paganism. We are moving from scientific discovery to spiritual exploration. Godly discernment and wisdom are greatly needed. See Tom Wright's examination of the resurgent pagan gods and the challenge to the church, *Bringing the Church to the World: Renewing the Church to Confront the Paganism Entrenched in Western Culture* (Minneapolis: Bethany House, 1992), and Jeffrey Satinover's exposé of the Gnostic pagan resymbolisation taking place, *The Empty Self: C.G. Jung and the Gnostic Transformation of Modern Identity* (Westport: Hamewith Books, 1996).

[12] From Hebraic thought to Platonic and Gnostic dualisms, pagan mysticism and medieval superstition, scholastic naturalism and Aristotelian logic, the Enlightenment and modernism, and now postmodernism and forms of Eastern, Gnostic and occultist mysticism (once again). For a basic understanding of Gnosticism, see Appendix 1.

for people to fall over when they are prayed for. It is not "natural" to hear God speaking to us, to feel his presence, to be healed by his power. That is supernatural (so we think). If there is no natural cause-and-effect explanation for what happened, it is not real. Or we have to have "proof" from Scripture ("show me chapter and verse") for a spiritual experience or miracle to be real, to be from God. We believe it because it happened *in the Bible*. So we consign God and miracles to history. Now we have modern medicine, science and psychology!

Has God changed because the times have changed and "the laws of nature" have been discovered? Has science replaced God as the ultimate authority – even for most Western Christians? They have been conditioned by critical scepticism, becoming suspicious of healing miracles and those who do them. Western missionaries ran into (R)reality when they were confronted with open spiritual battle in the Two-Thirds World mission field. They felt powerless in the face of raw spiritual and social evil because of their rational and naturalistic worldview. Philip Jenkins shows how the spiritual and theological leadership of global Christianity is shifting from the First to the Two-Thirds World because indigenous Christians and "independent churches" (Pentecostals, Charismatics and Empowered Evangelicals) have a spiritual worldview and life praxis in keeping with the biblical paradigm.[13] They are by far the fastest growing segment of Christianity *due to their practice of "power ministry"* in evangelism, church planting, healing the sick and casting out demons. This is the "next Christendom".

To summarise, the search for power is arguably the dominant quest for human beings. All worldviews provide a framework for this power quest, for controlling the causes behind things. The following diagram shows the contrasting worldviews, each with three spheres of power and causality: the spirit sphere (including God), the human sphere and the material sphere.[14] The lines between the spheres are porous, indicating an interactive reality, not separate spheres.

In biblical and Two-Thirds World societies more or less equal value is given to the three spheres, reflected in the space given to each in

---

[13] In *The Next Christendom: The Coming of Global Christianity* (New York: Oxford University Press, 2002).
[14] Taken and slightly adapted from Charles Kraft, p. 199.

the diagram. Since spiritual causality is primary over the human and material spheres, power flows "down". The main difference between the two is that Hebraic society focuses more on God in contrast to the "mediating middle" of gifts of the Spirit, angels, dreams, revelations, spirits, ancestors, demons, spells, magic, witchcraft, which is the main focus of Two-Thirds World societies.[15]

In Western societies the focus of power is primarily on the human and material realms, to harness material resources through science and technology for human benefit and control – power flows "up". There is minimal focus on God, with a "missing middle" of no or very little concept of spiritual powers interacting with human beings and nature. This "excluded middle"[16] is the reason why Westerners tend to see anything supernatural as religious or superstitious – although this is now changing to what is being called "spirituality".

Contrasting worldviews

BIBLICAL SOCIETY	⅔ WORLD SOCIETIES	WESTERN SOCIETIES
(God focused) Spirit Sphere	Spirit Sphere (Spirit focused)	Human Sphere
Human Sphere	Human Sphere	Material Sphere
Material Sphere	Material Sphere	

God Sphere ← Excluded Middle (pointing to top of Western Societies column)

---

[15] For example, 80% of all black South Africans are Christians, or claim to be, and yet 80% of all black South Africans consult sangomas (traditional herbalist-witchdoctors). It shows the power and fear that the ancestral African worldview has over them, or the powerlessness of Western Christianity, or both.

[16] See Paul Hiebert, "The Flaw of the Excluded Middle" (January 1982), *Missiology: An International Review,* American Society of Missiology, vol. X, no. 1. pp. 35–47. A discussion with diagrams on this concept – the lack of a spiritually interactive and mediated reality in Western culture – can be found in John Wimber and Kevin Springer, *Power Evangelism* (San Francisco: Harper & Row, 1986), pp. 75–81.

Part One: Introduction

In conclusion, we must not underestimate the power of our particular worldview, the lenses that determine how we see things. Through power encounter, when God breaks into our reality, our paradigms and worldview can be shifted, assuming we do not resist, but are open to such changes. We do not need to remain in powerless Christianity. We can embark on an exciting adventure with God in being naturally supernatural and supernaturally natural[17], in keeping with the biblical paradigm.

Personal reflection, application and group discussion

1. What do you understand by "worldview"? What are the key factors that make up a worldview?
2. What is your worldview? Can you describe its main features?
3. What is a "paradigm" and "paradigm shift"? How does a paradigm shift take place? Use a paradigm shift that you have been through as an example.
4. Why are worldview and paradigm shifts important for our discussion on, and understanding of, human sickness and God's healing ministry?
5. What obstacles to change and transformation (paradigm shifts) are there? Can you identify any in you? Do you *want* to change? How can you?
6. *An individual exercise:* Pray for a person who is sick, and see what happens. Did anything change in terms of the way you saw and experienced things?
7. *A small group exercise:* Invite another group that is culturally or ethnically different to your group. Sensitively explore the differences in worldview and life practice with them. At a later meeting discuss what your group learnt, how your paradigms and worldview were challenged.

---

[17]Phrases from John Wimber, now popularised in Gary Best, *Naturally Supernatural: Joining God in His Work* (Cape Town: VIP, 2005).

3

Definitions: A Position on Disease and Healing

*Beloved, I pray that in all respects you may prosper
and be in good health, just as your soul prospers.*
– 3 John 2 NASB

One of my first attempts at healing prayer was with an elderly gentleman. He called the church office saying he was depressed. I accompanied the Baptist intern pastor, a friend of mine. We found that he had cut his little toe and it was festering. He assured us it was not a problem, although it was obviously very painful and (in our minds) part of his depression.

When I innocently offered to pray for his toe, he was astounded, saying that he had asked for a pastoral visit for prayer for his spiritual wellbeing. The doctor had seen his toe a few days before and said it would be fine. How dare we bother God with a little toe when he is so busy with important things in his universe? He had irresponsibly cut his toe, so it was his problem, not God's. "I need spiritual help with my depression, and you want to pray for my toe? It's ridiculous!"

My naïve interference had messed up the pastoral visit, but my friend stood by me. We persisted, quoting Jesus (Matthew 10:29–30): A sparrow cannot fall to the ground without God's concern and likewise with the hairs on his head – God had numbered every one of them. He smiled; there were not that many left! Eventually he relented and we prayed for his depression *and* for healing in his toe. The next day the gentleman phoned to say that his depression had lifted *and* his toe had vastly improved – the pain had gone, much to his surprise.

When I reflected on the incident, I was amazed at his fixed ideas:

- A pastoral visit was *spiritual* care – the doctor takes care of the physical.
- His problem was depression – physical pain had nothing to do with it.
- God was concerned with big problems, not little things like sore toes; he would certainly not help if we caused the pain.

He struggled to see things differently. He could not see the biblical paradigm of God's concern for sparrows and human hair, and *therefore* how much more God is concerned for us, who are made in his image and likeness. The sentiments he held so strongly kept him in suffering and pain, as it does to untold millions.

Understanding human disease and divine healing

Sickness, healing and health is one of the most important issues occupying people's minds and pockets. Billions of dollars are spent annually, going beyond healing and health to youthfulness, beauty, exercise, weight loss, and many other forms of body focus. The obsession with the body is unprecedented in all of human history. People are desperate to remain healthy and young, and will do anything to achieve this. Others have lost hope and have a view of sickness that passively accepts the inevitable.

Having alluded to various attitudes and understandings of sickness and healing, I will summarise them and then focus on the biblical understanding.

Like the elderly gentleman, most *Westerners* view sickness as a physical problem for the doctors to heal – a result of the dualism separating the spiritual and material dimensions of reality. Spiritual challenges are matters of faith for pastors and theologians, while sickness is a matter of cause and effect for medical scientists to resolve. Modern medical practice traces its origin to Hippocrates, the father of medicine. Arguably Jesus' healing ministry and the Judaeo-Christian view of nature has empowered modern medicine and scientific discoveries more than any other culture or religion.[1] It is when the material view is divorced from spiritual reality that science becomes the authority (a god in the Western mind, as in, "The doctor said …"). Although psychology and para-psychological studies have undermined this material understanding of sickness and healing, most psycho-emotional disorders are still treated chemically.

Disillusionment with this naturalistic view has led to *alternative medicines and healing practices*. Homeopathy, acupuncture and most other forms of alternative medical practice are based on belief systems rather than on scientific research and method. The assumed beliefs about human nature and spiritual reality determine the practice of healing – working with energy fields, power points, "meridians", "chakras", "the Divine in us", "universal consciousness". These New Age beliefs and Gnostic spiritual experiences view sickness as negative energy or being out of sync. Healing comes by reading auras, balancing or releasing energies, using crystals and magnetic rocks, practising yoga and transcendental meditation, communing with your angel and pursuing "spirituality". The result is a "holistic" – not merely material – understanding of sickness and healing. It is a mixed bag of beliefs and practices, ranging from the good to the benign, the bad, and the outright demonic.[2] The devil blurs the lines with a mixture

---

[1] Ironically Jesus' thinking and practice with regard to healing was "material" – his interest in the physical, mental and material wellbeing of people was "greater than that of any other leader or religious system from Confucius through Buddha to Zen and Islam", Hippocrates and the Greeks included, Morton Kelsey says in *Psychology, Medicine and Christian Healing*, p. 53. Likewise the Judaeo-Christian view of nature differs from other religions: Creation is *not* sacred, or evil, or inferior, but God-given and good, to be stewarded, explored and used for the benefit of all. This view gave rise to the historical Western practice of scientific research leading to the industrial revolution, modern medicines and technological development.

[2] It is not the place to work through the mixed bag of New Age thinking and alterna-

of truth and falsehood, making his offer so seductive.

The *Two-Thirds worldview* (with their traditional religions) sees sickness and healing in spiritual terms affecting every aspect of the person. The causes of disease and the means of healing are not immediate and material, but ultimate and spiritual, involving gods, ancestors, dreams, spells, traditional herbs, muti (potions), "good" or bad spirits, "white" or black magic.[3] People are at the mercy of a relational universe in which sickness is due to offended powers, and healing is due to appeasement of the gods through rituals and sacrifices (to be in harmony with the interactive socio-spiritual-material world). It is a world of superstition and fear, punishment and reward, manipulation and control. Healing is mediated through the holy man, shaman, spirit medium, witchdoctor or mystic – depending on the religious culture – exercising great power in their community.

The biblical understanding of sickness and healing

The quote at the head of this chapter points to the biblical understanding of sickness and healing. John greets his friend Gaius with a common Jewish blessing: May you be prosperous and healthy (in a wholistic sense, inwardly, bodily, socially, materially).[4] It implies an

---

tive healing practices from a Christian perspective. Others have done this well: Vishal Mangalwadi, *In Search of Self: Beyond the New Age* (London: Spire, 1992); Russell Chandler, *Understanding the New Age* (Dallas: Word Inc., 1988); Roy Livesey, *Understanding Alternative Medicine: Holistic Health in the New Age* (Chichester: New Wine Press, 1985); Samuel Pfeifer, *Healing at Any Price? The Hidden Dangers of Alternative Medicine* (Milton Keyes: Word Publishing, 1988); John Drane, *What Is the New Age Saying to the Church?* (Great Britain: Marshall Pickering, 1991).

[3]From a Christian view, there is no "white" magic or "good" spirits. The only good spirits are God's *angels* who are "ministering spirits sent [from God] to serve" Christ-followers (Hebrews 1:14). *All* other spirits are evil, fallen with Lucifer. Magic is an evil category, the opposite of miracle, a God category. Miracles are God's direct intervention in nature and human affairs for redemptive good. Magic is witchcraft: using spiritual power to influence others for destructive purposes as in spells and curses (black magic), or for supposed good as in breaking spells and curses (white magic). Biblically, there is no such distinction – contrary to what J.K. Rawlings and *Harry Potter* teach. *Any* dabbling with, or use of spiritual power outside of God's Holy Spirit given through Jesus Christ, is witchcraft, occult, divination and sorcery. Millions turn to this falsehood to satisfy their deep longing for spiritual reality – the material-rational church has not addressed their needs.

[4]See footnote 7 in the Preface.

interrelated understanding of human nature based on the Hebraic worldview of *Shalom*: Yahweh's wholistic peace and prosperity, health and harmony, experienced through right relationships. Beginning with Adam and Eve, we see throughout the biblical witness how fractured relationship with God, the source relationship, ourselves, each other, and creation itself, leads to "the curse" – the chaos of sin, sickness, demons and death. We also see how restored relationship (reconciliation) through Messiah's life, death and resurrection breaks the curse and leads to forgiveness, healing, freedom and eternal life. *Shalom* is God's reign of wholistic order and wellbeing, the opposite of disintegrating chaos and destruction, the rule of evil.[5]

Simply stated, *a biblical understanding of human disease is disease – a lack of ease in the whole person.* Sicknesses are disorders, the opposite of *Shalom*, a disruption of God's wholistic harmony and relational wellbeing in the human being. Disease is a result of human sin, Adam's original disobedience. The curse of death intruded and spread throughout creation: "Sin entered the world through one man, and death entered through sin, so death came upon all people and all creation because all have sinned" (Romans 5:12 RAP). As death is an intruder in God's creation, so sickness is not natural to human beings – we instinctively resist it. Sickness is the foretaste and curse of death, at war with us and our world in a destructively wholistic sense. Therefore, disease is a human issue, affecting all of us and God's creation. *We* must take responsibility – with God's help – to address it in a wholistic sense.

How do we define healing, biblically speaking? *Healing is the event and/or process of restoring wholeness to the whole person.* Healing is God's *Shalom* – experiencing and ministering God's wholeness, order and wellbeing. The New Testament word for this *Shalom* healing is "salvation", God's work in saving us and creation from sin, sickness, demons and death, the focus of the next chapter. Such healing can only come to us, both immediately and ultimately, through the life, death and resurrection of Jesus Christ, by the power of the Holy Spirit. That is why we speak of divine healing, not faith healing – although

---

[5] I discuss *Shalom* in *Doing Reconciliation,* pp. 86–87, 145–149. For a full study of the *Shalom worldview*, see Walter Brueggemann, *Living Toward a Vision: Biblical Reflections on Shalom* (New York: United Church Press, 1976).

working with God in healing requires faith in him.

The biblical perspective of sickness and healing implies that we, who believe in God through Jesus Christ, are *called to work with him in a ministry of wholistic healing*. I believe this with all my heart, but not all Christians agree with me. I discuss various views on healing ministry in the next chapter.

At this point we need to further our understanding of sickness and healing by contrasting two models of human nature: the Greek-Hellenist versus the Hebraic view.

Human nature, disease and healing

Our particular assumptions with regard to human nature underlie our approach to sickness and healing. The Greek and Hebrew view of human personality have in different ways been foundational to modern thinking. Paul was a Jewish Rabbi. He thought Hebraically, but wrote his letters to the churches in Greek, sometimes using Greek categories, *but in a Hebraic manner.* In 1 Thessalonians 5:23 he says: "May God himself, the God of peace [*Shalom*], sanctify you through and through. May your whole spirit, soul and body be kept blameless at the coming of our Lord Jesus Christ." Paul uses the categories of spirit, soul and body in a wholistic way to affirm the dynamic unity of human nature: the God of *Shalom* sanctifies and keeps us through and through. He is not teaching a tripartite view of human nature *as such,* that we are made of three or more distinct parts. Using Paul's categories in 1 Thessalonians 5:23, we can illustrate the *basic view of human nature* as in the following diagram:

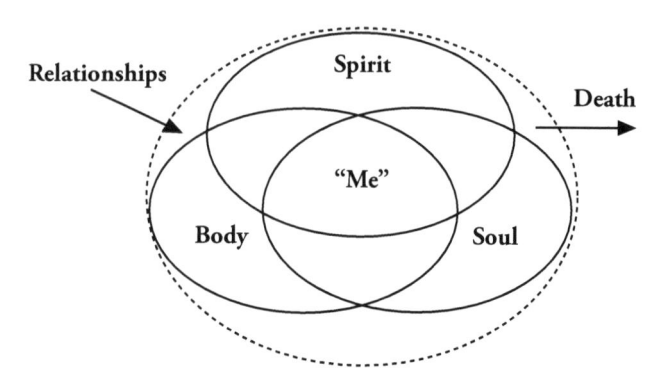

It is self-evident that we have capacities or dimensions to our human nature. Paul does not deny that, but asserts that they "overlap" in an integrated wholeness, a unity of "me". I am spirit, soul, body, *and more* – the sum total of my relationship with God, others and creation. My relational reality touches every aspect of who I am (the enclosing circle). Death is separation from my relational world in terms of my Space-Time-Energy-Mass experience (STEM reality).

This diagram can be applied in one of two ways: either towards fragmentation – imagine the circles moving apart to a state of separation, the tendency in the dualistic view; or towards integration – imagine the circles moving closer together to a state of oneness, the goal in the Hebraic view. Both these models have serious implications for our approach to sickness and healing.

The dualistic fragmentary model

Plato's (428–348 BCE) *Hellenistic view of human nature* was dualistic: The body or material world is a temporal shadow of the real world – the spiritual realm. We are seen as *souls imprisoned in bodies*. Aristotle (384–322 BCE) added logical analysis to this dualism, further dividing the human being into categories. Aristotelian logic entered the Western church through scholasticism and natural theology (Thomas Aquinas, 1224–1274 CE) and matured through Renaissance and Reformation thinking into modernism, reinforced by Descartes's dualism of "I think therefore I am". This led to the rational, analytical and scientific worldview discussed in the previous chapter.

The result is fragmentation in which the human being is categorised as having *a spirit* (spiritual capacity), *a soul* (the psyche – mind, emotions and will), living in *a body* (bodily organs, the five senses and social capacities).[6] In terms of sickness and healing, this categorisation of human personality has led to the treatment of one or more "parts" of the person in isolation from the other "parts". We are seen as an amalgam of parts rattling around under the skin – we are "fixed" by changing "bad" parts. This categorical-compartmentalised view has contributed to the rise of the specialist medical professions, who often

---

[6]The logical conclusion is disintegration into sub-personalities – each "instinct" or "part" of human nature becoming semi-autonomous – a return to pagan polytheism and Gnosticism. See Jeffrey Satinover, *The Empty Self*, pp. 53–57, 62–75.

treat "the problem" without regard to its effect on the whole person. The orthopaedic surgeon who successfully reconstructed my hip after my motor accident gave me a "hip prognosis" with no regard to my faith or emotions: "You will probably walk with a limp, and you'll have a hip replacement operation in ten years." He was wrong on both counts!

Christians also have their list of specialist healing ministries ("my deliverance ministry", "my inner healing ministry"). The tendency is to "reduce" healing to the particular specialisation – one approach addresses all illnesses.[7] This often results in ignoring those who are not healed, giving them a glib "spiritual" reason for their lack of healing, or treating them in a superficial and dismissive way. This not only reveals our prejudices, but causes serious damage. Because the human person is dynamically interrelated and complex, healing is not a simple issue, a one-cause or one-answer and easy-explanation event.

The wholistic integrating model

Derived from Yahweh as "One" in the *Sh'ma Israel* (Deuteronomy 6:4), the *Hebraic view of human nature is an embodied unity of personhood* – experienced in eternal life with God. Yahweh made human beings in his image by "in-breathing" them as "in-spirited-bodies" or "living beings" (Genesis 2:7), with no dichotomy between spirit and flesh. Because of the intrusion of sin and mortality, the spirit separates from the body in death. Christ's physical resurrection and the gift of his indwelling Spirit is God's guarantee of an eternal embodied existence. Healing is the foretaste of the future resurrection in this present age.

The mystery of human nature as one wholistic reality is illustrated in Hebrews 4:12 (cf. Jeremiah 17:9–10). Only God's Word can penetrate and expose hidden stuff in the complex unity of human nature. The writer is *not* giving us a basis to distinguish and divide between spirit and soul, heart and mind, body and emotions, as is

---

[7]There are variations of this "one solution fixes all" approach. Some Christians attribute most diseases to demonic causes and do deliverance for almost everything. Others reduce all physical disorders to sinful/spiritual causes, so repentance and forgiveness heals all disorders. An example of the latter is Henry W. Wright, *A More Excellent Way: Be in Health – Pathways to Wholeness, Spiritual Roots of Disease* (Thomaston: Pleasant Valley Publications, 2005).

taught in many churches.[8]

The point in this Hebraic model is that one "part" of the human being cannot be affected without affecting the whole. The whole person is involved in all that happens. Although sickness comes through different dimensions (spiritual, emotional, mental, physical), it affects other dimensions. Most long-standing disorders need treatment at many levels because multiple causes, both immediate and ultimate, are involved. Compensatory side effects must also be ministered to. Our focus is *not* on fixing the problem, but on healing *the person* – restoring wholeness. The person's social and environmental context (relationships and work situation), also affects, and is affected by, the dis-ease. Our mortality in terms of death (and its fear) is also a factor to be taken into account.

The wholistic approach to sickness and healing honours human dignity by the practice of a comprehensive, balanced and effective ministry. Because of the complexity of human nature, healing is more a process than an event. So we take time with people and do not rush the healing process. And we do not neglect natural and human means to healing (except spurious, deceptive and demonic means), working with God and others to receive and impart wholeness.

Classes of illness and Jesus' healing ministry[9]

To deepen our understanding of sickness and healing, I compare Jesus' healings with the three basic classes of human illness in medical science: psychic (or mental), organic and functional disorders. The Gospel writers used different words to describe Jesus' healing of various kinds of sickness: severe pain, demoniacs, epileptics and paralytics (Matthew 4:24). Although they may have used different

---

[8]Church leaders need to teach biblical anthropology (the Hebraic understanding of human nature) that reverses Platonic dualism in all its Gnostic forms, which is widespread in contemporary Christianity. I recommend Derek Morphew, *The Spiritual Spider Web* (E-Publication, Cape Town: VIP, 2003); G.C. Berkouwer, *Studies in Dogmatics – Man: The Image of God* (Grand Rapids: Eerdmans, 1962). They show how the Bible uses spirit and soul (*ruach* and *nephesh*) interchangeably, and how choices, thoughts and emotions are often referred to in "inward" bodily terms as "heart", "kidneys", "bowels of mercy", indicating a wholistic embodied view. See also Appendix 1.

[9]I summarise Morton Kelsey, *Psychology, Medicine and Christian Healing,* pp. 55–69.

words, they recognised various classes of illness, claiming that Jesus healed "every kind of disease and every kind of sickness" (Matthew 9:35 NASB). The healings they recorded were the more dramatic and meaningful encounters, but Jesus performed many other healings (John 20:30–31).

Psychic illness

Times of emotional stress and socio-political change – as there was in Jesus' day – contribute to psychological disintegration in people. Forms of personality disturbance were a serious issue in the first century – as it is in our day. It was a common malady healed by Jesus, generally described in the New Testament as "demonisation", the influence of spiritual powers in a person to one or another degree.[10] Our Western mind attributes this kind of explanation to the primitive mindset of "those days". However, psychological disturbances are manifested in one of three ways (the categories of psychic illness).

Psychosis: A person's mind may retreat from reality to such a degree that s/he cannot function. This may be marked by states of wild frenzy or dazed withdrawal (catatonic stupors). Jesus healed this kind of condition by expelling demons from the person (Matthew 8:28–34; 15:22–28; Mark 1:23–27). Biblically, this is a strong form of demonisation, as in "possession" or "control".

Psychoneurosis: A person may not break with reality, but experience a troubled mind characterised by anxiety, compulsiveness and depression. The neurotic worries about castles in the air, while the psychotic (above) lives in them! Neurosis can have emotional and other contributory factors. In biblical terms, it is seen as spiritual powers "troubling", "afflicting" or "oppressing" people in one form or another (Luke 6:18; Acts 10:38).

Hysteria: These are physical conditions resulting from mental/emotional states (psychogenic causes), as with my stuttering impediment. There is no organic damage, only the *unconscious* idea that a

---

[10]This does *not* mean the Bible attributes *all* psychological disorders to demonisation. Much of the psychic distress and disorder comes from our fallen world, our global state of disconnection from God, others and creation. It is a *spiritual* cause, not demonic per se. See Larry Crabb, *Connecting: A Radical New Vision* (London: Word Publishing, 1997).

particular organ cannot be used. Biblically it is understood as deception by an evil spirit (via fear or trauma) – a "stronghold" or "bondage" that must be released. Jesus healed some forms of blindness, muteness and paralysis by driving out spirits – these conditions were not attributed to organic causes (Matthew 9:32–33; 12:22–23; Luke 13:10–13).

Organic illness

In this second type of illness the structure, tissue or organs of the body are damaged in some way. These disorders cause actual physical alteration of the organism, including the deterioration resulting from germ invasion or long-term functional disturbance. Jesus cured many afflicted with this class of illness: various forms of skin disease and leprosy (Matthew 8:2–4; Mark 1:40–42), paralysis and lameness (Matthew 12:9–13; Mark 2:3–5; John 5:2–9), fever and blindness (Mark 1:30–31; 10:46–52).

Functional illness

Functional illness results from a malfunction of one organ or part of the body. It includes a variety of disorders in which a malfunction in one part disturbs the whole organism. Most of the commonly recognised diseases fall into this category, such as headaches, heart disease, high blood pressure, peptic ulcers and allergies. In terms of Jesus' healings, there are no specific references to what we call functional illness. But there are references to Jesus healing large crowds of people (some detail the disorders).[11] Because functional illness is the most common disorder, it is certain that he healed this class of illness.

Sources, causes and categories of healing

In conclusion, I must clarify the sources of healing, the interrelated nature of causes, and list the key biblical dimensions of healing.

There are four basic sources of healing:

- From *God's Spirit* – directly or through human agency (prayer).

---

[11] Matthew 4:24; 8:16; 9:35; 12:15; 14:14, 35–36; 15:30; 21:14; Mark 1:32–34; 3:10–12; Luke 4:40–41; 6:17–19; 7:21.

- From *scientific medicines* – herbs, plants, natural medicines and chemical drugs that overcome germs, bacteria and certain kinds of illness. Divine healing/God's power is not opposed to elements God created, that can be used for healing. We work *with* medical science, not against it.
- From *human faith and psychic power* – what doctors call the placebo effect (a sugar-coated pill with no medicinal properties that makes people feel better because of their faith in it). The innate power of the human spirit/psyche is at work, as in positive thinking. It operates through faith in self, pills, doctors, faith healers, crystals and many other means of healing. The healing lasts as long as self-faith and the psyche can hold off the symptoms; a "reverse hysteria", as the thought affects the body.
- From *demonic power* – the devil has power to "heal" people,[12] only to win them into trust and dependence on him. He comes as "an angel of light" by doing "good", to deceive and enslave. This kind of "healing" is no healing – even if the symptoms never return. Satan "heals" directly or through human agency, as in white magic, potions and witchdoctors.

Both God and the devil work with, and through, human faith and the power of the psyche. God heals in response to faith *in him* – not faith in self. The person's faith is not the source of healing, God is. Satan works through *anything* that removes the person from faith in and dependence *on God*.

In terms of the causes of sickness and healing, the "presenting problem" can be caused by sources other than the *apparent* class of illness. Various causes and compensatory effects must be taken into account in the healing process. For example, the elderly man's presenting problem was depression, but his sore toe contributed to, if not caused, his condition. Healing his toe lifted his depression and brought him closer to God. Allergies are treated symptomatically, but they are increasingly seen as emotionally based.

Psychosomatic causes and forms of healing are better understood

---

[12] The quotation marks indicate that it is not authentic healing from God – it is healing for ultimate destruction. Satan has real power to do *counterfeit* healings and miracles: Exodus 7:8–12, 22; 8:6–7, 16–19 cf. 2 Thessalonians 2:9–10.

Definitions: *A position on disease and healing*

in our day. In the 1980s I prayed for a young man with recurring migraine headaches. He was not healed until I heard that his father had died and he had to leave school to support his mother and siblings. Getting him a job and giving the family financial support healed him.

Addressing the symptoms in healing prayer does not always work. Physical symptoms can have psychological or economic causes. Emotional symptoms can be spiritually or socially based. The permutations are endless. We cannot be categorical about classes of illness and their causes. People are complex – there are levels of causes and compensatory effects *behind* every presenting problem. Our approach to healing must be thoroughly integrated and wholistic – to heal the whole person, not just the "affected part". I can now list the categories of healing from a biblical perspective as it relates to the whole person:

1. Healing of the spiritual/moral aspects – caused mainly by sin.
2. Healing of the emotions – past hurts and painful memories.
3. Healing of the demonised – deliverance in all dimensions.
4. Healing of the body – organic and functional disorders.
5. Healing of relationships – social pain, forgiveness and reconciliation.
6. Healing of the dying and the dead – helping people to face their mortality, and to die well. This dimension of healing includes raising people back to life when God so prompts (resuscitation, not resurrection).

Other kinds of healing, such as sexual, marriage and financial, can be placed in the above core categories. I deal with each core category in Chapters 14 to 19, highlighting their interrelationships. Categorisation helps in our *understanding* of sickness and healing, but wholistic integration is crucial in our *practice* of healing. Let's turn now to the biblical theology of healing (Part Two).

Part One: Introduction

Personal reflection, application and group discussion

1. How would you have handled the elderly gentleman with the sore toe? What would you identify as his core issue?
2. What exposure do you have to understandings of sickness and practices of healing outside the Christian tradition? What is good or bad about them?
3. What are the key underlying factors or assumptions that determine how any person understands the nature of sickness and healing?
4. To what extent have you held a Hellenistic or Hebraic view of human nature in your understanding of sickness and the practice of healing?
5. Having read this chapter, write your own definition of sickness and healing. What has changed from your previously understanding?
6. Comparing the classes of illness from medical science with the healings of Jesus, what have you learnt that is new?
7. Take time to minister to someone in your small group, practising some of the insights you have gained from this chapter.

Part Two:
Theology

We have seen how our underlying beliefs and perspectives determine our choices and lifestyles. Good theology leads to good practices or praxis; bad theology leads to bad practices. Our praxis reveals our theology – what we *really* believe, not what we *say* we believe. Actions do not lie; they reveal our beliefs. We look at our praxis of healing in Part Three. Part Two examines the basis of our beliefs in terms of a biblical theology of sickness and healing.

My goal in this section is to:

- Give a working knowledge of the biblical paradigm or framework of reality, the theology of the kingdom of God.
- Show how Jesus ministered the kingdom of God to people.
- Show the principles and patterns, means and methods Jesus used to healed people.
- Show how the kingdom healing ministry of Jesus was imparted to his followers, the church.
- Show how the church has (and has not) continued Jesus' healing ministry throughout its history.

4

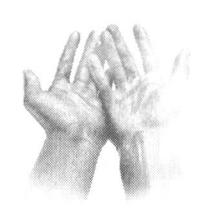

THEOLOGY: UNDERSTANDING THE KINGDOM OF GOD

*For this reason the Son of God appeared,
to destroy the works of the devil.*
– 1 John 3:8 RAP

*But ... the Pharisees ... said, "It is only by Beelzebub,
the prince of demons, that this fellow drives out demons."
Jesus knew their thoughts and said to them,
"Every kingdom divided against itself will be ruined, and every city or
household divided against itself will not stand. If Satan drives
out Satan, he is divided against himself.
How then can his kingdom stand? And if I drive out demons by
Beelzebub, by whom do your people drive them out?
So then, they will be your judges. But if I drive out demons by the Spirit
of God, then the kingdom of God has come upon you. Or again, how
can anyone enter a strong man's house and carry off his possessions unless
he first ties up the strong man? Then he can rob his house."*
– Matthew 12:24–32

The correct context to understand sickness and healing is the theology of the kingdom of God. In essence, this is war with evil to liberate human beings and the earth from the power of evil. Jesus came into the world for that very reason, to destroy the works of the devil. He saw his mission as an invasion of Satan's kingdom or "house", to tie him up and defeat him. Jesus then plunders his "possessions" – we who are held captive to evil by the curse of sin, sickness, demons and death. Jesus defeats Satan by his kingdom "coming upon" people, and he empowers his followers to continue doing the same.

The following story illustrates the explosive idea and reality of God's kingdom. It will give us an overall picture of God's dealings with human beings and the earth.

A story from ancient Israel

There is an interesting law tucked away in the Hebrew Bible. It deals with the emotive issue of land ownership and the concept of the Kinsman-Redeemer (from Leviticus 25, with insights from Ruth and Jeremiah 32). This parabolic story shows the biblical view of God's work in human history. Israel has always been a parabolic witness to the other nations.

Property was *the* most basic means of economic viability in Israel. *Every* family received a plot of land after the conquest of Canaan. To be landless or exiled was to be cursed or cut off from God – as Israel was for 400 years in slavery in Egypt. Yahweh's Kingship over Israel was established through the Exodus, the Sinai covenant, and gift of the Promised Land. "The land must not be sold permanently, because the land is mine and you are but aliens and my tenants" (Leviticus 25:23).

The land was a barometer of Israel's relationship with God. Faithfulness to God in the land – by its just usage and care of the poor – meant *Shalom, God's manifest presence* among them (Leviticus 26:11–12). Continued broken trust meant exile and slavery, a cursed land – withdrawal of God's manifest presence. Therefore the land was held in trust before God. Whenever it was sold or changed ownership, the seller gave his sandals to the buyer to symbolise the transfer of property rights, and to symbolise the original family name remaining on the land (Ruth 4:7). All land was from God, belonged to God, and would ultimately be returned to its rightful owner.[1]

The story went like this: If a person or family in ancient Israel fell into debt and could not repay what he owed, he had a choice. He could sell the land that God had given to him and his family, and repay the debt with the money from the sale of the property. But he and his family would then be landless. He would have to become a hired servant on another property in order to feed his family. Often this was tantamount to slavery, although God forbade it. Alternatively, he could enter into a kind of mortgage agreement with his creditor, who would then take the title deeds of his land, seal them and keep them, while he would work for his creditor to repay the debt in full. In effect, he would be a slave on his own land with the creditor ruling the roost – a usurper taking advantage of the poor. Amos 2:6, 8:6 calls it "buying the poor … for a pair of sandals".

The only hope was to look forward to the day when the debt would be paid off, title deeds taken back, seals broken, sandals returned, and the land restored to its rightful owner. Or the person could wait until the Year of Jubilee – the fiftieth year when all debts were cancelled and the land was returned to its rightful owner. The radical provisions and rationale of the Year of Jubilee are described in Leviticus 25. The redemption of the land every fifty years was assured in a radical manner, no matter what may have preceded.[2] It guaranteed the return of every property to its original owner, insuring justice and freedom for all, especially for the poor and oppressed. The Jubilee was The End, the final hope!

However, it did not need to go that far – in terms of working off the debt, or waiting that long for the Jubilee. Why? Because of a remarkable provision in the law for such an eventuality. If a person or family ran up a debt and lost their land, their nearest relative was obliged to bail

---

[1] See Walter Brueggemann's comprehensive biblical study, *The Land – Place as Gift, Promise, and Challenge in Biblical Faith* (Minneapolis: Fortress Press, 2002).
[2] The Jubilee brought about a revolutionary realignment of the economy and a just redistribution of wealth every fiftieth year. Its full meaning and liberating fulfilment in Messiah Jesus is discussed in Andre Trocme, *Jesus and the Non-violent Revolution* (Scottdale: Herald Press, 1973); John Howard Yoder, *The Politics of Jesus – Behold the Man! Our Victorious Lamb*, 2nd ed. (Grand Rapids: Eerdmans, 1994). To what extent it was practised, and for what length of time, is not known.

them out of trouble – the Kinsman-Redeemer was to redeem the land and restore it to its rightful owner. The Kinsman-Redeemer law is tucked away within the greater context of the law of Jubilee (Leviticus 25), revealing God's merciful intervention right now, before "the end" (the fiftieth year). Because the family name was at stake, the closest relative would redeem the land by paying the debt in full. He would take back the title deeds and sandals, evict the usurper and free the oppressed family to rule their own land once again. The land itself was liberated into harmony and fruitfulness (restored *Shalom*) due to the intervening grace of the nearest kinsman.

What if the debt was settled and the creditor (if he were deceptive and obstinate) remained on the property and continued his oppressive rule? He would be occupying the land illegally. The nearest kinsman would then go and gather all the other relatives and return to forcefully drive the usurper from the land and reinstate the rightful owner. If all the above did not happen, for whatever reason, the Year of Jubilee was still the final guarantee that justice, liberation and full restoration would take place.

The meaning of the parable

God created the heavens and the earth in five days. On the sixth day God created humankind in his image and likeness as the climax of his creation. God rested on the seventh day. *Then* it was over to us: Adam and Eve were created to care for creation. As creator, God is King/Ruler over all things. But he rules *through* human beings. God gave us this particular plot of land in trust, to have authority and ownership, to be his rule of love, his reign of *Shalom*. The Garden of Eden (meaning "delight") embodied this perfect state.

In Adam and Eve we broke trust with God by sinning against him. Through sin we sold out to the devil. We gave away our God-given authority to *Satan* (Hebrew for "opposer" or "adversary"). Having failed in his attempt to grasp the title deeds of heaven – to be God – Lucifer came to earth to grab the title deeds from us. He sealed them, stuck them in his pocket, and settled on our turf to rule and reign in our place. He walks the earth wearing our sandals, making us his barefoot slaves on our own land! The Garden of Delight was replaced by thorns and thistles, the Desert of Slavery. Jesus says: "Everyone who sins is a slave to sin" (John 8:34). In v. 44 he calls Satan the "father" of all sinners. The earth and all on it came under "the curse" of Satan's rule of sin, sickness, pain, poverty, demons and death. Chaos disrupted all aspects of God's creation.

Satan became "the god of this age [who] has blinded the minds of unbelievers" (2 Corinthians 4:4). We live in "the present evil age" (Galatians 1:4), in contrast to the future age in which God's kingdom reigns. The future age is God's eternal cosmic Jubilee. Paul says "*we know* that the whole creation has been groaning as in the pains of childbirth … [and] we ourselves groan" (Romans 8:19–23), waiting for the resurrection of our bodies, and the restoration of all creation. There will be no more slavery. All suffering will cease. Satan and his demons will be banished from the earth – it will be restored to its original owner. We will more than fulfil our created purpose on a new earth, ruling with God forever.

Jesus is our Kinsman-Redeemer who pays the price

We do not have to wait for the end of the world, for that final Jubilee. The provision in the law is of a Kinsman-Redeemer who comes to bail us out of trouble here and now, before the final judgment when everything is put right. Because we are made in God's image, Jesus of Nazareth is the nearest relative of every human being. He is closer than a brother or sister. God's family name has been at stake ever since human beings sold out to the devil. Our nearest Kinsman-Redeemer could do no other but to leave his home and come to redeem us from Satan's tyranny. Jesus did not grasp at equality with God – as Lucifer did – but he let go. He stripped himself of position, power and glory, and came to earth to buy us back (Philippians 2:7–11). Paul says: "You know *the grace* of our Lord Jesus Christ, that though he was rich, yet for your sakes he became poor, so that you through his poverty might become rich" (2 Corinthians 8:9).

Two thousand years ago Jesus came to redeem us and our land, the earth, through his incarnation, ministry, death, resurrection and ascension.[3] He began his ministry by announcing the Jubilee, then

---

[3] The early church creeds emphasize Christ's incarnation, death, burial, resurrection

enacted it: forgiving sins, preaching good news to the poor, healing the sick, delivering the imprisoned and enslaved. He literally drove Satan out of God's territory, human bodies.

In his death Jesus satisfied every legal requirement of justice, paying the full price for our sin, drinking the cup of God's wrath to its dregs. He died *our* death on *our* behalf, suffered *our* exile from God and the land: "My God, my God, why have you forsaken me?" (Matthew 27:46). Jesus took on himself the full force of evil as darkness covered the earth and the Spirit brooded over the chaos. Jesus spoke from the cross, beginning the new creation: "Father, forgive them …" (Luke 23:34). In doing so he disarmed Satan, stripped him of his power, publicly shamed him, triumphing over him by the cross (Colossians 2:15). Jesus reconciled us with God *and* the land: the earth quaked in anticipation of its liberation, tearing the curtain in the Temple from top to bottom, ending humanity's separation from God (Matthew 27:50–53). *Then* Jesus cried out: "*Tetelestai* – it is finished," bowed his head and gave up his spirit (John 19:30). That is to say, he rested. It was the seventh day, the Sabbath. His work of *recreation* was over. It was now over to us who believe.

Jesus was buried and "descended into hell", as the Apostolic Creed says. This was the harrowing of hell, *not* in the sense that he suffered under Satan (that would be heresy), but that he announced to Satan and all his trembling demons that the Day of Judgment, the Year of Jubilee, had occurred. The debt had been paid. Jesus then took back the title deeds of the earth and led the "captives" who died in faith (waiting in Abraham's bosom) into God's presence.[4] This happened

---

and ascension, saying nothing of his life and ministry. The kingdom was powerfully present in these events, but Satan's defeat also happened in Jesus' ministry life by the preaching, signs and wonders of the kingdom, important for a theology of healing. This latter emphasis has been recovered in the resurgent theology of the kingdom in the 20th century. Some scholars argue that Luke 4:16–21 (fulfilling Isaiah 61:1–2) was Jesus' announcement, and his ministry an enactment, of the *actual* Jubilee in Israel – which had not happened or been practised for centuries – see Andre Trocme, pp. 19–66, and John Howard Yoder, pp. 60–75.

[4] Jesus' "descent into hell" – what happened between his death and his resurrection – is not a clear doctrine in Scripture. From Psalm 16:8–11, Acts 2:25–31, Ephesians 4:8–10, 1 Peter 3:18–22, 4:6, Luke 16:19–31 and Matthew 27:50–53, we can give an indication as I have done in my brief comment – which represents a Lutheran view. For a detailed discussion on this issue, see Derek Morphew, *The Spiritual Spider*

when he ascended into his body and rose again, re-entering God's presence (John 20:17), defeating the power of death and the grave. As Hebrews 2:14–15 says: "He too shared in [our] humanity so that by his death *he might destroy him who holds the power of death – that is, the devil –* and free those who all their lives were held in slavery by their fear of death."

The resurrection accounts connote the new creation (Luke 24; John 20): Jesus was resurrected in a garden of spring flowers, was seen as "the gardener", and breathed a new species into being as God did in the first garden.[5] The Last Adam in-breathes us with his Spirit and we are "born again", a "new creation; the old has gone, the new has come!" (2 Corinthians 5:17). The curse has been broken, the earth has been restored to its rightful owner, the title deeds have been re-entrusted to us, and our sandals have been returned so that we can walk to the ends of the old earth bringing the new creation.

Jesus gives us authority and responsibility

On the day of his resurrection, Jesus breathed his Spirit into his disciples and said: "Go and forgive people people's debts and they will be forgiven and restored to this new creation. Those whom you do not forgive will remain in debt, in slavery to Satan. Announce the Jubilee and people will experience it! Announce the kingdom and people will enter it!" (John 20:21–23 RAP).

God has given us astounding authority and awesome responsibility. Before his ascension to God's throne, Jesus said: "*All* authority in the heavens and on the earth has been given to me; therefore *you* go in *that* authority and liberate people in all nations. Plunge them into the reality of the Trinitarian God; teach them to live God's life on earth; and I personally will be with you by my Spirit, to the end of the age" (Matthew 28:18–20 RAP). Then Jesus ascended to God's right hand, and with the Father he poured out the Holy Spirit on the church at Pentecost. This made Christ's authoritative headship in the heavens *real on earth, through the body of Christ*. We must exercise this "all authority" of God's kingdom by "the powers of the coming ages",

---

Web, pp. 81–88.
[5] For an exposition of the new creation/Eden connotations, see N.T. Wright, *The Resurrection of the Son of God.*

until all God's enemies become his footstool (Hebrews 6:4–5; Acts 2:31–35; Ephesians 1:18–23).

If Jesus has been given *all* the authority, then Satan has no more authority! The *only* authority he has is his influence over people through deception – he is the father of lies (John 8:44). His lies keep people ignorant of his demise through Jesus our Kinsman-Redeemer. He *continues* to rule people *illegally* through sin, sickness, demons and death, despite the price having been paid. He is a stubborn imposter. We must blow his cover! We are the newly authorised custodians of the earth enforcing Satan's defeat. We must preach the truth that sets people free. We must be aware of his deceptive schemes and crush him under foot (2 Corinthians 11:14; 2:11; Romans 16:20). We are to destroy the works of the devil as Jesus did, to "heal all those who are oppressed by the devil" (Acts 10:38).

If we keep quiet, if we keep the good news to ourselves, we empower Satan's illegal rule; we keep people in their ignorance and slavery. We have the very words of eternal life. We can speak order to chaos, bringing the new creation into existence. Our silence and passivity with regard to the good news of God's kingdom could be the greatest scandal in human history, equal only to Satan's deceptive cover-up since his defeat at the nail-pierced hands of Jesus.

If Jesus has done all this, why is the devil allowed to continue his evil reign? Why did it not all end two thousand years ago? I will answer this shortly, but what can be said briefly is that Jesus is coming back with our entire extended family from all of human history – God's angels included – to evict forcefully Satan and every last demon from the face of the earth. *Then Shalom will reign; every knee will bow and every tongue confess that Jesus Christ is Lord* (Philippians 2:10–11).

We turn now to a summary of the biblical theology of the kingdom of God and how it defines sickness and healing.

Summarising the theology of the kingdom of God[6]

"The kingdom of God" in both the Old and New Testament means God's *Kingship*. It is a dynamic reality, rather than a static idea. God rules over all he made, but the Bible emphasises *the action* of his rule. His kingdom or will is challenged and opposed on earth. We are taught to pray: "Your kingdom come, your will be done on earth as it is in heaven" (Matthew 6:10). Kingdom is the act of ruling, the manifestation of God's presence, more than the place, sphere or realm of rule. It is King*ship*, authority, power (Luke 19:12).

The biblical theme is: God *is* King, and God *will become* King. It leads to a two-age or two-kingdom framework of reality and human history: the present evil age (kingdom of evil), and the future age (God's coming kingdom).[7] The idea is that, through the fall of humanity, Satan has become "the god of this age", "the prince of this world" (2 Corinthians 4:4; John 12:31). God promises he will intervene and overthrow Satan's kingdom, re-establishing his rule over humanity and the earth. The Old Testament prophets spoke of the new age of God's kingdom as "the Day of the Lord". All the promises centre on God's Messiah-King,[8] who will bring about his kingdom on earth at *the end of the age*. Kingdom theology is part of eschatology, the study of the end or the last things. King Jesus is God's *Eschaton* – "the Last (One)" in Greek (Revelation 1:17). He not only brings the end of the world, he *is* The End. *Therefore* he is also The Beginning, making all things new.[9]

In the New Testament God's kingdom is fulfilled – called "realised" or "inaugurated" eschatology. The end has been realised or inaugurated *in history*. In Jesus of Nazareth, the Hebrew prophecies

---

[6]For a full theology of the kingdom, see Derek Morphew, *Breakthrough – Discovering the Kingdom* (Cape Town: VIP, 1991); G.E. Ladd, *The Presence of the Future* (Grand Rapids: Eerdmans, 1974).
[7]See Daniel 2:44; Mark 10:30; Matthew 12:32; Ephesians 1:21; Colossians 1:12–13; Hebrew 6:5.
[8]In Hebrew *Meshiach* (Messiah) is "the Anointed" or "the King". It is the same in the Greek: *Christos* (Christ) means "the Anointed", "the King". Therefore "Jesus Christ" is Jesus Messiah or King Jesus.
[9]This is Adrio König's point of departure in his excellent study of the kingdom, *The Eclipse of Christ in Eschatology – Towards a Christ-Centered Approach* (Grand Rapids: Eerdmans, 1989); also a VBI course in the Kingdom of God certificate.

were fulfilled: the future age broke through into the present evil age. When Jesus came to people, it was the end of Satan's rule over them and the beginning of God's reign. By destroying the works of the devil, Jesus set people free: "If I drive out demons by the Spirit of God, then the kingdom of God *has come upon you*" (Matthew 12:28). Paul says "the ends of the ages have come" upon us (1 Corinthians 10:11 NASB). In short, Jesus, God's King, spoke the words, did the works, and demonstrated the wonders of the kingdom of God.

However this happened without this age coming to an end. Jesus brings the future kingdom into this present age, confronting and defeating Satan, but without bringing the age to an end. It is a provisional and principled fulfilment of the kingdom. We still await that consummation of God's kingdom when Jesus comes *again* finally to banish Satan and his demons from the earth. This fulfilment *without* consummation is "the mystery of the kingdom of God" that Jesus taught in his parables (Matthew 13). Therefore "the last days" are from the first coming through to the second coming of Jesus (Acts 2:17; Hebrews 1:1–2). In these last days the wheat and the weeds grow side by side, good and bad fish are netted together, only to be separated at the end of the age. We live in the "mystery" between the times, the overlapping of two ages that exist side by side.

Although Satan has already been defeated, he is not yet banished from the earth. We are at war with him; and he is more dangerous now than ever, going around like a roaring lion, seeking whom he can devour (1 Peter 5:8). He is illegally making his "last stand" on our land. We experience the battle within ourselves, between our new nature in Christ and our old sinful nature. Theologians call this "eschatological tension". John expresses it well when he says we are "already" God's children, but what we will be has "not yet" been revealed. "We know that … the whole world is under the control of the evil one", but "the evil one cannot harm" God's children because he "keeps [us] safe" (1 John 3:3; 5:18–19). This tension or mystery has implications, especially for a proper understanding and praxis of healing. The following diagram illustrates the framework of the kingdom:

The biblical framework of the kingdom of God

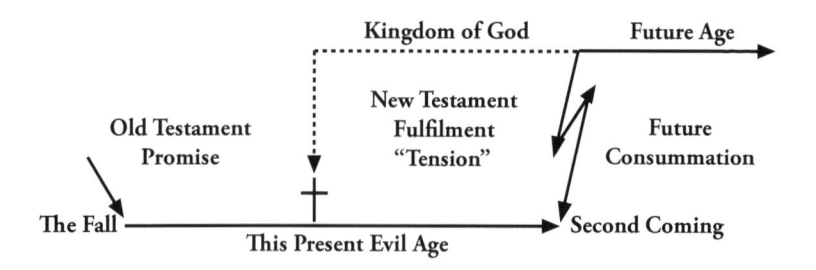

```
                    Kingdom of God              Future Age
                 ┌─────────────────┐─────────────────────→
                 ⋮                 ⋮
                 ⋮  New Testament  ⋮
   Old Testament ⋮   Fulfilment    ⋮      Future
      Promise    ⋮    "Tension"    ⋮   Consummation
            ↘    ▼                 ▼↗↙
   The Fall ─────┼─────────────────────→ Second Coming
                 This Present Evil Age
```

Summarising a theology of sickness and healing

From this kingdom framework I can summarise a theology of sickness and healing.[10] *In the beginning* God's *Shalom* (wholeness) reigned. This was disrupted by sin and death. The result was sickness, a foretaste of mortality and corruption. Sickness is our enemy, aimed at destroying us – the domain of Satan.

The Old Testament has a developing view of sickness and healing. Disease is part of the fall, allowed and even used by Yahweh as a means of discipline of (his) people. Healing is conditional on Israel's return to Yahweh in repentance. The strength of this theme is seen in the covenantal blessings and curses in Deuteronomy 28. Satan is *not* Yahweh's equal opposite, but a fallen angel opposing *humanity*. Satan and his messengers (sickness) are seen ultimately as Yahweh's servants – God remains in control. *But Yahweh's true nature as deliverer and healer* emerges in his Kingship over Israel through the Exodus and beyond. He defeats Israel's enemies, including sickness, false gods and death (Exodus 15:26: "I am *YHWH Rapha*, the Lord who heals you."). The psalmist affirms this view: Yahweh "heals all your diseases" (103:3).

This theme takes root in the prophets. The promised Messianic kingdom is characterised by God defeating evil and sickness with wholistic healing – restored *Shalom* – which is God's revealed nature

---

[10] John Wimber not only based a theology of healing on the kingdom, but also the way we do church, ministry and mission. See John Wimber, *Power Evangelism* and *Power Healing*; Venter, *Doing Church*; Bill Jackson, *The Quest for the Radical Middle – A History of the Vineyard* (Cape Town: VIP, 1999).

and purpose for Israel and the world.[11] Isaiah 35:4–6 poetically prophesies this:

> *Say to those with fearful hearts,*
> *"Be strong, do not fear;*
> *your God will come,*
> *he will come with vengeance;*
> *with divine retribution*
> *he will come to save you."*
> *Then will the eyes of the blind be opened*
> *and the ears of the deaf unstopped.*
> *Then will the lame leap like a deer,*
> *and the tongue of the dumb shout for joy.*
> *Water will gush forth in the wilderness*
> *and streams in the desert.*

At the end, in the Age to Come, God "will wipe away every tear from their eyes. There will be no more death or mourning or crying or pain" or sickness (Revelation 21:4). Heaven comes to earth, making all things new, more glorious than in Eden. Healing is definitely God's will, a foretaste of the end.

In the New Testament the future age breaks into the present, heaven comes to earth in Jesus of Nazareth. Sickness is seen as Satan's domain – it victimises and enslaves. Healing is part of God's kingdom, realised in Jesus' ministry, death and resurrection. The word for "salvation"/ "saved" (*sozo*) is also used for "healed" and "made whole".[12] Healing is not just physical but wholistic, a breakthrough of "the powers of the coming age" (Hebrews 6:5); signs and wonders of the kingdom's presence in fulfilment of the Hebrew prophets. When John the Baptiser doubted if Jesus was the Messiah, Jesus quoted Isaiah 35:5–6, pointing to the healing miracles he was doing (Matthew 11:2–6). However, there is the minor theme of sickness as discipline from the

---

[11] See Kelsey's Old Testament view of sickness and healing in *Psychology, Medicine and Christian Healing,* pp. 27–36. Michael Brown has done a comprehensive study on it in *Israel's Divine Healer, Studies in Old Testament Biblical Theology* (Grand Rapids: Zondervan, 1995). *Appendix 2 includes all the references to healing in the Old Testament.*

[12] In Acts 4:9. See also Mark 5:23, 28, 34; 6:56; 10:52; Luke 7:50; 8:36, 48, 50; 17:19; 18:42 (and John 11:12; James 5:15).

Lord (1 Corinthians 11:27–32).[13] In short, sickness and healing *is kingdom warfare* against evil in all its forms, restoring wholistic *Shalom* to people and creation.[14] It is also a kingdom mystery because we live and minister healing in eschatological tension.

The tension and mystery of the kingdom is critical to a proper theology and praxis of healing. We cannot dictate or control healing, yet we cannot accept or surrender to sickness. We pray with confident authority and expectation of healing for everyone, yet we are humble and honest, trusting God with the results – *only* God can heal. We do both *at the same time.* We instinctively try to resolve tension by tending to "either/or" ("and/both" is messy). Too much "kingdom now" leads to arrogance and presumption, demanding healing as if on tap. Too much "kingdom then" leads to pessimism and fatalism, leaving healing to "if it is God's will". "Balance" leads to a neutralising of the radical edges, loss of risk-taking, a passive middle road and theologically correct approach to healing. We too easily explain lack of healing by kingdom tension when we ought to push through in faith. "Tension", embracing *both* the "already" and "not yet" of the kingdom, makes us living paradoxes. It is learning to live and minister in the overlapping of two ages: the power of the kingdom *and* the resistance of this evil age. It leads to persevering faith, optimistic realism, dependence on God, discerning the moment, honouring people's dignity, respecting the unknown, and leaving the results with God.

In summary, sickness is the result of death; healing is the result of

---

[13] Some major themes or emphases in the Old Testament are minor in the New Testament, and vice versa. Some things in the Old Testament continue in the New, while others are discontinued, e.g. ceremonial law. The key to correct interpretation of Scripture is: The Old is fulfilled in the New, the New interprets the Old – *not* the other way round.

[14] The wholistic nature of *Shalom* means thinking of sickness and healing in political, economic, social and ecological terms, defeating evil in socio-economic structures and public policy, *not* only in spiritual, psychological and physical terms. Sickness and healing are about poverty and justice in terms of pollution, gender violence, equal access to health care, social welfare systems, affordable medical insurance and hospitalisation, multinational pharmaceuticals, the politics/economics of the HIV/AIDS pandemic, to mention a few. These dimensions are beyond the scope of this book, but we need to be aware of them to keep us from a dualistic view of healing (spiritual versus social). For healing and justice issues, see Walter Brueggemann, *Living Toward a Vision*, pp. 103–112, 141–153, 175–183.

resurrection. Sickness and healing are the war of the "middle ground" between death and resurrection; between spiritual resurrection in the now kingdom (at conversion) and bodily resurrection in the yet-to-come kingdom (at the Second Coming). "If the Spirit of him who raised Jesus from the dead lives in us, then he will also give life to our mortal bodies by his indwelling Spirit: as healing now, full resurrection later" (Romans 8:11 RAP).

The most *important conclusion* is that Christian healing is *ministering the kingdom of God* to people – *not* just "ministering healing". Hence the book's subtitle, because it defines *Doing Healing*. I conclude with alternative Christian views on healing, and how – by implication – kingdom theology answers them.

Various Christian views on healing[15]

1. *Healing as medical science:* Many churches have a dualistic, materialistic worldview in which there is no need for Christian healing ministry. Christian ministry is for the spiritual health of people and (real) healing is the domain of orthodox modern medicine, including psychology and psychiatry, which by and large have replaced the counselling healing ministry in many churches. However, healing is *God's* domain and he has authorised the church to bring wholistic healing to the world – not with the exclusion of medical science.

2. *Healing as God's sovereign will:* This takes two forms. Liberal theology says Jesus' healing miracles are mythical stories told as a means of preaching the gospel. If a miracle has any historical basis, it has to be scientifically explained through natural cause and effect – likewise with apparent modern miracles. If it cannot be explained in this way, it may be God's sovereign will overriding nature. Alternatively, many conservative Christians say God can, and occasionally does, heal the sick. But it is a fatalistic view of "the will of God", with no value placed on Christian healing ministry.

3. *Sickness as God's chastisement; healing as reward for repentance:*

---

[15] Although there are others, these are the main views influencing Christians. I mention the views without detailing how the theology of the kingdom challenges and answers them – this chapter has equipped you to do that exercise.

This takes a minor view in the Bible and makes it the major view. Sickness equals sin which equals punitive suffering from God. Suffering is "redemptive" in that God uses sickness to chastise us, to bring us closer to him. On repentance, we are healed. Paradoxically, this is both a spiritual and humanistic view: God is responsible for sickness and human beings are responsible for healing, via repentance.[16] This view results in a highly spiritual and even cruel practice of Christian healing without consideration of the major biblical view that sickness is an expression of the domain of evil which Jesus came to defeat.

4. *Healing ceased with Jesus and the apostles:* Healing miracles were given to Jesus and the early church to authenticate their kingdom message. With the formation of the New Testament canon in the 4th century, healing miracles ceased – called cessationism (the Bible now "proves" God's existence and truth). This view is part of dispensationalism, a theological system in some evangelical churches that says God deals with humanity, Israel and the church in separate times or dispensations. Signs and wonders were for a specific period.

5. *Healing as a result of the atonement and exercising faith:* The view that Jesus died not only for our sins, but also for our sicknesses. Like personal salvation, healing is through Christ's atonement on the cross, to be received by faith, as we receive forgiveness of sin, because "by his stripes we are healed". This Pentecostal and Charismatic view of healing has been popularised in the Word of Faith/Prosperity movements. The result is an aggressive healing ministry in which faith is the key – even the magical – factor. In fact, it is often faith in faith or in some formula, not faith in God. This view reduces healing to one event in Christ – his death.

6. *Healing as the restoration of the gifts of the Spirit:* This is an extension of view 5, found mainly in Pentecostal and Charismatic circles. It is based on a particular eschatology: Spiritual truth, gift ministries and healings were "lost" to the church during the medieval period.

---

[16] The Anglican healing service in *The Common Book of Prayer* is built on this view; Kelsey, *Psychology, Medicine and Christian Healing*, pp. 11–17.

From the Reformation, God restored salvation to the church (1500s), believer's baptism (Anabaptists, 1600s), evangelism and mission (Evangelical Revivals, 1700–1800s), Spirit baptism and gifts (Pentecostals, 1900s), the "Five-fold Ministry Offices" of Ephesians 4:11 (Charismatic church-planting networks, 1970s onwards), and now the great revival of signs, wonders and world evangelisation. "The last days" are seen as being just before the Second Coming of Christ, producing a "wind up" view of "the end times". It leads to a triumphalistic revivalist approach that believes a final generation of God's elite will do great signs and wonders to bring about world evangelisation for the coming of Christ. Healing is seen as increasing spiritual warfare through God's anointed end-time church, and those not in "this flow" of this restoration will miss out![17]

---

[17] See J.T. Alblas, *A Different Breed* (E-Publication, Cape Town: VIP, 2006) for a study that compares the Pentecostal Restoration framework ("New Apostolic Reformation" and related movements) and the evangelical kingdom framework (Vineyard, New Wine and other Empowered Evangelical movements).

Part Two: Theology

Personal reflection, application and group discussion

1. What has God said to you, or what has captured your attention while you read this chapter? Why has this impressed you?
2. How would you summarise, in your own words, the essence of the theology of the kingdom of God? What is the most exciting or difficult aspect for you?
3. Does the story of the land and Kinsman-Redeemer to illustrate the kingdom work for you? What weaknesses do you see in using this parable to explain the kingdom? Try to come up with your own illustration to communicate the kingdom, then share it with your group.
4. What has been your view or theology of healing prior to reading this book? Has your view changed in any way since reading this chapter? If so, how?
5. See my challenge in footnote 15. How does a kingdom theology of sickness and healing challenge and answer the various alternative Christian views of healing? Choose one or two as a practical exercise.
6. Is there anything you need to do or change in your life and ministry as a result of reading this chapter?

5

Modelling 1: Receiving and ministering the Kingdom

*The beginning of the good news about Jesus Messiah, the son of God …
After John was put in prison, Jesus went all around Galilee,
proclaiming the good news of God. "The time is now fulfilled,"
he said. "The Kingdom of God is at hand, right near you.
Repent and believe this good news!"*
– Mark 1:1, 14–15 RAP

Jesus is our model for ministry

Before I met my wife, she was a professional ramp and photographic model. After she stopped modelling, Jesus met her and changed her life. Then I met her and she has never been the same! Listening to Gilli's modelling stories, I was struck by the power models exert over people's minds and young people's bodies. What we see is what we want. Marketing knows the power of positioning and modelling. The church is naïve in comparison.

John Wimber repeatedly said, in relation to church, leadership and ministry, "models rule". We should be careful how we do things, who or what program we put up front in the church. It forms the minds and kindles the desires of our people, especially if it is successful. Pragmatism says: If it works and is successful, do it and do not ask questions. Defining success requires effort and honesty as no model is value-free. All models are package deals: they come with hidden assumptions, beliefs and contexts of formation. I discuss healing ministry models in Chapter 13. In this chapter I focus on Jesus as *the* model for all Christians.

Jesus' life and ministry is history, so we need imagination and interpretation to emulate his model. Reading the stories of Jesus makes us fall in love with him, causing us to pursue him passionately, to live and love as he did. I retell representative stories of *how Jesus ministered the kingdom of God to people* from Mark's Gospel. Mark recorded Peter's eyewitness accounts and the "sermons" he preached (as Peter's scribe).[1]

Mark begins with three key understandings: "The beginning of the good news of Jesus Christ, the son of God" (1:1). *Firstly,* he uses the same word from Genesis 1:1 in the Greek Septuagint: "In *the beginning* God created …" Mark is saying that it is a new beginning – God is (re)creating the heavens and the earth in Jesus' life and ministry. "The beginning" also implies that the new creation (the good news of Jesus), *continues* through his followers who emulate him until he returns. As Adam and Eve were entrusted with continuing God's good creation, so we are to continue God's new creation begun in Christ.

Secondly, Mark uses the political word "gospel" (*evangelion*, 1:1), derived from the Emperor cult: the "good news" that "Caesar is Lord" – the *Pax Roma*, the Peace of Rome wherever Caesar ruled. Heralds would go to the ends of the Empire announcing Caesar's "gospel" – the good news of his birth, life and victories over his enemies. Mark uses *this* word to announce the carpenter-rabbi from Nazareth: "*Yeshua* is Lord"! *The* gospel is that Jesus is *the* Messiah King who defeats God's enemies, bringing his kingdom – the peace (*Shalom*) of YHWH – to Israel and the world. The word "good news" recalls

---
[1] Sound tradition holds this view of how Mark wrote his Gospel. This is not the place to discuss other views. In relating the stories, I do not debate technical points citing sources, although I have consulted various commentaries.

Isaiah 52:7–10, the promised messenger announcing God's salvation: "Your God reigns!" This announcement is *an act of creation in itself, inaugurating the reality which it proclaims* – the kingdom of God.

Thirdly, Mark calls him "Christ, the son of God", a Jewish term from God's promise to King David regarding a Messianic son (2 Samuel 7:14 cf. Psalm 2:7). This title does not refer to a divine figure per se, but a human being anointed with God's Spirit as king, to bring his kingdom in fulfilment of all Israel's anointed deliverers and kings before him.[2] *It means that Jesus lived and ministered as a human being by the Spirit's power.* In this sense he is the consummate human being, the New Adam, the true Israel as God intended Israel to be, our model for life and ministry. Jesus was totally dependent on God *for* the Spirit's presence and power – just as we are. He was totally dependent on God, *by* the Spirit, *for* his life and ministry – just as we are.

Although Jesus was God's Son, he was affirmed as such *with the anointing of the Spirit* at his baptism (Mark 1:9–11).[3] Therefore *he* will "baptise … with the Holy Spirit" all those who follow him (1:8). The Spirit drove Jesus from his baptism into the desert to meet and defeat Satan (1:12–13). This stark account of the desert temptations conveys the brutal nature of the battle, implying that *this* was Jesus' ongoing war with evil in his kingdom ministry. Peter's summary is: "God anointed Jesus of Nazareth with the Holy Spirit and power, and he went around doing good and healing all who were tyrannised and tormented by the devil" (Acts 10:38 RAP). It was power against power – the Spirit's liberation overcame Satan's oppression in fulfilment of Isaiah's prophecy (61:1–2), which Jesus *consciously and intentionally* lived out: "The Spirit of the Lord is on me, because he has anointed me to …" (see Luke 4:14–21).

---

[2] To us "son of God" is the post-resurrection Christian understanding of "The Son of God" – *of Jesus as God*. Then we read that back into Jesus' ministry, which misleads us. Yes, Jesus was both fully divine and fully human during his earthly life, but he lived and ministered, *not* by his divine power – which he laid aside when he became incarnate (Philippians 2:6–11) – but by the anointing of the Spirit (Anointed = Messiah). If he had used his divinity, he would not be a model that we could follow. However, he was *a sinless man* under God's anointing, so in a certain sense he remains unique.

[3] Fulfilling the Messianic promises in Psalm 2:7 and Isaiah 42:1, joining Son and Servant: "You are my Son … my chosen one in whom I delight; I will put my Spirit on him, and he will bring justice to the nations."

Announcing and enacting the kingdom

Mark 1:14–15, quoted at the beginning of this chapter, is the summary statement of Jesus' ministry – the key that unlocks the stories of Jesus. Wherever Jesus went, he repeatedly announced the kingdom as stated in 1:15. His announcement made it happen; he enacted the kingdom by healing people and driving out demons. Words and works are *inseparable* in kingdom ministry. The following representative stories of Jesus' ministry illustrate this reality. But first, what did Jesus mean by this announcement, and how did the Jews understand it?

- *"The time is come, the kingdom of God is near":* History has reached its climax! It is the Day of Yahweh! The prophecies of Israel's times and destiny are *now* being fulfilled. God has come to judge and defeat evil, to save and restore Israel and the nations. He is asserting his rule. His Kingship is active, near you, within reach ("at hand"). The Jews would have heard: "Messiah is here to overthrow the Romans!" But God was defeating a greater enemy than Caesar and Roman oppression: Satan and his oppression. It meant: "The end has come," not meaning that everything will be destroyed, but rather a radical new beginning. King Jesus is "the First and the Last, the Beginning and the End" (Revelation 1:8, 17; 22:13). He is announcing *the end* of Satan's reign of sin, sickness, demons and death (judgment), and *the beginning* of new life, the restoration and recreation of all things (salvation).

- *"Repent and believe this good news":* Therefore, turn from your sins and return to God. Israel was already aware of this repentance from John's baptism. "Repentance" means more than turning from our sin. *Metanoia* means "change of mind", to see things differently – a paradigm shift. The Jews had to change their thinking, their preconceived expectations of a nationalistic military Messiah and kingdom, or they might "not recognise the time of God's coming" (Luke 19:41–44) and oppose it – which is what happened. "Believe" meant opening and entrusting yourself to what God is doing – this "gospel" of Jesus Messiah doing God's kingdom thing!

In effect, Jesus was saying: "God is actively present, asserting his Kingship over evil in all its forms. *To experience and receive this kingdom,* turn from your old ways and mindset, *change your thinking and open yourself to God's possibilities, entrusting yourself to what he is doing right now.*"

Receiving and ministering the kingdom

The first thing that Jesus did after he began to announce the kingdom (Mark 1:15), was to call followers – his emerging community of the kingdom (1:16–20). Rabbi Jesus drew a band of disciples to live with him, learn from him, become like him; to speak the words, do the works, see the wonders and suffer the wounds of the kingdom. Jesus chose them "that they might be *with him* and that he might *send them* out to preach and to have *authority* to drive out demons" (3:14–15).

This explains their calling ("Come, follow me", 1:17), their formation ("I will make you", 1:17) and their purpose (to be "fishers of people", 1:17). Jesus contextualised their occupation into their *kingdom vocation:* The "fishers" would complete the end-time/eschatological task of bringing God's judgment[4] by destroying Satan's works and saving people. Like Jesus, wherever his followers went, they represented the end (judgment) and the beginning (salvation). The church is not only the sign, but the instrument of the kingdom.

With a community of disciples in place, Mark tells the stories of Jesus to show:

- How God's rule in Christ defeats evil's rule in all its dimensions.[5]
- How Jesus models ministering the kingdom of God.
- How he uses ministry to train his disciples to receive and minister the kingdom *just as he did* – then to send them out to do the same.

---

[4] In fulfilment of Jeremiah 16:16; Ezekiel 12:13; 29:4–5 (cf. 47:8–12); 38:4; Amos 4:2; Habakkuk 1:14–17.

[5] King Jesus rules over evil by the word of his command (kingdom authority). "Spiritual warfare" is not merely driving out demons, as many Christians suppose. It is the wholistic engagement with, and defeat of, evil in *all* its forms, as seen in the stories of Jesus.

Part Two: Theology

Jesus rules over evil spirits (1:21–28 RAP)

The first story is of Jesus going to synagogue in Capernaum. He was invited to preach from the set Scripture reading that day. As he taught, the people became aware of the authority of this thirty-year-old Rabbi. He did not quote other authorities (previous Rabbis) as other teachers did, but spoke with insight and wisdom directly from God. This provoked a reaction.

Suddenly a terrifying shriek pierced the air. It sounded as if all hell had broken loose! A regular member of the congregation was screaming, "What do you want with us, Jesus of Nazareth? Have you come to destroy us? I know who you are: the Holy One of God." The people were shocked – this doesn't happen in church! They did not know it was a demon speaking. For years it had hidden and resided in that suffering man. The demon was exposed by Jesus' presence and authority, which was superior to the demon's authority to enslave. How many sit like this for years in church in silent suffering? What would happen if Jesus *really* came to your church one day?

In contrast to the congregants, the spirit world not only recognised and knew who Jesus was, but confessed it openly – in terror: the Messiah of God (see Luke 4:41). In contrast to human beings, demons know all about judgment and believe in God's Word – with trembling (James 2:19). As his followers, they know of Lucifer's rebellion and God's eschatological judgment of evil. So they were terrified: "What do you want with us? Have you come to torture us *before the appointed time?*" (Matthew 8:29). The demons pulled out their calendars to check: "What's up? You've come way before *the time!*" They knew it was not the end of the world, but meeting Jesus was meeting the end. The good news ("*The time* has come") was bad news for them. It was the end of *their* authority and torment over Abe and the beginning of their torture in "the Abyss" of judgment (Luke 8:31). It was the end of Abe's demonisation and the beginning of his freedom – God's kingdom "came upon" him.

How did Jesus respond to this interruption? His spiritual worldview told him it was not the man screaming, but a demon. He sternly rebuked the demon saying: "Be quiet!" (literally "be muzzled"). Jesus did not shout at the top of his voice to show his authority. In a

Modelling 1: *Receiving and ministering the kingdom*

controlled voice, he commanded the demon to be quiet. Jesus did not want the demon to create a disturbance, so he silenced his attempted control. Nor did Jesus want his identity to be made known in this way – it could hinder his mission.[6] Then he commanded: "Come out of him!" The spirit shook the man violently and came out with a further shriek. The people were astonished: "What authority! He even gives orders to evil spirits and they obey him." They had seen or heard of Jewish exorcists making demons leave people by magical incantations and techniques. This was no exorcism. It was direct expulsion – Jesus drove them out by *his authoritative command*.

Mark significantly begins Jesus' kingdom ministry – "the *beginning* of the good news of Jesus Christ" – with the expulsion of demons. In the beginning, chaos and darkness covered the earth. God spoke, and by the power of the brooding Spirit, *Shalom* triumphed over chaos, light drove out darkness. In this first story, Mark sets the pattern for Jesus' kingdom ministry: speaking the new creation into being, day by day asserting God's rule over disorder by driving out demons "throughout Galilee" (1:39). The face-off with demons was a raw and open confrontation between the two kingdoms. Although evil spirits are known in the Old Testament, this expulsion of demons is not mentioned.[7] Hence Jesus' deliverance ministry was powerful and controversial in Israel – a regular feature of his kingdom enactment, *and* that of his disciples.[8]

In doing deliverance, Jesus modelled it, training his disciples to expel demons. They did it well (6:12–13), but later were unable to drive out a spirit that made a young boy mute and caused seizures (9:14–29). Jesus was exasperated: "O *unbelieving* generation, how long must I go over these things? How long must I put up with you? Bring the boy to me!" He cast the demon out with a command. Their

---

[6]Jewish exorcists said spiritual powers are subdued by naming them. Some scholars say the demon tried to subdue Jesus in this way. I disagree. They could not help but acknowledge who Jesus was in fearful anticipation of the day when "every knee should bow ... and every tongue confess that Jesus Christ is Lord" (Philippians 2:10–11). See Mark 1:34; 3:11–12.
[7]The *only* reference that comes close is 1 Samuel 16:23. But David bringing temporary relief to Saul's torment by an evil spirit is not the same as Jesus' expulsions – they were unique in Judaism.
[8]Mark 1:32–34, 39; 3:7–12; 3:14–15 cf. 6:7–13; 5:1–20; 7:24–30; 9:14–27.

89

failure was attributed to "unbelief". Perhaps they presumed their gifting (6:7) was under their control, but previous successes are no guarantee of continued power.[9] Later they sheepishly sidled up to him: "Why couldn't we drive it out? Give us the inside track, what was *really* going on?" Jesus replied: "This kind comes out only by prayer – and fasting if necessary." This type of stubborn demon can only be expelled *by full reliance on God's unlimited power through prayer* (with fasting). Besides weakening evil powers, prayer transforms our unbelief into real faith making "all things possible to those who believe" (v. 23). Prayer helps us to change our thinking and open ourselves to God's possibilities. Jesus expected his disciples to operate in kingdom authority as he did, but they were slow learners and at times they failed.

Jesus rules over sickness (1:29–35 RAP)

After the meeting, they went to Peter's home. His mother-in-law was sick with a high fever and she could not prepare the meal. The disciples told Jesus, believing he could help, after what they had witnessed. Jesus went into her room and took her hand in his. The fever immediately left. She then prepared the meal.

Matthew 8:15 says Jesus "*touched*" her", a phrase for laying on hands for healing. Luke 4:39 says he "bent over her and *rebuked* the fever, and *it left her*". These references teach that her sickness was not of God; Satan was afflicting her. Just as Jesus rebuked the demon, so he "rebukes" the fever and "it leaves her". His rebuke was a command, his pattern for all subsequent healings.

Jesus rules over sickness as he does over demons, fulfilling the Hebrew prophets (Isaiah 35:3–6). Mark affirms this by telling how people brought "all the sick and demonised" to the house. "Jesus healed many who had various diseases and drove out many demons" late into the night. Very early the next morning Jesus was out in a quiet place praying, showing his utter dependence on God.

---

[9] That is why Jesus taught his disciples how to pray *daily*: "Give me *today* what I need for *today*." The context of "deliver us from evil" is "daily bread" (Luke 11:1–13), asking daily for the *charisma* of the Spirit *to help others.*

Modelling 1: *Receiving and ministering the kingdom*

Jesus rules over sin (2:1–12 RAP)

A few days later Rabbi *Yeshua* was back in Capernaum. Many gathered at Peter's house to hear Jesus "preach the word" of the kingdom (1:15). Four men came carrying their paralysed friend on a mat. Because they had heard or seen that Jesus healed the sick, they changed their thinking and opened their minds to God's possibilities: "He doesn't *have to* remain lame! God can do something – the Rabbi says God's kingdom is near!" But they could not get into the house due to the crowd. This did not deter them; their faith and different thinking led them up the stairs onto the roof. They dug a hole above where Jesus was standing and lowered their friend down.

When Jesus saw *their faith*, he responded by saying to *their lame friend*: "Son, your sins are forgiven here and now!" Some leaders thought: "What? How can he say that? It is blasphemy! Only God forgives sins! Doesn't he know the Word?"[10] Jesus knew in his spirit – by the Spirit – what they were thinking. He confronted them: "Change your thinking! God's kingdom is here! Which is easier to say to a paralytic: 'Your sins are forgiven' or 'Get up and walk'?" It is easier to pronounce forgiveness as no one can see if it happens. To say: "Get up and walk" is risking – everyone sees if it happens – or not! They judged Jesus to be a blasphemous "dispenser of cheap grace",[11] not believing he could heal the man. But the kingdom was near.

To show that God had given the "son of man"[12] *authority on earth to forgive sins,* Jesus turned to the paralytic and said: "Get up, take your mat and go home!" God's power entered his body, overcoming

---

[10]Exodus 34:6–7; Psalm 103:3; 130:4; Isaiah 43:25; Daniel 9:8–9. Only God forgives sins, but priests spoke forgiveness to people at Temple sacrifices. Prophets also spoke God's forgiveness (2 Samuel 12:13). Like a priest and prophet, Jesus pronounced what *God was doing* (forgiving), thus actualising it (the kingdom came on the man). But in so doing, Jesus bypassed the Temple (forgiveness) system, which was "blasphemy" – misusing God and leading his people astray.

[11]William Lane's phrase in The Gospel of Mark, *The New London Commentary Series* (London: Marshall, Morgan and Scott, 1974), p. 96, one of the better commentaries on Mark.

[12]The phrase Jesus used of himself (simply means "human being", as in Ezekiel's usage). But drawn from Daniel (7:13), it had messianic meaning in Jesus' day. It referred to "one like a son of man" who represents Israel, and after suffering and vindication, was given kingly power and authority to dispense God's judgment. Here he judges sin and forgives the sinner.

the paralysis. The man got up, took his mat and walked free. The crowd said: "We've never seen anything like this!"

The critics had to recognise that Jesus' forgiveness of sin had been effective. The story shows that *Jesus rules over sin* – he brings the kingdom as he feasts with sinners, offering them God's forgiveness and fellowship (2:15–17; Matthew 8:11–12). It also reveals the relationship between sin and sickness, forgiveness and healing,[13] implying that Jesus knew, by the Spirit, that this man needed forgiveness to effect his healing. *Jesus imparts authority to his disciples to forgive sins,* to speak what God is doing (Matthew 9:8; 16:19 cf. 18:15–20; John 20:22–23).

Jesus rules over nature (4:35–41 RAP)

A few days later, after a day of teaching a Kingdom Conference, Jesus told his disciples: "Let's cross over the lake to the other side." He went to the back of the boat, lay his head on a cushion and fell asleep. A furious storm arose and the boat was almost swamped. These experienced fishermen panicked! They were all bailing water when they realised: "Where's Jesus? Why isn't he helping?" They ran to him, shook him, shouting above the storm: "Rabbi, wake up! Do you not care if we all drown? How can you sleep through this?"

Jesus got up, faced the storm, "rebuked the wind and said to the waves: 'Quiet! Be still!' Then the wind died down and it was completely calm" (v. 39). He turned to his disciples and saw a terrified crew staring back at him. They were muttering: "Who is this man? Even the wind and waves obey him!" They were more in awe of him and his authority than in fear of the storm and death.

Jesus further traumatises them: "Why are you so *afraid*? Do you *not yet* have faith? How much more must I teach and model the kingdom to you? Repent from your fear! Believe God's presence and possibilities in this situation. God's kingdom is near you, on your lips. Rebuke the storm. I expected you to silence the storm – I was sleeping! The truth is: *It was a setup.* God tested you, allowing Satan to attack us via nature's corruption. I slept peacefully, trusting God,

---

[13]Original sin is the cause of all sickness and suffering. At times *a* sickness is caused by *specific sin,* so healing is often a sign of forgiveness: 2 Chronicles 7:14; Psalm 41:4; 103:3; 147:3; Isaiah 19:22; 38:17; James 5:14–16.

while you panicked in fear. Do you get it?"

Jesus "rebuked" the storm, as he did demons and sickness, using the same command to silence the storm: "Be muzzled" ("shut up"). Mark shows that *Jesus rules over nature,* especially when it is used by evil for its purpose, fulfilling the Old Testament idea of YHWH ruling over chaotic nature.[14] In Jesus, Yahweh's Kingship over creation is present and active, *anticipating* the eschatological renewal of God's *Shalom creation*. As Jesus drives demons and sickness from *people's bodies*, anticipating the resurrection, so he drives the demonised curse *from nature*, anticipating creation's liberation (Romans 8:19–23). He equips (and expects) his disciples to do the same.

Jesus rules over death (5:21–43 RAP)

Jairus, a synagogue leader, came to Jesus for help. He fell at Jesus' feet and pleaded: "My twelve-year-old daughter is dying! *Please* come and put your hands on her so that she will be healed." Jairus had changed his thinking about the synagogue opposition to Jesus since the healing on the Sabbath (3:1–6). He put faith in Jesus to save his daughter. Jesus responded to his repentance and faith by going with him, but their journey was delayed by a crushing crowd (Luke 8:42) and a sick woman.

The woman's twelve years of "bleeding" had made her socially and spiritually "unclean". She changed her thinking. Defying Torah prohibitions (Leviticus 15:19–33), she pushed through the crowd, reached out and touched Jesus' clothes. Power entered her and instantly she was healed. Although God remains in control of his power, using Jesus as an instrument, it is released *through human faith reaching out to the kingdom of God "at hand"*. In his kingdom consciousness, Jesus knew power had left him. But he was not aware of who touched him (the "not yet" of the kingdom). "Who touched me?" he asked. The disciples responded from a different consciousness: "Everyone's jostling you! How can you ask who touched you?" Then she came forward, fell at his feet trembling, and poured out her shameful, intimate story. They all stared in silent embarrassment, edging away

---

[14]Psalm 33:7; 65:7; 77:16; 89:9; 93:3–4; 107:23–30; 147:18; Proverbs 30:4; Nahum 1:3–6.

from her. She hadn't made Jesus "unclean"; rather, by touching him, God made her clean – the kingdom reversed the flow! Jesus affirmed her: "Daughter, *your faith* has healed you.[15] Go in God's *Shalom*."

Just then some men came to Jairus saying: "Do not bother the Rabbi. Your daughter has died." Jesus overheard it and intervened: "Do not fear! Hold onto the confidence that first brought you to me. Banish fear – trust God." Jesus decisively shut fear out because it is unbelief, the enemy of faith. He turned the crowd away and went to Jairus' house. The funeral preparations had begun – the flute players and mourners were wailing. He spoke into the confusion and chaos: "Why this commotion? Stop it! The child is not dead, but asleep!" Again Jesus calmly operates in kingdom awareness, open to God's possibilities, in contrast to the others, who laughed at him.

Jesus and the parents and three disciples went into the room, where the girl was lying. He took her by the hand, without regard to the law (Numbers 19:11–22, touching a corpse was the worst defilement), and said: "Little girl, I say to you, get up!" Immediately "her spirit returned" (Luke 8:55, the enemy of death left). She got up and walked around. Everyone was astonished, except Jesus – he expected it to happen. The news spread like wildfire (Matthew 9:26).

This story shows that *Jesus rules over death*. It was not a once-off miracle (see Luke 7:11–15; John 11). Jesus moves in the calm, assertive authority of the kingdom, not anxious (in contrast to those around him), but in tune with God's action, moment by moment. Thus he equipped his disciples to go and "raise the dead" (Matthew 10:7–8). These resuscitations (not resurrections) were foreshadowed by the prophets (2 Kings 4:18–37), who predicted God's victory over death when the Messianic kingdom came (Isaiah 25:7–8; 26:19; Daniel 12:2; Hosea 13:14). The future age, in which there will be no more death (Revelation 21:4), was being realised in Jesus' victories over death.

---

[15] The Greek word for "healed" means "saved". Both spiritual salvation ("go in peace") and physical healing ("be freed from your suffering") happen in this wholistic kingdom encounter.

Jesus rules over hunger and circumstantial need (6:30–56 RAP)

After a year of modelling kingdom ministry, Jesus imparted authority to his twelve disciples and sent them out, as apostles, to announce and enact the rule of God. On their return, Jesus took them to a remote retreat, but a large crowd followed. He had compassion, healing and teaching them. In the late afternoon, the apostles grew concerned: "The people are hungry and this is a remote place. Send them home so that they can buy some food." But Jesus said: "No, you give them something to eat!" He said to Philip: "Where shall we buy food to feed all these people?" *(He said this to test them as he already had in mind what he was going to do.)*

Philip took the initiative and called an "apostolic meeting" to discuss feeding the people. Operating on the assumption of scarcity and limited resources, they listed the reasons why they could not feed the people, e.g. it would cost eight months' wages; there were too many people – the "five thousand men" meant over twelve thousand if women and children were counted. Philip returned to Jesus to present his answer (the findings of the meeting). Along the way he met Andrew. "You weren't at the meeting – where were you?" Andrew replied: "Jesus told us to feed the people, so I went looking for food." Philip then saw Andrew holding five fish sandwiches. "A little boy gave me his lunch to share!"

Andrew repented and believed when Jesus spoke the word: "You feed them." He changed his thinking and opened his mind to God's possibilities, acting on the presence of God's kingdom. Jesus took the sandwiches and instructed the twelve to seat the people in small groups of between fifty and a hundred. He lifted the bread to heaven, gave thanks, broke it, and gave each of the disciples a piece of sandwich, saying: "Go! Feed the people."

Some say that, when Jesus blessed the bread, thousands of fish and buns rained down from heaven. Not so! The miracle happened progressively *through their hands* – as long as they kept sharing, they had food in their hands to share. The kingdom is "at hand", within our reach, if we repent and believe. After they had all eaten, Jesus instructed the disciples to pick up the leftovers. They gathered twelve big basketfuls! *Then* it *really* hit them. Some miracles happen slowly but surely, unnoticed at the time, but evident after the event; other miracles are instant and outwardly powerful.

This story shows that *Jesus rules over hunger and circumstantial need.* The "good news" is that he brings the future feast of the kingdom (as prophesied in Isaiah 25:6–9 cf. Revelation 19:9), here and now. He breaks the curse of hunger with kingdom abundance, enacting God's new creation. Jesus regularly feasted with people, making *their* table *his* table, celebrating the joyful fellowship and all-sufficiency of the kingdom with them, in anticipation of God's feast at the end of the age. *This* happened *that day* – the kingdom came. The crowd wanted to take Jesus by force to make him King when they saw the miracle. Jesus dispersed them, sent his disciples across the lake, and went up a mountain to pray.

Finally, walk on water!

Resisting the temptation to be the kind of King the people wanted (to use power for popularity, to indulge their appetite for the spectacular),[16] Jesus sought solitude with his Father. It made him reflect on how his body would be broken to feed the world, so he prayed the night away. In the early hours of the morning, he saw his disciples struggling in a storm on the lake, and decided to go to them. They had only covered about three miles (5 km) in seven or eight hours of exhausting rowing against the wind. This was another divine setup!

Through the wind and the waves, the disciples saw a figure walking towards them. They were terrified, believing that ghosts of drowned fishermen hung around the lake. At first this ghostly figure seemed to "pass by them",[17] but Jesus turned to them and said: "It's me! *Do not be scared!*" Peter turned from his fear and opened himself to what God was doing. Seeing God's kingdom was near, before another thought

---

[16] See John 6:26–33: "You're looking for me, not because you saw the miracle *and thus* put your faith in me, but because your tummies were filled – the miracle entertained you and now you want more Miracle Conferences! I refuse to make you miracle and conference junkies!" (RAP).

[17] Mark uses this phrase from YHWH's self-revelation to Moses, Elijah and Job (Exodus 33:19–22; 1 Kings 19:11; Job 9:8, 11), where his glory "passes by them". He implies this meaning in Jesus' self-revelation (Mark 6:50): "It is I" or "I am he" (see Isaiah 41:4f, 13f; 43:1f; Psalm 115:9f; 118:5f). *In the midst of the crisis, do not fear – God reveals himself – to save you!*

entered his mind, he said: "Lord, if it's you, tell me to come to you." Jesus replied: "Come!" (Matthew 14:27–33).

Peter took Jesus at his word, climbed overboard and walked up and down the waves to him. *Now* the disciples' eyes were really big! Then Peter thought: "This is wonderful – I'm walking on water! But … I don't normally do this! Do you realise what you're doing?" He took his eyes off Jesus and looked at the wind and the waves. Reacting to his five senses, he lapsed from faith back into fear and sank into the water. Jesus watched. Peter cried out: "HELP ME, JESUS!" *Immediately* Jesus reached out his hand and pulled Peter up to stand beside him. Then he rebuked Peter: *"You of little faith, why did you doubt?"* Why so harsh – a little encouragement might have been better? Jesus again attacks our mortal enemy: fear and unbelief. We must defeat it before it kills us. We can walk on water – *all things are possible to those who repent and believe!*

Mark's concluding comment is important (6:51–52): "The wind died down" and the disciples "were *completely amazed*". Why so amazed? Because "they had not understood about the loaves; *their hearts were hardened*". Mark's brutal honesty probably reflects Peter's later commentary on the event. He is saying that they just did not get it! They should not have been so amazed at the presence and power of the kingdom in Jesus – especially after the feeding miracle. The supernatural had indulged them; it had *not* converted them. Miracles as such do not transform us; we are transformed by faith-full relationship(s). *Signs and wonders* point us to *Jesus*, so that we put our faith fully in *him* – not in miracles or faith itself.

In conclusion

These stories illustrate *the* good news (gospel) that Jesus brings God's kingdom to those who repent and believe. They show *how* Jesus ministers the kingdom to people by the Spirit's power (not by his divine nature), as a model to equip his followers to do the same. The basic message is: The kingdom of God is "at hand" (reach out), it is "on your lips" (speak it out), it is all around you (step out and walk on water!).

Part Two: Theology

Personal reflection, application and group discussion

1. Why is Jesus' *model* of kingdom ministry so important for us today? Is it accessible to us – can we do what he did? Explain.
2. Summarise in your own words the essential message that Jesus preached in Mark 1:15. How would you say it today in your context so that it has the same impact and implications that it had in Jesus' day?
3. Do *you* enact the kingdom of God, not only announce it? *How* are you learning to receive and minister the kingdom of God in power?
4. Jesus rules over evil in its major forms: demons, sickness, sin, nature, death, hunger and circumstantial need. What personal experience have you had in any of these dimensions of kingdom breakthrough,
   a) in your own life, and
   b) through you to others in need?
5. Which of the stories of Jesus' kingdom ministry that I have retold has touched you and made the most sense to you? Why?
6. Put yourself in the disciples' shoes. Do you think you would be any different? How? Do you *really* believe that Jesus is training *you in the same way* to do the same things? How is he doing this?

6

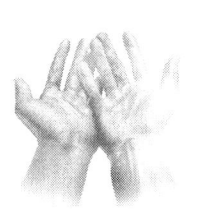

MODELLING 2: THE SECRET OF SUCCESS IN JESUS' MINISTRY

"My Father is always at his work, to this very day;
and I too am working – with him ...
I tell you the truth, although I am the Son,
I can do nothing by myself – on my own initiative.
Only what I see the Father doing, that's what I do ...
(the Father loves the Son and shows him all he does)
and only what I hear the Father saying, that's what I say ...
As the Father has sent me into the world,
in the same way I am sending you."
Then he breathed on them and said, "Receive the Holy Spirit."
– John 5:17, 19–20, 30; 8:26–28; 20:21–22 RAP

Consciousness precedes being, and not the other way round,
as the Marxists claim.
– Václav Havel, President of Czechoslovakia (1989–92)
and Czech Republic (1993–2003)[1]

---
[1] Quoted in Parker Palmer, *Leading from Within: Reflections on Spirituality and Leadership* (Washington D.C.: Servant Leadership School, 1992), p. 2.

Part Two: Theology

The secret of success – means or method?

As an enthusiastic young pastor, I saw healings and manifestations of the Spirit in various models of ministry. I was eager to learn, so I copied what I saw – even down to the mannerisms of the "man of God"! My quest was for the secret of their success, their power. Conference after conference repeatedly taught the "how to", but I slowly realised that *it was not about methods and technique, but about means and purpose*. Healing and miracles do not happen because we do one, two, and three. If it genuinely happens, it is because of the gracious presence and mysterious power *of God* – not because of the man/woman of God, or the right way of doing it.

We can understand why the disciples were dazzled by Jesus, in awe of his miracles. We can forgive them if they copied his methods when he sent them out to heal the sick and drive out demons, *believing that the power was in doing it the way he did it*. Jesus did not model a method or technique; he modelled kingdom ministry. When we are new to such things, we tend to follow the form without thought of the substance. We copy the method without regard to the means – we want to look good![2] Learning to heal the sick and minister the kingdom is not about "how-to's" – it is about learning to walk on water – all the best methods will not keep you afloat! The ability to transcend the laws of nature is not discovered by mastering spiritual laws, principles and techniques. It is about raw faith in God. "Did you *receive* the Spirit by obeying the law, or by faith in God? Does God *give* you his Spirit and work miracles because you do the right things, or because you believe?" (Galatians 3:2–5 RAP)

As I said in the Preface, Jesus' healing ministry was war, mystery and mercy, in the sense that it was dynamic, unpredictable and unconventional. It was a relational and interactive reality. There was no secret of success to Jesus' ministry, despite all the intrigue around such esoteric pursuits. (I confess: I gave the chapter this title to grab

---

[2] Kelsey says of Jewish exorcists who copied a method without the power (and were beaten up by the demons, Acts 19:13–16): It is "dangerous to imitate apostolic methods without the apostolic Spirit and power … the difference between magic and healing" is "trying to control spiritual powers" via methods which "can lead to destruction" (*Psychology, Medicine and Christian Healing*, p. 95).

your attention!) If there is a source, an explanation, it is: *Jesus did what he did, was who he was, through the indwelling presence of his Father, by the power of the Holy Spirit.* This is not a special formula; it is a lived life – the whole of your life for the rest of your life.

Jesus' goal was not only to entrust his kingdom *ministry* to his disciples, but to impart his kingdom *reality*, infusing them with his Spirit. He not only modelled and equipped his disciples to minister to the sick. More importantly, he modelled intimacy with the Father by the Spirit, and equipped the disciples to live in, and operate from, *that* relational reality. Skills and methods are important, as we will see later, but the source and means are as essential as the branch abiding in the vine – it can literally do *nothing* without that abiding.

Jesus is calling ordinary people to move above and beyond the natural and the normal, to walk with him in the realm of the miraculous, overcoming the chaos of evil. He is calling us to follow him as he followed his Father. In this Spirit realm, one thing is certain: *Not much is certain. Much more is unknown than is known. It is a relational reality of "trust and obey, for there's no other way ..."*, in the words of the hymn. The more we respond to him in relational trust, the more we begin to hear the Spirit as Jesus heard, and see the Father's works as he saw them. We learn to speak his words and do his works, just as he worked (and works through us) with his Father in his kingdom.

Relational oneness with Father by the Spirit

This chapter is a study in John's Gospel, as the previous chapter was a study in Mark's Gospel. Of the four Gospel writers, John is the mystic in the true Christian sense – he gives us "the secret", *the genuine* inside track. He shows Jesus' relational oneness with the Father by the Spirit as the source and means of his life and ministry. The core message of Mark (and Matthew and Luke – the Synoptic Gospels) is *the coming of the kingdom of God* in the Messiah by the Spirit's power. The core message of John is *the revelation of God as Father and his eternal life* in the Messiah (John 1:18), by the Spirit. John's key phrase is eternal life, *zoe aionios* ("life of the ages"), the equivalent of the Synoptics *basileia tou theou*, "kingdom of God" (eschatological life and rule).

My point of departure in John's Gospel is: "As my Father sent me, so send I you." Then Jesus breathed his Spirit into his disciples (20:21–22; 17:18).[3] If we can see how Jesus was sent, then we know how we, his followers, are sent to continue his ministry. Jesus was sent by the Father to reveal the true God to Israel and the world: the loving, redeeming and ruling Father. *This* Father destroys the works of the devil through his Son (1 John 3:8), giving his *zoe aionios* to those who believe in him through the Messianic Son (John 20:31).

Exactly how was this done? The Father *literally indwelt* Jesus by the Spirit, and all that Jesus said and did was from *that indwelling presence*, that relational oneness and intimacy with Father. This is the heart of the matter.

The quotation at the head of the chapter captures it (5:17, 19–20, 30). Jesus had a moment-by-moment consciousness of God as his Father, dwelling in him and operating through him. Havel's "consciousness precedes being" means that spirit and awareness are life, giving identity, growth, transformation. External forces, such as conformity to ideologies and behavioural standards, do not produce being. Jesus' *Father-consciousness* was not an escape into subjective superspirituality or a withdrawal into esoteric mysticism. It made Jesus intensely world conscious, deeply moved by the world's pain and need – a self-conscious and deliberate "I am working with my Father", moment by moment, to free people by destroying evil in all its expressions. He was profoundly conscious of "being sent" by the Father,[4] knowing he could do *nothing* on his own initiative or from his own ability. He knew he was utterly dependent on his Father – for his and the world's sake.

The above assumes a developing consciousness. Jesus did not wake up one bright morning and "discover" who he was (the Messiah). His identity and calling, his relationship with God *as his indwelling Father*, was a growing awareness. From an early age Jesus learnt that his own initiatives and abilities were ineffective compared to Father's. By the age of twelve, he was conscious of working with his Father

---

[3] The Risen Lord, the Last (or New) Adam, as God's gardener in the New Eden, breathing into being a new species *after his own kind* – "born again" of his Spirit – working with him in the New Creation already begun (a repeat of Genesis 2:7).
[4] "When a man believes in me, he does not believe in me only, but in the One who *sent me*. When he looks at me, he sees the One who *sent me*" (John 12:44–45). John uses "sent" (*apostello*) 18 times, and "to send" (*pempo*) 28 times.

(Luke 2:41–50). He learnt to "repent and believe" (Mark's version): how to turn from his own thoughts and initiatives, trusting Father for *his*. He knew the Messianic prophecies and intentionally sought to fulfil them – as in Isaiah 50:4f: "YHWH has given me a trained tongue to know the word that refreshes the weary, that heals the sick. He wakens me morning by morning; he wakens my ear to listen to him as his disciple. YHWH has opened my ears and I have obeyed – I have not rebelled or drawn back" (RAP).

Jesus learnt through spiritual disciplines (Scripture memorisation, meditation and constant prayer) to live with Father. He practised Father's presence moment by moment, developing a profound God consciousness in which he began to see what Father was doing, hear what Father was saying, feel what Father was feeling, in various situations. By taking risk and trusting, he learnt to act on what he believed were Father's thoughts, feelings and actions. Thus he increasingly lived, worked and ministered in unison with Father, changing the world.

Was his oneness with the Father due to his divinity? Or due to his human efforts through spiritual disciplines? As we saw in Mark's Gospel, it was neither – it was by the empowering Spirit. John says Jesus' baptism in water and anointing with the Spirit is what revealed him to Israel as Messiah (1:31–34); "for God gives the Spirit without limit" to Jesus (3:34). It was the indwelling Holy Spirit who enabled intimate oneness with the Father, making it subjectively real and objectively visible in Jesus' life and ministry. Again, I must acknowledge Jesus' sinlessness (divinity) made him unique, adding to oneness; on other hand, Jesus' spiritual disciplines were used by the Spirit in growing oneness with the Father – it did not drop out of heaven as a gift of effortless grace! It is always God-human cooperation, never one-way God magic! Jesus teaches this in "abiding in the Vine" – *the discipline* of mutual indwelling (John 15) – in the context of teaching us to receive the gift of the Holy Spirit (14 – 16).

The bottom line is: "*As* my Father sent me, *so* I send you." Jesus is our model of the source and means of life and ministry. We can, up to a point, have *the same* God consciousness in relational oneness with Father, through the Son by the Spirit. God intends it. Jesus modelled it. And died and rose again for it. It is not for us to be "spiritual", "fulfilled" or "happy", but for God's glory and for the world's salvation – to recreate it in God's image.

The principles – summarising how it worked

This is a rich study in John's Gospel. I briefly summarise the insights into how Jesus was sent, and thus how we are sent.

1. *The sense of mission,* being "sent" by God: "I came from God ... I haven't come on my own; he sent me" (8:42, see footnote 4). Jesus knew why he was born, his life purpose, and his returning to his Father to account for his life and work (John 13:3f); *therefore* he poured out his life to save Israel and the world (1:29; 3:16–17). We are invited into the same mission, into the same sense of being sent into the world and of accountability to God.
2. *The source* of his life and ministry was the indwelling Father by the Spirit's presence and power, for "God gives him the Spirit without limit" (3:34). The consciousness of the Father *actually* living in Jesus' body by the Spirit cannot be overemphasized. The "in", "indwelling", "one" reality applies to us. We are indwelt by Jesus *and* the Father in the Spirit – we are one with him.[5] This is made real through "drinking" the Spirit (7:37–39), "abiding" (15:1–8) and "feeding" (6:57: "As the living Father has sent me, and I live because of my Father, so the one who *feeds on me* will live *because of me*"). We live in, from and by the Father's eternal life, just as Jesus did.
3. *The initiative* in all things is with the Father by the Spirit (5:17–22). Jesus lived by explicit revelation (seeing and hearing) and implicit obedience (doing and speaking). He consciously and intentionally *worked with* his Father to save people. By seeing, listening and acting on it, he learnt to distinguish Father's initiative from his own; to discern Father's saving activity from his own (messianic) fantasies. This became so real that he could say: "If you believe me, you're believing my Father; if you've

---

[5] See 10:30, 38; 14:10–11, 17–20, 23; 17:11, 18, 20–26 (also 1 Corinthians 6:17–20).

seen me, you've seen my Father; if you've heard me, you've heard my Father" (12:44–50 RAP). This is incarnation, *not* a robotic obedience under Father's remote control. The relationship reaches a unity of will, a mature mutuality in which the initiative shifts back and forth: "If *you* remain in *me* and *my* words remain in *you*, ask whatever *you* wish, and it will be given to *you*" (15:7).

4. *The basis is relational integrity* – love, truth and trust (to "believe"). Jesus was deeply conscious of *Father's love and trust*, based on truthfulness. "For the Father loves the Son and shows him all he does" (5:20). This reality was nurtured by interactive intimacy, constant communion and implicit obedience – his gift of returned love to the Father. Jesus' relational integrity determined his experience and exercise of authority and power *in real terms*. God trusted Jesus and backed him up (see 6:63). The same relational reality applies to us, determining our authority and power *in real terms*.[6]

5. *The goal* is God's honour and glory, in the world being saved (3:16–17). As "a man of truth" (7:18), Jesus worked for the Father's honour, refusing praise and glory from others – he condemned those who sought it. He consciously sought his Father's glory, which was profoundly revealed in his death, the salvation of people and the healing miracles.[7]

6. *His credibility* depended on him *doing* his Father's works (miracles), not just talking about it: "*If* I do not do the works of my Father, *do not believe me*" (10:25, 30, 37–38; 14:11). It was evidence of their oneness and of Jesus' "sent-ness" (5:36). Likewise *our* credibility is tied up in our doing the "works of Jesus" – and even greater works (14:12). *God's* credibility in the eyes of the world is dependent on *our* expressed oneness with him in Christ – by doing his works; and by our expressed oneness with each other as believers – in unity and fellowship (17:20–24).

7. *The result was an incarnate modelling of God as the loving Father*. Jesus was God in skin: "The Word became flesh and dwelt

---

[6] Jesus "not alone ... with the Father": 8:16, 26–29, 38; 16:32. The Father's love for Jesus: 3:35; 5:20; 10:17–18; 17:23, 26. Love and obedience applied to us: 14:21, 23–24; 15:9–17; 16:27; 17:23, 26.

[7] 12:20–33; also 2:11; 5:22–23, 41–45; 7:17–18; 8:49–50, 54; 13:31–32; 14:13; 15:8; 16:14; 17:1–5, 22–24.

among us. We saw his glory … from the Father, full of grace and truth" (1:14). When Philip said: "You've talked so much about your Father, just show him to us and we will be convinced," Jesus replied: "How long have I been with you, Philip? If you've seen *me*, you've seen *my Father*!" (14:8–14). *Then* Jesus gives the real deal: "Don't you believe I am in the Father and the Father is in me? The *words* I say are not just my own, rather, it is the Father living in me who is doing his *works*. Accept our mutual indwelling or just believe it on the evidence of the miracles themselves" (vs 10–11 RAP). Jesus is saying that the Father who lives in him gives him the words to speak, which create the works of God, displaying the wonders of God.

In summary, here are the four key factors ("the secret"):

- *Communion*: The indwelling of God's presence (the fact of oneness).
- *Conviction*: The inward revelation of God's thoughts (the faith of oneness).
- *Command*: The speaking of God's words (the flow of oneness).
- *Creation*: The manifestation of God's works (the fruit of oneness).

John's stories illustrating Jesus' "secret"[8]

The calling of Nathaniel (1:44–51)

After Nathaniel's initial dismissive attitude ("Can anything good come from Nazareth?" v. 46), when Jesus saw Nathaniel approaching, he said: "Here is a true Israelite, in whom there's nothing false." This amazed Nathaniel: "How do you know me?" "When you were standing under the fig tree, *I saw you* …" Jesus saw what the Father was showing him about Nathaniel: "He's an honest man – call him to follow you." Nathaniel was so impressed with this Rabbi's supernatural knowing, that he declared Jesus "the Son of God, the Messiah of Israel". Jesus responded: "You believe because I supernaturally knew

---

[8] Again, in giving my RAP interpretation of the stories I do not discuss technical points and list sources, although I have consulted a range of commentaries – a primary one being Leon Morris, The Gospel According to John, *New London Commentaries* (London: Marshall, Morgan and Scott, 1971).

you? You'll see greater things than this! You'll see heaven open and …" Jesus prophesied, flowing naturally in the supernatural, working with the Father as he encountered people.

The wedding at Cana (2:1–11)

Jesus and his disciples were invited to a wedding. The host ran out of wine (the feast could go on for a week), but Mary believed her son could help: "Son, they have no more wine." Jesus was indifferent: "Why do you involve me?" It was a social embarrassment due to poverty or bad planning, and could lead to a lawsuit against the host for not providing enough. "My time has not yet come; I am not ready to act and be revealed for who I am." This "mother distancing" from a grown-up son who had discovered his life purpose (he was thirty years old!) did not bother her. Ignoring his rebuke, she said to the servants: "Do whatever he tells you to do." What faith! This really affected Jesus – not only the tense exchange with her, but her confidence in him.

As he stood thinking, communing with his Father about this "mother incident" and the wedding need, he *saw* six 100 l (twenty gallon) water jars used for ceremonial washing. He *saw* in his mind (his thoughts suggested): Fill them with water; Father will change it into wine. He acted on it: "Servants, fill these jars with water." They obeyed. "Now pour some out and take it to the Master of Ceremonies." This was more difficult for them, but they obeyed. The MC tasted it and called the bridegroom in amazement: "This is **really** good wine, the best I have tasted! You've kept it for the end of the feast – most unusual!" Neither he nor the groom – who was the more surprised and relieved – knew where the wine had come from. But Jesus *and the servants knew.* The extravagant miracle – the six jars were equal to eight hundred bottles of the best wine – happened in the doing of it – somewhere between the filling, pouring and drinking – *because* Jesus *dared* to see and hear what the Father was saying and doing. The implication is: If *we are* obedient and trusting *servants*, we too will see and know, and do the Father's works.

The Samaritan woman at the well (4:16–34)

Jesus surprised this woman in more ways than one. As a Jew, he spoke to a despised Samaritan; as a Rabbi he talked to a woman in public. Their conversation moved from common need (water) to Jesus' offer of God's salvation (living water). We can see his assumed inner dialogue with Father in the way the conversation went, because when she said: "Sir, give me this living water you're talking about," he suddenly changed tack and asked her to call her husband. It seemed irrelevant, but Jesus had inside information from the Father by the Spirit. She was honest enough to say she did not have a husband. Then Jesus told her: "You've had five husbands and the man you're now with is not your husband!" Wham! Revelation! Blown away, she said: "Sir, I see that you're a prophet!" And she discovered more … then went and called her village: "Come! See a man who told me *everything I ever did*! Could *this* be the Messiah?" She exaggerated a little, but that is what it felt like. That was the life-transforming impact of meeting a person working with Father.

The lame man at the pool of Bethesda (5:1–15)

On entering Jerusalem for one of the Jewish feasts, Jesus passed by the pool of Bethesda (meaning "House of Mercy"). Sick, disabled, blind and paralysed people lay there waiting for healing. They believed an angel disturbed the water once in a while, and the first to jump in would be healed. Jesus stopped in and went to one person, a lame man lying on his mat. We have to ask: Why did he stop there, and why address (heal) only *one* man among all the sick, leaving the rest in their misery? Somehow he was drawn in there to *that* man – I assume Father was prompting him. Jesus had faith for *that man's* healing from an inner sense of seeing Father having mercy and healing him. Maybe the man's cry over many, many years (like Israel in Egypt) had moved God's heart, prompting Jesus (like Moses) to deliver him. Jesus moved in a spiritual consciousness of knowing where, who, when … and then obeying.

Interestingly, Jesus discovered through *natural* knowledge (interview) that the lame man had been lying there for thirty-eight years. Jesus asked him: "Do you *want* to get well?" He wanted to know *if* the sickness had conditioned him into fatalistic acceptance, *or* if the man had the will, the faith, to get better. His sad answer: "I do want to get well; but I have no one to help me get in when the angel stirs the waters – others get in before me." Then Jesus said to him: "Get up! Pick up your mat and walk! The stirring of the water is not down there – it is right here in front of you, within your reach!" Jesus *commanded* the man to do the impossible: to stand up, roll up his mat and walk – after thirty-eight years of lying there! As the man made the first attempt to move, the miracle began. God's power entered his body, enabling him to stand, roll up his mat and walk home!

This story is in the context of our theme text (5:17–20), showing how Jesus worked with the Father in seeing and hearing, doing and creating.

The woman caught in adultery (8:2–11)

Jesus was in the temple courts teaching a large group that had gathered around him. He was interrupted by some Pharisees and Scribes who dragged a partially clad woman into their midst. She was covered in grime, wet with tears of shame, caught in the heat of adulterous passion. They had let the man go – *only the woman* is sinful and evil in her seductive adultery – so they arrogantly believed, manipulating their Scriptures (Leviticus 20:10; Deuteronomy 22:22–24). "Rabbi, this woman was caught in adultery. Moses *commands us* to stone her to death. *What do you say?*" It was a trap to test Jesus; they wanted to accuse him to the authorities. If he said "yes", the Romans could hold him for execution without trial. If he said "no", he would be going against Torah. If he gave no answer, the men probably would have stoned her to death. It was a very tense situation.

Jesus appeared to ignore them, bending down to write with his finger in the sand. Why did he do this? Various scholars speculate about what he may have written.[9] I think that, because of the sudden disruption, he stopped and stooped to wait on his Father to know what to say. Jesus had learnt not to be rushed into doing anything from his own initiative, but to wait for Father's initiative. He doodled in the sand, asking Father what he was doing and saying in this life-and-death test, in this humiliating crisis. "When they kept on

---

[9] Jesus listed the sins of the accusers (Job 13:26); he wrote what he later spoke, like Roman judges who first wrote their ruling, then pronounced it; or he wrote some words from Torah.

questioning him" (v. 7), shouting biblical texts and threatening her and him, "he straightened up and said to them: 'If any one of you is without sin, let him be the first to throw a stone at her.'"

As it began to sink into their thick skulls, the Goliath of legalistic righteousness and murder fell to the ground at the hands of the son of David. Jesus let it *really* sink in – after giving his word of wisdom, "again he stooped down and wrote on the ground". They began to realize, one by one, from oldest to youngest, that they were not without sin – they too were in danger of God's judgment. They had caught her in adultery, but Jesus caught them in hypocrisy. When he saw that all had gone, with only the two of them left alone, he stood up. All the sinners had left and the only sinless man on earth stood before her. He did not pick up a stone, though it was his right to do so. Instead, he tenderly asks: "Woman[10], where are your accusers? Have any condemned you?" "No one!" "*Neither do I condemn you!*" Being who he was, he spoke for God, giving forgiveness. But that did not mean he condoned her sin: "Go and leave your life of sin."

This is profoundly symbolic. God in Christ *stoops* down from heaven to the dust and dirt of earth, identifying with our sin and shame (his life and death). Taking upon himself our venomous attack of evil, he *stands* to answer the Accuser (the cross). Then he *stoops* again as evil dissipates (the burial); and finally *stands* up again, having banished all evil (the resurrection), and tenderly forgives and restores us to wholeness. Few stories match the sheer beauty, wisdom, emotion, compassion, dignity and women's liberation of this one.

Finally, raising Lazarus from the dead (11)

We see Jesus moving moment by moment in conversational oneness with Father, riding the emotional roller coaster of another life-and-death situation. After his meetings, he used to relax in the home of three close friends, Lazarus, Martha and Mary (outside Jerusalem). The two sisters sent word to Jesus: "Lord, the one you love is very sick" – in other words, come quickly. Jesus loved them, yet when he heard that Lazarus was sick, he remained where he was *two more*

---

[10] A term of endearment, not an indifferent address – Jesus used it for his mother (2:4; 19:26).

days! Was it indifference or neglect? No, he was acting on his Father's initiative through interactive awareness, seen in his response to the news about Lazarus: "This sickness will *not* end in death. It is for the glory of God." I imagine Jesus inwardly praying: "Father, you hear what they are saying. What do you think?" "Do not be alarmed, son. This sickness will not end in permanent death, but will be an opportunity to defeat death. I have allowed it for our glory, for us to work a miracle that the people may believe I sent you." So Jesus rested, not allowing a close relationship or situational crisis to wrongly pressurise him.

On the fourth day after the bad news, he said to his disciples: "Let's go to Judea" (where Lazarus is). They naturally responded: "They tried to kill you there! You want to go back?" Jesus responded from a different consciousness: "I must go and do God's works while I can, soon I won't be able to … our friend Lazarus has fallen asleep and I'm going to wake him." Again their natural response: "Oh, you're going to Lazarus! But Lord, if he's resting in recovery, why wake him?" Jesus then shocked them: "Lazarus is dead!" They must have thought: "What! He said it would *not* result in death, *now it has*! This is serious!" Jesus knew by revelation from Father that Lazarus had died. He goes further, saying: "I am glad I was not there – for *your* sakes – that you may now see and really believe. Let's go to him." Jesus already knew what he (and the Father) would do.

When they arrived in Bethany, Jesus found that Lazarus had been in the tomb for four days. His spirit had left and decay had set in. (Jews believed the soul of the dead hung around the body for up to three days before departing.) Many people were in their home, wailing and grieving. When Martha heard Jesus had come, she rushed out to meet him on the road. "Lord, if only you had come when we told you, my brother would not have died! But I know that even now God will give you whatever you ask." What honesty and faith, what acknowledgement of disappointment *and* confidence! Jesus replied emphatically: "Your brother *will* rise again!" This conviction (as we will see) was not only a theological statement about the end of the age, but a promise of a present miracle, which could only have come from the inner reassurance of faith in seeing what Father was doing.

But Martha read it theologically, as most of us do: "I know he will rise again in the resurrection at the last day!"

Jesus responded: "I am that Last Day! That last day is present, here before you. I am the Resurrection and the Life. If a person believes in me, they will live forever – though they die, they will never die. Do you believe this?" Yes, she believed, confessing her faith in him as God's Messianic Son. She returned home and told Mary that Jesus was asking for her. Mary quickly got up and went out to him. When she saw Jesus, she fell at his feet repeating: "If only you had been here my brother would not have died!" She was weeping, wailing along with others who had followed her. This affected Jesus. He was deeply moved and troubled, groaning at death and its aftermath. "Where have you laid him?" They said: "Come and see." He wept, grieving at *their* grief, feeling Father's compassion for *them*. Some noticed and said: "How he loved Lazarus!" while others wondered aloud why he had not prevented Lazarus' death. He came to the tomb and was once more moved with deep empathy for the people. Keeping focus and faith in Father, he said: "Take away the stone."

Martha protested: "No Lord! He's been there for four days. By this time he stinks." Jesus warmly challenged her: "Did not I tell you that if you *believed*, you would see the glory of God – a miracle?" So they rolled the stone away. At that critical moment, Jesus looked upwards: "Father, thanks for hearing me. I know you always hear me. Our dialogue throughout the day helped me. But for the benefit of those standing here, I have said this; that they may believe you have sent me; that you are in me doing your works." He faced the open tomb, raised his voice in a command: "Lazarus, come out!" (Some have said that Jesus specifically called "Lazarus" or else *all* the dead may have come to life! John 5:25, 28–29).

They heard a shifting and shuffling. Lazarus appeared at the entrance! He was bound in linen strips, with a cloth around his face. Jesus said: "Take off the grave clothes and free him." As Jesus worked step by step with the Father in doing this miracle, so they worked with Jesus by removing the stone, and completing his work by setting Lazarus free. In this way they participated in the Father's work. Jesus and Father always seek to show us what they are doing – and include us in doing his works (miracles) with him.

Personal reflection, application and group discussion

1. What has God said to you through this chapter?
2. Why are *source and means* more important than *method and technique;* relationship more important than rules or how we do things? Think of – and describe – an incident when you put method above means.
3. How would you describe, in your own words, "the secret" of Jesus' life and ministry?
4. Meditate on the story of the healing of the man who was born blind (John 9). Tell it to your small group, using John 5:17–20 to interpret the story.
5. Take time to experiment and practise what this chapter is about. Sit in a group and ask Father and Son to indwell you afresh by his Spirit, and to show you what he is doing, to speak to you about one or two people in the group. Each person can share what they are seeing and hearing, acting on it in prayer ministry. When everyone has had a turn, take feedback and evaluate, learning together what was accurate, not so accurate, or plain off the wall. It is a safe environment in which to learn together – try it!

7

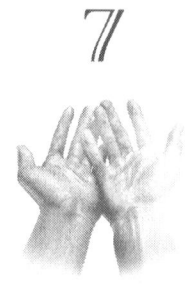

MODELLING 3: PRINCIPLES AND PATTERNS IN JESUS' HEALING MINISTRY

Jesus did many other miraculous signs in the presence of his disciples, which are not recorded in this book. But these are written that you may believe that Jesus is the Messiah, the Son of God, and that by believing you may have life in his name.
– John 20:30–31

This chapter is a break from the flow of thought and argument in the previous two chapters. Here I summarise in point form the important definitions and understandings we learn from Jesus' healing ministry. Besides the many other healings/miracles that Jesus did, the forty-one recorded in the Gospels are to bring us to faith in Jesus as the Messiah, the Son of God. However, we not only come to faith in Jesus through the stories, we learn the principles and patterns in his healing ministry that we can apply in healing the sick. We will summarise both the means and the methods that Jesus used.[1]

I give brief explanations of *which* words are used in the Greek New

---
[1] See Appendix 3 for the forty-one healing references and some key factors in healing.

Testament to describe Jesus' naturally supernatural healing ministry. Then I explain *why* Jesus healed, and tabulate principles and patterns regarding *how* he ministered.

Which words are used to describe Jesus' healings?[2]

- *Works of power (dynamis),* from which we derive the English words dynamite and dynamic. The New Testament uses *dynamis* to describe works of *God's* power over demons, sin, sickness, nature, people, and death, actions attributed to *the power of the Spirit, and of "the coming age"* breaking into our reality to accomplish God's purpose (Hebrews 6:5). The English word "miracle", derived from the Latin verb *mirari* ("to wonder"), is not used in the Greek New Testament. Some modern Bible translations (NIV) use the word "miracle" instead of "works of power".[3] We use "miracle" to mean almost anything that causes us to wonder, but it is specifically used for a happening that defies nature's laws and explanations – like blind eyes seeing.
- *Signs (semeia,* plural of *semeion)* means a distinguishing mark that reveals or points to something. In the New Testament it is used for unusual events that reveal divine, or at times demonic, powers. They are *miraculous signs* that point to Jesus and his Kingship – that God's reign has come ("signs of the kingdom", Matthew 11:2–5; Mark 16:15–20). Miracles are not an end in themselves, but point to who Jesus is and faith in him. "Signs" is John's key word for "miracles".[4]
- *Wonders (teras):* A marvel or happening that produces wonder

---

[2]For word studies: Colin Brown (ed.), *The New International Dictionary of New Testament Theology* (Exeter: Paternoster Press, 1978), vol. 2, pp. 163–172, 601–611, 620–635; Morton Kelsey, *Psychology, Medicine and Christian Healing,* pp. 83–89. For the critical debate, see Colin Brown, *Miracles and the Critical Mind* (Grand Rapids: Eerdmans, 1984), pp. 281–325; Graham H. Twelftree, *Jesus the Miracle Worker: A Historical and Theological Study* (Downers Grove: IVP, 1999) – his section on Miracles and the Modern Mind, pp. 17–56. I list Scriptures for you to see how each word is used.

[3]Matthew 11:20, 21, 23; 13:54, 58; Mark 6:14; 9:39; Luke 19:37; Acts 10:38; 19:11; 1 Corinthians 12:10, 28, 29; Galatians 3:5.

[4]John 2:11, 23; 3:2; 4:54; 6:2, 26; 12:18, 37; 20:30; also Matthew 12:38f; Mark 16:17; Acts 4:16, 22; 8:6.

and awe. In the New Testament it is only used together with *semeion*, "signs and wonders", or with "miracles (*dynamis*), signs and wonders". It is a supernatural or miraculous wonder of God's saving action.[5] Note that *these three words are also used of satanic powers* (2 Thessalonians 2:9).

Four other words are used (mostly synonymously) in the New Testament to refer to healing:

- *To give healing care (therapeuo):* An ordinary word for medical treatment, from which we derive the English word therapy. It is the most common word used by Matthew, Mark and Luke to refer to a ministry or service of healing – to cure a person.[6]
- *To heal or cure (iaomai)* was used almost exclusively as a medical term in Greek and was a favourite of Dr Luke. It was used to refer to various kinds of healings.[7]
- *To be in good health (hugiaino):* To be healthy, sound, or restored to health. "Hygiene" comes from this word, taken from the goddess of health, Hygeia. Again, it was a basic medical term used by the New Testament writers.[8]
- *To rescue, save or heal (sozo)* was used in various ways in the Greek world, including medically: to save a person from sickness or death. The New Testament writers used this word for God's salvation, both in its ultimate and immediate wholistic sense, which included healing and deliverance in all its forms.[9]

WHY did Jesus do healings, miracles and deliverance?

This is the most important question, as Jesus' attitude to sickness and healing reveals *God's* attitude to it. The answer to this question informs *our* reasons and motivations for doing healing in Jesus' name.

---

[5] Matthew 24:24; John 4:48; Acts 2:22, 43; 4:30; 5:12; 6:8; 8:13; 14:3; 15:12; Romans 15:19; 2 Corinthians 12:12; Hebrews 2:4.
[6] Matthew 4:23–24; 8:7, 16; 10:1, 8; Mark 3:2, 10; Luke 4:23, 40; 5:15; 6:7, 18; John 5:10; Acts 4:14; 5:16; 8:7.
[7] Luke 5:17; 6:18–19; 7:7; 8:47; 9:2, 11, 42; 13:32; 14:4; 17:15; 22:51; John 4:47; 5:13; Acts 3:16; 4:22, 30; 9:34; 10:38; 28:8; 1 Corinthians 12:9, 28, 30; James 5:16.
[8] Matthew 12:13; 15:31; Mark 3:5; Luke 5:31; 7:10; 15:27; John 5:4, 6, 9, 11, 14–15; 7:23; Acts 4:10.
[9] For a list of references, see footnote 12 in Chapter 4.

1. *For the glory of God:* Jesus healed for God's praise, not for his own glory. Jesus refused flattery and honour from people (John 5:41, 44 cf. 7:18). He healed people to glorify God, to show people who God is – in contrast to all other gods, powers and people.
2. *Because he cared for people:* Jesus suffered when others suffered. He was moved and motivated by *compassion* to help the poor, sick and demonised, literally embodying God's love and mercy for them (Matthew 14:14; 20:34).
3. *To destroy Satan's works and defeat his rule:* Jesus was hostile to what made people sick and oppressed, so he healed them. Jesus was at war with Satan and his kingdom, destroying the works of evil to set people free (Matthew 12:22–29; 1 John 3:8).[10]
4. *As a witness to God's future, and present, kingdom:* Jesus' understanding of God, the Hebrew Scriptures, his calling, and the times in which he lived, led him to heal the sick as a purposeful enactment of God's rule, intentionally fulfilling the prophets (Isaiah 35:4–6 cf. Matthew 11:1–6; Isaiah 61:1–2 cf. Luke 4:16–21). He self-consciously brought God's kingdom to people *by healing them;* demonstrating the kingdom not only as a future hope, but as a present reality in him. Healings are "signs of the kingdom" that point to Jesus, calling people to repent and believe in him as the Messiah.

HOW did Jesus minister? The principles and patterns

I summarise some things I have already said, along with new insights, from this overview of Jesus' healing ministry.

1. *By the Spirit:* Jesus began his healing ministry *after* his baptism and anointing with the Spirit, and *after* he defeated Satan in the desert. Full dependence on the Spirit, and learning to be led by him into confrontation with evil in all its manifestations, is a non-negotiable in healing ministry.
2. Jesus healed *every* kind of sickness and expelled every demon that he came across within a ministry context. *Healing and*

---

[10] In this context Kelsey says Jesus "did good" (Acts 10:38) to people – it is simply a good thing to help and heal people who are suffering. See *Psychology, Medicine and Christian Healing*, pp. 70–73.

deliverance worked hand in hand. It ought to be the same for us in our healing practice. Jesus healed physical, mental, spiritual, emotional and relational diseases and demonisations (Matthew 4:23–24; 8:16; 15:30–31; Mark 1:32–34, 39).

3. Jesus healed *all who came to him, all who asked for healing.* He was *always willing* to heal (Matthew 8:1–7; 15:30–31; Mark 7:31–37). His apparent reluctance on rare occasions can be seen as a test of faith, as with the Canaanite woman (Matthew 15:21–28). We should never turn away people who ask for healing ministry unless we have very good reason to do so.
4. Jesus' healing was *motivated by compassion* for the sick and demonised, for both individuals and "the crowd" (Matthew 9:36; 14:14; 20:34).
5. *Faith was critical in the healing process.* Jesus was more able to heal in *the presence of faith* in him and in his power to heal: the centurion's "great faith" (Matthew 8:8–13); the bed-carriers' faith (Matthew 9:2); the recipient's faith (Mark 5:28–34); the father's faith for his demonised son (Mark 9:12–29). One of the most common phrases in the records of Jesus' healings is: "Your faith has made you well." From the above examples, we see how Jesus discerned where there was faith, and *who* was exercising confidence in him for healing. Faith moves God. He responds to those who actively trust him for help.
6. Although Jesus looked for, and responded to, the faith of others, on occasion *he alone believed* and healed people. For the one ministering, these occasions are more difficult, but they happen through a gift of faith, which gives an inner assurance from God for the person's healing. Jesus healed the man born blind on this basis (John 9:1–7). Most of John's recorded miracles illustrate *Jesus' faith in the Father*, often in the absence of other people's faith.
7. However, Jesus' healing ministry was *limited by unbelief* – by a negative and critical attitude in unbelieving individuals. "He could not do any miracles there [in Nazareth], except lay his hands on a few sick people and heal them. And he was amazed at their lack of faith" (Mark 6:5–6; Luke 4:23–28).

Modelling 3: *Principles and patterns in Jesus' healing ministry*

8. Frequently Jesus would *heal many, many people at one time in large gatherings.* Often it was after people had walked long distances. On such occasions, he chose the time and place, while at other times he worked with spontaneous gatherings (Matthew 4:23–25; 12:15; 14:13–14; 19:1–2). He was aware of the power dynamics unique to large gatherings and kept his integrity when he needed to: he withdrew from the crowds (Matthew 8:18; Luke 5:15–16); dismissed them (Mark 6:45); demanded privacy to heal (Matthew 9:25); overruled a crowd's sentiments to heal (Matthew 20:29–34); escaped when they wanted to make him King (John 6:14–15). He knew what was in people (crowds), so he did not entrust himself to them (John 2:23–25). Jesus also healed people in synagogues, on the streets and in the marketplace.

    A comment: Charismatic leaders who do power ministry and large crowds are vulnerable to interactive dynamics that feed off their mutual brokenness. Large meetings are faith-filled with high expectations, and real miracles can and do happen. However, both the people and the (charismatic) minister come close to an invisible edge of psycho-spiritual dynamics and carnal group power, possible mass manipulation and even hysteria. The people give the preacher power and saviour status in their desperation for healing and their lust for the supernatural, making the preacher vulnerable to his ego needs (to be popular, heroic, spectacular). Few have *the discernment* to separate out the (S)spirit-carnal mix, or *the character* to respond with integrity to the Spirit and the people (and other "drives") in such a charged atmosphere. The bigger the crowd, the more rarefied the psycho-spiritual atmosphere, and the more vulnerable you are to unleashed powers that operate in, upon, and through you – powers that few people understand or can handle.

9. In contrast to large meetings, Jesus *ministered to individuals in isolated incidents,* giving them his full attention: the leper (Luke 5:12–13); blind Bartimaeus (Luke 18:35–43). We can learn much from Jesus' tenderness and interaction in these quality one-on-one encounters.

10. Jesus *withdrew to heal a person privately,* especially if there was a

negative environment (Mark 5:39–43; 8:23). In such cases, he included his closest disciples, presumably as witnesses, and for his support and their training.

11. *Jesus stopped or was stopped* by a person, to heal them – like Bartimaeus. He even *travelled distances to heal one person* – all the way to Tyre and Sidon, responding in the Spirit to the persistent cry of the Canaanite woman (Matthew 15:21–28, 29–31). Sensitivity to the Spirit will cause us to hear and feel certain cries of people, and lead us to them.

12. At times *he healed all* those who were sick in large gatherings (Matthew 4:24). On other occasions *he healed only one person*, leaving others sick, for example the lame man at the pool of Bethesda (John 5:1–9). These things are mysteries, not explained or reduced to a principle.

13. In the same mysterious way *healing flowed out of Jesus sovereignly by God's power,* without his conscious cooperation (Mark 5:27–29; Luke 6:19). It was released and received by the faith of those who reached out to touch him.

14. On occasion, in the rhythm of regular healing ministry, Jesus was *aware of a special anointing being present* and he consciously worked with it. Aware that "the power of the Lord was present … to heal", he responded to the Spirit and boldly worked miracles (Luke 5:17–26). Spirit-sensitivity makes us aware when power is present, and emboldens us to work miracles.

15. Jesus did not do miracles for those who wanted *to test him or to be entertained* by the supernatural (Matthew 12:38–42).

16. *Resistance* to healing the sick *grieved the Lord* (Mark 3:1–6; Luke 13:10–17). Jesus expressed godly anger at religious legalism, unbelief, sickness itself, demonic enslavement, and death.

17. Jesus employed *many patterns and methods in healing people,* tactile ways of communicating compassion, imparting power, engendering and releasing the person's faith to receive healing. They fall into two common practices, which worked together: the *laying on of hands* and *speaking the word of healing.*

   - *Laying on hands (touch):* He touched the untouchables (Mark 1:41), embracing some, holding others, tenderly touching withered limbs, firmly gripping arms, putting fingers into deaf ears (Mark 7:33). *People touched his garments* for healing (Mark 5:27–29; 6:56). Jesus used *spittle* (a known medicinal practice) on a dumb tongue and blind eyes (Mark 7:33; 8:23). Once he mixed spit with sand to make a *mud pack* to heal blind eyes (John 9:6), a possible symbolic use of creation material (Genesis 2:7). He sent out the twelve apostles to heal by *anointing the sick with oil* – also a known medicinal practice (Mark 6:13). Jesus used a variety of tactile "means of faith" to heal – some daring "acts of faith" – requiring people to do the same. He said to a man with a withered hand: "Stretch out your hand" (Luke 6:10; 7:14).

- *The spoken word:* Jesus healed by *a word of command*: "Stretch out your hand" (Luke 6:6–10); "Go" (Matthew 8:8–13); "Stand up" (Mark 2:8–12); "Arise" (Luke 7:11–17); "Be opened" (Mark 7:34). He rebuked sickness and demons (Luke 4:35, 38). At times, when healing people, he *looked up* to the heavens and prayed, sighed or groaned (John 11:41–42; Mark 7:34). Jesus made *declarations and pronouncements* by the authority of God's kingdom, and sent the twelve to heal the sick by pronouncing the kingdom of God upon people (Matthew 10:7–8).

18. Jesus *asked questions* of people, causing them to reflect. His questions about the need for healing indicated that, while at times he received words of knowledge from the Spirit, at other times he did not. It shows that he needed certain information in order to focus correctly in the healing process: "How long has he been like this?" to the father of the demonised son (Mark 9:21); "What do you want me to do for you?" to blind Bartimaeus (Mark 10:51); "Do you want to be get well?" to the lame man at the pool of Bethesda (John 5:6). Jesus *asked questions during and after the healing*, to work effectively with the healing process, to know what was or was not happen: "What is your name?" to the demons in (Mark 5:9); "Do you see anything?" to the blind man (Mark 8:23).

19. Jesus frequently did "*after-ministry care*" giving direction to those

he had healed: "Stop sinning or something worse may happen to you" (John 5:14). He directed people *to obtain medical proof,* to honour the socio-religious process within his Jewish context: "Go, show yourself to the priest and offer the gift Moses commanded, as a testimony to them" (Matthew 8:4 cf. Leviticus 13:49; 14:2–32). Jesus made positive comments about the work of physicians – he did not despise or work against them (Mark 2:17).[11]

20. The close *relationship between sin and sickness* was known in Jesus' day. He had a discerning approach, healing some sicknesses by forgiving sin – the person's sin evidently caused the sickness: the lame man (Mark 2:5–12); possibly the invalid at the pool of Bethesda (John 5:1–15, see v. 14). Note also 1 Corinthians 11:27–32; James 5:14–16. At other times Jesus said the person's sin, or their parents' sin, had nothing to do with their sickness, such as the blind man in John 9:1–3. Jesus healed many people *without* confession and repentance of sin, scandalous in the Judaism of his day. Sickness can be caused by other people's sin, and the community's sin: contracting HIV/AIDS from being raped; sickness from environmental pollution. Healing in these cases involves forgiving the perpetrator(s). Jesus treated some sicknesses as a direct result of the victimisation of demons (Matthew 9:32; 12:22).

21. At times Jesus *battled in the act of healing*, especially in expelling demons – it was not always instant. There was ongoing battle in driving out the legion of demons in Mark 5:6–13. We can take heart from the fact even Jesus had to *pray more than once* to heal a person: the blind man in Mark 8:22–26.

22. Jesus indicated that some maladies and demonic sicknesses would not leave immediately; that *longer prayer and fasting* was required for healing: the demonised boy (Mark 9:28–29). This emphasises Jesus' dependence on God for healing – *he actually withdrew from healing the sick to go away and pray* (Luke 5:15–16). How much more does this apply to us?

---

[11] Kelsey has a helpful discussion on Jewish and Greek healing and medicine, in comparison with Jesus' (Christian) healing ministry, in *Psychology, Medicine and Christian Healing*, pp. 26–40.

23. Lastly, a comment on Jesus and *the issue of discernment* (discussed in Chapter 20). Jesus warned not to wrongfully label or wilfully attribute healings done in his name (by the Spirit), to demonic powers and satanic deception. This would insult the Holy Spirit, placing the person in danger of permanent wrath (Mark 3:20–30). On the other hand, Jesus said people's character and life fruit would reveal who they really are; doing healings and miracles in his name is no proof of belonging to Jesus (Matthew 7:15–23). He also says of people doing healings *in his name apart from us* – who are *not* opposing us – that we should *not* oppose them. Leave them with blessing, assuming they are *for* us – their fruit will reveal their true character (Mark 9:38–41).

Part Two: Theology

Personal reflection, application and group discussion

1. What is the most important thing that you have gained from this chapter?
2. Think of *why* Jesus healed people, why he conducted such an extensive healing and deliverance ministry. Are there any other reasons or motivations that come to mind? What motivations have you seen in healing – both in you and in others ministering healing?
3. Comparing your experience and knowledge of healing with my list of principles and patterns in Jesus' healing ministry, what have you learnt that is different or new? What do you need to be aware of? Is there anything you need to change or do differently in your practice of healing?
4. As a practical exercise, take time to go through the Scripture references to the healing stories. As you read each story, compile your own list of the principles and patterns you discover in Jesus' ministry. What can you add to my list?

8

IMPARTATION: TRANSFER OF KINGDOM MINISTRY TO THE CHURCH

Jesus went through all the towns and villages, teaching in their synagogues, preaching the good news of the kingdom and healing every ... disease and sickness. When he saw the crowds, he had compassion on them, because they were harassed and helpless, like sheep without a shepherd. Then he said to his disciples, "The harvest is plentiful, but the workers are few. Ask the Lord of the harvest, therefore, to send out workers into his harvest field." He called the twelve disciples to him and gave them authority to drive out evil spirits and to heal every disease and sickness ... Jesus sent [them] out with the following instructions: "... As you go, preach this message: 'The kingdom of heaven is near.' Heal the sick, raise the dead, cleanse those who have leprosy, drive out demons. Freely you have received, freely give."
– Matthew 9:35–38; 10:1, 5, 7–8

> *"Very truly, I tell you, the one who believes in me will also do the works that I do and, in fact, will do greater works than these, because I am going to the Father.*
> *I will do whatever you ask in my name, so that the Father may be glorified in the Son."*
> – John 14:12–13 NRSV

Mentoring, training and impartation

Mentoring relationships are very important. Because we are seldom mentored in the home, many adults are looking for fathers and mothers. They are not aware that often they want the mentor to take responsibility for their lives, making them vulnerable to parent-child relationships (dominance and dependence, control and manipulation). When I asked John Wimber if I could come to Anaheim Vineyard for him to "spiritually father" me, he said I would be disappointed. Why? He said *Jesus* is the one who disciples and mentors us by his Spirit, via *multiple means* (for safety and balance) like community, leaders, spiritual disciplines and circumstances. One-on-one shepherd-disciple and father-son relationships have been abusive in the church – we need a different model of mentoring.

I went to Anaheim and learnt much through individuals, courses, small groups and the general environment. With regard to healing ministry, I found that coaching, training and impartation happened as we practised it in Sunday services, small groups, seminars, and in the marketplace. For example, one Sunday during ministry time, another person and I were praying for a young woman. (People ministered to each other all over the hall.) The Spirit was on her; she cried and moaned, moving her body rhythmically. I was embarrassed, as it felt seductive. We were not making progress, so I looked around to see if I could catch the eye of an experienced leader. I happened to see John and beckoned him.

He walked over, and stopped to look at her. Then stepped forward and spoke into her ear. She nodded her head. John began to rebuke a demon. The reaction was immediate. Her movements became pronounced and she fell to the floor, writhing violently. John told us to kneel beside her and hold her arms if we could. He touched her head, commanding the demon to come out. The confrontation produced weird body contortions, noises and a foul odour. After a while there was a sudden release and all was calm. John spoke again in her ear and called some women to take care of her.

I was amazed and asked him afterwards, "What happened? What did you say to her? How did you know it was a demon?" Seeing her movements, he knew from experience that it was a sexual confrontation – probably demonic. He asked God about it and instantly saw (in his mind) beach sand with two parallel markings. He concluded that God was showing him she had been sexually abused at the age of eleven, and it had led to her being sexually promiscuous (he surmised). He asked her quietly (to protect her dignity and test his assumptions) if what he "saw" and thought was correct. That is when she nodded and the unclean spirit reacted, and was later expelled. I learnt from the encounter and the after-reflection: John watched her while ministering; he drew on his experience; read her bodily manifestations; interacted with the Spirit and followed the promptings; did not get hyped up; was firm yet compassionate; protected her dignity, and stayed with the process till there was release.

That is how we learnt – the environment itself seemed to transfer skills, because ministry took place every time we gathered. John would periodically call people up who wanted to be anointed with oil for ministry, to impart the authority and power of the kingdom to "go, heal the sick!" The focus in those days was on "go heal the sick and drive out demons *in the homes, on the streets, in the shopping malls, the schools and workplace*". Doing it in church was for experimenting, training and re-empowering – but "the meat is in the street", Wimber said. When people ask why we do not see "the power" as in "the good old days", my answer is that we are church-focused more than world-focused.[1] Signs and wonders were meant for unbelievers, not for believers – they happen more naturally and powerfully in evangelism and mission (Hebrews 2:3–4).

---

[1] Gideon asked God: "Where are all the signs and wonders that our fathers told us about, especially when you brought us out of Egypt?" God answered, "Go as you are … and save Israel out of the hand of (evil)" (Judges 6:13–14 RAP). As you *go out to save people,* God's supernatural works will be manifested.

Part Two: Theology

Jesus' process of impartation and transfer

There are well-known mentoring relationships in the Bible: Moses and Joshua, Elijah and Elisha,[2] Paul and Timothy. We can learn much from them, but Jesus' mentoring relationship was of a greater spiritual wattage and scope – it included all who followed him. He was founder-leader of a prophetic messianic movement with clear aims, with a vision for Israel and the world – *through his followers* (John 17:20f). Jesus' goal was to impart and transfer his kingdom ministry to his followers, through training and deploying them. In fact, it was not only the impartation of kingdom authority and skills, but to entrust the kingdom itself to his followers: "Do not be afraid, little flock, for the Father has been pleased *to give you the kingdom … I confer on you a kingdom, just as my Father conferred one on me*" (Luke 12:32; 22:29). Jesus had a plan and strategy to explode his Father's kingdom outwards, through his little flock, in ever-increasing inclusive circles, from Israel to the ends of the earth.

Therefore, he intentionally called the twelve, so "that they might be *with him* and that he might send them out to preach and to have authority to drive out demons". He designated them *apostles*, "sent ones" (Mark 3:13–15). Jesus was only one person doing ministry at one time, in one place. After a year or so of modelling kingdom ministry – training his disciples – he multiplied the ministry by sending them out two-by-two to do what he had been doing in every town and village of Israel.[3] They were messengers of the kingdom, announcing and enacting it as Jesus did in Mark 1:15. They represented the end of evil and the beginning of freedom. This kingdom expansion had great impact, drawing the attention and opposition of the political powers (King Herod, Mark 6:12–14).

---

[2] The prophetic (signs and wonders) mentoring relationship between Elijah and Elisha can be seen behind the Luke-Acts narratives of Jesus and the early church. Craig Keener has helpfully laid this out in *Gift and Giver: The Holy Spirit Today* (Grand Rapids: Baker Academic, 2001), pp. 51–68.

[3] The sending of the twelve was both historically unique (offering God's kingdom to Israel) and the church's commissioning. Matthew 10 is a model of the later "great commission" of the church of all ages in Matthew 28:18–20: Given authority, go, make disciples (baptising), "teaching *them* to obey all that I have commanded" – which includes the commands of Matthew 10:7–8: preach the kingdom, heal the sick, cast out demons, etc.

Later Jesus sent out seventy-two other disciples to do the same (Luke 10:1f). They returned with joy that the demons submitted to them in Jesus' name (vs 17–24). This multiplied kingdom advance undermined and dislodged Satan's kingdom: "I saw Satan fall like lightning from heaven." Jesus affirmed what he had done to and through the disciples: "I have given you *authority* to trample on snakes and scorpions (demons), and to overcome all the *power* of the enemy (Satan); nothing will harm you." This filled *him* with joy and praise for God!

The transfer of kingdom ministry did not stop with the twelve and the seventy-two; it multiplied to the one hundred and twenty who waited in the upper room (Acts 1:15); to the five hundred who witnessed Jesus' resurrection (1 Corinthians 15:6); to the three thousand who came to faith at Pentecost (Acts 2:41). Jesus commissioned *all* his followers – the church – to go and speak the words and do the works of the kingdom, to the ends of the earth. The first transfer to the twelve (and seventy-two) is our model.

There are two dimensions to this transfer. The Synoptic Gospels show the *impartation of kingdom ministry* by commissioning (authority) and gifting (power) – the ministry Jesus modelled in Chapter 5. John's Gospel shows the *impartation of relational oneness* with Jesus and the Father by the Spirit – the intimacy Jesus modelled in Chapter 6. The book of Acts shows how these two dimensions worked together in the life of the early church (next chapter). Let us examine these two dimensions of transference, *as they apply to us*.

Transfer of kingdom authority and power (Matthew 9:35–10:10)

- *The mission, v. 35:* Jesus' mission was to go "through all the towns and villages" with the message and ministry of God's kingdom. Likewise, our (co)mission is to go to every town and village to the ends of the earth, to bring the kingdom to all who receive it. The word "mission" is not used in the Bible per se. It comes from the Latin *missio*, which means the same as the Greek *apostello*, "to be sent" to advance God's kingdom. We participate in the Missio Dei, God's mission. There is no doubt that doing ministry outside the church, or being sent on a translocal mission trip (as we call it), comes with "apostolic" expectations and happenings.

- *The model, v. 35:* Jesus modelled wholistic kingdom ministry: "Preaching the good news of the kingdom and healing every ... disease and sickness." It is proclamation and demonstration. Many churches have separated the two. The word is preached followed by the benediction – there is no demonstration of the kingdom. It is a rational Christianity without power, a far cry from Jesus and Paul, who practised both words and works.[4]

- *The market, vs 36, 37:* Large crowds flocked after Jesus because he met their needs. They were "harassed and helpless, like sheep without a shepherd", victimised and tormented by sin, sickness, demons and death. Jesus sighed: "The harvest is plentiful ..." We need to see people as Jesus sees them – see their real condition – and the potential kingdom harvest. Jesus came for sinners, the sick, not for those who thought they were righteous or well (Matthew 9:10–13). Once again: Our mission is ministry in the marketplace.

- *The motivation, v. 36:* "When he saw the crowds, he had compassion on them, because they were harassed and helpless." Jesus was purely and simply motivated by compassion, because of what he saw (the human need). *We ought to know what motivates us in ministry.* It is not easy, because "the heart is deceitful above all things, and desperately wicked: who can know it?" (Jeremiah 17:9 KJV). We all have mixed motives. I discuss compassion in Chapter 10, but ultimately, *God's love* for others, working in and through us, is the only authentic and sustainable motivation for mission and ministry.

- *The multiplication, vs 37, 38:* "The harvest is so vast but the workers are so few." Jesus said this knowing he was one minister at one time in one place, while many were dying without hearing of God's kingdom, without the opportunity to receive

---

[4] Paul says: "My preaching was not with wise and persuasive words, but with the demonstration of the Spirit's power, that your faith will not rest on human wisdom but on God's power ... For the kingdom of God is not a matter of talk, but of power" (1 Corinthians 2:4–5; 4:20 RAP).

Impartation: *Transfer of kingdom ministry to the church*

it. How could he multiply himself and his ministry to harvest the multitudes for the kingdom? It was not an immediate thought – he planned it all along – but he wanted to include his disciples in the process: "Ask the Lord of the harvest, *therefore*, to send out workers into his harvest field." Prayer is faith and working with God in his mission. Prayer makes us willing to be his answer to our own prayer: Jesus called his (praying) disciples to be the first workers in the harvest (10:1). He multiplied his ministry from one to the twelve to the seventy-two, reaching the multitudes.

- *The means, 10:1:* Comparing and joining Matthew 10:1 and Luke 9:1 (parallel texts), we get the following: "He called his twelve disciples to him and gave them power (*dynamis*) and authority (*exousia*) to drive out *all* demons and to heal *every* disease and sickness." Awesome! In sending out the twelve, Jesus gave them *the means of ministry* to drive out *all* demons and to heal *every* disease and sickness. It comes with "being sent" – we have God's backing (apostolic anointing) when we are in God's mission. I discuss authority and power, and how they operate in healing ministry, in Chapter 10.

- *The message, vs 7, 8:* Jesus gave his disciples a specific message to proclaim: the kingdom of God. We are not to preach our church, our ministry, our pet subject, or ourselves.[5] We are to preach the kingdom as Jesus did, through symbols, parables, explanations and enactments. We must preach that the kingdom is near, *actively present*. Pronouncing the kingdom on people is a power encounter. It naturally leads to enactment: "Heal the sick, raise the dead, cleanse the lepers, drive out demons."

- *The ministry, v. 8:* The ministry is to do the works of the kingdom by destroying the works of the devil in people's lives. Jesus did *not* say "*pray* for the sick, *pray* for the dead, *pray* for

---

[5]Jesus laid on us (his disciples) *the priority of the kingdom*: Pray the kingdom comes, *seek first* the kingdom, use the keys of the kingdom (Matthew 6:10, 33; 16:19). Jesus took on *himself* the priority of the church: "*I* will build *my* church" (Matthew 16:18). If we seek the kingdom, he will build *his* church. If we turn them around – we get preoccupied with building the church – then we neglect the kingdom and subtly it becomes *our* church built in *our* image and likeness. *Our* church becomes *our kingdom where we rule and reign* – that we preach and propagate.

the demonised ..." He said *heal* the sick, *raise* the dead, *cleanse* the lepers, *drive out* demons. How so? Because "freely you have received, freely give". We must use the authority and power of the kingdom we have freely received to heal and deliver people. We do that by directly rebuking sickness, demons and death, as Jesus did (we do it in his name). *Praying* for people is different to healing them. The former implies a posture of closed eyes talking to God. The latter implies looking at the person and speaking healing into them (more on this in Chapter 13).

- *The manner, vs 9, 10:* Jesus continued with clear instructions as to the manner in which they should minister. "Freely you have received, freely give" also means trusting God for your material support: do not charge or take money for your healing services or seek prosperity from kingdom ministry (vs 9–10).[6] In short, they were to be humble and trusting, yet discerning and strategic, wise and innocent, expecting opposition and suffering. (You can examine all the instructions Jesus gave them in Matthew 10.)

Transfer of Spirit-oneness and intimacy

John records no specific ministry transfer and sending out of the twelve during Jesus' earthly ministry as the Synoptics do. Instead he focuses on the "promise of the Father" (the *Ruach ha Kodesh*)[7] that Jesus prepared his disciples to receive at the resurrection and Pentecost. That was the impartation to the disciples, and the church of all ages, of the relational intimacy that Jesus had with the Father *by the Spirit*. It was essentially about Jesus' return to the Father to give the Holy Spirit to them – John's version of Jesus' multiplication of

---

[6]This raises the ethics of healing ministry, medical care and insurance. The sick are vulnerable and desperate; many will believe almost anything, pay anything, to be healed. Taking offerings in healing services ("give and it will be given to you ... in healing", "sow into this ministry") is an exploitation and abuse of the poor and sick. Asking for large fees and luxury hotels before agreeing to speak at a conference disobeys Jesus' teachings. For integrity sake, we must avoid any form of "Simonery" – offering or receiving money for supernatural power and healing (Acts 8:9–24).
[7]Literally "Spirit of the Holy (One)" in Hebrew. *Ruach* is a Hebrew feminine noun. *Pneuma* (Greek) is neuter; you can use "she" or "he". In keeping with the NRSV (inclusive language translation), I use "he".

himself; his transfer to, and commissioning of, the disciples, recorded in John 13–17, a profoundly intimate dialogue with his disciples the night before he was crucified.

This impartation of Spirit-oneness, whereby the Father and the Son indwell us, is a growing experience – of *the same reality and quality* of eternal life (*zoe aionios*) that Jesus had. It is captured in Jesus' words: "If anyone loves me, he will obey my teaching. My Father will love him, and we will come to him and make *our* home with him" (14:23); "As the Father has sent me, I am sending you" (20:21). How do we receive the Spirit, this transfer of relational intimacy?

Through believing

To receive the "promise of the Father" required *faith*, actual reliance on Christ. Those *who believed in him* would receive the Spirit when Jesus breathed into them at his resurrection and when he poured the Spirit on them at Pentecost, after his ascension to the Father. The Spirit was to indwell (resurrection life) and empower (Pentecost anointing) the *believers*. John uses faith (*pisteuo*) ninety times and the phrase "he who believes in me [Jesus] …" sixteen times. The key is "he who believes in me has eternal life" (5:24), and "he who believes in me will do the works [miracles] I have been doing, and greater works than these, *because I am going to my Father*" (14:12). Jesus ascends to the Father to send the Spirit to enable us to do God's works. It does *not* refer to having "great faith" to do Christ's miracles; it is being a believer in Jesus. *Therefore*, Jesus continues: "I will do whatever you ask in my name …" (v. 13). Jesus and the Father will do whatever *believers* ask for *in Jesus' name*, by the indwelling Spirit.

Through befriending

The Spirit gift is about "fellowship", the old English word better translated as "friendship". *Koinonia* means to participate, share and commune (1 John 1:3–7). The world does not know the Holy Spirit, but *believers* do, because he "lives *with* you and will be *in* you" (14:17). As Jesus was a true friend *with* his disciples, the Spirit will be a true friend *in* them. Jesus said the Spirit is "another *Parakletos*" (14:16), meaning friend, comforter, helper, counsellor, advocate. Jesus was one

Parakletos physically *with* them; after his resurrection and ascension, he will send *another Parakletos* to live *in* them.

The Spirit will think, feel and interact – be as real as Jesus was when he lived with them for three-and-a-half years. He will be Jesus *to* them, living *in* them, to be Jesus *through* them to the world – Jesus' multiplication of himself to the multitudes. Instead of having a physical mentor with them, they would have a Spirit mentor *in* them. They learnt to live under *visible* leadership by relational trust and growth; now they would learn to live under *invisible* leadership, as Jesus himself lived from the initiative of his indwelling Father by the Spirit.

In explaining this to his disciples, Jesus said: *"On that day,"* (when the *Parakletos* comes) *"you will realise* that I am in my Father, and you are in me, and I am in you" (14:20). The mutual Trinitarian indwelling would become subjectively real and objectively evident. Again, space does not allow me to unpack how Jesus detailed the nature of this *koinonia* friendship (in John 14–16). Suffice it to say we must befriend the *Parakletos*, who speaks, reveals, comforts, encourages, reminds, leads, guides, convicts, and glorifies the Father and Son through us.

Through receiving

Jesus also taught his disciples *how to receive the Spirit*, to live moment by moment in the flow of the Spirit, just as he did. The teaching on the Vine and the branches (15:1–8) is about relational "abiding". This intimacy and union with Christ is experienced *by receiving his words and Spirit into our very being* (the flow of "sap"). Then we can ask whatever we wish and it will be given to us (v. 7). The natural outflow is the fruit of Christ's character and works, produced in us in increasing measure. The Father's will is that we bear *much* fruit (v. 8).

There is perhaps a stronger image and more practical preparation that Jesus used to help his disciples receive and flow in the Spirit. It is found in 7:37–39. On the last day of the Feast of Tabernacles in Jerusalem, when the priests were pouring out water before the Lord, Jesus stood up and said in a loud voice: "If anyone is thirsty, *let them come to me and drink*. Whoever believes in me, as the Scripture has said, rivers of living water will flow from their inner being" (RAP). By this, says John, Jesus meant the Holy Spirit whom those who believed in him were later to receive. Up to that time the Spirit had not yet been given as Jesus had not yet been glorified (crucified, resurrected and ascended).

How do we receive the Spirit? Firstly, we must come to Jesus – the Anointed who baptizes with the Spirit – putting our faith in him as *believers*. Secondly, we must drink in the Spirit; and drink deeply, depending on how thirsty we are! The Spirit is promised as gushing water, freely poured out in the desert for all who are thirsty (Isaiah 35:5–7; 55:1); as God's wind that blows, his breath that he breathes (Ezekiel 37:9–10). We drink by lifting up our heads, opening our mouths and swallowing! We literally breathe in God's outpoured Spirit. We do not pray to receive the Spirit; we *actually receive* the Spirit by inhaling as we do not "pray for the sick" but "heal the sick" by speaking healing.

These are not mere lung exercises, if you are thinking that. Belief and body posture work together – what we experience or desire inwardly, we express bodily; and what we do bodily engenders an inward response. When we feel humble before God in worship, we bow down on our knees. This in turn engenders a greater sense of God's majesty and our humility. Because we believe Jesus breathes and pours *out* the Spirit, we breathe and drink him *in*. After preparing his disciples to receive the Spirit, Jesus *literally breathed on them* at his resurrection and said: "Receive the Holy Spirit" (20:22). At Pentecost the disciples received the Spirit as poured out wind, which they inhaled and then out-flowed (Acts 2:1–4).

Hebrew *ruach* and Greek *pneuma* both mean spirit, breath, wind, implying that to receive (Holy) Spirit, we inhale, and to expel (evil) spirit, we exhale. The more we drink in God's Spirit, the more we overflow with the Spirit as John 7:38 says: From our innermost being will flow rivers of living waters. (I discuss flowing in the Spirit regarding healing ministry in the chapters that follow.) The point is this: As Father was to Jesus by the fountain of his Spirit, for life-giving ministry to the world, so Jesus is to us by the fountain of his Spirit, so that we too are a free-flowing river of God's healing to the multitudes.

Personal reflection, application and group discussion

1. Do you really believe that Jesus has transferred and imparted his kingdom ministry to *you* as a believer in Christ? To us as a local church? Give your reasons.
2. In what ways do you see this kingdom ministry being expressed and practised in *your* life? In the life of your local church? Are there other aspects that you long to see practised? What would they look like?
3. Have you had mentoring in practising the healing and deliverance ministry of Jesus? How were you mentored and how has it helped you? Or how were you not mentored, and what sort of mentoring do you long for?
4. What did you learn from the Synoptic accounts of the transfer and impartation of kingdom ministry to the disciples? What did you learn from John's version of Jesus' impartation of Spirit relationship and intimacy? What longing does this arouse within you? What can you do about it?
5. What has God said to you through this chapter? How are you going to respond to it?
6. Do a practical exercise in your small group.
    - Have an evening where everyone receives (drinks) the Spirit afresh as described in John 7:37–38 and Acts 2:1–4. See what happens.
    - Get your group to do Matthew 10:7–8: Go out to a shopping mall, a public park, or a place where there are people. Ask God to show you what he is doing, who he is working with. Go and explain (pronounce) God's kingdom to the person. Then ask them what their need is, and heal or deliver them by actually doing healing as I have described.

9

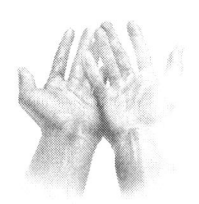

Continuation: Healing ministry in the early church and church history

*"Lord, are you at this time going to restore
the kingdom to Israel?"
He said to them: "It is not for you to know the times or dates
the Father has set by his own authority.
But you will receive power when the Holy Spirit comes on you;
and you will be my witnesses in Jerusalem, and in all Judea
and Samaria, and to the ends of the earth."*
– Acts 1:6–8

*After the Lord Jesus had spoken to them, he was taken up
into heaven and he sat down at the right hand of God.
Then the disciples went out and preached everywhere,
and the Lord worked with them and confirmed his word
by the [miraculous] signs that accompanied it.*
– Mark 16:19–20

Part Two: Theology

The impact of the transfer and multiplication of Jesus' kingdom ministry in Israel was enormous, challenging earthly and heavenly (evil) powers (Ephesians 6:12), which in turn led to Jesus' suffering and death. The impact of the kingdom transfer and multiplication *after* Jesus' death, resurrection and ascension was immeasurably greater.

Luke records the exponential explosion of the kingdom through the early church in the book of Acts – a direct result of the outpoured dynamite of the Holy Spirit by the ascended Christ. Beginning in Jerusalem at Pentecost, the Spirit's dynamic through the church advanced the kingdom to all Judea and Samaria, and to "the ends of the earth" (Rome and beyond). They were *not* to be preoccupied with God's dates regarding national Israel and the end of time. They were rather to be fully occupied with God's *transnational* kingdom by the *dynamis* of the Spirit, to the ends of the earth. This would provoke the powers even more, involving suffering and martyrdom. *Marturia* ("witness") is the root of "martyr" – the Spirit's power is not only to witness in speaking the *words*, doing the *works*, and seeing the *wonders* of the kingdom, but also the power to share in the *wounds* of Jesus, to endure persecution and martyrdom with joy.

Mark summarises this ongoing advance of the kingdom in the closing words of his Gospel. After his death and resurrection, Jesus was taken up into heaven and sat down at the right hand of God – crowned King in heaven over *all* things. His coronation was made real on earth through his subjects who, as heralds, went everywhere announcing and enacting the gospel of Christ's kingdom. The heavenly King *worked with them* by backing up their word – *his* word spoken from his throne – with confirming signs and wonders by the power of his Spirit. This was God's vindication of Christ's suffering at the hands of evil powers.[1]

---

[1] Mark 16:19–20 completes Mark's "Son of Man" usage (2:10; 8:31; 9:9, 12, 31; 10:33; 14:21, 41), fulfilling Daniel's messianic prophecy (Daniel 7:9–27). The son of man embodies and represents God's people (believing Israel). He suffers under evil "beastly" rule (ministry and crucifixion); then is vindicated by God (resurrection and ascension) as he "comes with the clouds" to God's heavenly court. He is given "authority, glory and sovereign power" so that "all nations and people from every language worship him. His dominion is an everlasting dominion that will never pass away" (7:13–14). *He did this on behalf of* "the saints, the people of the Most High", so that Satan's "power will be taken away and completely destroyed forever", and the saints given "the sovereignty,

The church is God's authorised instrument and empowered embodiment of Christ's kingdom on earth – as Jesus was in his ministry. The church is apostolic (missionary) by nature, by reason of its existence. When we cease doing mission, we cease being the church *of Jesus Christ*, and become something else. We are *Christ's body* on earth, led and governed by the heavenly head through his indwelling missionary Spirit. Christ's Lordship *over* the church is experienced by the Spirit's Lordship *in* the church – to the extent that we allow it. *Then* that Lordship/Headship spreads through us, over all things, to the ends of the earth – *not* in a triumphalistic all-conquering Crusader-spirit, but in the tradition of the Suffering Servant. We too are sent as humble servants on bended knee, naked in our vulnerability, with basin and towel, to wash the feet of the world. The church is Jesus to this world – nothing more, nothing less!

The Acts of the Holy Spirit in the apostolic church

Luke wrote his account of the early church as a continuation of his Gospel of Jesus. The "acts of the apostles" are really the acts of Jesus, the ruling head, by the empowering Spirit in the apostolic church. Luke emphasises the role of the Spirit and prayer, both in Jesus' life and in the early church. He portrays a dramatic picture of this naturally supernatural body of Christ continuing Jesus' healing ministry – with all the spiritual and political opposition that it generated. He structures his book on Acts 1:8: kingdom advance from Jerusalem (chapters 1–7) to Judea and Samaria (8–13), and to the ends of the earth (13–28). The dynamic behind each phase of advance is the coming of the Spirit "on all people" (2:17): on *Jewish* believers in Jerusalem (ch. 2); on *Samaritan* believers (*mixed race,* ch. 8); on a chosen instrument of the Gentile mission (Saul, ch. 9); and then the climax, on the *Gentiles* (ch. 10). Lastly, on a special category, a few remaining disciples of John the Baptiser (ch. 19). Luke uses these groups representatively,[2] to say two important things:

---

power and greatness of the kingdoms under the whole heaven …" (7:26, 27).
[2] See Howard Marshall's studies: *Luke, Historian and Theologian* (Exeter: Paternoster Press, 1970); The Acts of the Apostles, *New Testament Guides* (Sheffield: Academic Press, 1997).

Part Two: Theology

1. *The Spirit is poured out and available to every believer in Jesus* of *all* languages, races, genders, ages, classes (2:17–18). Pentecost reverses Babel, reconciling *all* types of people into one new nation, God's people. This "gift of the Holy Spirit" is for *all* who repent and are baptised, "for *all* whom the Lord … calls" (2:38–39).
2. *The Pentecost experience is the prototype for all believers* in receiving this gift – "baptism" (1:5) or "power" (1:8) – of the Spirit, in order to advance God's kingdom to the ends of the earth. This is the key to the story of Acts.

Pentecost was the experience of the Spirit that became *the principle power of their ongoing ministry: the intimate blending and working together of the divine and the human.* Luke records this prototype experience in 2:1–4. They were sitting in the upper room waiting on God (active human expectancy). The house was filled with wind and "all of them were filled with the Holy Spirit" (active divine initiative; passive human experience); *they* began to drink/inhale the Spirit (active human response; passive divine); "and *they* began to speak in other tongues" (active human initiative; passive divine); "as *the Spirit* enabled[3] them" (active divine; passive human). The Spirit spoke, or made the "tongues" meaningful, in the fifteen languages of those present (active divine, 2:9–11). The result of this interactive blending and partnering of the human and divine was supernatural witness – three thousand people entered God's kingdom.

In summary, *God's initiative* is the coming of the Spirit in wind, fire, filling, inner promptings, uttering words meaningful to people. *Human initiative* (response) is receiving and overflowing with the Spirit in the active waiting, expecting, breathing in, opening the mouth and speaking out. The Spirit did not *make* them speak in tongues; *they* spoke in tongues as the Spirit prompted them. It is like walking on water – the miracle *only* happens when *you* do it, as Jesus prompts ("Come!"). You have to trust and act! *That is how* they

---

[3] NIV translation of *apophtheggesthai*, "to utter forth". I like "prompted" (*The Message*). It is a word peculiar to Acts (2:4, 14; 26:25), used in the Septuagint for the "utterance" of prophets, not for normal speech (see 1 Chronicles 25:1; Ezekiel 13:9). Luke used it for "tongues" as the disciples experienced it, but it was *prophecy* to the hearers, understood in their vernacular, fulfilling Joel 2:28f (cf. Acts 2:14–21).

overflowed in the Spirit and his power: *They* spoke words in response and obedience to inner promptings – words they had not learnt or understood, but that made sense to others with the supernatural power of saving grace.

Luke shows how Pentecost (tongues) happened when the Spirit came "on all people",[4] reinforcing the principle dynamic: *Drink in the outpoured Spirit and respond to his enabling promptings by overflowing in speech and action, trusting God for the supernatural kingdom effect.* I am not proposing the classic Pentecostal position that tongues is the evidence of the baptism/empowering of the Spirit ("you must speak in tongues to be filled with the Spirit"). I *am* saying the evidence of Spirit infilling is Spirit outflowing in manifestations of supernatural *charisms* (grace gifts; tongues being a common "trigger").

Luke has a Hebrew theology of the Spirit: The Spirit comes primarily to empower people, by commonly giving *inspired utterance* (prophesying). When Moses appointed the seventy elders, God put his Spirit on them and they prophesied. Then Moses said: "I wish that all YHWH's people were prophets, that YHWH would put his Spirit on [all of] them!" (Numbers 11:29). The prophets predicted that this would happen: God will pour out his Spirit "on all people. Your sons and daughters *will prophesy* …" (Joel 2:28f).[5] It was fulfilled at Pentecost in the Spirit's coming with tongues (Acts 2:14–21). Luke shows the same pattern of Spirit infilling and Spirit outflowing in inspired utterance at Jesus' birth, in his life, teachings and ministry, and in the early church.[6]

All this to say: There is an important theology behind the tongues

---

[4]On Jews, 2:4; on Gentiles, 10:44–46 (*11:15–17*); on John's disciples, 19:6. Luke does not say the Samaritans spoke in tongues, but implies supernatural happenings as Simon offered money for the power to impart the Holy Spirit (8:14–18). There is no mention of tongues when Paul received the Spirit (9:17–18), but we know he spoke in tongues (1 Corinthians 14:18).

[5]Although this is the common Old Testament pattern (Numbers 11:25–26; 24:2f; 1 Samuel 10:6; 19:20–24; 2 Samuel 23:1–2; 1 Chronicles 12:18; 2 Chronicles 15:1–4; 24:20; Nehemiah 9:20, 30), *it is not exclusively so.* There are other manifestations of the Spirit's coming on people (Genesis 41:38; Exodus 31:3; Deuteronomy 34:9; Judges 3:10; 6:34; 11:29; 13:25; 14:6, 19; 15:14; 1 Samuel 16:13; 1 Kings 18:12, 46).

[6]Luke 1:15–17, 41–45, 46–55; 67–79; 2:25–32; 4:18–21; 12:12; Acts 1:2, 8; 2:4, 17; 4:8, 31; 5:32; 6:10; 7:51; 10:45–46; 11:28; 13:2, 4, 9; 20:23; 21:4, 11.

phenomenon. *Speech* is the unique evidence and expression of human personality made in God's image (compared to animals). God expressed himself by *speaking* all things into being. When the Spirit comes, he expresses his personality by speaking in us, to us, and through us, as we yield responsively to him, the *Parakletos* discussed in the previous chapter. Therefore …

> *Tongues enacts the principle of yielding control of ourselves in faith – even beyond our rational understanding – to the Spirit's initiative and government.* It confirms the exaltation of Christ's headship over all,[7] made real by his Spirit's rule *in* yielded people. It symbolises the humbling of human headship (our mind is "unfruitful", 1 Corinthians 14:13–17); and the taming of the most "unruly member" of the body, the tongue, for the most heavenly praise and purpose: the Spirit's control and use of our "whole body" for his enabling graces "just as he determines" (James 3:1–12 cf. 1 Corinthians 12:7–11). To illustrate the principle: Whenever I speak in tongues, as Paul regularly did (1 Corinthians 14:18), I realise I speak, but the Spirit speaks in me. I speak from my spirit in faith, via my yielded tongue, but my mind does not understand. God (and maybe others) hears with full understanding and responds accordingly! Tongues is *like the uncorking of the bottle to release the full flow – rivers of living waters – of John 7:38*.

> *Tongues enacts the kingdom mission to reach and reconcile all nations by the Spirit's enabling.* Pentecost reversed Babel (Genesis 11) by overcoming not only human pride, control and understanding, but God's judgment via the language barrier. It symbolises the breaking of all apartheid walls of principalities and powers that divide and rule; and the reconciliation and healing of the nations through *God's* eternal rule and reign, by the Spirit's supernatural power *in the church*.[8] For example:

---

[7] The Hebrews knew the sacrifice had been accepted in the Holy of Holies when they heard the tongues in the bells ringing on the High Priest's garments; he was alive, not dead! The joyful tongues at Pentecost signalled (and continue to signal) that Jesus' once-for-all atoning sacrifice has been accepted in the heavens; that *he is* interceding for us as *he* now reconciles and rules the nations *through us*.

[8] David heard God's Spirit (wind) in the balsam trees (a marching sound), which led

> Whenever I pray in tongues, I am reminded that I am not only mystically participating in the conversation of the Trinity, but I am mystically in communion with all God's people, even angels, everywhere![9]

Back to Acts. Luke shows how the early church experienced many supernatural phenomena – not just healings – through yielded co-operation with the Spirit. Space does not allow me to illustrate this human-divine interaction through the stories in Acts, as I did in Mark and John. They are listed in various categories and references in Appendix 4 for your own study. I show the direct effect that the supernatural had on kingdom advancement and church growth, including fourteen references in Acts where "signs and wonders" occurred with preaching and resultant church growth. The purpose of "signs and wonders" was *not* church enjoyment or personal indulgence.[10] It was for wholistic spiritual warfare to advance God's kingdom. As with Jesus, the dramatic happened in the marketplace, in evangelism and mission. The stories recorded in Acts are the prominent, representative ones – obviously much more happened. Healing was part of the normal life and ministry of the early church.

They performed the miracles that Jesus did: drove out demons; healed all kinds of sickness; forgave sins (and withheld forgiveness in judgment); ruled over nature; and raised (resuscitated) the dead. They did "greater works", like the healings and deliverance that came from the touch of Peter's shadow and from materials that had been laid on Paul's body (5:12–16; 19:11–12). They used Jesus' basic method of healing: speaking (commanding) and laying on hands (also used to

---

to his victory (2 Samuel 5:22–25). The leaves of the Tree of Life in the New Jerusalem are "for the healing of the nations" (Revelation 22:2). I see tongues as the rustling of those leaves in God's wind as it blows through the barrier-breaking, race-reconciling, nation-healing, worldwide church of Jesus Christ. Tongues is a sign of the end, when every tribe, language, people and nation will worship around God's throne (Revelation 5:9–10).

[9]"The tongues of mortals and angels" (1 Corinthians 13:1 NRSV); Romans 8:26–27 is participation in the Trinity through praying/groaning in/by the Spirit; Hebrews 12:22–24 is God's historic, eternal, cosmic communion.

[10]We must not presume on spiritual power and the supernatural; it is playing with dynamite, as the seven sons of Sceva discovered (19:13–16)! Entrustment of power is for spiritual warfare, both for salvation (healings) and judgment: death (5:1–11); blindness (13:6–11). See also 1 Timothy 1:20; 1 Corinthians 5:1–5; 11:27–32.

impart the Spirit, 8:17; 19:6). The key was the inner prompting and enabling of the Spirit as they "looked" at people (e.g. 3:4; 8:23; 13:9; 14:9).[11] The Spirit spoke to them in many ways: angels appeared and verbally directed them (8:26; 12:8: 27:23); demons opposed them (13:6–12). It was all-out war.

The kingdom signs and wonders affected political structures and spiritual principalities, causing a reaction. In Philipi Paul drove out a demon, causing a mini economic collapse, resulting in flogging and imprisonment (16:16–36). But as Paul and Silas sang and praised King Jesus, an earthquake opened the prison doors, leading to their release and the salvation of the jailer and his family. The earth was part of this *total* cosmic warfare – as it is today, if not more so!

Healing in the early church letters

References to sickness and healing, signs and wonders in the letters to the churches, can be summarised as positive awareness and problematic texts.

Positive awareness: Beginning with Paul's earliest letters, he affirms healing and miracles as part of the *normal awareness and practice* of the church – the "already" of the kingdom. Paul preached the gospel "not simply with words, but also with power, with the Holy Spirit" (1 Thessalonians 1:5; 1 Corinthians 2:4–5). Satan has real power for "counterfeit miracles, signs and wonders" – people were not to be deceived by them (2 Thessalonians 2:9). Paul was concerned that the Galatians were "bewitched" (by a religious spirit?) into believing that God "gives [the] Spirit and works miracles" by Jewish pedigree – as a reward for keeping Torah – not by faith in Messiah Jesus (Galatians 3:1–5). He did "signs, wonders and miracles" with "great perseverance", the marks of a true apostle (2 Corinthians 12:12; Romans 15:19). Healings and the supernatural are not only for evangelism and mission; they are also for the health and growth of the church via spiritual gifts, as part of the regular "body life" (1 Corinthians 12–14).

---
[11]A man crippled from birth, who had never walked: "Paul looked directly at him, *saw that he had faith to be healed* and called out, 'Stand up on your feet!' At that, the man jumped up and began to walk."

God confirms his "great salvation" through "signs, wonders and various miracles, and gifts of the Holy Spirit" (Hebrews 2:3–4). James speaks of healing as *a regular ministry practice* in the local church through its leaders (5:14–16). Not many churches have this *mindset and expectation*, that healings and supernatural gifts of the Spirit are a normal part of ministry in the church and mission in the world. It urgently needs to be recovered for both effective church ministry and our co-mission in the world.

"Problematic" texts: They reveal *a realism* in the early church with regard to sickness and healing – the "not yet" of the kingdom. Paul says to the Galatians that "it was because of an illness that I first preached the gospel to you. Even though my illness was a trial to you, you did not treat me with contempt or scorn. Instead, you welcomed me as if I were an angel of God, as if I were Messiah Jesus himself" (4:13–14). Despite being ill, Paul was not ashamed to preach the gospel and do signs and wonders in Galatia (Acts 14:3, 8f). He saw his sickness as an opportunity to preach the gospel. Many say his illness was an eye condition (Galatians 4:15 cf. 6:11). The fact that they did not despise or reject Paul and his message due to his illness – they received him as Messiah – reveals a mindset uncontaminated by the Judaisers and other pseudo-apostles. These travelling preachers and professional orators taught purity of pedigree, strength and success as God's will, and illness and weakness as failure.

The second letter to the Corinthians is Paul's defence in his battle with these "super/false apostles", whose real goal was power and prosperity – by exploiting people and churches. True (apostolic) ministry, spirituality and power is in weakness and suffering, in carrying the marks of Jesus: "death works in us that life may work in you" (4:10–12 RAP). Paul ends his letter with his "thorn in the flesh" explanation, showing how God's power is made perfect in his weakness (12:7–10). He does not specify his "thorn", which has led to debate and speculation. Some say it was his sickness (Galatians 3:13). From the context in 2 Corinthians it can be argued convincingly that it was the constant opposition of false brothers, "messengers of Satan" (12:7 cf. 11:14–15), and its toll in terms of struggle and weakness, so that he remained fully dependent on God (12:10).[12]

However, Paul warned the Corinthians that God can use bodily weakness, sickness and premature death as a discipline to keep them from being judged with the world – a serious consequence of celebrating the Lord's Supper "in an unworthy manner" (1 Corinthians 11:27–32). The context shows that "eating and drinking in an unworthy manner" means not discerning the Lord's body (the church) – not "irreverence toward the sacred" (the sacraments of bread and wine).[13] They dishonoured Christ in his sacrificial death by not honouring the hungry, the poor, the weak, when they gathered around the Lord's table. Eating selfishly and getting drunk neglects others and destroys community. The price of broken community is weakness, sickness and even death. God allows it as a discipline to turn us to him and one another, saving us from ultimate judgment.

Lastly, there are three references to sickness in Paul's co-workers. Epaphroditus "was ill and almost died. But God had mercy on him …" (Philippians 2:25–30). How he was healed, Paul does not say, but he was well enough to be sent to the Philippians. Paul told Timothy to "use a little wine because of your stomach and your frequent illnesses" (1 Timothy 5:23). The medicinal properties of a little wine were well known – a home remedy from the great apostle! In his last recorded letter, Paul says he left Trophimus sick at Miletus (2 Timothy 4:20). We do not know if he prayed for him (he must have!) or if Trophimus recovered.

In conclusion: There is kingdom realism about all of this, showing the serious warfare we are involved in, and the paradoxical nature of faith in expectation and perseverance, honesty and acceptance. If we accept sickness, it is only for a while. Like mortality and death, sickness can never be our friend. It will always be our enemy, to be

---

[12] This is consistent with the Old Testament: God left the Canaanites in the land as "thorns" to keep Israel from exalting themselves (Numbers 33:55; Judges 2:3 cf. Joshua 23:13; Ezekiel 28:24). For an in-depth discussion on Paul's thorn in the flesh, see Philip Hughes, The Second Epistle to the Corinthians, *The New International Commentary on the New Testament* (Grand Rapids: Eerdmans, 1962), pp. 442–454.

[13] Kelsey's phrase in *Psychology, Medicine and Christian Healing*, p. 90, which most churches believe, teach and practise. I follow Derek Morphew's interpretation, consistent with the Jewish roots and context of 1 Corinthians 10 and 11, in *Breakthrough*, pp. 293–302.

Healing ministry in church history

I have shown how the church continued Jesus' healing ministry in faithful obedience to his co-mission. Many of the questions that concern Christians today ("Is it God's will to heal?" "Can a Christian be demonised?"), never entered the minds of the early believers. Healing and deliverance were the normal practice of church ministry and mission, resulting in millions coming to faith in Christ. By the end of the third century, up to a fifth of the Mediterranean world had become Christian. It became the official religion of the Empire in 313 CE and then began to deteriorate. However, there have been major turning points towards restoration and health: the Reformation (1500–1600s), Evangelical Awakenings (1800s), the Pentecostal revival and Charismatic renewal (1900s).

Supernatural healing followed the same pattern: its explosion in Jesus and the early church; then a decline through to the 1800s when a renewed interest and practice in Christian healing began. *However, there are recorded incidents to show that healing never ceased completely – it happened throughout church history.*[14] The following graph gives an overview of *healing* and the supernatural *throughout church history*.

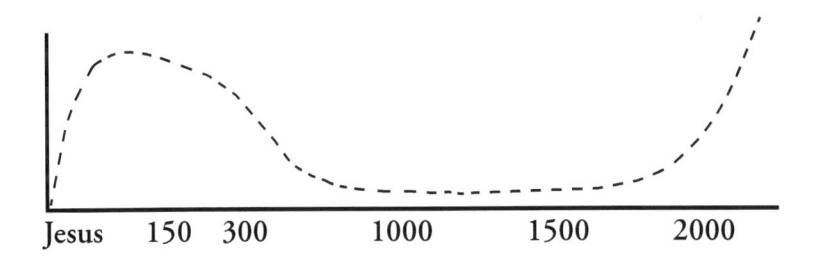

Jesus   150   300   1000   1500   2000

---

[14] We documented many of them from primary sources for the Fuller MC510 course (see my Preface) to show that they took place *in every period of church history*. Evelyn Frost was the first to research healing in the first few centuries, *Christian Healing: A Consideration of the Place of Spiritual Healing in the Church of Today in the Light of the Doctrine and Practice of the Ante-Nicene Church* (London: A.R. Mowbray, 1940). Morton Kelsey researched healing throughout church history in *Healing and Christianity* (1973), revised and expanded in *Psychology, Medicine and Christian Healing* (1988).

Francis MacNutt's summary is this: From "a lively belief in healing prayer" being central to the church, it "was taken away, not by the enemies of Christianity, but, surprisingly, by Christians themselves ... by holy leaders who nearly killed Christian healing; the monks, for instance, fled to the desert (400 CE) to escape the sinful cities and then refused, in the name of humility, to pray for the sick".[15] It seems unbelievable, but it is true as we see the key shifts that took place with regard to Christian healing in the church's history:

From believer's baptism to Christian confirmation

The normal pattern of people becoming Christians ("Christian initiation") in the early church was repentance and faith, water baptism and laying on hands for "the gift of the Spirit" (Acts 2:38–39). Many converts were freed from demonisation from their pre-Christian lifestyle before or at their baptism. Belonging in church community meant evangelising, healing and casting out evil spirits. Over the first few centuries, infant water baptism began to replace adult believer baptism, and catechism and confirmation was seen as the baptism of the Spirit, when the Bishop laid hands on the candidates. This became the norm by the eighth century, producing nominal Christians. The personal Pentecost-experience of the Spirit, with tongues and other supernatural *charisms* for every Christian, all but died out. Their lives no longer evidenced the power of the Spirit, which was the basis of healing ministry.

From believer's ministry to professional priesthood

The early church believed and practised *the priesthood of all believers* – Jesus, our High Priest, fulfilled Judaism's priesthood in his "new covenant" (Hebrews 7–10; 1 Peter 2:4–10). The mess of every-believer ministry led to restrictions and regulations in set prayers, prescribed blessings, and particular methods. By the fourth century, many or-

---

[15] In *The Nearly Perfect Crime: How the Church Almost Killed the Ministry of Healing* (Grand Rapids: Chosen, 2005), p. 11. Beside Kelsey and MacNutt, I recommend Killian McDonnel & George Montague, *Christian Initiation and Baptism in the Holy Spirit: Evidence from the First Eight Centuries,* 2nd ed. (Collegeville: Liturgical Press, 1994), and Frank Darling, *Christian Healing in the Middle Ages and Beyond* (Boulder: Vista Productions, 1990). I draw from these secondary sources for my broad-stroke summary shifts in Christian healing through church history.

ganic freedoms of every-believer ministry had been whittled away by the ordained priests and Bishops. Further professionalisation of ministry led to the comprehensive disempowerment of ordinary church members, creating a clergy-laity divide (seventh century). The church returned to the Old Testament temple priesthood – a fundamental reversal that produced the following destructive shifts.

From regular healing to a church sacrament

The practice of healing was *an organic* part of normal Christian living in the first three centuries.[16] Then healing became part of the church sacraments (baptism and the Lord's Supper), administered by leaders. Healing and deliverance moved from a *charism* exercised by individual believers to a *formal* church ministry: the anointing of oil by elders and recognised specialists (James 5:14–16). Later only the priests could anoint with oil. By the eighth century, only the Bishop could pray over the oil to make it "holy" for healing. Healing became a formal sacrament (anointing of the sick) administered by ordained priests and exorcists, taking healing out of the hands of ordinary Christians.

Then the unction (anointing) for healing evolved into the unction for the dying to prepare people for death, due to a shift from physical to *spiritual* healing (from ninth to eleventh century). A sacrament was a "means of grace" spoken into existence by the priest's blessing – the bread and wine literally becoming the body and blood of Jesus. When the priest spoke healing, and the person was not healed (physically), it was easier to explain it as "spiritual" healing. This shift found a basis in St Jerome's (342–420 CE) translation of the Bible into Latin. He used the word *salvo* for "heal" in James 5:15–16 ("… will *save* the sick"), making spiritual salvation more important than physical healing. As a result, preparing the person for heaven by anointing them – not healing their illness – became a formal church sacrament. The Unction for the Dying officially replaced healing at the Council

---

[16]Church leaders in the first three centuries all wrote of healings, deliverance and Spirit gifts as the normal life and ministry of the church (the Apostles to the Apostolic Fathers: Clement of Rome, Ignatius and Polycarp; to the Ante-Nicene Fathers: Justin the Martyr, Tertillian, Cyprian, Clement of Alexandria, Origen and Iranaeus). They said: "If you do not heal the sick, their blood will be on your hands!"

of Trent (1551). It remained in place in the Roman Catholic Church until the Second Vatican Council in 1962, when the healing ministry of the church was re-recognised and re-authorised.

From the humble healers to the prosperous powerful

Jesus multiplied his kingdom ministry to a few uneducated fishermen, resulting in a revolution of divine healing that advanced throughout the Roman Empire. Christianity spread among the poor, illiterate and uneducated. They believed, received and continued the supernatural ministry of Jesus, which led to great persecution and church growth. As the church grew, the educated and wealthy entered, making the church acceptable and respectable. Emperor Constantine became a Christian and declared Christianity the official religion of the Empire in 313 CE, giving the church political power and growing prosperity. This resulted in a progressive loss of spiritual authority and godly power, manifested in, among other things, a decline in healings and miracles.[17]

From the ordinary many to the holy few

As the church became increasingly worldly (post-313), with a loss of spiritual vitality and power, some Christians and church leaders left the sinful cities for the desert, to pursue holiness in new idealistic communities. In the early church healing was seen as a sign of "kingdom come", of the Spirit's power, via the many Christian practitioners. The pursuit of holiness led to healing becoming a sign of sainthood, a proof of holiness: "If God uses you to heal, it's a sign of purity" and "God only uses holy people (saints) to heal the sick". Although some Desert Fathers were known for healing and deliverance, e.g. Macarius of Alexandria, ironically many others turned away from praying for the sick not to appear proud, to be worthy of sainthood! The shift in

---

[17] This reversal is symbolised in the dramatic healing of the man crippled from birth (Acts 3:1ff). Peter and John said: "Silver and gold we do *not* have, but what we *do* have, we give to you. In the Name of Jesus Christ, WALK!" (RAP). He was instantly healed by these "unschooled ordinary men ... [who] had been with Jesus" (Acts 4:13). As the church became prosperous, it lost its godly power. The Constantinian church has implicitly been saying: "Healing we do not have, but what we do have we give to you. In the Name of Jesus Christ, here's some silver and gold (and medicines) to help you!"

healing from *the many* to *the few* was first from ordinary believers to deacons and elders; then to ordained priests; then only to priests who received permission from the Bishop; and then to authorised exorcists and those recognised as holy. It ended up in *the one* who healed people – "the royal touch" – the ultimate symbolic reversal of healing through the many. Kings and queens claimed divine authority to heal, not because of their virtue, but due to their position as monarch.[18]

This view of healing and spirituality emerged from the hierarchical medieval worldview of God, angels, saints, Popes, Cardinals, Archbishops, Bishops and priests – producing a spirituality of "climbing the ladder of holiness to perfection". The higher you go, the more God uses you. Sainthood was the ultimate, attained with proof of three verifiable *healing miracles*, as declared by the Pope (that is *post-death*, when a person prays to the dead saint and is healed). Healing shifted from the living to the dead, from incarnation and resurrection to incantation and ritual – healing through shrines, relics of the saints and mystical appearances. Millions have flocked to shrines for miracles.[19] This is a far cry from the simple healing ministry of Jesus and the early church.

From suffering as persecution to suffering as sickness

The holiness pursuit, with its need to deal with sin and guilt, became entangled with suffering and sickness. Originally suffering was viewed as circumstantial hardship and persecution by opposition to the kingdom – martyrdom for the truth as being a faithful witness to Jesus. This shifted to sin, guilt and penance: God not only allows us,

---

[18] See Marc Bloch, *The Royal Touch* (New York: Dorset Press, 1989). The practice occurred mainly in England and France, dating back to the 1100s. In one year King Edward I (thirteenth century) blessed 1 736 people with many testimonies of healing (p. 56). On Pentecost Sunday, 1698, King Louis XIV prayed for 3 000 people who suffered from scrofulous (p. 204). Calvinism put an end to it in England in the late seventeenth century; the French Revolution stopped royal healing services by chopping off Louis XVI's head in the late eighteenth century!

[19] The Church Fathers (see footnote 16) recorded healings through shrines and relics without questioning their authenticity. Biblically, the closest to this is 2 Kings 13:20–21 – a dead man came back to life after touching Elisha's bones when he was thrown into his tomb. The context and purpose was different to healing at shrines. God can do anything – he does empower or use objects like oil, water, cloth or Peter's shadow to heal – as does Satan. Discernment is always called for.

but even causes us to suffer, in order to cleanse us. We must willingly take on suffering – without complaint and with great fortitude – to help God purify our souls. The many forms of penance in self-inflicted mutilation and punishment are legion in church history – burning fingers over candles to stop lust. Origen dealt with this sin by castrating himself! Sickness was seen as part of God's chastisement, a suffering that causes us to repent toward godliness. This inverted the New Testament view of sickness as an evil expression of Satan's kingdom into a means of purifying grace. Suffering – as sickness – became a sacrament for those who aspired to holiness and sainthood.

The confused meaning of suffering and sickness went beyond personal piety. Colossians 1:24 was misunderstood as *vicarious suffering for others*, to "make up that which was lacking in Christ's sufferings" (RAP) by doing penance for other people's sin and sickness. It was a twisted sense of compassion: to "suffer with" in a vicarious redemptive way.[20] The result was a quest for suffering, and even other people's sickness, *to mark you as a saint*.

From Hebraic wholism (Shalom) to Platonic and Gnostic dualism

I will not repeat what I said about Platonism and Gnosticism, and its effect on Christian healing in Chapters 2 and 3. Intellectuals who became Christians brought their pagan assumptions into Christian faith, eroding the biblical worldview. The radical effect that various philosophies had on the church, as it developed through the ages, can hardly be overstated.[21] The replacement of Hebraic wholism by Platonic and Gnostic forms of dualism meant that spirituality was viewed as escape from the body, resulting in a devaluing of healing ministry. The body was despised – not worth caring for.

From "God is dead" to the restoration of Christian healing

Western church leaders did not develop a theology of healing, which led to the demise of healing ministry in the Catholic Church. *Eastern leaders did develop a theology of healing, resulting in a sustained*

---

[20] Only Jesus, as God's sinless Son, could suffer vicariously for us. He is our substitute, taking our sin and sickness on himself, making *his* suffering redemptive.
[21] See Colin Brown's historical study, *Philosophy and the Christian Faith* (Downers Grove: IVP, 1968).

practice of healing in the Orthodox Church to this day.[22] Thomas Aquinas (1224–1274) built a theological system on Aristotelian logic, replacing the spiritual/magical worldview that had taken hold in Medieval Europe. His scholasticism separated God and supernatural healing from the natural world. John Calvin (1509–1564) developed cessationism on Aquinas's natural-rationalism: Healing miracles *ceased* with the apostolic era;[23] God has now given us doctors and medicine for healing. No healing ministry emerged in Reformed circles. Many Protestant churches to this day have no healing ministry for the same reason. The Enlightenment entrenched the dualism of faith/spirit and science/medicine, leading to the scientific study of the Bible (in "Biblical Criticism"), which later declared Jesus' miracles as myths, with some theologians concluding that "God is dead" (late nineteenth and twentieth century).

A renewed interest in healing and the supernatural began in the early 1800s. It came from both outside *and* inside the church through various influences ("discoveries") that challenged the modern scientific worldview – like hypnosis and the unconscious; psychosomatic medicines and parapsychology; New Thought and Christian Science; Evangelical revivals and Pentecostalism with tongues, healing and deliverance, and the pursuit of the historical Jesus and the recovery of kingdom theology ("inaugurated eschatology"). Western missionaries also encountered the reality of spiritual power and a spirit worldview in the Two-Thirds World – with some "return flow" to Western churches. The emerging indigenous native churches naturally took to the biblical worldview and practised power ministry. When Pope John XXIII opened Vatican II (1962) with the prayer: "Come Holy Spirit, give us a second Pentecost," the "signs and wonders" Char-

---

[22]The key *Western leaders* were Ambrose (339–397), Augustine (354–430), Jerome (340–420) and Pope Gregory the Great (540–604). The key *Eastern leaders* were Athanasius (296–373), Basil the Great (329–379), Gregory of Nyssa (330–395), Gregory of Nazianzus (330–389) and John Chrysostom (345–407).

[23]John Calvin said: "But those miraculous powers and manifest operations, which were distributed by the laying on of hands, have ceased. They were only for a time. For it was right that the new preaching of the gospel, the new kingdom of Christ, should be signalised and magnified by unwonted and unheard-of miracles." *Institutes of the Christian Religion*, trans. Henry Beveridge (Christian Classics Ethereal Library, 1998), pp. 1015.

ismatic renewal began to flow sovereignly across all denominations (Catholics, Protestants, Evangelicals and others). This has resulted in a recovery of Christian healing and the practice of the supernatural Spirit gifts in the church.

Personal reflection, application and group discussion

1. Give an overall impression of what this chapter has meant to you.
2. Identify and reflect on two strands within you:
    a) the desire to be powerful, intelligent, respectable, professional, safe and secure; and
    b) the deep hunger for God, for raw trust in him – to walk on water and taste the power of God working through you to others.
    In what ways do these two desires manifest in your life and ministry? How can you discipline the former and feed the latter?
3. What has been your personal experience of the Holy Spirit? Has it had any similarities with what you have read in the book of Acts? Describe.
4. Do you agree with my interpretation of Acts, in terms of Pentecost and Spirit baptism and its manifestations? What is your personal experience of speaking in tongues? Do you agree with my theology on tongues?
5. Choose a story of a healing miracle in Acts. Apply the "interpretative key" (the divine/human cooperation by the Spirit) that I have proposed, and tell the story revealing the inner dynamics of what might have happened.
6. Do you have any problems with the "problem texts" with regard to sickness and healing that I commented on? Would you have anything different to say?
7. What strikes you about the picture of healing and the supernatural through church history? What can you own as the formative roots of your belief and praxis with regard to sickness and healing? What needs to change for you?

Part Three:
Praxis

Praxis simply means practice – our practice of healing ministry. At the beginning of Part Two I said that good theology leads to good praxis, and bad theology leads to bad praxis. In Part Three I apply our good kingdom theology to develop a good healing praxis. Theology leads to praxis, but when we reflect critically on our praxis, it causes us to (re)examine our theology, which in turn can adjust our praxis. At times we first act and then reflect, uncovering our underlying motivations, beliefs and values. Alternatively, we first get things clear mentally and then we act accordingly. Such a circular process is called Practical Theology. We reflect on our praxis *in the light of Scripture* and we reflect on Scripture *in the light of our praxis*.

Part Three is an exercise in Practical Theology in order to develop a responsible and effective healing praxis in the light of Scripture. My aim is to:

- Communicate the key factors in being a practitioner of Christ's continuing healing ministry.
- Explain how to work with the enabling grace gifts of the Holy Spirit so that we can be effective in Christ's healing ministry.
- Discuss various models of healing in the church, and present a simple five-step model of ministry for ordinary believers in Jesus.
- Give a clear description of each of the main areas of healing, and a step-by-step method to minister healing in each of these dimensions.
- Impart tools for discernment in spiritual phenomena and healing

practice, so that practitioners can cooperate with what the Spirit is doing.
- Commission and empower every reader and every healing ministry in the local church that is exposed to this book.

10

PRACTITIONERS 1: THE KEY FACTORS IN THE PRACTICE OF HEALING

*Jesus ... gave them power and authority to drive out all demons
and to heal every disease and sickness ...
and he sent them out ...
Freely you have received, freely give.*
– Joining Luke 9:1 and Matthew 10:1, 8

*"Therefore, my brothers and sisters, stand firm.
Let nothing move you. Always give yourselves fully to the work
of the Lord [healing and deliverance],
because you know that your labour in the Lord
is not in vain."*
– 1 Corinthians 15:58

Part Three: Praxis

Practitioners

When John Wimber first proposed the word "practitioner" for Christian healers, I was excited. It sounded right! We were discussing the language we needed to use as we developed the Healing Seminars in 1982. I immediately thought of our family doctor in South Africa – referred to as a GP, general practitioner. I respected him for his sensitive manner, empathetic listening, diagnostic skills and restrained use of medicines. He was an effective healer.

The thought that every follower of Jesus is called to continue his healing ministry *as a spiritual GP* made me take Christian healing ministry seriously. It comes with responsibilities, because we use *God's* power, which does not oppose, but complements medical science. I questioned: What would a Christian healer, as a spiritual GP, look like? This raised the issue of qualifications and training, the means and manner of healing, and *especially the idea of praxis*.

"Practitioner" put the emphasis on *practising* healing, not merely analysing and studying it. We think we know healing if we understand it, if we have been taught what the Bible says about it. When Jesus commissioned his followers to heal the sick and drive out demons, he said: "Go do it," *not*: "Go study it." Biblical thinking emphasises correct formation rather than information. We know and have been well taught when we are obeying and practising, and by practice we come to know. Christians are *practitioners*, not theoreticians. So the way to learn about healing – to heal others – is to practise, practise, practise!

Therefore, says Paul, we must stand firm by not allowing ourselves to be moved away from continually *doing* the Lord's work of healing, as we know that our work is not in vain – a humble privilege recognised by God! It is all about *doing* healing. It is not about status, title, privilege, position or power ("Doctor", "Evangelist", "Prophet", "Pastor" or "Bishop").[1] Rather about *function, the privilege of practising* the ministry of Jesus in humility and servanthood. It is all about Jesus and *his* ministry of healing, not about us and *our* ministry.

---

[1] Jesus expressly told his followers to *avoid* dress, place and titles as means of authority and honour – it detracts from God's glory and Messiah's ministry (Matthew 23:1–12). The church's ongoing use of titles, position and dress is worldly.

The idea of "practitioner" also raised the fact that every Christian is a *general* practitioner rather than a *specialist* healer (a dentist, cardiologist or surgeon). Followers of Jesus are GPs in *his* ministry of healing – not specialists in our own ministry (my "Inner Healing Ministry"). Specialisation can develop through growth in gifting and track record *in an area of ministry*, but people quickly treat such specialists as special, as gurus. It becomes their identity and profession (money for services). They end up operating outside the local church without accountability – see some dangers of specialisation in Chapter 3. The point is we should *all* have the basic skills needed to practise Jesus' wholistic kingdom ministry, the focus of Part Three. We are *all* spiritual GPs, learning to work with *God's* power to bring wholistic healing to the whole person. Let us look at the qualifications and the key factors that make for effective healing practitioners.

Qualifications

In South Africa it takes seven years to qualify as a medical GP – five years of academic study and two years of practice. How long does it take for ordinary Christians to qualify to heal the sick? Jesus modelled healing, training his rural followers for a year or so before he sent them to "drive out all demons and heal every disease and sickness". Christian initiates (converts) in the early church engaged in kingdom ministry with the rest of their new family as a normal part of their belonging and growth, in obedience to King Jesus' (co)mission. From Day 1 it was relational "apprenticeship" through practice with others.

The earliest evidence of a preparation or training "catechism" for new believers (Hebrews 6:1–3) shows immediate inclusion and practice in kingdom ministry. The foundational "elementary teachings of Christ" were: repentance and faith; baptism and laying on of hands to receive and impart the Holy Spirit, healing and deliverance; resurrection and eternal judgment. Short and simple! We have seen how this changed as the church grew and its context evolved through the centuries. Initial restrictions on and qualifications for ministry developed into years of catechismal training before release with laying on of hands. Professionalisation and institutionalisation killed the church's healing ministry. History shows that revivals generally begin with organic ministry among the poor and uneducated. Church growth leads to the qualifications bar being lifted higher and higher in the name of "respectability", "purity", "doing things in the right way". The free-for-all-anything-goes approach is equally irresponsible. What is required is *honest feedback and correction, adjustment and growth in healthy community where on-the-job training is the normal culture.*

There is a tension in the qualifications for Christian healing practitioners: the bar must not be too high, allowing only the trained to minister; nor can it be so low that anyone can lay on hands. The key is community – inclusive, empowering, mentoring community. It is about the freedom and joy of discovery, trying and failing and trying again, within the safety and security of relational love, learning and accountability. Some find this far too organic, undefined and messy. To help, I will list *the most basic qualifications* according to the Scriptures, as I understand them, for Christian healing practitioners.

1. *Every believer:* Every person who believes in Jesus can and should practise the laying on of hands for healing. A believer is a committed follower of Jesus through water baptism and Spirit empowerment – Christian initiation. Jesus makes it clear in Mark 16:16–18: "Whoever believes [the gospel] and is baptised will be saved … and these signs will accompany *those who believe* [believers in Jesus, *not* those who exercise great faith]: In my name they will drive out demons; they will speak with new tongues … they will place their hands on sick people, and they will get well."

2. *At every level – the obedience of discipleship:* Believers at all levels of growth are called to heal the sick and drive out demons. It does not require a high degree of spirituality, purity or maturity; rather "the obedience of faith" (Romans 1:5) to Jesus' commission, from Day 1 of our discipleship till we die. New believers should be initiated into healing ministry from their spiritual birth – they get hooked for life! We can never grow beyond ministering healing to others.

3. *"Thirsty" and receptive:* I have shown how those who "repent and believe" receive and minister the kingdom. Openness, receptivity, hunger and faith qualify us to minister healing – God uses such

people. The "thirsty" are filled with, and flow in the Spirit (John 7:37–39). Paul says we must be *desirous* of spiritual gifts to help others (1 Corinthians 12:31; 14:1).
4. *Faithful and persevering:* This is not so much a qualification for healing the sick as how to be an effective healer. Being a practitioner means perseverance in practising healing. After the first flush of excitement and success, the real challenge is regular practice – to push through all the doubts, difficulties and mysteries that arise. Real faith is *faithfulness.* Paul did "signs, wonders and miracles *with great perseverance*" (2 Corinthians 12:12). Do it "in season and out of season … with great patience" (2 Timothy 4:2).
5. *Willing to be trained and coached:* This does not mean that *only* those who are trained can lay hands on the sick – *any believer* can. However, anyone who is unwilling to learn, refuses training and coaching, is not teachable and accountable should not be allowed to minister. Unaccountable ministry is dangerous, both in leaders and ordinary believers. Biblically, ministry is always *authorised*: it comes from belonging, equipping, recognition and accountability, as we have seen with Jesus and his disciples.

Training

The first key factor in healing ministry is equipping. Training is not verbal teaching; it is on-the-job apprenticeship. Jesus equipped his followers through a simple *show-and-tell method of coaching and mentoring*:

- *Show:* Jesus did it – modelling healing ministry – while they watched.
- *Tell:* He interacted with them so that they learnt from what they saw.
- *Show:* Then he got them to do it, while he watched.
- *Tell:* They interacted with him, learning from what they had done or did not do.
- Then he sent them to do it, and they reported back to give account – periodic interaction for further learning and ongoing accountability.
- He told them to repeat the process – get others to watch them

– to model and impart ministry via show-and-tell apprenticeship.

We should do church in this way, equipping every believer with the basic skills and practices of the kingdom. This is seldom done because of inadequate theologies, outdated models, professionalism and institutionalisation. However, we practise *this* method of training *organically* – we intentionally include others in ministry every time we lay on hands – and *structurally* – do training seminars, workshops, healing clinics on the streets. If we do show and tell, we will see an exponential multiplication of Christ's healing via every-believer ministry.

Faith

This second key factor is critical in receiving and ministering healing. To be an effective practitioner, we must understand faith and how it operates in the healing process. In Chapters 5 and 7 I showed how Jesus worked with faith and healing.

Biblical faith is belief, reliance, confidence, trust – to *en*trust to someone. We trust *in* God and people, trusting them *for* things, such as salvation and healing. It is *not* faith in concepts or things, such as ideologies, doctrines, power, money. Only persons break trust, *not* things. That is why trust in idols is *un*belief. Faith is relational, *not* a formula (the laws of faith), a manipulative mechanism, a magical power to get God or people to do things for us. When used in those ways, it is not faith but witchcraft. Therefore faith in the power of positive thinking, in a formula, religious ritual, faith in faith itself, faith in healing, or faith in a person as if they are God is all idolatry.

Real, biblical faith is a powerful mystery *because* it is God-related. God only relates in trust. He evokes confidence and imparts faith. He is profoundly moved by faith, responding to all who rely on him. "Without faith it is impossible to please God, because anyone who comes to him must believe that he exists and that he rewards those who earnestly seek him" (Hebrews 11:6). Therefore, "*all things* are possible for those who believe" (Mark 9:23 RAP), *because of who God is*, not because of our faith.

Faith involves knowledge and expectation. People came to Jesus for healing as they heard of his compassion and power to heal. "Faith comes from hearing ... the word of Christ" (Romans 10:17); "the word", *rhema*, is the spoken or enlivened word. That is why we are commissioned to speak *this* good news, *the* word of the kingdom, as it leads to faith and expectation *in God*. God does not disappoint – he acts on behalf of those who trust him. His integrity is at stake! He is faithful to all who believe, even when he does not act or intervene as and when we expect. In that case a deeper test of faith is at work, teaching us to be faithful to God beyond our understanding and expectations, beyond healing or no healing. This does not mean easy acceptance if faith is not (apparently) answered, but rather perseverance in faith by persistent request until God does something, as Jesus taught (Luke 11:5–13 cf. 18:1–8).

Faith is *a decision*, a trusting *attitude*, expressed in *actions* – in commitment, obedience, baptism (Romans 10:9–11). For example, Peter moved from fear to faith: "Jesus, if it is you out there, tell me to come to you" (Matthew 14:28 RAP). He took Jesus at his *rhema* word ("Come") and walked on water. His faith released *God's* power – was honoured by it – and the miracle happened in the doing of it. Even when he lapsed from faith to fear and sank, he cried out: "Lord, save me!" and was saved. Faith is *not* admiration of someone else's faith in action or mental assent to truth. It is an act of entrustment to God in *his* abilities on the basis of *his* Word – beyond our logic, abilities, control and experience. Faith is spelt R-I-S-K. This does not mean *presumption*: acting "in faith", presuming to speak for God and do miracles, when he has not initiated or spoken. This results in embarrassment and shame on God and us. Jesus only acted on his Father's initiative. Elijah's miracle of heavenly fire that defeated Baal's prophets was "at your command" (1 Kings 18:36; cf. Lamentations 3:37–38: "Who can speak and have it happen if the Lord has not decreed it?"). In summary: "Faith is *being sure* of what we hope for and *certain* of what we do not see" (Hebrews 11:1). It is a *conviction* that makes unseen hopes – future kingdom healing – a present reality.

This is what we must cultivate and work with in the ministry encounter and healing process. Jesus always worked where there was faith; God rarely heals sovereignly without human participation.

- There is "lack of faith" that resists God's healing (Mark 6:1–6).
- There is "little faith" that fails to receive or work God's miracles, and is rebuked (Matthew 8:26; 17:20).
- There is "wavering faith" that is challenged and strengthened for healing (Mark 5:35–36).
- There is "faith as small as a mustard seed" that can move mountains (Matthew 17:20).
- There is the "measure of faith" that we all receive and must put to use (Romans 12:3).
- There is "great faith", based on confidence in God's authority and power, which breaks social conventions and persists till it receives healing (Matthew 8:10; 15:28).
- And there is the "gift of faith", an impartation of *God's* faith, that receives or works miracles despite all opposing factors (1 Corinthians 12:9).

As practitioners, we learn to work in the ministry encounter with the faith that *we* have, that *the recipient* may have, or that *others* have for the person's healing. Sometimes there is faith and heightened expectation *in the atmosphere* that unleashes spiritual powers. We must discern where faith lies and how to release it, receiving and activating spiritual gifts, causing people to reach out and receive healing. Jesus did this when he touched people, spoke words, spat on tongues, and did other acts as "means of faith". Any act of faith must *not* impose *our* faith on others; it should release *their* faith and/or *God's* power. Acts of faith should not violate values such as personal dignity and relational integrity.

Compassion

Now we come to the heart of it all: *God's love* in action, seen in Jesus. I intentionally began both my preface and story with the compassion of the Wounded Healer. Compassion is foundational to healing ministry. Any other *motivation* in healing and *manner* of ministry is problematic and even dangerous. What is compassion and how does it operate in the healing process?

The word compassion comes from the Latin *compassio*, "to suffer with". The New Testament word is *splagchnizomai*, "to be moved in the bowels", moved to our depths by the plight of a person. The suffering, "passion", moves us with deep emotions of empathy, sadness, and even anger. Some texts in certain early manuscripts had "moved with *anger*" instead of "compassion" (Mark 1:41).[2] Jesus' compassion was a profound mix of anger toward the evil of leprosy and sorrow for the man, because of what leprosy had done. He viewed sickness as Satan's merciless victimisation of people. *He felt their suffering in his body* and freed them from evil by the power of God's love.

Other related Hebrew and Greek words convey the same reality, translated as "mercy", "pity" and "spare" (to spare from pain or punishment). This broader understanding is based on the Old Testament experience (theology) of *YHWH's mercy and compassion*, fulfilled and embodied in Jesus.[3] Compassion in Hebrew connotes "womb" or "wombishness": giving life, nurture, tenderness, deeply carrying (caring for) others – not without labour pains! This is how YHWH gave birth to Israel and carried her from Egypt, *throughout her history*, culminating in Messiah Jesus, who was mercilessly killed to mercifully save Israel and the world. Jesus' ministry and death were the fullness of the fountain of compassion that flowed like hot healing springs from the womb of God.

Compassion is more than a feeling; *it is an action* of intervening grace. A feeling of pity that stops short of action is mere human sentiment. Whenever Jesus was "moved with compassion", he acted: he healed, forgave and fed the multitudes. He often acted contrary to social norms and apparent rational thinking – like embracing the lepers. Compassion transcends human convention and logic. It is the *emotional fire and energy* that motivates both the action and the manner in which healing is done: assertive but sensitive and merciful; never manipulative or abusive. By nature, God *and* humans

---

[2] For a technical explanation of this, see William Lane, *The Gospel of Mark*, pp. 84–87.

[3] For some of this background, see David Bosch's exposition of God's compassion as the fount of the *Missio Dei*, in *Witness to the World* (Atlanta: John Knox Press, 1980), pp. 50–57 and Marcus Borg, *Jesus: A New Vision* (San Francisco: Harper, 1991), pp. 100–103, 129–141. See Hosea 6:6 cf. Matthew 9:13, 36; 14:14; 15:32; 18:27, 33; 20:34; Mark 1:41; 5:19; 9:22; Luke 6:36; 7:13; 10:33, 37; 15:20.

have compassion, so it is both gift (Romans 12:8) and cultivation in healing ministry.

As practitioners, we learn how to discern and work with *God's* compassion more than our own – otherwise we burn out of our own energy. This is not easy as our brokenness – our need to be needed and recognised – blurs the process. Natural caregivers, due to their warm temperament and/or past wounds, are especially vulnerable in this regard. When they suffer from compassion fatigue, it has been more of them than God, with little or no spiritual renewal. Alternatively, there are others who do not feel much, who have little or no compassion, for whatever reason. Then things are less blurred – if they feel *God's* compassion, they know it! *Their* challenge is to become *emotionally* vulnerable and accessible to God and others, as unnatural or painful as this may seem.

The Wounded Healer story says that getting in touch with our own suppressed wounds and pain, and processing them with God, helps us to identify with others in their pain – compassion is born and develops. In this way God's power is mysteriously active in and through our weakness. Often when I am weak or tired, or when I least expect it, in a ministry context, I feel God's compassion moving in me. It is also aroused when I look carefully at a person as Jesus did, with the eyes of Father, intuitively seeing things about them. Compassion is an emotional-physical-spiritual encounter, experienced in tearfulness, groaning,[4] grief, gentle assertiveness, a gut-wrenching, a yearning and burning, or even a physical pain. These "compassion manifestations" move me to ministry, often pointing me supernaturally to what God is doing.

The point is: *God's compassion is a powerful source of healing.* No matter what our temperament, personality or past pain, we are *all* called to participate in the mystery of God's suffering love. Let us be *available* to God's compassion.

---

[4] Compassion is the heart of intercession: to "come between" God and others in need, with the Spirit groaning in us for them, for God's will to be done (Romans 8:26–27).

Authority and power

Since authority and power go hand in hand in Scripture, I will discuss them together. Many years ago I witnessed a concrete-mixer truck coming screaming down a steep hill. A traffic officer stepped into its path. He lifted his hand, ordering the truck to stop. I covered my eyes, thinking it would flatten him. Then I looked and saw white smoke rising from the screeching tyres as this massive truck came skidding and grinding to a halt. Fortunately the truck stopped. The officer was alive. I breathed again! I began to think …

What brought the truck to a sudden halt? Was it the power of the brakes? The obedience of the driver? Or the authority of the officer? Although all three factors worked together, the officer's authority was decisive. My mind played: What if the officer did not put on his uniform and appeared in his underpants? He would be dead! The uniform did the trick. *But* he had to put it on – the sign of his authority – *and* he had to risk using it by stepping out into the road. What would have happened if the driver defied his authority? The full might of the law and police would have come down on him, enforcing his submission and judgment.

What is the biblical understanding of authority and power?

Authority and power are crucial in healing ministry as they stop evil in its tracks. Authority (*exousia*) is the right or freedom or power to act (authorisation). It is either conferred by law, position and structure (the traffic cop), or it comes from within – from personality, skills, morals ("charisma"). Or it comes directly from God (spiritual authority, true charisma). Power (*dynamis*) is ability, strength, might, energy. It can be spiritual power (God or Satan's); material/physical power (muscles, dynamite); socio-structural power (politics); or psychological power (manipulation, intimidation). Authority is about influence; power is about force. Obviously authority that is not backed up by power is as meaningless as it is powerless. In this sense authority is power and power is authority.

All authority and power in creation belong to God, Creator and Ruler of all things. *All* use of authority and power is accountable to God. They are *kingdom* realities: God delegates authority to angels and

Part Three: Praxis

humans *to rule* with appropriate power at varying levels over various realms. In creation God authorised humans to rule over the earth as his representatives, delegating authority to governments, families and other "orders". In Adam and Eve's rebellion, we gave away our God-given authority to Lucifer, who misused his God-given authority to deceive us, that he might rule the earth with his destructive powers. In God's King, Messiah Jesus, Lucifer and his hordes have been disarmed and defeated – their authority and power is bound – and a new human race has been born again, Christ's followers, reinstated as the rightful rulers of the earth.

The risen and ascended King commissioned *them* with "all [his] *exousia* in the heavens and the earth" (Matthew 28:18; Ephesians 1:17–23), and with the *dynamis* of his Spirit (Acts 1:8), to advance his rule to the ends of the earth.[5] We are to use *Christ's* authority and the *Spirit's* power to enforce evil's defeat. Jesus said: "I have given you *exousia* to … overcome *all* the *dynamis* of the enemy" (Luke 10:19). The basis of our authority is Jesus: his victory, his name and his Word. The basis of our power is the Spirit: his indwelling presence and his gifts. This present spiritual warfare against evil in all its forms is our training for reigning in the new heavens and the new earth.

What have we been given authority and power over?

When we have faith in Jesus, we are given *exousia* to become God's children, born of his Spirit (John 1:12–13). On baptism and drinking the Spirit, we are given *dynamis* to be God's "rivers of living water" (John 7:37–39). Through being in the church, joined to God's people, we are given *"the keys of the kingdom"* (Matthew 16:19).[6] We open the kingdom to those who respond to us bringing freedom and close it to those who reject us, bringing judgment on themselves (Matthew 10:7–15). Whatever we "bind on earth will have been bound in the heavens and whatever we loose will have been loosed …"[7] We use

---

[5] Daniel 7 is key to how *exousia* and *dynamis* are used in the New Testament – how evil is defeated and authority and power are given to God's people through the Son of Man (see footnote 1 in Chapter 9).

[6] Jesus gave Peter the keys to open, in a unique sense, the kingdom to Jews (Acts 2) and Gentiles (Acts 10), but the authority (keys) is given to *the church* to conduct *Christ's* ministry (Luke 12:32; 22:29).

[7] This applies to church government/discipline: to give or withhold forgiveness

King Jesus' delegated *exousia* to speak into existence on earth what he has already done (or is doing) in the heavens. The church has been given *that* authority to rule over sin, sickness, demons, death, nature, hunger and circumstantial need (Chapter 5).

Keys commonly symbolised authority to open and close. Jesus quoted Isaiah 22:22 and Revelation 3:7. To modernise the image: When we use the keys of a vehicle, as with the truck driver, we enter a world of power. We unlock and release an empowering mobility beyond our own limits and power, to be used responsibly or it can run away with us and cause great harm to ourselves and others. So we *learn* to drive and acquire a license for accountability. By using our kingdom authority, we activate, work with, and are carried along by *God's dynamis*. We are empowered way beyond our own abilities.

What is this power? It is God's dynamite displayed in creation, far greater than the Big Bang. As God spoke, his "hovering Spirit" powerfully created all things (Genesis 1:2ff; Psalm 33:6). God's *dynamis* is also seen in the *re*creation of all things, historically demonstrated in Jesus' bodily resurrection by "the Spirit of holiness".[8] This was the inbreaking foretaste and guarantee of the end of the age: the resurrection of all humans and the consequent liberation and recreation of the earth (Romans 8:11, 19–23; 1 Corinthians 6:14). This was *the powers of the coming age* that came on the Hebrew deliverers and prophets; that was fulfilled in Jesus as he received the Spirit in fullness; that was imparted to his followers at Pentecost and to us today. God's *dynamis* is his "empowering presence",[9] working through us to do his works of resurrection and recreation.

How do we exercise Christ's authority and the Spirit's power?

We receive Christ's authority and the Spirit's power by risking, stepping out, lifting our hands and ordering evil to stop. Jesus did

---

(Matthew 18:18; Acts 5:1–11; 1 Corinthians 5:1–5), and to permit or forbid certain things (Acts 15). However, it also applies broadly in kingdom ministry, binding sickness and demons, loosing people in healing and deliverance.

[8]See Romans 1:4; Ephesians 1:18–23; Paul prays that our eyes will be opened to know God's great power *in us*: the power that raised Jesus from the dead and seated him far above all other powers.

[9]Gordon Fee, *God's Empowering Presence: The Holy Spirit in the Letters of Paul* (Peabody: Hendrickson, 1994).

not heal by praying for people – he spoke healing, ruling over evil by confronting and commanding: "Your sins are forgiven"; "Demons, be quiet"; "Sickness, go"; "Eyes be open"; "Lazarus, come forth". We use authority by speaking the word (command in Jesus' name); we impart power by laying on hands (releasing the Spirit's gifts). The Father creates and rules by speaking the word (authority) and the Spirit does the work (power). Like Jesus, we must work with the Father, seeing and hearing what he is creating, and speaking it into existence, as the Spirit empowers it (John 5:17–20).

I picture authority and power *in healing ministry* in terms of creation (Genesis 1:2ff). When I look at an individual or a congregation while ministering, I see them as "formless and empty, darkness over the face of the deep". It is nothing personal – most people are in chaos to one degree or another. Jesus saw people as "harassed and helpless, like sheep without a shepherd" (Matthew 9:36). I look for where God's *Ruach* is brooding, waiting for God's word, to enact what he says. This "looking" to see what God is doing leads to compassion, promptings, feelings, intuitive seeing and hearing. I act on it, exercising authority by speaking *in faith*: "Let there be light! Be healed in Jesus' name!" The Spirit backs me up in power – *so I trust* – shining God's light, bringing order out of chaos, driving out the darkness. This must be practised humbly and gently, not presumptuously.

Jesus modelled and taught his disciples *a kind of authority*, and *manner of usage*, that was different to what was practised in his society. Kingdom authority is *spiritual* – it comes from God through submission and service. In this world's system, it is *structural* – based on position, title, wealth and knowledge, through asserting authority over others – "lording it over" (Mark 10:42–45; Luke 22:24–30). The centurion knew that Jesus had great authority: "Just say the word and my servant will be healed" (Matthew 8:8–10), because he saw that Jesus was *under* God's authority, obedient to Father. To the extent that we are under God's authority, yielded in service to his will, we are given and exercise *that* authority *in real terms*. Otherwise we exercise authority without power. Spiritual authority is not static; it is relational and dynamic, requiring integrity and faith for (back-up) power *in real terms*.

Samson flirted with the symbol of his God-given authority – his uncut hair (Nazirite vow). As long as he kept the integrity of his uncut hair, the Spirit of God "came upon him in power" to do God's works of deliverance (Judges 13:5, 25; 14:6, 19; 15:14). He compromised that integrity by the seduction of his enemies, allowing his hair to be cut, and lost his power (16:19–20, "he did not know that the Lord had left him"). Tragic! Water baptism is our outward sign of submission to Christ and of his authorisation of us. By compromising its integrity and meaning – taking off our uniform – we lose our authority *in real terms*. We either cease exercising it, or bolster it by raising our voices, doing "shows of power", hyping, manipulating, and repeating empty phrases like: "In the name of Jesus", which is not a magical formula, as the seven sons of Sceva discovered (Acts 19:13–17). We simply cannot presume on God and his authority.

The same applies to *power*. Jesus modelled and taught *a kind of power* and *manner of usage* that was different to the world. He fully relied on *God's* power, not on his own human power, using it for God's purposes in defeating evil and freeing people. He refused to misuse it to "show a sign" to be accepted or to satisfy a lust for the supernatural. Jesus exercised God's power in weakness, not in his strength or bravado and presumption.[10] After receiving the Spirit's power at baptism, Jesus resisted the temptation to use it:

a) to indulge (feed) himself;
b) to be spectacular; and
c) to receive more power to rule the world (Matthew 4:1–11).

Instead, he chose a long obedience in worshipful service to his Father, trusting *God's* power in his weakness and death. It is dangerous to want power. Few can resist its temptations. Power corrupts and absolute power corrupts absolutely. God's way to power is powerlessness, seen in the Suffering Servant of Isaiah (42, 49, 50, 52–53), fulfilled in Jesus.

In ministry practice, we are reliant on God's power through the gifts of the Spirit. We cannot possess or control his power or gifts. We are servants of God's power, partnering with him in mutual trust.

---

[10] In 2 Corinthians Paul develops a theology of power that manifests through weakness, in contrast to the false apostles, who were triumphalistic, relying on outward shows of power, motivational oratory, success and prosperity.

Neither can we manufacture or manipulate it into action. God's power either operates or it does not; sometimes surprising us, sometimes not in evidence as we suppose it should be. We want the dramatic stuff! Kingdom power is often like the seed or yeast that operates beyond human feeling and observation, working in a hidden and silent way during and after ministry, bringing into being what we speak in Jesus' name.

This means that, when we feel weak, it is a good time to minister to others. Why? Because we are totally reliant on God – his power is free to work through us without our enthusiastic interference!

Personal reflection, application and group discussion

1. Are you really a *practitioner* of Christ's healing? If not, why not?
2. Do you agree with my qualifications to practise Christ's healing ministry? What were your qualifications before reading this chapter? Has anything changed for you?
3. Have you been trained in healing? In what way? How can you practise show and tell?
4. How have you understood and exercised faith in healing ministry? What have you learnt in this regard, after reading my discussion on faith?
5. What has been your experience of God's compassion? How does it work in healing?
6. What is your understanding, and experience, of authority and power in healing?

11

Practitioners 2: Working with the Spirit in the grace gifts

Now to each one the manifestation of the Spirit is given for the common good. To one there is given through the Spirit the word of wisdom, to another the message of knowledge by means of the same Spirit; to another faith by the same Spirit, to another gifts of healing by that one Spirit, to another miraculous powers, to another prophecy, to another the ability to distinguish between spirits, to another the ability to speak in different kinds of tongues, and to still another the interpretation of tongues. All these are the work of one and the same Spirit, and he gives them to each one, just as he determines.
– 1 Corinthians 12:7–11

Follow the way of love and eagerly desire spiritual gifts, especially the gift of prophecy.
– 1 Corinthians 14:1

Part Three: Praxis

As a new believer in Christ, the Baptists taught me the evangelical gospel of forgiveness of sin and "winning souls for Jesus". After a year or so, the core message got through: It is all about becoming holy like Jesus to bring others to him. The more I tried to pray, get holy and evangelise people, the more I felt a distinct lack of "something". As I read the stories of Jesus, I was deeply moved by how he helped people. I saw the same healings in the book of Acts, and realised the power of the Holy Spirit was the source behind it all.

At that time a Pentecostal Christian in my class began talking to me about "The baptism of the Holy Spirit – with speaking in other tongues!" Apparently I needed to "have this" to experience the power to witness and pray and even heal the sick. I was not aware we could do that! I decided to go for it, wanting more of God and having nothing to lose. He laid his hands on my head and encouraged me to receive the Spirit and speak out whatever God prompted me to say. ("No English words, okay?") As he prayed over me in tongues, I breathed in and felt an excitement building. Then I praised God … in English! After a few explanations and further prayer, I decided to "let my tongue go" and speak whatever came. Strange sounds and words began to flow. It was weird and wonderful! I broke out of my self-consciousness and my Baptist bounds.

My worship and prayer life was transformed, connecting me directly with God, my emotions and my body. I breathed in God's Spirit daily, overflowing in my prayer language with joy, praises, intercessions, groanings and tears. God felt so close. It led to "witnessing" with passion and conviction, urging people to turn to Jesus for help. I began to experiment with Spirit gifts and healing prayer.

What followed was instructive. Tensions grew with my fellow Baptists as I exercised and explained spiritual gifts. The minister was rightly concerned for his people and for correct doctrine. Christ-likeness in character, in love and purity was the emphasis. As good Bible-believing Christians, they pursued this, but were silent on the Spirit. It was an open secret that "those over there" (the Pentecostals) were illegitimate and carnal, always seeking "experiences".

The more I went to "those over there", the more I heard about the Spirit's power and gifts (and grew in them), and the less I heard about character. I joined the Pentecostals and discovered that "those over there" (the Baptists) knew nothing of the Spirit and his power – that is why their church was dying and ours was growing! Then a person who spoke in tongues and healed the sick was "caught out" living a double life (sexual sin), and I found myself caught in a dichotomy, as though there were two opposing options for Christians.

Fruit or gifts?

What would you prefer: a fruit tree full of delicious fruit, or a Christmas tree with many wonderful presents? I prefer a fruit tree full of fruit *and* Christmas presents! Many Christians subconsciously think and live as if there is a choice between the nine fruit of the Spirit (Galatians 5:22) and the nine gifts of the Spirit (1 Corinthians 12:8–10); between growth in Christ's character (fruit) or pursuit of the Spirit's power (gifts). We can be either holy and powerless, or powerful and unholy. There is no such choice. They are both the work of one and the same Spirit in the person. Jesus was full of God's character (authority) and gifts (power).

Both fruit and gifts are for others, not for ourselves – for our own enjoyment, popularity or spirituality. *Others* are transformed by Christ's character in us – the love, joy, peace, patience, kindness, goodness, faithfulness, gentleness and self-control, and by the Spirit's gifts operating through us – wisdom, knowledge, faith, healing, miracles, prophecy, discernment, tongues[1] and interpretation.

Fruit is a process of growth and cultivation through spiritual disciplines and life's hardships. Fruit is not instant, but gifts are. We receive and impart God's supernatural gifts by faith from the day we are empowered or baptised with the Spirit. As presents are put on and taken off a Christmas tree in a moment, so spiritual gifts are exercised and received in an exchange between persons. There is no direct correlation between the tree and the gifts, except willingness to carry the gifts. A Christmas tree may be a fir tree carrying dolls – gifts do not tell us about the nature or quality of the tree (the person). Fruit does; it tells us the type and quality (good or bad fruit) of the

---

[1] Tongues in personal prayer is for self-edification. When practised in church, it must edify others (1 Corinthians 14:4–5).

Part Three: Praxis

tree. In short, fruit reveals the character of a person, while gifts show their ability.

Therefore, we must not be wowed, let alone deceived, by those who do signs and wonders, by large numbers and "success". Gifts and power are not signs of spirituality or integrity. As Peter said, they did not heal the lame man due to their "own power or godliness", but by exercising "faith in the name of Jesus" (Acts 3:12, 16). Miracles are not a comment on character – they are gifts exercised by faith. We can do signs and wonders in Jesus' name, yet he might deny knowing us; fruit does not lie (Matthew 7:15–23). The Corinthian church was rich in gifts, but carnal and divisive (1 Corinthians 1:7; 3:1ff). Some can live a double life (habitual hidden sin) while exercising a healing ministry – God's grace and patience in this regard never ceases to amaze. He generously gives callings and gifts without revoking them (Romans 11:29). We do not take our children's gifts away when they misbehave – at least not immediately! It eventually does catch up with us when God acts to protect others (and us) from the growing integrity/credibility gap and abuse of authority and power. As with Samson, God eventually "hands us over" to our sin, to our demons, who then rule over us.

Paul says the gifts are functional and temporal, but the multifaceted character of God's love remains forever, determining our being and becoming (1 Corinthians 13). He is *not* saying it is love *or* gifts;[2] rather that love, with its related fruit, must govern the motivation and operation of the gifts, or else they become meaningless, divisive and destructive. That does not mean we can concentrate on character and ignore the gifts – this would grieve the Lord! We "quench the Spirit", *not* by rejecting his fruit, but by having contempt for his gifts – prophetic ministry in all its dimensions (1 Thessalonians 5:19–20).

---

[2]This book is about healing and related gifts – I hope to write *Doing Spirituality*. For helpful discussions comparing the fruit and gifts, see Derek Prince, *Faith to Live by* (Fort Lauderdale: Derek Prince Publications, 1977), pp. 37–39; Howard Erwin, *These Are not Drunken As Ye Suppose* (New Jersey: Plainfield, 1968), pp. 149–156.

The Spirit in salvation and empowering

Before I discuss the gifts and how they work in ministry, I need to clarify the Spirit's work in salvation and empowering. Since Pentecostalism in the mid-1800s through 1900s, there has been confusion about the biblical understanding of "the baptism in/with the Spirit". What does it refer to?[3]

Roman Catholics and traditional churches practise infant baptism to receive children of believing parents into Christ's body (salvation), then adult confirmation to impart the baptism of the Spirit by the Bishop's laying on of hands. Wesleyans and Methodists believe in regeneration by the Spirit at conversion and then a subsequent experience of the Spirit, "The Second Blessing", for entire sanctification. Anabaptists and Evangelicals teach the baptism in the Spirit as salvation, from 1 Corinthians 12:13, with no need for any subsequent experience. Pentecostals teach we are born again by the Spirit, but need a subsequent experience, the baptism in the Spirit, to receive the Spirit in power, evidenced by speaking in tongues. Charismatics (people from all the above) have an "applied" Evangelical theology: We receive the baptism of the Spirit at salvation, but experience "the release" of the Spirit later, with ongoing infillings/empowerings as and when needed.[4] It has never been an issue for the Eastern Orthodox, as they have always been open to mystical experiences of the Spirit, believing they "proceed" directly from the Father.

These differences are not trivial. Beliefs determine practice. If we "get everything" at salvation and do not need any more, then we will not want, let alone expect, more from God. If we do not believe in laying on hands for every Christian to impart the Spirit and to heal the sick, then we will not do it. Many churches are powerless as a result. If we believe that we need the Spirit's power, we will want it, we will ask, seek and knock till we get it (Luke 11:5–13). If we believe the Spirit

---

[3] This is an extensive study, so I *briefly summarise* my view without discussing arguments or sources.
[4] This was Wimber's position, called Empowered Evangelical. See *Power Evangelism*, pp. 139–149. For a thorough study of all views, see Henry Lederle, *Treasures Old and New: Interpretations of "Spirit-Baptism" in the Charismatic Renewal Movement* (Peabody: Hendrikson, 1988). For a well-argued Pentecostal view, see Howard Erwin; and a qualified Charismatic view, see Craig Keener.

comes with freedom to speak, pray and praise in tongues, releasing "the gifts", then we will expect, teach and practise it whenever we lay on hands. We will also work sensitively and responsibly with those who do not experience it, just as we do with those who are not healed when ministered to.

One reason for this confusion is spatial thinking: "In", "out", "on", "when". Do we receive the Spirit (in us) at salvation? Or only when he comes on us in power?[5] Greek language tends to material concepts, rather than Hebraic relational theology. The apostles wrote the New Testament in Greek but thought in Hebrew from the Old Testament foundation. In relational theology, we see YHWH sending "the Angel" with "the Word" to save and deliver, call and commission individuals to the work of deliverance (prophets, judges and kings). These were manifestations of the pre-incarnate Son of God ("theophanies" or appearances of God).[6] Then YHWH sent his Spirit, anointing them with power to fulfil their commission;[7] and promised to pour his Spirit on all his people "in the last days", empowering them as "kings and priests" to reconcile all the Babel nations to YHWH (Joel 2:28; Exodus 19:16; Revelation 1:5; 5:10). God relates to us in salvation by the work of his Son, and in empowering us by the work of his Spirit.

Tertullian said the Son and the Spirit are the right and left hands of God. The primary work of the one hand is relationally enabled by a secondary work of the other hand, and vice versa. The Father communicates the primary work of the Son (salvation) by the Spirit; we are "born again" of the Spirit (John 3:3–8; Titus 3:5). He communicates the primary work of the Spirit (empowering) by the Son, who baptises us with the Spirit (Acts 1:5, 8). Jesus is the model for all

---

[5] Gary Best and Peter Davids argue that Luke uses "baptism with the Spirit" in the Old Testament sense of the Spirit coming "on" a person for empowering; while Paul tends to use "baptism in/by the Spirit" in the New Covenant sense of the Spirit "in" a person for regeneration, in *Implications of the Kingdom* (Cape Town: Vineyard Bible Institute, 2000), pp. 76–88.
[6] See Genesis 16:7ff; 19:1, 21; 21:17; 22:11; 31:11–13; Exodus 3:2–4f; 14:19–24; 23:20–23; Joshua 5:13ff; 6:2–5; Judges 2:1–5; 6:6–12ff; 13:2–9ff; Zechariah 1:12ff cf. 2:1f; 3:1–7.
[7] For the Spirit's coming on people, mostly *after* (angelic) commissioning, see footnote 5 in Chapter 9.

believers: he was born of the Spirit (at conception) and empowered in the Spirit (at baptism), to bring kingdom salvation to earth. We too are born of the Spirit (at conversion) and empowered in the Spirit (at baptism, or ought to be), commissioned to take kingdom salvation to the ends of the earth.

In the language of "baptisms", the early church theologised and practised three experiences as one initiation or baptism into Christian faith (Acts 2:37–39; Ephesians 4:4–5):

1. The repentant/believing sinner is *baptised into Christ* by the Spirit for salvation – into Christ's death, resurrection and body of believers (Romans 6:3–11; 1 Corinthians 12:13).
2. That obedient believer is *baptised into water* by another believer for public confession of faith and belonging in Christ's body (Matthew 28:19–20).
3. That "thirsty" believer is *baptised into (with) the Spirit* by Jesus Christ for power to witness, to advance God's kingdom (John 1:33; Acts 1:5–8; 2:1–4f).

The early believers initiated Christ-followers via this "package deal", with some exceptions as to the order.[8] It was close to, but distinct from, salvation by water baptism ("baptismal regeneration"). In our day we experience these three – or only one or two of them – separately, often years apart. However, the point is that it is not about "in", "on" or "when". It is about trusting Jesus (by the Spirit) for our salvation, sanctification and life calling; and trusting the Spirit (by Christ) for power, gifts and kingdom come. Then the Spirit progressively forms Christ's character (the fruit) in us and releases his power (the gifts) through us, backing up our authority in being Jesus to this world – speaking his words, doing his works, seeing his wonders and sharing his wounds. However we understand Luke, John, Paul and Peter in terms of "the baptism in the Spirit", the issue is not correct terminology, but experiencing the Spirit in power.

---

[8] See Acts 2:37–41; 8:12–17, 26–39; 9:1–18; 10:44–48; 16:13–15, 29–34; 18:7–8; 19:1–7. Paul uses the Exodus as a type or model of Christian initiation (1 Corinthians 10:1–4).

Part Three: Praxis

The Spirit and the grace gifts (1 Corinthians 12:1–11)

At Pentecost the church received the Gift of the Holy Spirit from the Father via the Son. The Gift brings the gifts – commonly *charismata*, meaning "grace gifts". They are not earned; they are graces from God received by faith to benefit others. Paul lists three major groupings of spiritual gifts, each with some differences.

- Jesus gave *ministry gifts* to some to lead and equip the church (Ephesians 4:7–11).
- He gave one or more *motivational gifts* to each member of the body as their motivation or regular function (Romans 12:3–8; 1 Peter 4:10).
- He gave *manifestation gifts* to "each one" (1 Corinthians 12:7–11).

These are not firm categories and fixed lists. Paul mixes it up and throws in two other gifts – helps and governments – in 1 Corinthians 12:28–30. However, the first two groupings identify the gifts with the persons themselves. The nine manifestation gifts are identified with the Spirit: the anointing "overflows" through us in any given manifestation, at any given time, to meet any given need. It is mainly these manifestation gifts that are the *dynamis* of the Spirit to enact the "signs and wonders" of the kingdom.

The context in which Paul discusses *manifestation gifts* is the gathered church – order in worship, correcting excesses in usage of the gifts, especially "tongues" (1 Corinthians 10–14). He asks: "Do all work miracles? Do all have gifts of healing? Do all speak in tongues?" (12:29–30). No – he is talking about the gathered body. "In the church" (12:28) there needs to be diversity of gift functions for the good of the whole. One member cannot manifest all the gifts, or all members only manifest one gift! Paul says the Spirit gives "to one … to another … and to yet another … just as he determines" (vs 8–11). The Spirit "manifests" or "shines forth" (*phanerosis*, v. 7) God's multifaceted light through the prism of the gathered community, driving out the darkness "for the common good". So the Spirit flows through receptive and responsive believers to give supernatural gifts to those in need: wisdom, healing, revelation and faith.

Paul is not saying that individuals have only one or two gifts. The gifts are not ours. We partner with the Spirit in delivering them to those in need. We receive the Person of the Spirit with all his abilities (potential manifestations), not a portion of the Spirit with one or two gifts. Furthermore, Paul is not addressing how these graces operate through the believer "out there" during the week, in the scattered church. What happens in the gathered church applies to the scattered church – the individual believer. The church is the temple of the Holy Spirit; our bodies are also temples of the Spirit. As Spirit-filled individuals, the Hebrew prophets, Jesus, apostles and other believers all practised these gifts "out there" wherever the need presented itself, advancing God's kingdom with supernatural power. In sensitive partnership with the Spirit, when ministering to a person, we too can "shine forth" with whichever gift meets the need before us, both in church (the training ground) and in the world (the real battleground).

Therefore, we must not be ignorant about "spiritual gifts" (v. 1). Paul's word *pneumatikon* is "spirituals", spiritual phenomena, Spirit manifestations.[9] They are known by their content, not by ecstatic "shows of power" as in pagan practice (vs 2–3). If the content glorifies Christ, God's Spirit is inspiring it, whether we feel inspired or not.[10] We can only say "Jesus is Lord" by God's Spirit, and "Jesus is cursed" by another spirit (vs 2–3). Spirit manifestations can happen simply as a belief or thought – the intent and content reveals its source. For example, Peter responded to Jesus by declaring him as God's Messiah – without ecstatic shaking (Matthew 16:15–23). Jesus said it was a supernatural revelation by God's Spirit. In the next verse Peter rebuked Jesus for saying that he (Messiah) would suffer and die. Jesus responded: "Get behind me Satan! You don't have your mind on God's interests, but on human interests" (RAP).

God's Spirit inspires and uses us with "different kinds of *charismata*"

---

[9]Gordon Fee is helpful in discussing 1 Corinthians 12:1–11, The First Epistle to the Corinthians, *The New International Commentary on the New Testament* (Grand Rapids: Eerdmans, 1987).

[10]Paul may be reassuring them that, although tongues are "ecstatic utterances", coming from God's Spirit, they glorify Christ. But later he says *whatever happens "in church"* (meetings) must be "intelligible" so as to edify others, by being evaluated, and thus tongues must always be interpreted (14:5, 12–13, 27–28).

(v. 4) to glorify Christ, not ourselves, and to help others, not serve our interests. That is how we know they are from God. They happen as inner promptings or thoughts that enter the mind and are spoken out – with our inner censor active, or we could think and speak from another spirit. Paul goes on to say that, just as there are different gifts, so there are different "ministries" (v. 5 NKJV). Gifts that are practised regularly can become a recognised ministry of Christ, as a specialisation. There are different effects ("workings" v. 6, *energemata*) that the Father "works" in all people. God determines the energy, effect and scope of our ministries. We must not go beyond our God-given capacity by performing, promoting, comparing or competing with others (vs 14–26).

Paul lists the supernatural (not natural talents) manifestation gifts (vs 7–10). I categorise and define them as follows, in application to healing ministry.

Gifts of revelation from the mind of God

The word of knowledge: A word ("utterance") of God's knowledge, commonly operating in the teaching gift. Applied to personal ministry, it is revelation of a truth or fact about a situation or person. God literally shares with us a little of what he knows. Why? To show us what he is doing, what is going on; to release the person's faith to receive from God as they realise God is revealing this. A typical example is Jesus "knowing in his spirit" people's thoughts (Mark 2:8). Reading the biblical examples will give you faith to practise it.[11]

The word of wisdom: This is the same as knowledge, except that, in personal ministry, it is God's wisdom or insight into a situation; a revelation of what should be done; a pronouncement of God's direction and purpose. It unlocks mysteries, resolves problems and warns people. Wisdom is knowledge skilfully applied, as in Jesus' word of wisdom with the woman caught in adultery (John 8:1–11).[12]

---

[11] See 1 Samuel 9:15–20; 10:22; 2 Samuel 12:1–7; 1 Kings 21:17–18; 2 Kings 4:27; 5:20–26; 6:8–23; Matthew 1:20–21; Luke 1:13; John 1:46–49; 4:16–19; Acts 5:3–4; 9:10–11; 10:19–20; 16:9. The examples show "words of knowledge" are "prophetic ministry" in the tradition of the Hebrew prophets speaking God's mind to a person or group, as Mark Stibbe argues in *Prophetic Evangelism: When God Speaks to Those Who Don't Know Him* (London: Authentic Media, 2004).

[12] Also dream interpretation: Genesis 40, 41:2 (especially 20–23), 4, 5, 7, 8. See

Discernments of spirits (plural): To test or distinguish between spirits (1 John 4:1); to see into the spirit world; to judge who or what is motivating a particular phenomenon, person or situation – either God, human or demonic – as in evaluating prophecy (1 Corinthians 14:29; 1 Thessalonians 5:19–22). An example is Jesus discerning a demonic cause behind a paralysis (Luke 13:10–16).[13]

Gifts of inspiration from the mouth of God

Prophecy: Inspired utterance commonly speaking God's mind for a community, person or situation; or to predict future events (uncommon). Prophecy is for strengthening, encouragement and comfort (1 Corinthians 14:3). Other applications (1 Corinthians 14:24–25), to expose hearts, bring correction and direction, confirm that prophecy is the primary means through which most of the other gifts flow. I discuss this below.

Different kinds of tongues: Also inspired utterance, but in languages not learnt by the person. Paul clearly sees two applications: tongues for personal worship and prayer, and tongues that God uses to minister to others if they are interpreted – made meaningful (1 Corinthians 14:3–6, 12–13, 18–19, 27–31).

Interpretation of tongues: Inspired interpretation of the tongue being uttered, giving the meaning and not the (direct) translation. For example, see the "tongues writing" on the wall and Daniel's interpretation in Daniel 5:22–28.

Gifts of demonstration from the hand of God

Gift of faith: An infusion of God's faith that enables a person to "move mountains" in a given situation (1 Corinthians 13:2). It emboldens the person to speak and act in demonstration of God's power – often without thinking or you would not do it! In terms of healing ministry, it prompts the command to be healed or "prayer of faith" (James

---

2 Samuel 12:10–14; 1 Kings 3:9–12, 24–27; 1 Chronicles 12:32; Matthew 2:22; 22:15–22; 27:19; Luke 21:14–15; Acts 9:15; 13:9–12; 15:13–29.

[13] Also 1 Samuel 16:7; 1 Kings 22:16–27; 2 Kings 6:15–17; 1 Chronicles 28:9; Nehemiah 6:10–13; Ezekiel 13:1–7; Matthew 16:15–23; Luke 9:51–55; John 2:24–25; Acts 5:3; 8:18–23; 16:16–18; 1 Corinthians 14:29; 1 John 4:1; Revelation 22:6.

5:15; Acts 3:4–6).[14]

Gifts of healings (plural): Graces for all kinds of healings; manifestations of *God's* healing in one or more of its wholistic aspects; a partial in-breaking of the future resurrection reversing an aspect of the curse of death and mortality. The plural could indicate that the Spirit gives faith in different Christians to heal different kinds of sicknesses. This gift is commonly imparted through the spoken word and the laying on of hands.[15]

Workings of miracles (plural): Ability to do various "miracles". Paul uses *dynamis* – works of power. The examples show it is difficult to differentiate the gifts of miracles, faith and healings. Probably miracles are more creative, as in Peter helping the lame man to his feet – then the miracle happened (Acts 3:6–8). It is "working" miracles (*energemata*): God energises us to effect a demonstration of his power to meet human need and rule over nature.[16]

Flowing in the Spirit

Paul is describing Spirit phenomena via various labels. From the biblical examples it is clear that Paul did not have in mind a fixed list and defined categories as I have presented them. The gifts overlap and work together. The emphasis is not on "the gifts" per se, but on the Spirit and his flow, or rather our overflowing with the Spirit to meet people's needs. It is "rivers of living waters flowing from our inner being" (John 7:37–39 RAP). As a flowing river carries various things along with it, so the Spirit flows from us with "words": a revelation, healing, faith and wisdom, as the Spirit prompts and determines.

How do we "flow in the Spirit"? By opening our mouths and speaking! By following inner Spirit promptings, we yield our most unruly faculty, the tongue, to the Spirit, receiving "wisdom from

---

[14] See Genesis 22:6–13; 1 Kings 17:1–6; 18:20–39; Daniel 3:17; 6:16–22; Matthew 14:29; Mark 4:37–40; 11:12–14 cf. 20–24; Acts 3:4–6; 16:24–26; 27:20–25; 28:3–6; Hebrews 11:32–35.
[15] See 2 Kings 5:1–14; 20:1–6; Matthew 8:6–13; 9:18–22; 15:22–28; Mark 10:46–52; John 5:1–13; Acts 5:11–16.
[16] See Exodus 4:28–31; 7:1ff; Joshua 10:12–15; 1 Kings 13:1–6; 17:8–16; 2 Kings 4:18–37; 20:8–11; Matthew 14:15–21, 25–33; 15:32–39; John 2:1–11; Acts 3:1–10; 5:12, 15–16; 6:8; 8:6–7; 19:11–12.

above" (James 3:1–18). It is like uncorking the bottle and allowing the fountain to flow: first a few drops, then a trickle, then a stream, and then rivers of living waters! I frequently pray the following prayer: "Father, make my mouth a fountain of life. Let my mouth bring forth wisdom. Let my lips know what is fitting. Let my tongue bring healing and be a tree of life. Whenever I open my mouth, may words be given to me" (from Proverbs 10:11, 31, 32; 15:4; Ephesians 6:19).

The Bible broadly designates this as *"the prophetic", "prophetic ministry", or "being filled with the Spirit"*. It is God's answer to Moses' prayer in Numbers 11:29 that *all* God's people would be prophets, filled with his Spirit, fulfilling Joel 2:28 – God's outpoured Spirit enables us to prophesy. That is why Paul says: "Eagerly desire spiritual gifts, especially the gift of prophecy. I would like *every one of you* to … prophesy … be eager to prophesy" (1 Corinthians 14:1, 5, 39). Why? Because prophecy "speaks to people for their strengthening, encouragement and comfort. While everybody is prophesying, [the person] will be convinced by all … and the secrets of [their] heart will be laid bare" (1 Corinthians 14:3, 24–25). *The point is that "inspired utterance" (prophecy) is the primary means through which all the charismata manifest and flow* (see footnote 11).

Attitude and appetite are critical to flowing in the Spirit. Paul repeats three times that we must "earnestly desire spiritual gifts" (12:31; 14:1, 39). By ignoring or despising the prophetic, we "put out the Spirit's fire" in us (1 Thessalonians 5:19–20). Rather, "fan into flame" the gifts, for "God did not give us a spirit of timidity, but a Spirit of power, of love and self-discipline" (2 Timothy 1:6–7). We do this by continually "praying in the Spirit", in tongues (Jude 20; 1 Corinthians 14:4, 14–15, 18); by being thirsty and drinking deeply of the Spirit (John 7:37ff); by asking, seeking and knocking persistently for the gifts of the Spirit, banging on God's door for power to help others (Luke 11:5–13).

This is precisely how we obey Paul's command: "Be continuously filled with the Spirit" or "flow continually in the Spirit" (Ephesians 5:18). Paul uses the present continuous tense. He is *not* saying we need regular refillings as if we "use up" or "leak" the Spirit (material theology). Rather, we must be continually under the Spirit's intoxication, influence and flow, evidenced first in our speech. The word that follows: "Be filled with the Spirit" is: "Speak …" (v. 19). Secondly, it is evidenced in our behaviour (vs 20–21f). Being "filled" with the Spirit is continuous mutual relationship (relational theology) – "flowing in the Spirit" in ministry to others.

All this implies intimacy with, and sensitivity to, the indwelling Spirit; how we hear and follow God's inner promptings in order to work (super)naturally with him as Jesus did – the focus of the next chapter.

Personal reflection, application and group discussion

1. What has been your biblical understanding of the "baptism in the Spirit"? How have you experienced this empowering of the Spirit?
2. Compare, in your own words, the fruit and the gifts of the Spirit. What is the relationship between them?
3. What has been your understanding of the manifestation gifts of the Spirit? Having read this chapter, what has changed for you?
4. Which particular gifts of the Spirit have manifested through you in ministry? How can you exercise faith to be used in other manifestation gifts?
5. Reflect on how you "flow in the Spirit" in the ministry (or how you do not flow!). How can you flow confidently and freely in the Spirit? What must you do or cultivate?
6. *An exercise*: Take time to read some of the biblical examples I have listed in footnotes 11 – 16. Pray about them and ask God to enable you to flow in the Spirit's supernatural gifts as the prophets of old did. Then go and "try it out" at the earliest opportunity. Report what happens to your small group.

12

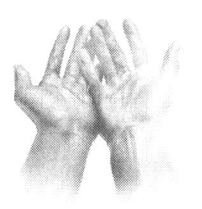

Practitioners 3: Spirit intimacy, sensitivity and exercises

*The Sovereign Lord has given me an instructed tongue,
to know the word that sustains the weary.
He wakens me morning by morning,
wakens my ear to listen like one being taught.
The Sovereign Lord has opened my ears,
and I have not been rebellious; I have not drawn back.*
– Isaiah 50:4–5

*Train yourself to be godly.
For physical training is of some value,
but godliness has value for all things,
holding promise for both the present life
and the life to come.*
– 1 Timothy 4:7–8

Part Three: Praxis

The challenge

Preaching one Sunday as a young pastor, I was aware of a pain in my knee. After a while it dawned on me: God may be indicating someone else's pain. I stopped and said, "Is there someone who has pain in the right knee? God wants to heal you. Be healed in Jesus' name!" I waited. No one responded! I was embarrassed. I cut my sermon short and closed the meeting. Afterwards an elderly lady came to me and said she had had a thrombosis lodged in her right knee for a few days – verified by her doctor. She said that, as the words came out of my mouth, an electrical power came down into her right shoulder, through her body into her right knee. She was under a power, unable to respond – but the pain had gone! The next day the doctor verified that the thrombosis had disappeared.

Recently I was in Soweto – the city near Johannesburg that housed three million black people under apartheid. A teenage girl came to me for healing prayer. She was almost blind (only 10% sight) due to a degenerative disease. Her eyes seemed blank as she tried to focus, desperate for healing. I placed my fingers over her eyes and commanded them, in the name of Jesus, to be restored to sight. I broke any generational curse that might have caused it, but nothing seemed to be happening. My mind, spirit and body groped to hear or see what God was saying and doing. Total powerlessness overcame me as I felt my fingers wet with her tears. I cried, "O God, please heal her! Show me what's going on. Have mercy, Lord!" Two others who were ministering with me sensed nothing specific from God. After extensive prayer, nothing had changed.

This came on the back of my wife and me praying weekly for a baby that was born brain damaged. It generated the same desperate feelings. There was no observable change – our ministry seemed futile. I have had similar feelings when my wife and children have fallen ill. (Why is it so difficult to minister healing to your family?) While I have been writing this book, they have challenged me: "You're writing about healing for the whole world, why can't you heal me? You're the expert!"

These incidents have made me feel like tearing my clothes and saying, "I'm not God! I can't do what only he can do! Where is your power, Lord? What's wrong? Why don't you heal?" Then it swings to,

"Lord, even if, for whatever reason, you're not healing, *I* want to heal this person! They're suffering and need healing now!" I do not mean to be presumptuous or disrespectful, but there are times when I would do things differently to what God apparently does or does not do. I say "apparently" as I see only a miniscule slice of God's Reality and must respect the mystery of not knowing. We want instant miracles but I realise that many healings are hidden and progressive – the seed or yeast of the kingdom.

I believe and practise, with all my heart, all that I have written in this book, but *why can we (I) not perform genuine healing miracles reasonably regularly as Jesus and the apostles did?* The answer is complex, but reflection over years, from my subjective experience and perspective, has led to three conclusions. This is besides the explanation of the "already" (the first story above) and "not yet" (the second story) of the kingdom and the consequent warfare.

1. We are not consistently intimate with God, knowing him and what he is doing. It connects us with our deepest desire and need: to know God's love – to love and be loved in oneness with him as instruments of his healing love in the world – responsive co-workers or co-lovers with God.

2. It exposes the authority-power or the belief-performance gap. We command healing without effective power. We believe in God's healing and practise it, but cannot perform it when needed – random, not regular healings. We are not fit or sufficiently conditioned to perform healings when required.

3. We practice healing in church and not enough in the marketplace, on the streets. The unchurched receive healing easier than the churched – they seem to believe and receive more naturally than believers do. Besides, signs and wonders are for not-yet-believers, not the converted! I have commented on this in precious chapters, so I will elaborate on the above two points.

Part Three: Praxis

Spirit intimacy, consciousness and sensitivity

Having explained the intimate oneness between Jesus and the Father by the Spirit as the source of his life (his ministry success was the overflow, Chapter 6) and the transfer of that same relationship to the disciples (Chapter 8), the question is: *How* do we develop this intimacy with God by the Spirit?

We were all created for this intimacy.[1] Intimacy is *knowing* God at ever-deeper levels of disclosure, which is eternal life (John 17:3). *The key to intimacy is self-disclosure*, based on God's self-disclosure to us in Christ (John 1:18). We cannot know another person, let alone God, unless they reveal themselves to us. We self-disclose by going beyond superficial and factual communication – talk about others – to talk about ourselves, our thoughts, beliefs, secrets, *and especially our feelings/emotions*. It is being truly vulnerable, entrusting your real self to another. Disclosure invites and requires *mutual disclosure* for intimacy to grow. God not only disclosed himself to us in Jesus, but continues to disclose himself to us daily, if we listen, by relational interaction with his indwelling Spirit. This calls for growing disclosure *from us* day by day if we are truly to know God in his thoughts, feelings and actions. It results in kinship or union with God, whereby we know him, instinctively hearing him with growing clarity in all dimensions of our personhood, in any given situation.[2]

Intimacy leads to *a shift in consciousness* from unhealthy self-sensitivity to the Father-consciousness and Spirit-sensitivity that Jesus cultivated and lived from. This shift is a journey from unconsciousness, to conscious awareness, to conscious effort, to unconscious habit. For example, when we are young, we are unconscious of the fact that we cannot drive a car. Then we become aware of it and want to drive. So we consciously engage, learning to drive, going through every

---

[1]English "intimacy" comes from Latin *intimare,* made of two words: *intimus,* "to be inside of" and *intimidare,* "to be in awe of". Intimacy is mutual interpenetration in awe-filled love, respect and sharing.
[2]God longs to share his feelings and thoughts, to "*confide* in those who fear him" (Psalm 25:14; Proverbs 3:32). YHWH confided in Abraham ("God's friend") when he was going to destroy Sodom (Genesis 18:17–19; 2 Chronicles 20:7; James 2:23). Job knew God's "intimate friendship" (Job 29:4). David's psalm-prayers are examples of profound emotional self-disclosure.

motion with concentration and effort. By persistence, it becomes easier, eventually becoming an unconscious habit, a "natural instinct", so that we can multitask while we drive. Similarly, we carefully, deliberately and persistently "practise the presence" of God,[3] moment by moment, disclosing to him and listening for his disclosure in every situation, till it becomes, over years, an unconscious *state of being*.

In this way sensitivity to the Holy Spirit – interacting with our senses in each moment – grows into oneness of thought, feeling, word and deed. Jesus said: "I no longer call you servants, because a servant does not know his master's business. Instead, I have called you friends, for *everything that I have learned from my Father I have made known to you*" (John 15:15). This depth of disclosure is made real by the *Parakletos*, who "makes known to us all that belongs to the Father and the Son" – what they have, think, see, say and do (John 16:13–15). The question is, practically, how do we hear the Spirit in ministry?

How we "hear God" in ministry

Hearing God is a learning process. Young Samuel heard God calling him, but did not know it was God until Eli, his mentor, identified it for him (1 Samuel 3). Jesus says his sheep not only "hear" his voice, but "know" (recognise) his voice, as opposed to other voices – "hirelings", our lower nature and the devil (John 10). The best way to get to know the Spirit's voice in ministry is

   a) from others who are practised in it;
   b) to study biblical examples as listed in the previous chapter; and
   c) to practise it consciously, moment by moment, as discussed above.

We hear the Spirit primarily from within, not from "outside" of us. He indwells us. The Spirit prompts and speaks through the way God has created us – through our faculties. I am not dividing the human being into categories – in practice we hear God in a diffuse and

---

[3]From Brother Lawrence, *Practicing the Presence* (Albany: Books for the Ages, Ages Software, 1996). He was a seventeenth-century monk who learnt to practise God's presence in and around him in a noisy monastery kitchen in unbroken communion and union, until his consciousness was fundamentally altered, so that he lived from God's presence.

integrated way in the whole of who we are:

1. *Our mind:* Through revelation and knowledge that comes as thoughts and words, and even a voice – the most direct form of God's communication – as opposed to visions and dreams (Exodus 33:11; Numbers 12:6–8).[4]
2. *Our imagination:* Spontaneously seeing ideas, words, a sentence, pictures, visions, dreams – indirect communication, needing interpretation. Sometimes it is a "video" in the mind, where you see conditions God is healing.
3. *Our memory:* Remembering a Scripture, past experience, word or dream – the Spirit "reminds you" of relevant things as and when needed (John 14:26).
4. *Our will:* A strong conviction, desire, "willing" something into being, a clear sense of direction, decision or choice.
5. *Our spirit:* An intuition, hunch, gut feel, impression, just "knowing", sudden infusion of power or faith, spontaneous flow of words from the Spirit that you speak without thinking, like: "Pick up your mat and walk!"
6. *Our emotions:* God uses the whole range of our emotions – compassion, joy, grief, anger – indicating his feelings regarding a person or situation, showing us what he is doing or healing, or as a discernment of what is happening.
7. *Our body:* We experience God in bodily sensations – see, hear, smell, taste and touch – indicating what people are suffering, what God is healing.[5]

The five physical senses embrace all the above means of hearing God because *they are also psycho-spiritual senses*: taste the Lord's goodness; feel his touch; see what God is doing; hear what he says; smell his

---

[4] "Face to face" referred to Moses' intimacy with YHWH, *the source of his miraculous works of deliverance* (Psalm 103:7). The prophet that God would "raise up like unto Moses" (Deuteronomy 18:15) was Jesus, who embodied "face-to-face" intimacy with God (John 1:18) – *the source* of his miracles, the new Exodus from Satan's oppression. See Pope Benedict XVI's reflection on *this* as "the mystery of Jesus", Joseph Ratzinger, *Jesus of Nazareth* (New York: Doubleday, 2007), pp. 1–8.

[5] The opening story in this chapter illustrates "sensational" or bodily hearing from God. Space does not allow me to illustrate the other ways in which we hear God. Think of your own experiences in this regard.

fragrant presence. The Hebrews experienced God (spirits and people) wholistically, not just "spiritually" – hence they used these tactile terms. Westerners call this the "sixth sense of faith" or ESP (extrasensory perception): receiving knowledge/experience apart from our physical senses, described as intuition, enlightenment, "religious" or psychic experiences. Satan and his demons tempt and interact with us in the same way, through both our physical and psycho-spiritual senses.

Evaluating our hearing from God

In ministry we operate from *revelation* (Spirit's promptings, thoughts, pictures, feelings), to *proclamation* (speaking "the word"), to *demonstration* (doing "the works"). It happens in the "already" and "not yet" of the kingdom: We know and prophesy "in part", seeing obscurely as through tinted glass as it comes through our fallen humanity. When "perfection comes", we will see and know "face to face"; then the gifts fall away (1 Corinthians 13:9–12). Consequently we have to interpret and discern what the Spirit is saying.

When the Spirit prompts, reveals or speaks, we consciously (and unconsciously) evaluate, interpret and apply it:

- What am I hearing, seeing or feeling?
- What does it really mean?
- Is it God, or am I making it up?
- What if it is wrong?
- Should I say it?
- How do I say and apply it?

It is here that we can get things wrong, make mistakes or, at worst, hurt the recipient of ministry. I have made some terrible mistakes! While ministering to a young man, I sensed things regarding his father and spoke words of protection and blessing over his dad, until he stopped me: "My dad died ten years ago." I felt like disappearing! If I had asked him about his father before I interpreted the Spirit's promptings via my *human sympathy*, I would have better understood and applied my "sensing".

This makes some people reluctant partners with the Spirit – they back off hearing from God in case they miss it. Like the man who buried his talents, if we do not use it, we lose it (Matthew 25:14–30). The more we use, more is given to us. Our accuracy rate goes up as we learn to trust, practise, and grow in self-knowledge and in the Spirit's interaction with us as unique individuals. I take Jesus at his word (Luke 11:5–13): If we ask for bread (the Holy Spirit), we get bread, not another spirit. If we ask for fish ("What are you saying Lord?"), we do not get a snake (poisonous, demonic). When I ask the Spirit to reveal, to speak, I trust what comes next – but with my interpretative censors active. I would rather err on the side of going for it in faith and tidying things up afterwards, than being overly cautious, hesitant and doubtful.

We are answerable for what we say and how we say it, when ministering in God's name. Working in team, being accountable and teachable, means we trust others to help interpret what the Spirit is saying. Prophetic manifestations must be evaluated (1 Corinthians 14:29–33).[6] Few think God's thoughts or hear his voice so clearly that it needs no interpretation ("face to face", Numbers 12:8). The point is that we grow in hearing and obeying God through practice and honest feedback, adjustment and more practice. However, hearing God accurately is no guarantee that healing will happen – it is not a fail-safe formula. Healing is a mystery because other factors are involved.

Spiritual exercises and their role in ministry

One of the other factors is the authority-power gap, the belief-performance gap. God *gifts us* with authority and power in Christ but, subjectively speaking, it only operates consistently *in real terms* to the extent to which we obey God in relational integrity. We believe in healing, but cannot perform it when needed, partly because we are not fit to work with God in performing the healing. Athletes not only believe they can perform *and* win, they are properly conditioned by regular exercise and training to win. God obviously has to come through or nothing happens, but our conditioning to cooperate skilfully with him is crucial. He works in partnership with us, seldom

---

[6] Especially if "the words" are *predictive, directive or corrective* – then pastoral leadership is required.

apart from us.

Spiritual exercises (disciplines) are basic to our co-life of intimacy with God – with the overflow of ministry. Some say Spirit gifts and healing are by God's grace and our faith; we do not need human effort in spiritual gymnastics like prayer and fasting "to earn healing". They confuse grace with effort. The truth is that grace denies *earning* – we cannot earn grace gifts. It does not deny *effort*.[7] *In fact, grace calls for faith effort in human cooperation to be an effective instrument of God's grace.* We cannot earn or determine God's grace gifts – they come sovereignly, like the man generously sowing the seeds of the kingdom. However, we can determine the quality of soil that the seeds fall into. By disciplined effort, we can plough and prepare our hearts, be ready and responsive, so that when the seed gifts come, they have maximum effect and fruit through us – God's grace is not wasted on us. If *Jesus*, God's Son, needed to practise so much spiritual discipline to work effectively with Father in healing, how much more must we?

God gives us a honeymoon or childhood period, in which we exercise faith and people are healed relatively easily. Then challenges arise and it starts drying up. We lose our innocence and naïveté, realising that by *trying* on the spot, we cannot heal people – we need *training* off the spot to learn how to do it. Training involves exercises/disciplines, which are "activities that we can do that enable us to achieve indirectly, what we cannot otherwise achieve by direct immediate effort" (Willard's definition). I cannot sprint 100 m in ten seconds by trying, by direct, immediate effort. But by training daily – probably for many years – I will indirectly achieve that if I am a talented or gifted athlete. To the extent that we train off the spot, we can (super)naturally perform on the spot when we need to do healings, by God's gifts. When we "pray in secret", we are "rewarded openly" (Matthew 6:6) – God backs us up publicly with answered prayer. The result is: *A disciplined person is able to do what they need to do when they need to do it!*

Again, it is not so much training in the gifts as in oneness with the Giver. We need training in the presence more than in the presents

---

[7] I owe this and subsequent understandings to Dallas Willard, *The Spirit of the Disciplines: Understanding How God Changes Lives* (San Francisco: Harper, 1988).

of God. They flow naturally from his presence.[8] We seek God's face, not his hand. "Train yourself to be godly. ... [It] has value for all things ... both [in this] life and the life to come" (1 Timothy 4:7–8; 1 Corinthians 9:24–27). Paul uses *gymnazo* for "train" (the root word is "naked"), from which we get "gymnasium". Strip yourself of all encumbrances and engage purposefully in spiritual exercises to be fit to partner God in all that he does in and through you in any given situation. What exercises will enable us – indirectly and over time – to perform what Jesus commanded: "Heal the sick, drive out demons"? I mention two foundational disciplines, and propose two sensitivity-training exercises.

The Word of God

The Hebrews believed that what comes out of the mouth is an overflow of the heart – both sinful *and* godly words and works. Behind this is a theology of the rehabilitation and re-formation of "the heart", the core and the whole of the human being, *by God's Word and wisdom*. A lifelong devotion to read, study, meditate and memorise God's Word should be normal for Christians. This is not the case for most Christians, in my experience. We hear God most clearly and directly through his Word as, over time, it forms our worldview, beliefs, values, thoughts, feelings, attitudes, words and actions. *This* is *the* context in which we hear the Spirit as he speaks and leads throughout the day.

There is *a way of reading* for *spiritual formation* that Eugene Peterson calls "the art of spiritual reading".[9] It is slow, pondering, repetitive reading, praying the text back to God, like leisurely sucking a lozenge. Hebrew meditation *is* memorisation ("eat this book"), whereby God's Word enters and transforms our mind, emotions, will and body. Every thought is brought into captivity to the obedience of Christ (2 Corinthians 10:5). The Word becomes flesh as, morning by morning, we awaken, asking God to open our ears as one being

---

[8] See Willard on the presence and presents of God, *In Search of Guidance: Developing a Conversational Relationship with God* (San Francisco: Harper, 1993), pp. 37–39, one of the best books on *Hearing God* (republished under that title).
[9] Eugene Peterson, *Eat This Book: A Conversation in the Art of Spiritual Reading* (Grand Rapids: Eerdmans, 2006). Eugene has brought Scripture back to its central place in the life and formation of the Christian and the church.

taught, so that we receive an instructed tongue to know the word that sustains the weary. It is a "long obedience in the same direction" (Nietzsche's phrase). I end this chapter with a Scripture memorisation that I recall and pray through the day.

The practice of prayer

For the Hebrews, prayer was and is the native breath of the soul (Genesis 2:7). Prayer is inhaling the Breath (*Ruach*) of God, moment by moment, giving us God's life. If we stop praying, we die – in more ways than we realise! The more we pray, the more we are infused, indwelt and empowered by the Spirit to see, hear and do what the Father and the Son are doing. The practice of prayer takes two basic forms:

"Praying alone in secret" (Matthew 6:6f): Pray in your room, shutting all else out. The open secret is that not many Christians do this. Fewer do it consistently enough for transformation to take place. People are too busy. They do not know how to pray, needing practical methods to help. The deliberate and vulnerable act of bringing our body, our whole self, before God's presence, to engage him in naked face-to-face communion for an extended time, is an indispensable daily discipline. Prayer is "answering God",[10] listening and responding to his Word to us, teaching us dialogue, not monologue, with God.

"Pray without ceasing" (1 Thessalonians 5:17 KJV): Paul's phrase for what others have described in different ways.[11] I once heard a young man preaching on this verse, using a classic malapropism: "Pray without seizing! We need the oil of the Spirit to pray so that we do not seize up like a machine, that we can run smoothly throughout the day." His sermon was about ways to pray in which we do not seize up. Paul *commands*: Cultivate an attitude of prayerfulness, a consciousness

---

[10] Hans Urs von Balthasar's definition of prayer in his profound book, *Prayer* (New York: Paulist Press, 1967). It has been popularised in Eugene Petersen, *Answering God: The Psalms as Tools for Prayer* (San Francisco: HarperSanFrancisco, 1989). This teaches you *how to pray* by giving practical methods of prayer.

[11] The most well known is Brother Lawrence's "Practicing the Presence". Eastern Orthodox Christians are to pray The Jesus Prayer *continually*: "Lord Jesus Christ, Son of God, have mercy on me, a sinner." See Archimandrite Leviticus Gillet, *The Jesus Prayer* (New York: St Vladimir's Seminary Press, 1987). Praying in tongues is another way.

of God's indwelling presence. Our listening prayer eventually moves beyond words and thoughts to a union of intuitive knowing.

Can we realistically live in this kind of unbroken communion with God, while busy at work all day? Yes! By persistent, conscious effort, disciplining our minds to find God – include him – in all that we do, moment by moment. It eventually becomes an unconscious habit of listening to, and working with God in all things. Most Christians kid themselves into believing they pray on the run throughout the day, largely to sooth their guilt for not having a specific "quiet time" with God in private. That is far from the real thing! If it were, the world would be transformed. From experience and reading, I have learnt that "praying without ceasing" is dependent on our practice of "praying alone in secret".

Two exercises to train our senses

We must "train our senses" (*gymnazo*, Hebrews 5:14) to discern and distinguish, not only good from evil, but what God is saying and doing in any given situation. It is training both our physical *and* psycho-spiritual senses. Due to busyness and blockages, desensitisation and damage, most of us are not in touch with what we are sensing much of the time, let alone moment by moment. No wonder we cannot hear God speaking to us! Try these two exercises. If you do them consistently and long enough, they will enable you to sense God.

Practise extended periods of solitude and silence: Take two or more hours *every week* to be alone in a place where you will not be disturbed. Enter into silence before God in prayer. Become still. Picture him before you. Wait on him. Do it long enough to allow all other noises and disturbances – without and within – to come and go, until you enter that inner still point. By persistent practice you will get there! Then rest in God's loving embrace, sensing him through as many of your faculties as you can, and respond to him. Plan a six to eight week cycle of taking *a full day* in a retreat centre for this practice of solitude and silence.

Practise "sensing" through the day – whenever you are with a person. Stop at least five times during the day and ask yourself: What am I feeling right now (emotions)? Describe it in a word or two. What am

I sensing right now (body)? Answer. What am I thinking right now? What is God saying to me? In this way you can "sensitise" yourself to God and yourself. Practise it whenever you are with a person. Listen carefully to them, but inwardly sense what you are feeling, thinking, seeing. Ask God what he is doing with them, if he wants to say anything to them through you. Risk and walk on water!

In conclusion, I hope you are not feeling guilty and exhausted at the effort being called for: "I've got to do all these exercises!" That is the wrong message! Companionship with God is a healthy marriage, a joyful adventure of growth in love and intimacy. We have to slow down to live in the present moment, to *enjoy* God and ourselves. We still do all the things we have to do, but we learn to do them in a different way – "contemplatively" with God in all things. Christian spiritual leaders speak of "contemplative prayer"[12] (centring prayer, mental prayer, prayer of the heart) as *the* essential discipline that enables us to live in effective daily intimacy and partnership with God, bringing his kingdom, doing his will on earth as it is done in heaven.

A RAP Scripture memorisation

My Father is always working, to this very day, and I, too, am working with him.

I tell you the truth, the Son can do nothing by himself; he can only do what he sees his Father doing, because whatever the Father does the Son also does. For the Father loves the Son and shows him all he does.

I do not speak of my own accord, but the Father who sent me commands me what to say and how to say it. I know that His command leads to eternal life. So whatever I say is just what the Father has told me to say.

Do you not believe that I am in my Father, and that the Father is in me? The words I say to you are not just my own; rather, it is the Father, living in me, who is doing his works. (John 5:17, 19–20; 12:49–50; 14:10)

---

[12]The essence of Von Balthasar's exposition on prayer. A helpful book on the history and ways of practising "contemplation" is Thomas Keating, Basil Pennington & Thomas Clark, *Finding Grace at the Center* (Massachusetts: St Bede Publications, 1978).

Part Three: Praxis

Personal reflection, application and group discussion

1. Consider the struggle regarding healing that I describe at the beginning of the chapter. Do you experience anything like this? Do you agree with my conclusions to the questions I raise? What would be your answers?
2. Do you struggle with being intimate with others, with God? If so, how and why? How might you nurture more intimacy with God?
3. What is your dominant consciousness? In what ways might you develop an ongoing God consciousness?
4. How do you most commonly hear from God? Through what faculties?
5. When last did you hear God speaking to you – that you were conscious of? What did he say? How can you hear his voice more often and more clearly?
6. How do you respond to what I have written about spiritual disciplines – and specifically the exercises I have discussed?
7. Learn the Scripture memorisation I have recorded. Write it out on a card and keep it with you throughout the day, quoting and praying it as often as you can. Do this every day for one week, and then record in your journal what difference it made in you, and around you.

13

MODELS: HEALING MODELS AND A FIVE-STEP ORDINARY BELIEVER MODEL

"Be imitators of me as I am of Christ."
– 1 Corinthians 11:1 NRSV

Paul sees himself and other leaders (1 Corinthians 4:6) as a model for life and ministry: "Follow my example to the extent I imitate Christ." As discussed, Jesus is our model of kingdom ministry. People follow models, the way we do things, whether they are conscious of it or not. It has great power in forming beliefs, values and practices. Reflecting on our models and practices of healing ministry helps us to see if they communicate what the Bible teaches.

We need to be aware of, and learn from, the various models of healing ministry in the broader church. It calls for honest discernment: God's blessing (apparent success) does not necessarily mean his endorsement. *Every* model of ministry has human fingerprints; it is never "pure kingdom". So we honour the whole church, and are humbly self-critical about our own values and model.

Part Three: Praxis

The following overview is a general characterisation of the primary healing models, summarising the research I did while working with John in 1982.[1] The models are not fixed. There is development and crossover of personalities and healing practices, due to mutual influence.

An overview of various healing models[2]

- *Evangelicals:* From conservatives like A.J. Gordon, to "holiness" like A.B. Simpson and dispensationalists like John MacArthur. Their worldview is Western modernist, not allowing for manifestations of God's supernatural power as an expected norm in ministry. Cessationist-dispensationalists believe God only heals sovereignly, because healing and miracles through human agency ceased with the apostolic era. Where there is a theology of healing, it is based on the atonement (Gordon and Simpson). There is generally no practice of healing in more educated circles; but where there is often in poorer circles, the pastor is the one who prays. Evangelicals react to Pentecostal TV healing evangelists, tending to throw the baby out with the bath-water, sceptical of healing ministry. The exception is the Empowered Evangelicals' model, as represented by Wimber and related kingdom-paradigm movements.[3]

- *Pentecostals:* From classic Pentecostals like F.F. Bosworth, T.L. Osborn and Oral Roberts, to Faith and Prosperity preachers like Kenneth Hagin, Kenneth and Gloria Copeland and Benny Hinn. They have a spiritual worldview, open to supernatural intervention as a normal part of Christian ministry. Their theology of healing is based on the atonement of Christ, received by assertive faith. Their healing practice is event and crisis oriented, through preaching and words of knowledge,

---

[1] The research is found in the manuals: John Wimber, *Signs and Wonders and Church Growth, Parts 1 & 2* (Anaheim: VMI, 1984); *Healing Vol. 4: Models and Methodology* (Yorba Linda: VCF, 1982).
[2] In each model I mention representative personalities; see their books in the Bibliography.
[3] See the Bibliography: John Wimber, Ken Blue, Gary Best, Jack Deere, Charles Kraft, Barry Kissel, Rich Nathan, Mary Pytches, Kevin Springer, John White.

laying on of hands, outward "shows of power" and other means of releasing faith. It takes place mostly in big meetings, with promotion and high visibility around the "man of God" or woman of God, e.g. Aimee Semple McPherson, Kathryn Kuhlman. In local church practice, healing is also centred on the platform. Some Pentecostal churches equip their members to practice the gifts of the Spirit, especially for evangelism.

- *Charismatics as in Neo-Pentecostals:* From deliverance ministries like Derek Prince, Bob Mumford, Don Basham and Peter Horrobin, to neo-Pentecostal healers like the international leaders (usually "apostles") of Charismatic church-planting movements. Although their theology of healing is similar to Pentecostals, some have a kingdom awareness, but interpreted within a restorationist framework: healing is God's restoration of the gifts and ministries to the church, leading to the end-time revival that will usher in the return of Christ. Their healing practice is also focused on the preacher and elders doing healing up front, but not with the same hype, promotion and mass meetings. They include counselling in healing ministry, and some equip their members to minister. Healing Rooms have recently emerged. Contrary to some Pentecostals, they practise demon expulsion from Christians.

- *Charismatics as in Neo-Mainline:* From deliverance and healing ministries like Francis MacNutt, Michael Scanlan, Agnes Sanford, to psychological and inner healing ministries like Ruth Carter Stapleton, Dennis and Matthew Linn and Leanne Payne. These healers operate within the Charismatic Renewal paradigm, continuing to exercise their ministries in the mainline churches. The model is characterised by a wholistic approach to healing, seeking to heal all interrelated levels of brokenness. Their worldview is spiritual, and they integrate theology (use of Scripture) with psychology and other disciplines for wholistic healing. The atonement is still central to healing, but many have broadened into a kingdom understanding of healing. Healing is a process, rather than an event or crisis. They have a pastoral approach, with a primary emphasis on inner healing of memories, past hurts, demonisations, abuse and forgiveness. Their practice is varied: counselling, role-play, guided imagery, "soaking" prayer ministry (extended time with one person) with laying on of hands and exercising the gifts of the Spirit. Equipping people to do healing ministry is generally part of their practice, although it tends to selection, training and deployment of the few, not the many.

- *Liturgical/sacramental:* Represented in Morris Maddocks, Father Edward McDonough, Morton Kelsey and Mike Endicott.[4] Many of these healers overlap with the above Charismatic model, having a spiritual worldview and similar theological paradigm, but with greater use of liturgy and the sacraments in ministering healing. Consequently they see healing more in terms of official church ministry, as a function of the ordained priesthood. Their practice is through liturgical services – recipients kneel at the altar to receive healing through the sacraments of the Eucharist, Penance (confession and absolution), and anointing with oil. Often there is a mystical encounter with God via other "signs of his presence": priestly robes, incense, candles, the crucifix, icons and stained glass windows. For obvious reasons this model does not equip ordinary believers to minister healing.

A five-step ordinary believer model of ministry

As the church grows worldwide, so healing theologies and practices develop and shift, hopefully towards a recovery of the healing ministry of Jesus and the early church. Wimber has made a contribution through a simple five-step model of ministry that embodies our kingdom theology and praxis.[5] Before I discuss the model itself, I list the values that determine its practice.

---

[4] Categorising Kelsey and Endicott is difficult. Their practice is (or was, Kelsey) eclectic and nuanced.
[5] First recorded in *Healing vol. 4: Models and Methodology*; then changed (reshuffled) in Wimber's *Power Healing*, pp. 209–244. *My presentation goes back to the original*, with an adjustment in wording for ease of usage.

Some undergirding values and guiding principles

- *Accessible to all believers:* Most of the healing models are priestly, revolving around the individual who ministers the healing – the "man of God", ordained priest, specialist healer. This has disempowered ordinary Christians – the models are inaccessible or out of reach. Few, if any models, have intentionally "equipped the saints" to do the ministry of healing. We are committed to do ministry in a way that
    a) does not draw undue attention to the platform or the person leading the ministry, and
    b) draws ordinary believers into practising ministry in a method that is accessible, real and responsible.
- *The value of ministering in teams:* We believe in the democratisation of ministry "by the people, for the people, to the people".[6] It is best practised in twos and threes, except if we are alone, spontaneously engaging in ministry. One person should initiate the ministry and keep a facilitating role, while the others give words and minister. Teamwork is sensitivity, listening to one another, not dominating or cutting across, but giving space to listen to God and engage, each in turn. Team means drawing in others who are uninitiated in ministry and want to learn, watch, participate and be coached.
- *Honouring and loving the person:* People must never be treated – or used – as objects of our ministry. They are not clients that we are "doing things to". We minister to persons, not masses, numbers or conditions. People are unique, with names, faces, histories and pain, to be treated with respect and dignity in any given ministry exchange. We minister with compassion and mercy.
- *Ministering wholeness more than resolving the presenting problem:* By loving people in ministry, we bring a little wholeness to the whole person, as opposed to merely resolving their felt need. The presenting problem is often a symptom of deeper issues, so we take time with the person to heal the related causes with a view to restoring *Shalom* to the person.

---

[6]We call it "every-believer ministry". Biblically it is "the priesthood of all believers" (1 Peter 2:5, 9).

- *Depending on the Holy Spirit in mutual partnership:* We are midwives facilitating people's experience of God, helping to birth what the Spirit is doing. We work with God *and* the person, secure in the knowledge that only God can heal. It is about responding to the Spirit *and* the person as we observe, listen, initiate, encourage, step back, let it happen, and intervene if necessary – *the art* of not being too present and directive, and not being too reticent and retiring. Working with God in facilitating people's healing is a deep mystery, a great privilege and responsibility.

- *Using disclaimer language and not absolutist language:* We minister by speaking to conditions as Jesus did, not in arrogance or presumption, but in humility and honesty, with quiet confidence in God. Because we see and know "in part", we avoid using absolutist language – speaking as if God is talking directly through us: "God says this is your problem"; "The Lord says: 'I am going to heal you.'" That is top-down and intimidating, leaving no room to be corrected – if *God* is saying this, as you claim, how can it be wrong, even if we know it is wrong? Disclaimer language is: "I sense the Lord is saying …"; "I feel God is doing …"; "I see this picture. Is it applicable to you?" It includes and invites, leaving the door open to have misheard or misinterpreted what God is saying. In short, we must be real and simple, not religious, hyped and complicated, both in our words and style of ministry.

In describing the five-step model, we do not apply it mechanically or legalistically. "What step am I on? Am I doing it correctly?" If we have seen it in action and have it clear in our minds, by reading this carefully, it operates as a background guide, like the railway tracks on which the ministry train runs. Practice will make it flow easily and unconsciously.

Step 1: Contact and setting

The first step is contact with the person. Either the person comes for ministry (wants it), spontaneous contact with a person may lead to ministry, or you feel led by God to go to a person to offer ministry.[7] People asking for healing show faith in God (James 5:14f). Jesus worked with such faith, never refusing anyone who came to him. The spontaneous ministry situation, mutually agreed to, is exciting because faith has entered and risk is being taken. Initiating contact to offer ministry requires greater sensitivity, integrity and faith.

The setting in which the contact is made is important: Is it conducive to ministry? The setting may be a church meeting, conference or home group – all conducive to ministry. Or the ministry contact may be made in an office, on the street or in a shopping mall, which may or may not be conducive. We must assess the appropriateness of the environment, as it can cause self-consciousness and discomfort, disabling the person from receiving from God. Then it is better to schedule ministry at a time and place that secures and enables the person to receive.

Step 2: Interview and diagnosis

The second step is to find out what the person is asking from God, what their particular need is. In a team context, one person must initiate the interview and ministry. It means getting enough information to engage in ministry with some sense of direction. Like a doctor who is ministering to a sick person, we do a brief interview and diagnosis – the emphasis is on brief – not more than two or three minutes. This is not a "chat"; a long litany of complaints (gently bring the person back to the point); a counselling situation (a different process), nor is it the time to give advice or tell your story ("Oh, have you tried this …?" or "I had a similar problem …" or "That reminds me of …"). Ask a few key questions to identify the issue and what is possibly behind it:

- What is the problem? What do you want God to do for you?
- How long have you had this? When did it start/happen?
- Did anything else happen at the time it started? Are you aware of what may have caused this? Is it in your family (bloodline)?

---

[7] You should not go to a person and say, "God told me to minister to you. Let me lay hands on you." Rather share the sense of leading and allow the person to invite ministry or to turn it down.

> ❧ Do you want to be made well?

Each answer should be two or three sentences. Gently restrict them if they carry on. An extended dialogue undermines the ministry moment. Jesus asked these kinds of questions before he healed people, showing that he needed certain information, while at other times he received revelation from the Spirit.[8] We listen on two levels simultaneously: to the person and to the Spirit, discerning and diagnosing the issue and its underlying causes.

Step 3: Engagement and selection

The third step is to engage in ministry with a preliminary selection in mind from the interview and diagnosis of what area to minister into, whether spiritual, emotional, deliverance, physical or relational healing.

You begin ministry by putting the person at ease: "We are going to lay hands on you and invite Jesus to heal you." Tell them to relax and receive. If they get prayerful and intense say, "Dial down. Lift your head and open your hands to receive from God." Invite the Lord: "Come Holy Spirit …" and bless the person: "I bless you with God's Spirit. The kingdom of God be upon you." As you engage in ministry in this way, you do three things:

1. *Keep your eyes open* to see what God is doing. Look for outward evidence of God's touch. Various physical manifestations indicate different spiritual confrontations and healings (described in Chapter 20). See psycho-spiritually for what the Spirit may be showing you. Looking at the person, often you intuitively see and know certain things. In keeping your eyes open, you are ministering healing, speaking to things ("Pain, go in Jesus' name!"), not praying for or with the person (closing your eyes and talking to God).[9]

---

[8] See Chapter 7 point 18 in the text for the details and biblical references.
[9] The distinction between *ministering* versus *praying* becomes blurred in practice because we mix it up: "I speak to the pain and command it to go … please Lord, come with your power … Is anything happening in your body?" Like David in the Psalms, we speak to our enemies, to God, to ourselves, all in the same breath! I emphasise the distinction to break the old paradigm and posture of "praying for sick people", to establish the posture of "heal the sick, drive out demons".

2. *Lay on hands appropriately.* We lay on hands to tangibly impart the Spirit. The way you and the ministering team lay on hands is important. It can make the person feel uncomfortable and crowded, detracting from their encounter with God. Or it can be a means of love and comfort, releasing their faith, imparting blessing and healing. There is obvious sensitivity with cross-gender laying on of hands, especially from men to women, due to the prevalence and history of male abuse of women. There should be no touching of any sensitive areas in communicating healing, unless you get the person to lay their hands on their own body, or invite other women to do so, like touching the tummy to heal ulcers.[10]

3. *Start from the general and move towards the specific.* Begin with general statements of blessing that secure and affirm the person: "Receive the Spirit … I bless you with God's power … Jesus loves you … he's touching you … more, Lord …" These statements are all true and safe, creating an environment of warmth and love, allowing the person to feel God's presence, to enter the "anaesthesia" of the Spirit. When you see the Spirit working or you feel prompted, begin to address the issues. Start with what the person told you, the presenting problem: "Headaches go, in the name of Jesus."

Getting specific with your words increases the risks, but it is safe to start with the presenting problem. Like turning on a hot water tap, you first run cold, then warm, then hot. From pronouncing general statements of blessing, you speak to the presenting problem, which leads to specific words in addressing the issues and underlying causes. Often when you say one thing ("Headaches, go in Jesus' name"), God shows you another thing ("I have a picture of nodules in your neck and shoulders – I break tension in your body"), and then on the tail of that comes another more specific word, going to the cause ("I sense that you need to forgive someone … is it your boss? Did he betray

---

[10]In the early days of the Vineyard we laid hands "off" people, holding hands above and apart from them, because of the abuse in Charismatic circles of people falling "under the power" due to pressure laying on of hands and/or auto-suggestion in the minds of the receivers. If people were going to fall under the power or whatever in responding to the Spirit, it was not going to be because of manipulation from us!

your trust, or am I missing it here? Forgive him and the headaches will go!").

By this time, you are so specific that it is either right or wrong. If you are right, the person will be crying with astonishment at God's love, knowing that only God could have shown you that – "the secrets of their heart" are revealed (1 Corinthians 14:25). Specific and accurate revelation leads to power encounters that release faith to receive gifts of healing. Because you have used disclaimer language, asking questions and not making statements, if you are wrong, the person can disagree with you without feeling intimidated. We are like surgeons using words with laser precision by God's "finger" (Spirit, Matthew 12:28; Luke 11:20), penetrating ever deeper to touch the darkest recesses of the human psyche. These levels of ministry require great sensitivity. The person is so vulnerable and psycho-spiritually open that they could "bleed" profusely if we say the wrong things insensitively or presumptuously. However, profound miracles happen when we exercise faith to flow in the Spirit with ever-increasing supernatural accuracy and compassionate power.

In illustrating how we start with the general and move toward the specific, I have described what I mean by ministry selection. We select, from the given information *and* the Spirit's leading, which area to focus on: spiritual, emotional, deliverance, physical or relational healing. Once the area of sickness is identified, with possible underlying causes, we engage in a method of healing suited to the particular area of dis-ease. I present a practical method for each of these in the following chapters.

Before moving to the next step, I must re-emphasize that *in practice* ministry flows in a wholistic, integrated way, not in a fragmented, compartmentalised manner. Although each area of sickness has a method of healing, they are interrelated in terms of compensatory effects and causes. Here are some examples:

- Spiritual sickness can be caused by emotional elements, which in turn can be caused by a physical condition: feeling cut off from God as a result of deep-seated anger resulting from physical sickness or suffering.
- Emotional sickness can be caused by relational factors, which

can be caused by sin or even demonisation: immobilised in rejection and self-pity from a divorce, stemming from a husband who was a serial adulterer.
- Demonisation caused by unresolved emotional hurt, caused by circumstantial trauma: an irrational fear stemming from a violent attack that was not processed after it happened – the bad memory terrorises the person.
- Physical sickness caused by demonisation caused by relational sin: arthritis stemming from a spirit of bitterness, caused by unforgiveness of an abuser.
- Relational sickness caused by spiritual sickness, caused by emotional hurt and even demonisation: unreconciled relationship, due to hardening of the heart toward God, stemming from a cynical spirit because of past hurt.

Step 4: Interaction and re-engagement

This step involves getting feedback from the person during ministry *in order to re-engage with greater precision.* It is *not* stopping the ministry encounter, rather refocusing it with updated information to work more accurately with the person and the Spirit to penetrate the root issues. This interaction and re-engagement can happen a few times – as many times as is needed or naturally happens.

My normal practice is to do the initial interaction and re-engagement after having moved from the general to the specific presenting problem ("Headaches go, in the name of Jesus"). After addressing the headaches, I wait for a while and watch to see what happens. Then I ask, "How are you feeling? Has the headache gone?" There is no problem asking for feedback if you do it sensitively. Sometimes they give you subtle signals that they need a little encouragement or interaction; or there is a lull in ministry and/or you feel prompted by the Spirit to ask them a question. You obviously *do not* want to do it when it will interrupt or distract from a God encounter that is powerfully and evidently happening. You let God do his thing and you watch with wonder and learn from him!

As with Step 2 (the interview), the interaction must be very brief and to the point, or it can lead to discussion with the ministry momentum being lost. Jesus asked for feedback after addressing the presenting problem with the blind man in Mark 8:22–26. If the condition has gone, praise the Lord and stop ministry – unless they want more. We do not have to find a deeper cause behind every symptom or presenting problem! If nothing has changed, or there is partial change, re-engage in ministry. Jesus did exactly that with the blind man. Ask for feedback again.

During interaction I also ask, "Are you sensing anything in your body? Are you seeing something in your mind? Is God showing you anything?" Or you might say, "I am sensing this … seeing this picture … what does it mean to you?" Often this opens things up and shows what God is doing at deeper levels. Be careful not to make them feel they *have* to feel or see something! Do not pressurise them. They must be honest and we must not apologise for God if they do not sense anything. I reassure them that, if they do not feel anything, it does not mean that God is not doing anything. He is in fact doing much more than they would ever realize – beyond their senses. Like spending time in direct sunlight, they can *never* expose themselves to God's Spirit in ministry without *something* happening, which only becomes evident later.

As you do this – minister, feedback and more ministry – the person relaxes, opens up and becomes vulnerable to God. Interaction with the person *and the Spirit* helps identify related causes and blockages, eventually uncovering root issues.

Step 5: Closure and care

The last step is to bring the ministry to proper closure, with debriefing and some pointers as to the way forward. Jesus spoke to people after ministry at times, giving them instructions (John 5:13–14).

Learn to read the signs that tell you it is time to bring the ministry to an end. The person may open their eyes and look at you; they may get tired and disengage; a circumstantial element may intrude (children interrupting); you may sense from the Spirit it is time to close it down. Do not prolong the ministry when it should *evidently* end. We must not make the opposite mistake of closing it down when the person needs to soak more in God's presence!

Ask how they experienced the ministry. Put into perspective anything that might have concerned them, especially if they did not subjectively experience much. That often leaves them insecure. You need to reassure them that it is not necessarily their fault, nor God's fault; rather, it is a battle with evil. Persistent ongoing ministry can break blockages and open up healing processes; at least it will bring a measure of wholeness, even if the problem is not resolved. At times you need to protect their minds from rejection, doubt and condemnation from the devil's attack. Leave the person feeling understood, loved and valued. If they were healed, they may need simple instructions on how to keep and further their healing, as Jesus did in John 5.

If necessary, offer them direction as to what they should do next, like waiting on God at home, soaking in his presence, and returning for further ministry. Or they may need therapy or pastoral counselling to uncover issues, resulting in more effective ministry. You may recommend a healing/recovery course that you are aware of. I always check if they are part of a home group, as ongoing community (loving friendship) is crucial for healing and growth.

This step, like the interview and interaction, must be brief as they have already undergone an extended time of ministry. Be careful not to allow this to become a prolonged discussion, advice giving or counselling. It is merely to tidy up any concerns, secure the person and point them in the right direction in their journey to healing and wholeness.

Part Three: Praxis

Personal reflection, application and group discussion

1. What model(s) of healing ministry have you been exposed to in your Christian life?
2. Do you practise ministry to sick people? How do you do it? Have you examined the undergirding theology and values determining your approach to, and practice of, healing ministry?
3. Do you agree with the values that I have explained, that underpin the five-step model?
4. What do you think of the five-step ordinary believer model of ministry? What do you agree or disagree with – or would you change? Why?
5. An exercise: Plan a session with friends, or your home group, to practise the five-step method of ministry. Ask for one or two who are sick in any way. Get threes or fours to minister to them, systematically working through the steps. Have a time of group feedback to see what happened – what God did – and what you can learn from it. Then practise it as often as you can!

14

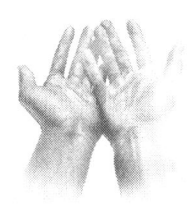

Method 1: Ministering healing to the spirit

The Lord God commanded, "You are free to eat from any tree in the garden; but you must not eat from the tree of the knowledge of good and evil, for when you eat of it you will surely die."
– Genesis 2:16–17

*Have mercy on me, O God, because of your unfailing love.
Because of your great compassion, blot out the stain of my sins.
Wash me clean from my guilt. Purify me from my sin.
For I recognise my rebellion; it haunts me day and night.
Against you, and you alone, have I sinned;
I have done what is evil in your sight.
You will be proved right in what you say,
and your judgment against me is just.
Create in me a clean heart, O God.
Renew a loyal spirit within me.*
– Psalm 51:1–4, 10 NLT

Part Three: Praxis

I need to point out that the Bible does not categorise sickness and healing in the six dimensions addressed in the following chapters: spiritual, emotional, demonisation, physical, relational, and death and dying. I do so for logical explanation, keeping in mind the wholistic understanding of human nature discussed in Chapter 3. The six dimensions flow into one another – they are not compartmentalised – thus we struggle with terminology and definitions of spirit, heart, soul (see Chapter 3, footnote 8). I am working from praxis, explaining phenomena; do not "stumble" over my categories and definitions!

We learn about sickness and healing *in the Scriptures* via the stories. There is no systematic exposition of sickness and healing in the Bible. I use homiletical licence in selecting biblical stories to illustrate each of the six dimensions, applying the emerging principles *to give a practical method of healing in that area of dis-ease*. I also use the stories to show the interrelated effects on the person, both in terms of sickness and wholistic healing. My purpose is to give a concise understanding and method of healing in each of these areas from the perspective of praxis – without being simplistic or superficial. They are each a book in their own right!

Understanding spiritual sickness and healing[1]

Sickness of the spirit is about our spirituality, *our sin* and its effect upon us, with the consequent need for restoration of *our relationship with God*. What distinguishes humans from other earthly creatures is that we are made in God's image as embodied *spirit* beings. The core of human nature is our *spiritual* capacity: our ability to relate to God and spirit beings, to make moral choices (willpower), distinguishing right from wrong (conscience and character). It is *the most fundamental and powerful factor* affecting all dimensions of our personhood, both in sickness and in health.

Biblically, there is first spiritual death and resurrection/life, then spiritual sickness and healing/health. Let me explain.

The human spirit comes from God's Spirit. Adam became a living soul (*nephesh*) by God's breath (*ruach*, Genesis 2:7). Our spirit is "the

---

[1] See John and Paula Sandford, *Healing the Wounded Spirit* (Tulsa: Victory House, 1985).

Method 1: *Ministering healing to the spirit*

candle of the Lord", God's light within us (Proverbs 20:27). *It is a relational spiritual reality* of eternal life and light *from* God as we are made in his image. Sin brought death: "If you eat of that tree you will surely die" (Genesis 2:17; 3:1ff). Death means "separation". Sin separated Adam and Eve from God. Their lights went out, plunging them into the darkness of corruption and death in their thinking, beliefs, choices, emotions, body, behaviour and relationships, and creation was cursed.

Paul says: "You *were* dead in your ... sins, in which you used to live ... but ... God ... made us *alive* with Christ" (Ephesians 2:1–6). God so loved us that he sent his Son, the Life and Light of the world, to reconcile us to him. Jesus died *our* death, for *our* sin, in *our* place, and physically rose again to give us eternal life and light. As we put our faith in Christ, God forgives our sins and we "cross over from death to life", from "darkness to light" (John 5:24; 8:12). We are *spiritually* resurrected and re-ignited by God's Spirit indwelling our spirit ("born again"), *the source for all other dimensions of healing,* from the inside out. It is *the progressive transformation* of our will, mind, emotions, body, relationships and creation itself. It happens to the extent that we entrust ourselves to God *in Christ* for healing, and not to other gods – ourselves and other spirit beings.

Biblically, all who are *not* born again are spiritually *dead* – they cannot be spiritually *sick* no matter how "spiritual" they may claim to be, in the New Age understandings of "spirituality". All who are born again are spiritually alive, united with God in one (S)spirit (1 Corinthians 6:17). Growth in Christ ensures spiritual life and health, but *spiritual sickness* can occur. How? *The common causes are:* sinful choices, patterns of unresolved sin, guilt and shame, a broken or weak will, hardness of the heart, character flaws and failure. So "let us purify ourselves from everything that *contaminates* body and spirit, perfecting holiness out of reverence of God" (2 Corinthians 7:1); "put off" (put to death) sinful desires and "put on" our new nature in Christ (Ephesians 4; Colossians 3).[2]

---

[2] Paul prays that we will be "*sanctified* ... through and through", that our "whole spirit, soul and body *be kept blameless* at the coming of our Lord Jesus Christ" (1 Thessalonians 5:23). Peter says we must "*make every effort* to add to [our] faith ..." key qualities to grow productively in our faith (2 Peter 1:5–11), and thus be kept from spiritual sicknesses.

Christians from the early church to the present have been aware of the forms and causes of spiritual sickness. The Desert Fathers spoke of "illnesses of the heart": ignorance, forgetfulness, hardness, blindness, contamination and imprudence.[3] The seven deadly sins are well-known causes of spiritual sickness and death: pride, greed, lust, anger, gluttony, envy and sloth.

Biblical examples

The story of Adam and Eve (Genesis 3:1–24)

This story shows the elements involved in spiritual death, the prototype of every subsequent temptation, sin, spiritual sickness and healing.

Created in God's image and likeness, Adam and Eve tended the garden during the day and walked with God in the cool of the evening – a picture of pristine purity, peace, spiritual health and wholeness. It was heaven on earth, *Shalom*: relational unity with God, themselves, each other and creation.

The serpent came and challenged God's word, causing Adam and Eve to doubt God: "Did God *really* say … but do you not know if you eat of that forbidden tree you will *not* die! God knows that your eyes will be opened and you will be like him, knowing good and evil." Temptation always questions God's Word and integrity via an enticement of the senses – they "saw that the fruit was good for food and pleasing to the eye" (v. 6), and an appeal to human pride – "desirable for gaining wisdom" to be like God (v. 6). Being tempted is being "led astray" by our senses, appetites and pride, to trust ourselves – our wisdom and knowledge – more than God – what he knows and says. Sin is responding to temptation, *not* resisting it; *choosing* to act in disobedience to God and his Word, breaking faith with him. Sin rejects God, making us god. Behind every sin, whether we realise it or not, is the belief that we are like God. Temptation is enticement of our corrupted senses, which leads to sin, resulting in death (James 1:13–15).

Adam and Eve's death was separation from God (spiritually and

---

[3] See Kyriacos C. Markides, *The Mountain of Silence: A Search for Orthodox Spirituality* (New York: Image Books, 2001), pp. 53–66.

Method 1: *Ministering healing to the spirit*

ethically), within themselves (mentally and emotionally), from each other (relationally and socially), from nature (ecologically), and eventually from the body (the spirit leaves the body in death). Their sin "opened their eyes", *not* to what they wanted, but to a rude awakening of disorder and chaos at all levels of created reality:

1. They immediately suffered *guilt and shame*: "They realised they were naked" and felt ashamed (v. 7) – psycho-spiritual dis-ease.
2. They consequently *covered up* to hide their shame – a total makeover with the latest fig-leaf technology and fashion (v. 7) – self-justification.
3. *Fear* gripped them when they heard God walking in the cool of the evening – "I was afraid" (vs 8, 10) – emotional disorder.
4. They *withdrew* and *hid* from God (vs 8–10) – spiritual alienation.
5. When confronted, they *projected and shifted blame*. Adam said: "The woman *you* put here with me … gave me … fruit from the tree" (v. 12). Eve said: "The serpent [you made] deceived me, and I ate" (v. 13) – relational/social disorder. It affected their children – Cain *murdered* Abel (4:1ff).
6. The earth was *subjected to corruption* due to their sin. They were expelled from Eden Garden, symbolising human alienation in the desert exile of a cursed creation (vs 14–18) – ecological disorder.
7. The wholistic effects of spiritual death and sickness are summarised in vs 16–19: ongoing enmity between Satan and human beings; physical pain in childbirth; dependency and dominance in relationship; sweat and toil in work and survival; and physical mortality.

God responded and dealt with this spiritual death by:

1. *Not* withdrawing in anger, but mercifully *seeking and calling* Adam and Eve.
2. *Confronting* them with their sin – getting them to own up – confess.
3. *Forgiving* them through blood sacrifice – by covering their sin and shame with "garments of skin" that *he made and provided* (v. 21), foreshadowing the "Lamb of God, who takes away the sin

of the world" (John 1:29), as he "crushes the serpent's [Satan's] head" in the "bruising of his heel" (v. 15).

The stories of King Saul and King David

Both Saul and David were chosen and anointed as king; both had spiritual life and health; both fell "spiritually ill" through disobedience to God. Saul did not recover – he deteriorated to the point where his spiritual sickness killed him. David recovered his spiritual health and wholeness. Here are the key elements:

- *Spiritual health:* When God chose Saul as king, he poured his Spirit on him and Saul prophesied, becoming a different man (1 Samuel 10:10–11). David was a man after God's own heart from his youth – intimate with God – as seen in his many psalms.
- *Temptation and sin:* Saul's spiritual sickness began when he presumptuously offered the burnt offering before Samuel arrived (1 Samuel 13). Later he disobeyed God's command to annihilate the Amalekites (1 Samuel 15). He was tempted by seeing "everything that was good" and kept it. For David it began when he was tempted by seeing Bathsheba bathing, when he should have been at war. His lust led to an adulterous affair. On hearing Bathsheba had fallen pregnant, David resorted to deception, cover-up, lies and even the murder of her husband. David's sin caused relational destruction, affecting his children and family for generations (2 Samuel 12:11–12). David's eldest son Amnon raped his own sister (2 Samuel 13:1ff). David's sin caused spiritual, emotional, mental and bodily dis-ease,[4] evidenced in his penitential Psalm 32 – I quote vs 3–5 (NLT):

  > When I refused to confess my sin, my body wasted away, and I groaned all day long. Day and night your hand of discipline was heavy on me. My strength evaporated like water in the summer heat. Finally, I confessed all my sins to you and stopped trying to hide my guilt.

---

[4] There are two New Testament examples of sin being the probable direct cause of paralysis (Mark 2:5–11; John 5:14).

Method 1: *Ministering healing to the spirit*

- *God's response – confronting the sin:* God was grieved by what Saul and David did, and revealed it to prophets who confronted them. God sees all that we do and, sooner or later, for our own sake, he confronts us with our sin – often through others as a test of our pride. With Saul the confrontation was immediate (1 Samuel 15:10–14). With David it was after a couple of weeks, after he had thoroughly messed up (2 Samuel 12:1ff).

- *Their response – avoidance and ownership:* Saul avoided responsibility when Samuel confronted him. He lied: "I have carried out the Lord's instructions" (1 Samuel 15:13); blame-shifted: "The soldiers … spared the best of the sheep and cattle" (v. 15); used spiritual pretence: "… the best … to sacrifice to the Lord" (v. 15); and insisted: "But I did obey the Lord" (v. 20). Saul humbled himself only when Samuel pronounced God's judgment on him: "I have sinned … Now I beg you, forgive my sin …" (vs 24–25). Apparently it was too late because, although God forgave Saul, his repentance was based on self-pity, evident from his consequent spiritual deterioration.[5]

    David took responsibility when Nathan confronted him, immediately owning his sin: "I have sinned against the Lord" (2 Samuel 12:1–14). He wrote Psalm 51 at the time, tearfully repenting with godly sorrow, asking God for mercy and restoration to spiritual health (see the quote at the head of the chapter).

- *The outworking – death and healing:* God's Spirit lifted from Saul and an evil spirit tormented him (1 Samuel 16:14f), making him neurotic and insecure, driving him to hatred and rage. He tried to kill David (1 Samuel 18:6–11). He systematically hunted David to kill him, having moments of extreme remorse and self-pity (1 Samuel 19–26). Saul ended up consulting a witch (1 Samuel 28), and killed himself in utter defeat, despair and humiliation (1 Samuel 31).

    David received his forgiveness *and* bore his judgment with a contrite heart, seeking God with fasting and prayer until the

---

[5]Paul refers to "worldly sorrow [that] brings death" (*false* repentance), and "godly sorrow [that] brings repentance that leads to salvation" (*true* repentance, with its seven-fold fruit, 2 Corinthians 7:9–11).

child born of Bathsheba died (2 Samuel 12:13–25). God gave David and Bathsheba a second child, naming him "Beloved of the Lord" (Solomon), confirming David's forgiveness and spiritual healing. Psalm 51 lists the wholistic nature of spiritual healing: a new spirit (vs 10–12); restoration of the mind and emotions (vs 8, 12, 14, 15); healing of the body (v. 8) and relationship (v. 13), with societal impact (v. 18).

A contemporary example

Years ago a middle-aged man came to me for ministry on a number of occasions. He presented a slightly different problem every time, like stress, depression and apathy. A common theme emerged: "I am out of sorts with myself and God." I got desperate and asked God to show me what this man was not disclosing. As I invited the Holy Spirit and blessed him, moving from the general to the specific, I saw a picture of a sticky spiderweb over his head, over his mind. I asked the Spirit what it meant and intuitively knew it was condemnation due to unresolved sin sticking to him like slime, oppressing his mind and life. I told him the picture and asked if he had abiding guilt and shame. He confirmed this, "Yes, I do." "Is it because of some pattern of sin or a habit that you're ashamed of?" I asked. "Well … yes … I'd better tell you … but will you keep it strictly between us?"

He told me of his dark struggle with a secret life of anonymous homosexual encounters in public toilets. It had been going on for years, while he was a "happily married" family man. This was extremely painful – he could not look me in the eye – but he had taken the first step, breaking the silence and saying it. We are as sick as the secrets we live with. What is pushed into the dark is demonised; what is brought into the light is forgiven and healed. We are *not* set free by acknowledging the truth – that is part of it. It is *God's* truth in Jesus and his teachings that sets us free (John 8:31–47).

I had two instinctive responses: revulsion and compassion. Instantly I gave my revulsion to God, feeling guilty about it. I realised I did not have to choose between the two feelings. The revulsion was *not* against this man. I was feeling *God's* revulsion for what Satan had done to him, making him sick with sin and shame. I was feeling *God's* compassion for him, to free him from the tyranny of the spider that had caught him in a web of living death.

I reached out and embraced him. He began to shake and shudder, breaking down uncontrollably as I held him. I asked him if he wanted to be forgiven and free. He nodded, yes. "Verbally confess your sin and struggle to God. Be specific and name them all." He did this while breaking down, pouring out the details to God, remembering various incidents, as the Holy Spirit showed him. When he was finished, I spoke forgiveness and cleansing over him, over his whole spirit, mind, emotions and body, by the blood of Jesus. He wept with utter relief.

We spoke through the implications of what it would mean for him to get spiritually well: commit to a healing journey with God; disclose to his wife in an appropriate context (entrusting his marriage and children to God); and receive extensive counselling. With God's help he would have to turn (repent) from this pattern of secret sin, identify the driving forces and heal the wounds behind his homosexual struggle. He would enter a life of accountability for his thoughts, feelings and spiritual life, pursuing various spiritual disciplines in community and mentoring. We initially made good progress with God doing some amazing things, but he relocated and I lost contact with him.

Human beings are strange, sophisticated beings. Born-again Christians can live for years in a schizoid accommodation with lies of Satan and serious spiritual sickness. We "make peace with" racism, materialism, sexism, sexual immorality and perversions, rage, jealousy, greed, witchcraft and addictions at our peril. Paul warns us: These "acts of the sinful nature" will not only make us spiritually sick, but will actually kill us, keeping us from entering the kingdom of God (Galatians 5:19–21; 1 Corinthians 6:9–11).

A step-by-step method of healing

Once you have identified *spiritual death* in a person, lead them to Jesus as the only one who can give them spiritual life through his life, death and resurrection.

1. *Recognition:* Get them to acknowledge
    a) their spiritual death in separation from God by their sin (they

are sinners), and
b) their faith in Jesus as God's Son, who reconciles them to God through what he has done for them.
2. *Confession and repentance:* Lead them in prayer to
   a) confess their sinful reality before God;
   b) ask for his mercy and forgiveness, and
   c) commit to turn from their independent (sinful) way of living, with God's help.
3. *Faith and commitment:* Lead them to
   a) entrust themselves to Jesus, receiving the gift of eternal life in faith, and
   b) commit to follow Jesus in his person and teachings, within a community of his believing people.
4. *Thanksgiving and follow-up:* Get them to thank God for his forgiveness and eternal life. Follow-up with any ministry and direction as needed.

Once you have identified *spiritual sickness* while ministering to a person – in any form as described above and more – take the following steps:

1. *Confrontation of sin:* Face the person with the specific sin causing their particular spiritual illness. This is not always easy – it requires sensitivity, compassion, courage and wisdom. I warn people that, if they conceal their sin, it will eventually catch up with them or kill them. But if they confess and renounce their sin, they will find mercy (Proverbs 28:13).
2. *Confession and repentance:* Get them to
   a) confess their sin – to agree with God that he is right in what he says about them; that they have done wrong! And
   b) repent – turn from their sin and ask God for forgiveness and help.
   I assure people from 1 John 1:9 that, if they confess their sin to God, *he will forgive* them. James goes further: "Confess your sins to each other and pray *for each other* so that you may be healed" (James 5:16).
3. *Commitment to an act of repentance and restitution if needed:* The person must commit to

Method 1: *Ministering healing to the spirit*

a) an act of repentance, such as confessing to another person *if they wronged them*, and
b) to appropriate restitution to put things right if so needed – if they have stolen something.

As John the Baptiser says, there must be fruit – or actions – of true repentance (Luke 3:8–14).

4. *Cleansing and forgiveness – to speak and receive it:* Speak forgiveness and cleansing over them: "The blood of Jesus Christ cleanses you from your sin. You are forgiven – receive it now from God." Jesus authorised this (John 20:23). Encourage the person to take God at his word and thank him for forgiveness. Sometimes a symbolic act, like sprinkling water, helps the person to receive God's cleansing (Hebrews 10:22). I speak cleansing to their body – the "parts of the body" that were "instruments of unrighteousness leading to wickedness" – and dedicate them now as "instruments of righteousness leading to holiness" (Romans 6:12–13, 19).

5. *Forgiving themselves and others:* I make sure that they forgive themselves, because God has forgiven them. They must break the inner tapes of guilt, self-condemnation and disqualification – often the direct accusation of the devil (Revelation 12:10–11; Romans 8:1). If necessary, I break the lies and condemnation of the devil by the blood of Jesus. They must also forgive any other person who has wronged them, because God has forgiven them. In fact, God will *not* forgive them if they do *not* forgive others who have sinned against them (Matthew 6:14–15). I discuss forgiveness in the next chapter. Sometimes our spiritual sickness is due to our sinful *reactions* to other people's sin against us – our sinful acting out of the pain that we have received in being a victim of another person's abuse. Unforgiveness can block our healing from spiritual sickness.

6. *Heal related affected aspects:* Minister healing in other areas affected by their spiritual sickness as per the following chapters, like healing past hurts, breaking soul ties, and doing delivserance.

7. *Continue the healing journey:* In after-ministry care impress on the person the need for a journey to grow into spiritual health and wholeness, *not* to relapse into old patterns of sin and sickness. Get

them to commit to certain processes, tailored to their particular needs, like community accountability in small group belonging, counselling and recovery courses, and growth in the disciplines of biblical devotion and prayer.

Personal reflection, application and group discussion

1. What is your understanding and definition of spiritual sickness and healing? List some causes and probable symptoms of this dis-ease.
2. How do you relate to the biblical stories I used to explain spiritual sickness and healing? What did you learn from them?
3. What patterns, or aspects of these stories, could you identify in your own life story? Do you have any unresolved sin or form of spiritual sickness that you need to deal with? You can apply the steps to healing to yourself.
4. Have *you* ministered to a person with spiritual sickness to a point of healing? Reflect on how you ministered to them. What can you learn from it?
5. Do a James 5:16 exercise: Plan with your small group to read this chapter, then to confess your sins (failings, weaknesses) to one another, and to minister to each other, so that you may be healed. If you are not part of a small group, go to a trusted friend and do James 5:16, asking them to pray for you.

15

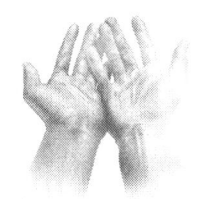

METHOD 2: MINISTERING HEALING TO THE EMOTIONS

"The Spirit of the Lord is upon me, because he has anointed me to preach good news to the poor, heal the bruised and brokenhearted, speak release to the captives, open the eyes of the blind, free those who are oppressed, and to announce God's Jubilee."
– Luke 4:18 RAP

Understanding emotional sickness and healing[1]

This category of sickness and healing is commonly called "inner healing": to bring a person to psycho-emotional wholeness by healing past hurts, painful memories, damaged emotions and broken self-esteem – *in general terms, healing the destructive effects of life's hurts.* This includes the effects of the sins of parents, inherited family conditions, soul ties and emotional dependencies.

---

[1] For resources see Bibliography: Backus, Bradshaw, Harris, Kelsey, Leman & Carlson, Linn (brothers), MacNutt, Padovani, Payne, Sandford, Sanford, Seamands, Smith, Stapleton, Tappscott and Scanlan.

We *all* suffer the consequences of living in a fallen world. The rain falls on the righteous and the unrighteous. We cannot stop life's hurts coming upon us, no matter how godly we may be; but *we can decide how to respond to them*. We can find God's meaning and purpose in what happens to us. He is present with us in it all. Jesus comes to us on the water *in the midst* of our storm. He can turn it for our good. God saves us *through* life's trials and struggles, not *from* them.

The symptoms of emotional dis-ease are many and varied: From inferiority to superiority complexes; from dominance to dependence; from sadness and grief, to moods and depression, rejection, anxieties and fears. The list is endless. The symptoms or presenting problem can be spiritual, emotional, mental, demonic, physical and even social. Only when we uncover the root cause of unresolved emotional pain can we heal it.

What are the causes of emotional dis-ease? Whereas *spiritual* sickness is mainly caused by our own sin, *emotional* sickness is largely the result of other people's sin against us and the effects of life's hurts in general. Abuse traumatises us, causing long-term damage. Psycho-emotional sickness can also be caused by the effects of the parents' sins passed through the bloodline (Exodus 20:4). Our responses to the above causes can exacerbate the emotional dis-ease by suppressing, ignoring, acting out our pain in sinful choices, or bring healing by talking it through, finding God in it and seeking help.

What are emotions? The Bible sees emotions wholistically and yet paradoxical.

1. There is recognition and empathy for emotional pain and brokenness.
2. There is no accommodation of "negative" or self-indulgent emotions.
3. There is the command to cultivate "positive" emotions like joy, love and peace.

This is *not* to suppress or negate painful or negative emotions as "ungodly" or "sinful". They are real and valid. We are to acknowledge and bring them to the light, so that they can be healed and rehabilitated, trained and transformed, for the glory of God and the good of creation. Life with God is committing to growing transformation into

Method 2: *Ministering healing to the emotions*

Christ-likeness, by knowing God's love and obeying his commands (Matthew 28:19–20; John 14:21–24), *no matter how we feel!*[2]

Emotions are like children: They are delightful gifts from God, but if they are not disciplined, they can develop into delinquent dictators, running riot through our bodies, destroying our self-image and holding our minds and relationships ransom.[3] In one sense emotions are "innocent" or "amoral"; what we do with them is good or bad, right or wrong. They are vulnerable to misuse and abuse, to hurt and damage, especially when we are young. In another sense, like children, our emotions are corrupted, tending to sin and selfishness because of our sinful nature. They need to be redeemed – intentionally disciplined and trained, rehabilitated and transformed, with God's help. We need to grow up before we grow old by training our emotions to be cooperative servants of God.

In terms of medical science, emotions are body chemicals ("feelings") the brain releases in response to outward stimuli.[4] Emotions are the energy that fuels the body (the whole person), healthily or destructively, depending on how we handle them. These "flash" feelings tell us something has happened, that we can respond appropriately. Feelings of anger say something has upset us. We should not deny or suppress the feeling (*imploding*); nor ventilate or project them onto someone else (*exploding*). We must ask what the feeling points to, then *express* it responsibly in an adult manner with the appropriate actions – not react irresponsibly like a child. This is how we grow emotional intelligence or maturity.[5]

---

[2] The twenty-one "one another sayings" in the New Testament ("love one another", "forgive one another") are all *commands* with *no* reference to feelings ("if you feel like it"). In other words, obey God in faith as a choice of the will, *entrusting your feelings to God,* and your emotions will be brought into submission, healing and transformation – to feel *God's* emotions.
[3] We live in the most narcissistic and emotionally neurotic generation, with all the consequent fallout. Robert Bly has described this well in *The Sibling Society* (London: Hamish Hamilton, 1996).
[4] This is helpful, but medical science with its materialistic worldview cannot explain spiritual reality with the interaction of (S)spirit-body, mind-brain, emotions-will. Emotions are triggered *both* by the "outward" (body) five senses *and* by "inward" stimuli of spirit, will, thoughts and imagination.
[5] See Daniel Goleman, *Emotional Intelligence: Why It Can Matter More Than IQ* (London: Bloomsbury Publishing, 1995).

A flash feeling can become a *repeated pattern* of emotional response to certain situations. An emotional pattern can lead to a mood or habit, both positive or negative. Over time it becomes fixed and incarnates itself in *a body posture*, attitudes and actions. Anger is a powerful emotion to be expressed without sinning (Ephesians 4:26), but repeated *unresolved* anger leads to contempt, hatred, violence and murder; if not literally, then attitudinally, verbally and relationally (Matthew 5:21–26). Unresolved anger is seen in certain fixed facial features. Joy and other emotional states are seen in other body postures.

Habitual moods and unhealed emotions also become channels for our "corrupted desires", *affected* appetites of our fallen nature (Ephesians 2:3; Romans 6:12–14). They tend to form spiritual and chemical *attachments* to substances, people and/or spirits, resulting in dependencies, addictions and enslavements – means of demonisation.[6] They also give expression to or are the result of psycho-emotional predispositions and spiritual curses that are passed through the bloodline from the sins of the parents (Exodus 20:4). Children experience *the consequences and vulnerabilities* of the sinful strongholds.

Invasive traumatic experiences, like abuse and divorce, cause "chemical storms" that are imprinted on the memories of our body cells. If these emotions are not processed and healed, they become stuck in a "body memory". The body will have automatic (autonomic) chemical reactions (relapses) in the form of panic attacks, depression, fear and headaches, *whenever there is any association with the unresolved trauma*. Emotional devastation takes time, patience and cooperative effort to heal. Because we do not see emotions (the devastation), we think we will recover overnight, or we should "just get over it now". However, we also know that God can heal emotions instantly.

The primary way of healing emotions is to talk about them. In "disclosing" feelings, we not only release them, we see what is behind them, and what we can do about them. *Regular disclosure,* especially to God in prayer, can ensure emotional health. David's psalms reveal how his emotions and perspectives shifted as he prayed (Psalm 42, 43). We heal bad experiences by revisiting them in discussion, in the imagination, to re-interpret them in the light of God's truth, meaning

---

[6] See Gerald May, *Addiction and Grace* (San Francisco: HarperSanFrancisco, 1988).

and purposes.[7] In this way the pain goes out of the memory and the body, and is laid to "rest in peace". No matter how deeply we suppress bad memories, if they are buried "alive", they push their way up to consciousness over time, demanding attention through bodily pain, sicknesses, nightmares and relapses. Unhealed emotions "leak" through projection and outbursts, defensive attitudes, sinful actions, and relational dysfunction.

It is well known that up to 70% of all physical ailments that doctors treat are psycho-emotional problems – "psychosomatic illnesses" – *the* most common area of sickness. It is no different in Christian healing ministry. My own healing journey in Chapter 1 is an example. Sadly, this area of inner healing is generally neglected in church life, primarily for two reasons:

1. *Incorrect theology*: Because we are "new creations in Christ" (2 Corinthians 5:17) we do not have to deal with past pain – it was sorted out when we got saved.[8] So embrace the new nature in Christ by "positive confession" and avoid "negative confession" (bad feelings). To "live by faith" (2 Corinthians 5:7), we interpret as: "Not by feelings", so we deny our emotions as lies from Satan in the name of faith and godliness. The result is placing no value on inner healing. People with emotional issues are tolerated or treated harshly.

2. *Emotional disconnection or numbness*: We are not in touch with our feelings or our issues, due to accumulative unresolved damage, so we think we do not need inner healing. We do not know how broken we really are, how we "leak", until reality bites – when things go wrong or others say, "Enough!"

Emotional healing comes from God, through his Son and his Spirit. God suffered our emotional pain, and its effects, in the life and death of Jesus

---

[7]Finding meaning and purpose is similar to the logotherapy of Viktor Frankl, *Man's Search for Meaning: An Introduction to Logotherapy* (London: Hodder & Stoughton, 1964).

[8]Salvation is an event *and* a process. To be inward-focused and blame everything on our past (on our parents) is wrong; as is being only future-focused, embracing our new nature in Christ by ignoring our past. When present problems *probably* point to past pain (we "leak") or we have flashbacks of repressed memories, *then* we face it and seek God's healing.

of Nazareth. By God's Spirit, Jesus healed the bruised and broken, the victims of other people's sin, captives to emotional pain and oppression (Luke 4:18). God has compassion on us through "the man of sorrows, acquainted with grief". Jesus empathises with our emotional weaknesses as he carried them *in his own body* (Isaiah 53:3–5; Hebrews 4:15). Every hurtful experience finds perspective, meaning and purpose through Jesus' life, death and resurrection. In this way, God pours his oil, the Holy Spirit, into our wounds, soothing our emotions and memories. The Spirit, the "finger of God", is able to touch and heal our deepest parts. Healing also comes through a proactive process – renewing our minds, attitudes and actions in our new nature in Christ (Romans 12:1–2; Ephesians 4:17–32).

Biblical examples

The two disciples on the road to Emmaus (Luke 24:13–35)

The trauma of death, especially the sudden death of a loved one, can be devastating. God gives us the gift of tears to mourn our loss, to release our emotions of sadness and grief. The pain can be so acute that Scripture assures us: God himself comforts those who mourn (Matthew 5:4). However, we must receive his comfort to experience it, or grief and sadness can "get stuck" in us, with destructive consequences. Let us see how Jesus ministered emotional healing to his disciples with regard to his traumatic death.

Cleopas and his wife were walking home to Emmaus, 11 km from Jerusalem. It was the Sunday after the Friday crucifixion. They had witnessed the terrifying ordeal and *"were talking with each other about everything that had happened"* (v. 14). They verbalised their pain around Jesus' death, not clamming up in silent implosion, nor exploding in destructive outbursts. Then: *"Jesus himself came up and walked along with them; but they were kept from recognising him"* (vs 15–16). He saw their pain and came alongside them. God comes to us in our pain – we do not have to "feel" his presence to know that he is beside us. We often feel abandoned by God in our pain – so the devil would have us believe. At times our eyes and feelings are purposely kept from sensing God in what is happening, in order to test us. God *can* come to us in the form of a stranger. We struggle to disclose in the privacy and safety of trusted others, let alone with strangers!

He asked them, "What are you discussing?" (v. 17). Asking questions is a key method in healing wounded emotions, to get people to tell their story, to draw out the pain. We must also realise that sharing our stories, talking to others – even strangers – is talking to God, because he is present in our pain, carefully listening. *"They stood still, their faces downcast"* (v. 17). Jesus' question stopped them in their tracks. The right questions stop us living past our pain, pulling us out of our busyness, denial and escape patterns. When we "stand still", we feel, express, and face our pain.

They asked Jesus, *"Are you a visitor to Jerusalem?"* (v. 18). He did not seem to know what had happened. God acts ignorant to get us to talk; or he may actually choose not to know certain things! Jesus responded, *"What things?"* (v. 19). He was not going to be sidetracked by counterquestions or other generalities. He wanted them to be specific, gently pressing them: Tell me your story! In telling our stories, we relive what happened, feeling the emotions, disclosing and owning them. Most importantly, we see *the perceptions and beliefs* behind the emotions, that which caused us to experience and interpret the event in a particular way.

The two disciples shared their story, the pain, grief, and underlying perceptions of disillusionment and unmet expectations: Jesus was *God's* prophet (v. 19). Why did the chief priests and rulers kill him (v. 20)? Disillusioned? God did not protect him? They hoped he was God's Messiah, that he would redeem Israel (v. 21). Now all hope was gone! Defeated? Angry? Jesus let them – and the nation – down? And there was shocking news from some women disciples (women's testimony was suspect!): Jesus' tomb was empty! An angel told them in a vision that he was alive (v. 23)! Some men verified the empty tomb (v. 24), but they could not find Jesus. Cleopas and his wife were traumatised, confused, fearful, not knowing what to believe.

Jesus began healing them through honest feedback. *"How foolish you are, and how slow of heart to believe all that the prophets have spoken! Did not the Messiah have to suffer these things and then enter his glory?"*

(vs 25–26). Ouch! This was harsh! Maybe these people, this situation, needed that approach. I do not believe Jesus disregarded their pain – he loved them by exposing the perceptions and beliefs behind their emotions. They should have *known* better, which would have helped them to *feel* better. He goes further: They were *"slow of heart to believe"* God, God's Word. They *did* know better, but refused to believe God. That is why their experience of Jesus' crucifixion was so devastating. Their feeling was captured in Jesus' pain: "My God, my God, why have you forsaken me?"

Then Jesus re-interpreted their bad experience in the light of God's Word, systematically explaining that Messiah needed to suffer and die to save Israel and the world (v. 27). Their *perception* of the Friday ordeal shifted as they saw God's purpose in it, relieving their confusion, healing their pain. Later they said: *"Were not our hearts burning within us while he talked with us on the road and opened the Scriptures to us?"* (v. 32). The truth set them free! The truth is: Whatever happens to us has meaning and purpose in the light of Messiah's life, death and resurrection. The truth is: God works in all things for the good of those who love him, who have been called according to his purpose (Romans 8:28).[9]

"As they approached the village, Jesus acted as if he were going farther" (v. 28). This was a test to see if they would be hospitable, inviting a stranger into their home. Thereby, unbeknown to them, they would receive the Risen Lord into their dwelling, into their innermost being. Jesus had entered their story, walked in their shoes, and shared their pain. But did they want more? More healing, deeper trust, greater intimacy? God "acts" as if he is moving on to test if we want to risk more. *"But they urged him strongly, 'Stay with us …'"* (v. 29). Beautiful!

"When he was at table with them, he took bread, gave thanks, broke it"

---

[9] The context of this verse is what we suffer ("groanings") from fallen creation and our mortal bodies, from "trouble, hardship, persecution, famine, nakedness, danger, sword, death, demons … in all these things we are more than conquerors through him who loved us" (vs 18–39). We conquer these things, not by glib positive confessions, emotional denial and spiritual escapism, but by facing reality, acknowledging and owning our brokenness, feelings and perceptions; allowing them to die with Christ and to rise again with new understandings (paradigm), new feelings, a new creation.

(v. 30). Normally the host of the home does this, but this stranger was being his normal self. Jesus made every home he was invited to the Lord's home; every table he sat at, the Lord's table. He became the host, not presumptuously, but humbly taking the initiative, sharing his life, breaking his body for the broken people around him. He came not to be served, but to serve and give his life as a ransom for people. Jesus always gave thanks to his Father *for all things*, finding him *in all things, even in the cross of Calvary*.

"... and [he] began to give it to them. Then their eyes were opened and they recognised him" (vs 30–31). Was it his usual way of breaking the bread that gave him away? Or did the Spirit open their eyes? Or did they see the nailprints as he gave them the bread? Maybe all three. The reality is: The Spirit opened their eyes to see Jesus in the breaking of bread – they encountered the Risen Lord, completing their (emotional-perceptional) healing, bringing great joy.

Then *"he disappeared from their sight"* (v. 31). Ironically, this gave them even greater joy! His disappearance confirmed that he *had* appeared – he was alive and present. God's *manifest* presence is not permanent yet. We know this as it manifests then "disappears". God says: "It is over to you. Having been healed by power encounter, continue to live by faith and not by sight, till we meet face to face."

Their response was community reflection and accountability. As they reflected, they realised Jesus had been with them all along, healing them when they were not even conscious of it. Much emotional-perceptional healing takes place that way, as a growth process, a journey with the abiding but hidden presence. Now and then God opens our eyes by his manifest presence in the breaking of bread, by power encounter and other forms of sacramental ministry. Then we see the Lord for who he really is, and we see the healing and transformation that has happened along the way. They *"got up and returned at once to Jerusalem"* (v. 33) to reflect with, and account to, the community of disciples. By mutual storytelling and comparing notes, they confirmed the truth: "The Lord is risen indeed!" (v. 34). The end picture is a radical reversal of the opening picture.[10]

---

[10]Peter's experience of the crucifixion is similar: From his calling in the boat overflowing with fish (Luke 5) to his threefold denial of Christ around the fire and the crucifixion, and Jesus' post-resurrection appearance where he re-enacted Luke 5

Part Three: Praxis

A contemporary example

I was speaking at a youth camp when something dramatic happened during ministry time. A female voice screamed, "No! Get away from me! No! Leave me! Get away!" Through the dim lights I saw a group of young people gathered around a teenage girl. They had been ministering to her with outstretched hands. When she screamed, they upped the verbal tempo and began rebuking a demon. Someone was shouting, "Keep quiet, Satan! Come out of her in Jesus' name!" They all stretched their hands towards her and raised their voices in common cause. Then she screamed again.

I immediately felt disturbed. Her shriek was filled with fear and pain. "Lord, what's going on there?" My sense was to intervene. As I moved across the hall toward the scene, God answered: I saw a vision superimposed over the growing commotion – a picture of a dark room with a quivering little girl inside. That confirmed my inner sense that it was not a demonic situation, and that I needed to get the group to back off and give her space.

Having done that, I gently asked her if I could sit down and check if she was okay. She sat whimpering in the corner in a foetal position, knees tucked up under her chin. Slowly she nodded her head. I waited till she regained her composure. I asked her what had happened. She did not know: "I just freaked out!" Then I asked, "When you were a little girl, were you ever locked in a dark room, scared and alone?" Her body began to shiver and shake and shudder as she sobbed from her guts. The fear and pain at the core of her being was being exposed, was "coming up", as it were.

She calmed enough for me to ask what had happened to her in that room. Through gentle encouragement and interrupted, tearful dialogue, she came out with it. At the age of seven, she went to a friend's party, where she was pushed into a dark room. Some adults were having an orgy. Hands stretched out toward her to grope her. She could not get out the room and screamed, "No! Get away from me! Leave

---

(John 21), restoring Peter around the fire by a threefold question, confession and affirmation. By reliving, re-interpreting and reversing, Jesus healed Peter. See also how Joseph re-interpreted his adverse experiences in the light of God's purposes (Genesis 37:19–28; 39:1–23; 43:6; 45:1–8).

me alone!" She slowly finished her sad story. I pointed out God's love to her: He had "set up" the dimly lit hall and the crowding in of well-meaning outstretched hands, which led to a relapse into a "body memory", causing an automatic scream. She understood and wept. I said to her, "Through this God is saying: 'Face this bad memory, this abuse. I am here to help, to heal you.'" She nodded her head in agreement.

I led her through an exercise in which she went back to the traumatic experience in her mind and imagination. It was painful. "Why did Jesus let it happen?" she asked. I replied, "I do not know, but it wasn't him. Evil did that to you. Let's invite the Lord into this painful memory." She re-entered the experience in her mind and we invited Jesus into it. "Is Jesus doing or saying anything?" I asked. "The room is filling with light!" He came to her and pushed all the groping hands away. He bent over to comfort her, and spoke to her … she wept. Reliving the incident by reinterpreting it in the light of Jesus' intervening presence, step by step, brought her inner peace. It helped her come to terms with what happened, taking the pain out of the memory.[11]

I spoke cleansing and healing to her mind and memory, and especially to her emotions and body. I broke any sense of false guilt, if she blamed herself for what had happened – common in abuse survivors. With encouragement, she verbally forgave the men before God. I shared Scriptures with her: God works in all things for her good – he could make her a better person through this bad experience. I encouraged her to see a counsellor to deepen her healing journey.

A step-by-step method of healing

Once you have identified a form of emotional sickness – the effects of past hurts – as a cause of the person's brokenness, apply the following steps. You can apply them to yourself in God's presence to heal your own emotional dis-ease.

---

[11]H. Leuner named this method "guided imagery", in "Guided Affected Imagery", *American Journal of Psychotherapy*, 1969, 23, pp. 4–22. Ruth Stapleton and Betty Tapscott practised this in *Christian* healing; similar to a recent Christian therapy called Theophostics by Edward Smith (some Evangelicals criticise it as "unbiblical"); see also William Backus's Misbelief Therapy. The authors are in the Bibliography.

Part Three: Praxis

1. *Face it:* Help the person see the underlying cause of their malady so that they can acknowledge and own it, and work together with you in healing it.
2. *Revisit and re-interpret it with Jesus:* Talk and pray through the painful experience or bad memory before God. Invite Jesus into the incident, encouraging the person to see him in their imagination, re-interpreting what happened in the light of his intervening presence. Help them picture Jesus taking their pain on himself on the cross as they drink healing from the fountain that flowed from his pierced side.
3. *Expose and break any lie of Satan:* Affirm basic truths to break the lies of Satan: God did *not* abandon them, though they might have felt he did. What happened was evil, from Satan, not from God. God does not tempt us with evil (James 1:13). God allowed it for reasons we do not now know. He works in it for our good; he *can* bring meaning and value out of it (Romans 8:28). God does not allow us to be tested beyond what we can bear; he always provides a way out (1 Corinthians 10:13). God does not necessarily save us *from* pain, but *through* pain. If they were a victim of circumstance or other people's sin, they must *not* blame themselves for what happened. There is no hurt beyond God's power to heal and no sin beyond his ability to forgive, so they can forgive the sinner(s) in God's name.
4. *Give and receive forgiveness:* Talk and pray them through God's forgiveness for any sense of guilt they may have in terms of what happened, especially with regard to sinful choices they might have made in reaction to what happened. Help them forgive the person(s) who perpetrated the evil against them. Jesus made it clear that they can, and must, forgive the person *for God's sake*, because he forgives their sins – not matter how "big" the sin (Matthew 18:21–35). If they do not "forgive from the heart" those who have sinned against them, they will be tortured by unforgiveness: the growing torment of anger, bitterness and hatred, with all its consequences.

Explain that *forgiveness is a decision of the will before God* to let it go, to "cancel the person's debt", the literal biblical meaning. We "cancel debt" by "writing off" their sin (they owe us nothing), releasing the person to God in forgiveness. The obedient decision to forgive causes our feelings to catch up to the freedom and joy of forgiveness. Forgiveness is unconditional, even if the person has not apologised or taken responsibility for what they did. They may need to do Matthew 18:15f with the perpetrator(s) – with mediators if necessary – to confront and forgive "from the heart". I elaborate on forgiveness and Matthew 18 in relational healing in Chapter 18.[12]

5. *Break the power of any soul tie, emotional attachment or dependence:* Once they have received and given forgiveness – and you have spoken cleansing to them in Jesus' name – address harmful emotional attachments, dependencies and soul ties to anything or anyone. These often come about via the psycho-emotional wounding and due to our sinful choices. Rejection can lead to adultery which creates a soul tie, binding the person in various ways. Ask the person to renounce the dependency or soul tie, then "cut" them free by speaking the word of the kingdom.

6. *Break the power of any curse or bloodline:* Address any inherited effect of the bloodline that may have caused, or come to light as a result of, the psycho-emotional brokenness. A family history of alcoholism, violence, sexual perversion, child molestation, or other types of emotional-social abuse means the person has been a victim of their parents' sin and excesses. It will be evident in constant related struggles and sicknesses in the person's life, with the force of a curse or spiritual bondage and genetic predisposition. The person must renounce them and break their power in Jesus' name. Cut them free from their bloodline and "plug" them into Jesus' bloodline.

7. *Speak healing to the wounded area:* Pour the oil of the Holy Spirit, as it were, into the areas that have been opened up in this "ministry operation". Speak soothing recovery to the raw and exposed emotions. Speak God's peace and well-being: "*Shalom* be on you now; *shalom* to your emotions, to your mind, to your

---

[12]Forgiveness is a huge issue, marked by misbeliefs and subjective struggles. All the authors mentioned in footnote 1 deal with forgiveness; Matthew Linn's *Healing Life's Hurts* is especially helpful.

body." Speak resurrection to the emotions that were damaged. In bringing the ministry to a close, rededicate them to the Lord; especially their emotions and body. How to do this, in the next chapter.

8. *Talk through a follow-up healing process:* After-ministry care is important. Map out a way forward for them to further their healing. It means community belonging, more prayer ministry, counselling if needed and especially renewing their minds in God's Word – putting off the old patterns and putting on their new nature in Christ (Romans 12:1–2; Colossians 3:1–17).

Personal reflection, application and group discussion

1. What has been your understanding of emotional sickness and healing up to this point? Having read this chapter, has anything changed?
2. What has been your own experience of emotional pain? Of healing a past hurt, bad memory, an emotional dependence or soul tie?
3. Do you agree with my explanation of emotions, and how wounding takes place, with the consequent effects if not dealt with? What is missing, in your opinion, from my discussion on emotional wounding and healing?
4. What did you learn, that was new for you, from the biblical story of the two disciples on the road to Emmaus?
5. Take time to piece together and record in your journal the elements in Peter's story of calling, denial, restoration and emotional healing. I gave the broad strokes and references in footnote 10.
6. Plan to do this chapter with your home group. Encourage each person to think about their own story, life journey. Have a time of sharing stories of emotional wounding and damage. Apply the steps to minister healing to one another and see what God does. Reflect on what you learnt.

16

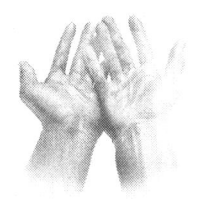

Method 3: Ministering deliverance from demonisation

*"Whoever believes and is baptised will be saved ...
And these signs will accompany those who believe:
In my name they will drive out demons ..."*
– Jesus, Mark 16:16–17

The reality of evil

This area of healing is difficult to accept or relate to as a common life reality. To "have a demon" is unthinkable. Our Western worldview dismisses it, giving it a social stigma. *"If* it is real, it only happens in primitive societies." The stigma is also due to the King James translation of "demon *possession*" in the stories of demonic expulsions. "Possession" conjures up terrifying pictures in people's minds. The Greek word so translated is *diamonizomai,* literally "demonised" – to be under the *influence* of a demon. The type and degree of influence is seen by the context and content of the stories (see Chapter 3, Psychic illness).

Part Three: Praxis

This issue is taboo for most people, as they do not believe in the existence of *personal* evil, in Satan and his demons. *If* acknowledged, evil is metaphorical and principle, *not* literal and personal. The New Testament stories of demonic expulsion are seen as "primitive myths" or "spiritualised" into symbolic teachings. The devil has deceived people into believing he does not exist! Hence many people are demonised without knowing it – they tolerate, accommodate and make peace with their inner darkness, compulsions and drivenness.

The other extreme is obsessive belief in personal evil – also a form of deception. Preoccupation and fascination with evil results in demonisation, in worship of Satan and his demons by glorifying him, making him responsible for everything. The balanced biblical approach is: "Do not look for a demon behind every bush. But if you find one, do not beat about the bush! Drive it out."

Scripture speaks of Satan, Beelzebub, the devil, fallen angels, principalities and powers, rulers, authorities, demons and its diminutive *daimonion,* little demon or god, wicked and unclean spirits.[1] Satan is Lucifer, the fallen archangel, who rules his kingdom via his hordes (above list). The origin of fallen angels is clear, but the origin of demons is not stated. Many think they are one and the same. Jews in the intertestamental period believed demons came from the angelic/human interrelations of Genesis 6:1–4 (1 Enoch 6–12; Jubilees 10). Others speculate that demons are spirits from a pre-Adamic race.[2] They are all spirit beings – literal persons without bodies, with will, emotions, intelligence, and speech. Demons/evil spirits seem to be "splintered" personalities (by God's judgment) with an insatiable appetite to inhabit human bodies so that they can express their particular appetite identity (hate, lying, lust).[3] Jesus "bound" and defeated

---

[1] Matthew 8:31; 12:24–28; Mark 1:26; Luke 4:41; 8:2; Ephesians 6:12; Colossians 1:16; 1 John 3:8; Revelation 12:4–11.
[2] See Derek Prince, *They Shall Expel Demons* (Tamil Nadu: Rhema Books, 1998), p. 91.
[3] Judges 9:23 (evil, treacherous); 1 Samuel 16:14–23; 18:10 (evil, tormenting, rage); 1 Kings 22:22; 2 Chronicles 18:20–22 (lying, deceiving); Isaiah 19:14 (distorting, perverse); Isaiah 29:9–10 (disorienting, slumber); Isaiah 61:3 (despair, heaviness); Hosea 4:10–12; 5:4 (adultery, prostitution); Zechariah 13:2 (impurity); Mark 9:17 (mute); Mark 9:25 (deaf and mute); Luke 13:11 (infirmity, crippling); Acts 16:16 (divination, foretelling); 1 Timothy 4:1 (deceiving); 1 John 4:3, 6 (antichrist, falsehood).

them in his life, death and resurrection. We experience this victory as "already" and "not yet"; therefore we are in an ongoing war with evil.

Understanding demonisation and deliverance[4]

Demonisation can be defined as a relational influence by an evil spirit, in one form or another, to one degree or another, in one or other area of human personality. The New Testament describes it in three ways: to "have" a demon; to be "in" a demon; or to be demonised – *diamonizomia,* the common usage. These are *not* spatial concepts: Is a demon "in" or "out" or "on" or "attached to" a person? The Hebraic idea behind these usages is relational – the influence that the demon has over the person or that the person has yielded to the demon,[5] ranging from mild to severe, from "driven" to "bound" (Luke 8:29; 13:16). Various words are used to describe the nature of the demonisation.

Can a Christian be demonised? A Christian cannot be "possessed"; it implies ownership and Jesus "owns" Christians. We can be "demonised" in one or other area of our lives if we give Satan a "foothold" (Ephesians 4:26–27). We must be aware of Satan's schemes so that he does not outwit us (2 Corinthians 2:10–11). If we do not rule over our own spirit, if we "lack self-control", then we are "like a city whose walls are broken down" (Proverbs 25:28). The enemy can enter and set up a "stronghold" in an area of our personhood. How do we know if it is a demonisation and not just another problem? By

---

[4]For resources see Bibliography: Basham, Friesen, Green, Horrobin, MacNutt, Montgomery, Prince, Scanlan, and Wimber. I am especially indebted to Derek Prince, *They Shall Expel Demons*, for this section. Friesen's *Uncovering the Mystery of MPD* is important with regard to discernment, diagnosis and ministry to multiple personality disorder (integrating the personalities) as distinct from direct demonisation (driving out personalities). Space does not allow me to discuss multiple personality disorder (now known as dissociative identity disorder) and Satanic Ritual Abuse (SRA), which Friesen does adequately. Suffice it to say, we must train our people, ministry teams and counsellors to know when they need to refer people for skilled and professional help before we damage them by acting on what we don't know, e.g. trying to "cast out" a legitimate part of the wounded dissociated self.

[5]The same as "having" or "being filled with" the *Holy* Spirit in Chapters 9 and 11 – the relational influence of yieldedness to the Spirit. Spirit (*ruach* and *pneuma*) is wind or breath: it is invisible, *but seen by its effects on the person*, as we see the effects of the wind on the trees, for better or worse.

identifying the source:

- *The world*: The pressures of life referred to in emotional healing, overcome by our faith in Jesus (John 15:18f; 16:33; 1 John 5:4).
- *The flesh*: The lower nature with its corrupted desires referred to in spiritual healing. We repent from, and "crucify", these sinful tendencies (Colossians 3:5–10).
- *The devil*: If these two – that the devil uses *indirectly* to oppose us – are not overcome by faith and spiritual discipline, it is almost certainly a *direct* demonisation, which must be renounced and driven out.

What are the symptoms of demonisation – how do we diagnose a demon? We need to be careful in our discernment as demonisation can "present" in the form of spiritual, emotional, physical and social diseases. There are ten verbs that help us diagnose the effects or signs of direct demonic activity:

1. *Entice:* An independent, persistent enticement towards certain things, like stealing. It goes beyond "natural" enticement of temptation (James 1:13–15).
2. *Harass:* Demons victimise/harass us via our weaknesses, causing sickness (Matthew 9:36) and things to go wrong beyond reasonable explanation.
3. *Torment:* Demons torture and torment beyond our ability to stop it – often through unforgiveness (Matthew 18:34; 2 Corinthians 2:10–11). It can be physical torment (pain), mental (fear of insanity) or spiritual ("You have committed the unpardonable sin").
4. *Compel:* Irrationally compulsive and controlling behaviour, like compulsive gossip, eating, drinking, lying. This produces chemical reactions in the brain which lead to dependencies and addictions – entrance points for demons.
5. *Enslave:* The fruit of compulsions. Demons enslave people to habits (pornography), substances (drugs), and to people (dependence-dominance).
6. *Defile:* Demons are "unclean spirits" that defile the mind,

imagination and mouth by filthy thoughts, pictures and words (even when praying!).
7. *Deceive:* Forms of destructive self-deception and deception of others, primarily via *spiritual* deception in terms of erroneous doctrines and religious beliefs (1 Timothy 4:1–5).
8. *Discourage:* The Holy Spirit never discourages; he convicts and encourages. Demons discourage, leading to accusation, condemnation and despair – to the point of suicide by a spirit of death (Isaiah 61:3; Revelation 12:10–11).
9. *Attack:* Demons attack through circumstances and people, especially via emotional wounding and weakness in our bodies (tiredness and sicknesses).
10. *In summary – restlessness:* If there is one symptom characteristic of the presence and work of demons, it is constant restlessness or drivenness.

What are the causes of demonisation – how does it take place? If we understand what is going on, we can submit to God, resist the devil, and he *will* flee from us (James 4:7). But demons work on us over time, weakening our will through various means (listed below), for both voluntary and involuntary demonisation, through invitation and invasion:

1. *Family background, occult and false religions:* The idolatry of false religions and occult practices are "sins of the parents" that affect the children (Exodus 20:3–5). They pass on spiritual strongholds and curses via the bloodline. The children must be delivered from them. We also bring curses upon ourselves by repeated sinful choices.[6] And all forms of *direct personal involvement* with the occult and idolatrous religions open the person to demonisation.
2. *Strong prenatal and childhood experiences:* Rejection in the womb, fear, violence and abuse in the home can lead to demonisations.

---

[6]Derek Prince lists seven signs that a curse may be at work, *They Shall Expel Demons*, p. 210: mental or emotional breakdowns; repeated or chronic sicknesses (especially hereditary); barrenness or repeated miscarriages and related female problems; marriage breakdown and family alienation; continual financial brokenness; being "accident prone", and a family history of suicides or unnatural or untimely deaths.

3. *Through sinful acts or habits:* Sometimes a single deliberate sinful act opens you to demonisation. When Judas decided to betray Jesus, "then Satan entered him" (Luke 22:3). Generally prolonged personal sin leads to demonisation.
4. *Trauma and sustained emotional pressure:* Spirits of fear, depression and hopeless can gain access through sudden emotional shock and terror, like accidents, rape and violent attack. Other spirits enter over time via persistent, unrelenting pressure.
5. *Binding oaths, soul ties and dependencies:* Demonisation can come from making ungodly binding oaths to people, organisations and beliefs (secret organisations like Freemasonry and cults). It can also come from strong soul ties via domineering relationships and other forms of dependencies (drugs).
6. *Idle words and inner vows:* Idle words are not innocent. What we *habitually* say has power (Matthew 12:36–37). "I wish I were dead!" invites a spirit of death. Inner vows, often due to hurt ("I will never trust again"), can lead to demonisation.

What areas of personality become demonised? Through lack of self-control and other weaknesses, demons break down our "walls", our inner defences and personality, seeking to influence, infest, drive and destroy us. They work in gangs: One is the door-opener and the "related others" gain a foothold – rejection lets in self-pity, loneliness, despair and even suicide. Anger is accompanied by aggression, hatred, rage and even murder. Sometimes a person is so broken and demonised that their personality and defences need to be totally rebuilt after deliverance. There are seven areas of personality that become demonised. This summarises my understanding of demonisation:

1. *Spirituality:* Our spiritual capacity and formation can be demonised via deception, erroneous beliefs, idolatry, religious spirits and occult practices.
2. *Emotions and attitudes:* They can be demonised through negative sinful moods and choices, as they become habitual, obsessive and driven.
3. *The mind:* This is the main battlefield (2 Corinthians 10:4–6; Philippians 4:6–9). Demons of fear or lust control our imagination (fantasy world). Doubt, unbelief, indecision, confusion and

insanity can torment our thoughts.
4. *The tongue:* The tongue is demonised through habitual, and then compulsive, lying, exaggeration, slander, gossip, criticism and being foul-mouthed.
5. *Sexuality:* Sex is God's good gift; it is not dirty. Because it is such a strong drive, God has set boundaries for its practice for our own good. It is a prime target of Satan – if he can gain control of it, he can wreck people and relationships. *Compulsive and addictive* pornography, fantasy, masturbation, adultery, fornication, homosexuality, lesbianism, paedophilia and other perversions are generally demonisations of our sexuality.
6. *Physical appetites:* Not only the sexual appetite, but any God-given appetite or desire can be demonised by habitually "giving them over" to sinful ways: eating (obesity), drinking (alcoholism), excessive sleeping. "Uncrucified flesh" (Paul's language) attracts demons like vultures to a carcass.
7. *Physical body:* Demons attack the body through weaknesses and sicknesses like epilepsy, muteness, blindness and curvature of the spine (Mark 9:17ff; Matthew 9:32f; 12:22f; Luke 13:10ff). We must distinguish between these causes (hysteria) and organic and functional causes of physical illness.

What is deliverance? It is the act or process of "driving out demons", as quoted at the head of this chapter. It is freeing the person from the destructive influence of an evil spirit. We do this on the basis of Jesus' defeat of Satan in his life, death and resurrection, by using his authority – pronouncing God's kingdom and commanding in Jesus' name – and the Spirit's power – giftings of discernment and faith. Jesus taught us to pray daily for our own deliverance: "Lead us not into temptation, *but deliver us from the evil one*" (Matthew 6:13).

A biblical example

The healing of the Gerasene demoniac (Mark 5:1–20)

This is an extreme case of demonisation. Every area of his life was affected: He lived in caves and tombs among the dead, cut off from *social relationship*; he slashed himself *physically* and tore his chains apart; he was tormented *emotionally* and *mentally* (with insanity), often screaming out loud; and he was cut off *spiritually* from the God of Israel. Although he was so severely controlled by "an evil spirit" (v. 2), he could still choose to seek help. When he saw Rabbi Yeshua *"from a distance, he ran and fell on his knees in front of him"* (v. 6). The truth is that, no matter how severe the demonisation, we can choose to turn to Jesus for help. He obviously must have heard about this particular Rabbi (his compassion and miracles) to have come to him.

"He shouted at the top of his voice, 'What do you want with me, Jesus, Son of the Most High God? Swear to God that you will not torture me!'" (v. 7). The man spoke (or shouted), but it was the demon that spoke through his voice. This is common when demons manifest, when pushed into the open by God's presence. Jesus represented God's presence and judgment of evil; they reacted in fear of their eternal punishment. As Christ-followers, we too bring God's presence, representing his judgment on evil. Demons will hide in people's bodies until they are pushed into the open. Then they shriek, talk, or perform all sorts of physical manifestations to challenge authority, negotiate, distract and induce fear.

"For Jesus was saying to him, 'Come out of this man, you evil spirit!'" (v. 8). The grammar implies an ongoing battle. Jesus commanded the demon to leave, but it resisted by trying evasive tactics. Demons commonly do this, but like Jesus, we must refuse prolonged dialogue with demons. Jesus asked him: *"What is your name?"* (v. 9). This caused the demon to identify itself. It was believed that knowing the demon's name gave authority over it – true up to a point. It is knowing and using *Jesus'* name that is the source of our authority. However, knowing the nature of demonisation (to name it) helps in the process of deliverance.

"'My name is Legion', he replied, 'for we are many'" (v. 9). The "my/we" shows gang activity. Weaker ones go easily; the "strong man" will resist till the end. When it goes, the whole pack normally leaves with it. A legion was a battalion of 6 000 Roman soldiers. Whether the man was literally infested with 6 000 demons, we do not know – it reveals our unbelievable capacity for spirit accommodation.

"He begged Jesus again and again not to send them out of the area"

(v. 10). Demons are fearful of being sent to eternal punishment, the Abyss of confinement for Satan and his hordes (Luke 8:31; Revelation 20:1f). God has not given us authority to send them there! Demons seem to operate in allocated areas, which they get to know – the people and patterns – becoming disoriented and ineffective in new areas. When they come out of a person, they wander around "in a dry place seeking rest" (Luke 11:24–26). If they do not find rest, they try to re-enter the person's body (their former "house"), bringing other spirits with them. They are so desperate not be "homeless" that they will settle for pigs' bodies! *"Send us among the pigs; allow us to go into them"* (v. 12). Jesus obliged. The two thousand pigs reacted, stampeding to their death. This revealed the reality of spirits entering material bodies and their destructive nature. They cannot automatically enter *human* bodies against our will; they entered the pigs, not the people standing there. Jesus expelled the demons by command (vs 8, 13).

The people found the man *"dressed and in his right mind"* (v. 15). His dignity was restored, mentally, emotionally, socially and spiritually. He told his family and friends what the Lord had done for him, and word spread throughout the area (v. 20) – it affected the entire region, socially, economically, and spiritually. God's kingdom came with power, defeating Satan and his hordes.[7]

A contemporary example

I asked my brother-in-law, Robin Snelgar, to share his story in his own words.

> It started with a problem of anger as a young boy: Through a brutally abusive stepmother; a father who refused to protect me; being discarded in a boarding school, where I was bullied and beaten in the name of "corporal punishment", and sexually abused. My inability to defend myself became an obsession. I learnt to distrust people as relationship seemed to bring nothing but pain and betrayal. My anger grew steadily and became volcanic, sitting in my belly like a fire of hatred. Sometimes I

---

[7] The deliverance stories are instructive: Matthew 9:27–34; 12:22–29; Mark 1:21–28; 7:24–30; 9:14–29; Acts 16:16–21.

would explode in violent fits of rage.

At university I found freedom through weight training and rugby, causing those who may otherwise have "messed with me" to fear me. Paradoxically I resented them when they stared at me and talked about my size. My relationship with girlfriends resulted in a few abortions, which reinforced my resentment and anger. They were **my** kids being killed. The sense of helplessness at not having a say in their "lives" drove me into complete rebellion. I got married – we had a traumatic relationship. The fact that my wife could not fall pregnant made me feel: "Well, I have had my share of children, and I am sure 'god' is not going to give me any more; but hell, it is infuriating!"

I felt I had absolutely no control over my life – it seemed to spiral all the time, and only downwards. While busy completing my doctorate, pushing weight training and living on a Spartan diet, my anger grew into a giant. It abusively threw its weight around in frequent tantrums. Then slowly I became physically weaker and weaker, and eventually it was discovered that I had cancer. It was very serious, detected too late. Terror came on me. I tried to run from it in every way. How could life be so unfair, so damned mean? And this "loving god" that everyone kept referring to – was this his idea of "love"? One day, standing in the shower, I balled up my fists, looked up and screamed, "Come on, come down here and take me on. What is your problem? Come on, take me on!" One day my father took me to a small church for prayer, and God miraculously healed me of cancer – can you believe it?

I continued to feel so out of control that **somehow** I had to take control of **something** in my life. I became obsessive compulsive, superstitiously believing that by controlling my behaviour, I could control everything. I became almost immobilised unless I obeyed the obsessive-compulsive rituals I had developed. The result was anorexia/bulimia. The point is: In trying to take control, I lost more control. Being aware of this, I began telling my family that someone else was controlling me. That "being" grew – it was easy to relate to another being, to talk to him about the issues and give up responsibility for life. After all, he "controlled" me, and there was nothing I could do about it.

Eventually, I was institutionalised. They called it "paranoid schizophrenia". I simply called him "Nibor" (my name spelt backwards). My experiences in the mental hospital fed my mania – this was like taking Satan to his feeding ground. I was institutionalised three times, and had become so openly aggressive that I ended up in "the cage" (a padded cell-like room). I had my own language, form of writing, and peculiar behaviour – all of which seemed very intriguing to the psychiatrist. He ignored "Nibor", who was so real to me! I felt as though I was burning up on the inside, the only way I can describe how I felt all the time. And I was incredibly restless. It was as though a groan was constantly in my mouth waiting to be uttered. I could not find any form of peace with my head in a constant state of funk (not a result of medication; I never took the medication I was given as I was far too paranoid, too suspicious of the psychiatrist).

At that time my wife became a Christian, and I met her pastor (Oscar). He had been involved in deliverance over the years, but I was not interested in that. Nor did he believe that I was demonised – so manipulative and sly had I become. One day, out of the blue, while agonising over life, I felt a small bit of sanity, as though the sun had broken through the clouds just for a short time. I shouted to my wife to call Oscar. Fortunately Oscar came, but he did not realise that he had to pray for deliverance. I screamed at him that I could not continue with this "Nibor" burning me up. He began to pray for me. As soon as he used the words "the blood of Jesus" and laid his hand on my head, I felt as though something rose up in my chest and expanded within me, with nowhere to go. I jumped into the air, although I am sure my legs did not do the jumping. I landed on the carpet on my back and went into a convulsion. I remember that I had opened my mouth to shout Oscar's name, but it was a long protracted scream. I was vomiting, but there was no vomit as we know it – but something was coming out of me.

*I always felt that I wanted to utter deep groans (that which was "sitting in my mouth" all the time); gibberish normally came from my mouth in those moments. If similar utterances occurred at the time of deliverance, it would not have surprised me. There were a couple of demons present as they addressed Oscar (it is difficult to recall details as I was "fuzzy" minded during those days). He ignored this completely and continued to pray in the name of Jesus. When I sat up, I felt the old terror of my life almost consuming me. I attempted to shout this out to Oscar. Immediately he laid his hand on my head again, and I felt as though a long and agonizing groan was literally **sucked** out of my body.*

This last long groan brought such relief! What peace! I cried in a way that I had been unable to for such a long, long time. To just lie and not feel the "burning", and to relax into a deep sleep – it was like heaven. After what seemed like a long time, I regained my composure and got up. Oscar talked and prayed with me, leading me to faith in Jesus Christ. I know that the change in my personality was immediate and visible to all who knew me. They commented on how my face had changed – I began smiling again. The compulsive swearing, aggression, anorexia/bulimia had gone. Although I was free, I knew I had a long way to go to rebuild my life and personality, and to grow into my full freedom in Christ.[8]

A step-by-step method of deliverance

If, in the course of ministering to a person, you discern a demonisation (God shows it to you); you observe signs of its presence (the symptoms listed above); the demon manifests, or the person asks for deliverance from a certain demon, once you have diagnosed demonisation, take the following steps. By applying these steps, you can also do "self-deliverance" for demonisation.

1. *Affirm faith in Jesus as Lord:* Get the person to affirm verbally their

---

[8]Robin is Professor and Head of Department of Industrial Psychology at Nelson Mandela Metropolitan University, Port Elizabeth, South Africa.

Method 3: *Ministering deliverance from demonisation*

faith in Jesus as Lord over their lives. If they are not believers, lead them to faith in Christ. Often that causes the demons to leave – with or without manifestation. If you baptise them and lay hands on them to receive the Spirit, the demons will either leave or manifest.

2. *"Humble yourself"; acknowledge the need:* The person must own their need for deliverance, humbling themselves before God by acknowledging their demonisation. Some who came to Jesus were so desperate that they *begged* for deliverance, not minding their dignity or what people thought of them. Pride and stigma, self-consciousness and control hinder deliverance. The person must trust God and submit fully to him (James 4:6–7; 1 Peter 5:5–6).

3. *Confess and repent from any known sin:* Verbal confession and turning away from any known sin is key to deliverance (1 John 1:9; Proverbs 28:13). Sinful entanglements are "legal ground" for demonisation and their refusal to leave.

4. *Receive and give forgiveness (and restitution):* The person must
   a) receive and affirm God's forgiveness in faith;
   b) forgive others who have sinned against them – unforgiveness blocks deliverance. In fact, over time it invites demonisation, and
   c) seek forgiveness from others if their sin against the other is linked to their demonisation. This might include making restitution. I have seen a man who had stolen goods be delivered from the compulsive demons only when he returned the goods and made full restitution.

5. *Renounce and revoke the demonisation:* The person must renounce any other grounds of demonisation: cut any soul tie that may hold them; renounce occult and idolatrous religious involvement; revoke any curse or inner vow that may bind them, and break evil attachments or enslavements that they have yielded to. At times this step involves removing and burning books, fetishes or objects that link the person to the demonisation (Deuteronomy 7:26). Years ago we drove demons out of a few sangomas – African spiritist herbalists. Only when we had removed the goat-

skin fetishes and other symbols, and burned them, did the demons scream and leave.

6. *Stand on God's Word and command the demon to leave:* Take your stand on the authority of God's Word and drive the demon out with a command. The person can also command the demon to leave. If there is resistance, I ask the person to look at me and keep eye contact as I address whatever I sense God shows me. That way they manifest and leave as I command. If necessary, we can command the demon to name itself. Then expel it by name.

7. *Expel and exhale – work with what happens:* Encourage the person to cooperate with the expulsion. Demons come out mainly through the mouth – "spirit" is "breath". Exhaling is the common way of expelling an evil spirit, as inhaling is the common way of receiving the *Holy* Spirit. They can also come out via other orifices, as in a "pop" of the ear and extremities of the body, as in shaking the fingers. Lesser spirits leave with little or no manifestation as we flow in words of knowledge rebuking various things – people may blink, sigh, yawn, belch, cough, sway, tremble, shake or fall. In this sense much more deliverance happens than we realise. Heavy-weight demons manifest in confrontation, resistance, aggression, voices, pleading, and various evasive tactics. They do not leave without a battle, coming out with shrieking, violent body reactions and retching. These deliverances are infrequent. My point is: People block the expulsion by not cooperating, like verbally praying when they need to stop speaking and exhale the demon.

8. *Persist till freedom comes:* Diligent persistence is needed when the demons resist. Do not enter into extended dialogue with demons. Avoid their evasive tactics by insisting they leave in Jesus' name – they *are* defeated by the blood of Christ. They can move around in the body – a spirit of pain does this. Persist in driving it to a body extremity and out. Often a demon will go and the person will relax, only for another to manifest. It can go on till all the demons are out. Usually the person will know when they are free.

If the demon does not go, after extensive time, or if the person is too exhausted, close the session and make another time for deliverance after preparation and prayer. A major reason why some people are not delivered is lack of proper preparation, where we weed out what prevents deliverance: wrong motives, attention seeking, theological hang-ups, hidden sin and lack of repentance, failure to break with the occult and other "spiritual ties". There is also the mystery of right timing for some, while others seem to be an ongoing battlefield of spiritual powers.

9. *Bless and rededicate their body as the temple of the Holy Spirit:* After deliverance I always speak *Shalom* (peace and protection) over them. I encourage them to breathe in deeply and receive the Holy Spirit, "filling up" the places "left empty" by the demonisation. I rededicate their body to the Holy Spirit by speaking a "blessing" over them (recorded below). My wife and I learnt it from Derek Prince. We often speak it over people after ministry. I bless the main body parts by name. In so doing I have seen spirits that were still "hiding", flushed out.

10. *After-ministry care:* Let them express how they feel. Clarify any confusion or concern. Reassure them if need be, and set another time for preparation and more ministry. Warn and prepare them for the demons to attempt a return (Matthew 12:43–45). To keep their deliverance, instruct them to "occupy their house" by
    a) seeking further emotional and other healing;
    b) renewing their minds and living by God's Word;
    c) cultivating thanksgiving and intimacy with God;
    d) committing to community belonging, accountability and support, and
    e) daily putting on "the whole armour of God" (Ephesians 6:13–18).

A confession and blessing over the body

My body is the temple of the Holy Spirit.
It has been redeemed, cleansed and sanctified, by the blood of Jesus.
The devil has no power over me, no hold within me, no unsettled claim against me.
All has been settled by the blood of Jesus.
I overcome Satan by the blood of the Lamb, by the word of my testimony,
and I do not love my life so much as to shrink from death.
The Lord is for my body and my body is for the Lord.
I am joined to the Lord, so I am one spirit with him.
I am not my own; I have been bought with a price, with the precious blood of Jesus.
Therefore I will glorify God with my body.
(1 Corinthians 6:13, 17, 19–20; Revelation 12:11; 1 Peter 1:19)

Personal reflection, application and group discussion

1. Have *you* ever consciously been delivered from a demonisation? What was it, and how did you experience it?
2. What was your understanding of demonisation and deliverance before you read this chapter? What has changed for you?
3. Having read this chapter, are you aware of any possible demonisation in your life at present? If so, apply the steps above and free yourself from it – or seek deliverance ministry.
4. Have you ever ministered deliverance to someone else? What was the experience like? What did you learn from it?
5. An exercise: Read this chapter with your home group. Then have a time to minister deliverance to those who may be demonised in one form or another.

17

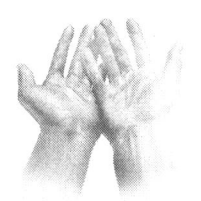

Method 4: Ministering healing to the body

*Jesus went throughout Galilee, teaching in their synagogues,
preaching the good news of the kingdom,
and healing every disease and sickness among the people.
News of him spread all over Syria and people brought to him all who
were ill with various dis-eases, those suffering severe pain,
the demonised, those having seizures,
and the paralysed, and he healed them.
Large crowds from all over the region followed him.*
— Matthew 4:23–24 RAP

This is an astounding description of Jesus' ministry of the kingdom. Matthew often said Jesus healed "every" disease and "all" the sick (8:16; 9:35; 10:1; 12:15; 14:35–36; 15:30). Healing all kinds of physical illness showed a concern for people's *material wellbeing* – a remarkable characteristic of Jesus' ministry. He gave us his authority "to heal *every* disease and sickness" (Matthew 10:1).

Part Three: Praxis

Understanding physical sickness and healing[1]

Sickness of the body has its root cause in physical or material factors, either organic or functional disorders (see Chapter 3). Healing the body is about changing and restoring the *physical* condition so that the body is restored to full function. As I have shown, physical conditions can be caused by spiritual, psycho-emotional or demonic factors. The bodily symptoms look the same, but the causes can be different. If they are not dealt with, they hinder or prevent *physical* healing from taking place, or they can cause the *physical* symptoms to "return" (as in "I have lost my healing"). They can also lead to organic damage and/or functional disorders that need to be healed.

Of all the types of healing, physical healing is simple and straightforward, but it can be the most challenging to believe in. It is easier to minister healing to what is "unseen" (inner healing), as no one knows if the healing takes place or not – it is only observable later in attitudinal, behavioural or other changes. As Jesus asked: "Which is easier; to say to the paralytic, 'Your sins are forgiven!' or 'pick up your bed and walk'?" (Mark 2:9 RAP). No one sees whether God forgives the man's sin, but everyone sees whether or not he picks up his bed and walks. If he does not walk, the credibility of the healer is in doubt (John 10:37–38).

Physical healing is tangible and verifiable – people know if and when they have been healed. That does not mean all physical healings happen immediately. Many healings are progressive, as body tissue and functions are slowly restored to wholeness. This is especially the case if related "unseen" causes are being healed. However, physical healing and raising the dead most clearly demonstrate the power of God. That is why the word "miracle" is used, "works of *power*" in the Greek. All genuine healing ultimately comes from God – he heals primarily, though not exclusively, through human and natural means, including natural and scientific medicines, and healthy lifestyles. In terms of Christian ministry, God heals the body in answer to prayer and faith, through the laying on of hands and speaking God's Word.

If we discuss *the symptoms* of physical illness, we enter the field

---

[1] See the Bibliography for Baxter, Bosworth, Brown, Endicott, Gordon, Hagin, MacNutt, Maddox, Osborn, Roberts, Simpson, Wimber.

of medical science with the many lists of organic and functional disorders that they have "discovered and described". *The causes* are also many and varied, but they can be summarised in lifestyle choices and responses, deterioration and malfunction of bodily organs, and "outside invasion" by trauma and germs (bacteria and viruses). The biblical focus is not on the symptoms and causes of sickness and healing, but on *God's power* to heal, both instantly and progressively, because it is a direct confrontation between Spirit power and material disorder.

We can *define healing of the body as the intervention of the Spirit's power in defeating bodily disorder and re-establishing God's order* (Shalom wholeness). Physical healing is a foretaste of the *bodily* resurrection from the dead: "The Spirit of him who raised Jesus from the dead … will also give life to your mortal bodies", both now in healing, and then in the resurrection (Romans 8:11). Because it is a Spirit-material power encounter, bodily sensations are commonly experienced in the healing process. It would be wrong to make them the focus of attention as God also heals without any bodily manifestations.

In summary, physical healing is a kingdom event: The future resurrection breaks into our bodies, defeating Satan's rule of mortal sickness, on the basis of Jesus' defeat of Satan in his *physical* life, death and resurrection. Physical healing also expresses God's nature: He simply loves to heal and restore people to wholeness. Jesus came to reveal YHWH's nature, who gives life in all its fullness; Satan's nature is to steal, lie, kill and destroy (John 10:10; 8:44).

A biblical example

The leper who came to Jesus (Mark 1:40–45)

This is a remarkable story of healing from an organic illness. In Jesus' day leprosy referred to various contagious skin diseases, as enumerated in Leviticus 13 and 14. This man "was covered with leprosy" (Luke 5:12), probably of the "real" kind: nodular and anaesthetic leprosy that caused large nodules under the skin, killing the nerves in parts of the body, grossly deforming and slowly rotting the flesh. It was a living death. Josephus said lepers were treated "as if they were in effect dead persons".[2] Torah gave strict laws governing the quarantining of lepers outside the walled cities and towns due to their "defilement". They had to shout: "Unclean! Unclean!" (Leviticus 13:45). The penalty for entering a city or town was forty lashes. Physical contact with a leper brought serious spiritual, ceremonial and social defilement.[3]

Leprosy had destroyed this man spiritually, mentally, emotionally, physically and socially. "When [the leper] saw Jesus" (Luke 5:12), he came to him amidst others milling around – revealing his desperation and faith – knelt down, fell with his face to the ground, and begged Jesus for healing. He broke all the religious rules and social taboos. Given what I said in footnote 3, it is astonishing that he even *dared* to come to this Rabbi – unless the more astonishing reputation of Jesus' radical compassion and healing power had preceded him. Faith comes from "hearing … the word of Christ" (Romans 10:17), leading to the leper's unorthodox actions. Jesus always responded to faith.

"*If you are willing, you can make me clean*" (v. 40). The leper believed Jesus was *able* to heal him, but he was not sure if Jesus was *willing* to heal him. Why? This is common in physical healing – God *can* heal me, but *will* he heal me now? The "if": Lord, *if* you are willing; *if* I am worthy enough; *if* I fast and pray and serve the poor, will you heal me? We cannot bargain with God. We need to believe *both* his ability *and* his loving willingness to heal, as a gift of grace and mercy. Doubt with regard to willingness is understandable: How do you face the pain and questions if you are prayed for and *not* healed? "God, why …?"

"*Filled with compassion, Jesus reached out his hands and touched the man*" (v. 41). Jesus' response was not to berate the leper for his doubt as to whether Jesus was *willing* to heal him. Rather, Jesus was moved with compassion for the man. As explained in Chapter 10, Jesus was

---

[2] Book 3, Chapter 11, verse 3, *The Works of Josephus: Complete and Unabridged*, trans. William Whiston (Peabody: Hendrickson Publishers, 1987), p. 97.

[3] "The Law enumerated sixty-one different contacts which brought defilement, and the defilement which contact with a leper brought was second only to the defilement caused by contact with a dead body," says William Barclay, *And He Had Compassion* (Edinburgh: The Saint Andrew Press, 1975), p. 35. Barclay cites the Talmud saying that Rabbi Meir would not eat an egg bought in a street where a leper had passed; other rabbis boasted that they would throw stones at lepers to chase them away; while others hid themselves or took to their heels on seeing a leper in the far distance.

Method 4: *Ministering healing to the body*

moved with a mix of *mercy* for this man and *anger* at what leprosy (the devil) had done to him. *That* moved him into action. He did the unthinkable: going against Torah prohibitions and social stigma, he tenderly touched the untouchable, without fear of defilement.[4] Rather than the flow of defilement entering Jesus, healing went from Jesus into the man – the *greater* power. What Jesus did was utterly remarkable, unheard of in all of Israel. Never underestimate the power of God's *compassion*.

"*I am willing. Be clean!*" (v. 41). Jesus indicated his willingness by touching the man, but he also gave verbal assurance of his willingness to heal the man. In so doing, Jesus represented YHWH's essential nature: healing is God's will for people. This was very different and contrary to the way other rabbis portrayed God: leprosy was defilement, even punishment from God, to be shunned at every turn.[5] Jesus used his authority and spoke the word of healing, releasing God's power.

"*Immediately the leprosy left him and he was cured*" (v. 42). It sounds so simple. At one level it is: physical healing either happens or it does not happen. Or it happens as a process, a progressive healing, therefore *repeated* ministry is helpful.

Jesus sent him away with a "strong warning" not to tell anyone about the healing, but to go and "*show yourself to the priest and offer the sacrifices that Moses commanded for your cleaning*" (v. 44). By doing this Jesus honoured Torah (Leviticus 13–14), wanting the priests to verify the healing, and to confirm the fact that only God can cure leprosy (2 Kings 5:1–14). The modern equivalent would be to work with the medical profession in the healing process. "*Instead he went out and began to talk freely, spreading the news. As a result, Jesus could no longer enter a town openly, but stayed outside in lonely places. Yet the people still came to him from everywhere*" (v. 45). This is breathtaking, showing the powerful effect of Jesus' *physical* healings.

---

[4] Jesus' touch was warm, full, lingering (Jewish style – maybe even embrace), not the momentary fingertip touch ("ET glowing finger") of many healing evangelists moving from one to the next: "Be healed! Be filled!"
[5] Suffering, sickness and sin were all connected in the Jewish mind. It would be beyond belief that God would treat a leper as Jesus did. They had not understood Isaiah 53 – that Jesus embodied it.

Part Three: Praxis

A contemporary example

I have chosen to share a documented story of physical healing from a man in another church where I was invited to preach. He wrote a five-page letter explaining what God had done for him, giving the names of doctors and telephone numbers to verify the authenticity of the healing.[6]

> *I am now 29 years of age. Approximately 15 years ago I began to notice a pain in my right leg which gradually became more and more irritating until it reached the stage where it worried me. So began a decade and a half of visits to doctors to diagnose a pain that was getting worse with the passage of time.*
>
> *At about the age of 16, I noticed that my back had started to ache as well and at times I found it quite painful to lie flat on my back on a bed. I had to deliberately relax my muscles from the base of my spine upwards to get relief. Both these conditions continued over the years and became progressively worse.*
>
> *Initial diagnosis indicated that I may have had the beginnings of diabetes, or a blood clot in my right leg. The pain in my back was attributed to spinal decay which showed up on x-rays. I also had a curvature of the spine. No immediate remedy was offered to either of these defects, so I let things go. Up to this point no fewer than three doctors had examined me and had taken x-rays.*
>
> *The pain got progressively worse so that four years ago I visited another doctor. He went through the usual tests with not much more success; until he asked if I had ever had my legs measured, or worn built-up shoes. I answered in the negative. He then measured my legs and found that my right leg was ¾ of an inch shorter than my left leg. This was subsequently confirmed by an orthopaedic specialist, to whom I was referred. As a result I got built-up shoes and wore them for three-and-a-half years.*
>
> *During this period I gave my heart to the Lord and an*

---

[6]He gave me permission to use the letter "if it can be of help to others". I have edited out unnecessary detail.

Method 4: *Ministering healing to the body*

incredible peace and joy entered my life. The long searching ended abruptly. I later joined the New Creation Community Church. At my first visit to this lovely body of people, the Lord touched me in a very powerful way. I forget what the talk was about that evening – it may well have been on healing – but I do remember at the end of it all, those with physical defects were asked to come forward.

I stood up, explained my physical handicap to the people and proceeded to receive prayer from three of the brothers present. Almost immediately I sensed a tremendous vitality enter my body, like an electric current that flowed throughout my whole being and focused onto my spine and right leg. Then a miracle happened. In front of my own eyes and the eyes of the three men (and the video camera, which I did not know was filming me until afterwards), my right leg grew! I was overcome! Shortly afterwards, as I was standing up, I felt a click in my spine and it "moved" towards the centre, all of its own accord, and the pain that had persisted for 14 years just vanished!

Since the healing I have thrown out my built-up shoes. I go running whenever I feel like it and I can relax normally with my back in any position, including propped up by straight-backed chairs which used to give me a great deal of discomfort. I really believe without question that **God** *healed me. But it is the* **inner** *healing that came out of this, which has meant more to me than anything. God has taken away grief, sorrow, anxiety, emptiness, and so many other negative aspects and replaced them with joy and fulfilment.*

From my perspective, I taught on healing and asked people with physical defects to stand. I got twos and threes to minister healing to those standing. I decided to minister to this particular man with the help of two others. On hearing his symptoms – from my experience, not from revelation – I thought it could be related to a short leg. I sat him down on the chair and measured his legs by holding both feet in my hands. Sure enough, one leg seemed shorter than the other, and we could see that he had a built-up shoe.

We laid hands on his legs and began to bless him with the

healing presence of the Holy Spirit. A visible sense of God's power came on him – he began to sigh, he moved his body and expressed emotion. We commanded the leg to grow in the name of Jesus. After commanding a few times, the leg began to grow. We watched it grow out – in a few seconds – to the same length as the other leg. Our faith was quickened and we laid hands on his head, shoulders and back, speaking healing into his body, wherever he had pain and weakness. The power of God was evidently on him. After a while we asked him to stand and test his legs and back, to walk and move and bend. He excitedly reported complete freedom from all pain, with a right sense of balance in both legs.

Subjectively, I did not have revelations or feel great faith or power in ministering to him. I often feel compassion and have learnt to follow the faintest promptings from God, but my usual experience in ministry is obedience to Jesus in quiet confidence that God will heal, mostly without sensations of faith or power.

Faith is important in physical healing, but we must avoid two extremes: A sense of faithlessness when confronted with challenging symptoms like paralysis, blindness, or full-blown AIDS (they can defeat our faith even before we begin ministry). Alternatively, we must not mistake presumption for faith by hyping people up, making claims or empty promises, raising false expectations, or trying to make something happen when evidently it is not. Rather, persistently practise the "obedience of faith" in which gifts of healings, faith and miracles often operate without subjective feelings of faith and power.

A step-by-step method to heal physical illness

Once you have identified organic or functional disorder, take the following steps:

1. *Bless the person* with Christ's healing presence: "Come Holy Spirit …" Watch what happens – give time for the person to receive God's presence and touch.
2. *Lay on hands:* Touch the affected area if it is appropriate. Sensitive areas of the body must not be touched. Rather lay hands on the head and shoulder. The person can lay their own hands on a

sensitive part of their body.
3. *Address the disorder:* Address the dis-ease directly. Jesus taught us to command the mountain: "Go, throw yourself into the sea" (Mark 11:22–24). "Mountain" was a Jewish metaphor for great difficulty. Depending on the particular condition, command whatever you want to have happen: "Pain, leave the body now!" "Tissues and ligaments, be restored." "Cancer, go in Jesus' name. I break your power. I curse cancer at its roots!"
4. *Watch and work with God:* Watch what God does in the person's body, and bless what he is doing. Physical healing often, though not always, involves manifestations of the Spirit in terms of bodily sensations, like heat, cold, trembling, shaking, dizziness or "resting in the Spirit" (losing balance and lying down). Different manifestations can indicate different kinds of healing, discussed in Chapter 20. Ask the person for feedback and work with what they are sensing, speaking the healing into being.
5. *Do an act of faith:* If prompted, do an act of faith that might release the healing. It releases the person's faith to receive. It is a "means of grace" like anointing with oil; giving them the sacraments of bread and wine; putting a finger into the person's ear if they are deaf.
6. *Address any blockage:* If necessary, address whatever might present itself as a possible hindrance to the physical healing: breaking a curse; rebuking fear, confessing unresolved sin; ministering deliverance from demonisation, calming the person if they are getting over-emotional or hyped up. This may include helping the person to take action to work with the healing process ("Get up and walk"), or to make restitution for wrongdoing.
7. *Feedback and aftercare:* Ask the person how they are feeling, and test whether healing has taken place. If not, make another appointment for further ministry. Some physical disorders are only healed through persistent ministry. If the person has been under medical care or taking medication, they should see their doctor. Never advise a person to stop medication unless they are evidently healed. The person may need counsel on how to keep their healing, especially if there were underlying psycho-

emotional and spiritual causes.

When healing does not happen: Why some are not healed

Commonly people are not physically healed or the sickness returns because the underlying causes are not addressed. This needs to be carefully examined and explained to the person receiving ministry. All sorts of feelings and questions arise when healing does not happen after sincerely asking God in Jesus' name. What do we say to them, besides the reason of underlying causes?

I encourage them to come for more prayer ministry *because healing is warfare* – sickness is part of Satan's domain in the "already" and "not yet" of God's kingdom. Jesus has defeated sickness, but it is not yet banished from the earth. This is the "mystery" of the kingdom, *the mystery of healing which we cannot really explain or control.* If we blame anyone for not being healed, we must *not* blame God, but the devil. Satan makes us angry and bitter towards God because we are not healed, separating us from the source of healing. He questions God's character and Word, sowing unbelief and rebellion in our hearts towards God.

However, our deepest struggle with not being healed remains with God: "If God is both able and willing to heal me, why doesn't he?"[7] I mostly respond sincerely: "I really do not know. Why not ask *him*?" God is well able to answer for himself! The explanation of the mystery of the kingdom (of healing) includes the mystery of selection, timing and place: Jesus healed one man at the Pool of Bethesda, leaving the others in their sickness (John 5:1ff). He often entered the Temple area through the gate called Beautiful, without healing the paralysed beggar that sat there daily. The man was only healed by Peter and John after Jesus' ascension (Acts 3:1ff).

---

[7]Similar to the age-old: "If God is love and all powerful, why doesn't he stop all the human suffering right now?" It is the problem of God, *suffering* and evil. I cannot discuss it here, but there are persuasive theological/philosophical answers to this question. See C.S. Lewis, *The Problem of Pain* (London: Fontana Books, 1957); Paul Fiddes, *Participating in God: A Pastoral Doctrine of the Trinity* (London: Darton, Longman & Todd, 2000), pp. 152–190, his chapter on "The Vulnerable God and the Problem of Suffering". Also Paul Fiddes, *The Creative Suffering of God* (Oxford: Clarendon Press, 1988).

Method 4: *Ministering healing to the body*

If we do not blame God, we quickly blame ourselves for not being healed: I am not worthy; I must have sin; God is punishing me; I do not have enough faith. This too is mostly the work of Satan, "the accuser". Or the one ministering healing lays these sentiments on the person to explain why they were not healed. All this is the cruel result of broken self-image and wrong God-image (bad theology). We need to help the person who has not received healing to process these feelings and beliefs, so that they do not feel alienated from God. *To entrust ourselves to God beyond whether he heals us or not, as per our expectations, and even beyond our understanding of him, is worshipping God in truth for who he is, and not for what he can do for us.*

It is true that specific unresolved sin can bring sickness and hinder healing (John 5:14; James 5:16). It is also true that some people are not healed because of their lack of faith or scepticism (Mark 6:1–6; James 5:15), or even because of unforgiveness and broken community – disunity and unresolved relational sin (1 Corinthians 11:30; James 5:16). If any of these elements emerge as blockages to healing, the person must put it right with God and others, if necessary, and healing will probably take place. But even if healing does not take place, to leave the person feeling loved and valued – to minister wholeness to the whole person – is ultimately more important than resolving their presenting problem.

Part Three: Praxis

Personal reflection, application and group discussion

1. Give your own understanding and definition of healing of the body.
2. What has spoken to you in this chapter? What has God said to you? And what have you learnt about physical healing through this chapter?
3. What has been your personal experience in *receiving* physical healing from God through laying on of hands? What did you learn from it?
4. What has been your experience in *ministering* physical healing to others by the laying on of hands? Give an example and the lessons you learnt.
5. Get your home group to do a practical exercise of ministering physical healing to those who have any form of bodily dis-ease.

18

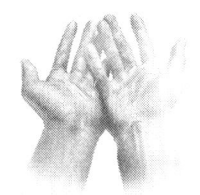

METHOD 5: MINISTERING HEALING TO RELATIONSHIPS

Make every effort to live in peace with all people and to be holy; without holiness no one will see the Lord. See to it that no one misses the grace of God and that no bitter root grows up to cause trouble and defile many.
– Hebrews 12:14–15

The absolute importance of relationships

Relationships either make us or break us. Mostly it is a bit of both. Relationships can be *the* most destructive force for pain and alienation this side of hell; *the* most loving source of healing and happiness this side of heaven. The tragedy is that we are such broken people because we are so unskilled at relationship. Dysfunctional people generally conduct dysfunctional and codependent relationships, creating dysfunctional homes where children grow up to become dysfunctional adults.[1]

---

[1]Dysfunctional means unable to function properly as a healthy, *interdependent* adult – stemming from brokenness and leading to dysfunctional or sick relation-

Part Three: Praxis

Why are some people so dysfunctional, constantly sick and neurotic? Experience has taught me that it is mostly the result of accumulated unresolved pain in relationships, the close link between relational and "inner" healing in Chapter 15. Few things have the power for wholistic destruction in all the interrelated dimensions of human personality as broken relationships. On the other hand, Dr Dean Ornish shows that the power of loving relationship to heal wholistically is unparalleled.[2]

Why are relationships so fundamental to our human existence? Because ultimate Reality is relational. Relationship – not money – makes the world go around. God, as Father, Son and Spirit, is an Eternal Community of Love. Human beings are the pinnacle of God's creation, made in his image and likeness, to take care of creation. "Male and female he created them" (Genesis 1:27). By nature we are relational beings, created in love, by love, for love. This is true for each of us, no matter what circumstance or motivation prevailed at our conception.

We live in one interdependent reality: interrelated with God, ourselves, each other, and creation (*Shalom*). When relationships thrive in love, we experience *Shalom's* order, harmony and wholeness. When relational integrity is broken, for whatever reason, it results in Satan's chaos, conflict and death. Relational breakdown in any of *these* four dimensions affects the others. To isolate it to one dimension or leave it unresolved is to fragment and disintegrate human personality, society and creation. This applies *especially* to our relationship with God, *the* source relationship, and with one another. How we relate to each other directly reflects how we relate to God (1 John 4:19–21).

---

ships – manifesting in dependence, independence or codependence, the perverse opposite of interdependence. I cannot discuss these and other *important* models of dysfunction from relational psychology: Games People Play, Transactional Analysis, Ecological-Systemic models. I merely give a concise theological view of relationships. See Melody Beattie, *Codependent No More* (San Francisco: Harper & Row, 1987); Eric Berne, *Games People Play* (New York: Grove Press, 1964); Thomas Harris, *I'm OK – You're OK* (New York: Avon Books, 1967); Gregory Bateson, *Steps to an Ecology of Mind* (Chicago: University of Chicago Press, 2000).
[2]In *Love and Survival: How Good Relationships Can Bring You Health and Well-Being* (London: Vermillion, 1998). This book contains important research on the healing power of intimacy in relationships.

Therefore, our healing and wholeness are profoundly tied up with one another.

If this is true of relationships in general, how much more is it true of relationships in the body of Christ? We who are joined to Christ are joined to each other by God's Spirit. We are *God's* born-again children; he is our Father. We are brothers and sisters: we love one another as *the* earthly model of the Trinitarian Community; as *the* reconciling and healing balm for all relational breakdown; as *the* integrating and uniting energy of *Shalom* in society and creation. That is why Jesus prayed that we would be one as he is one with the Father and the Father with him, "so that the world may believe" (John 17:20–23). By our *love* for one another, and our neighbour and enemy, "all people will know" that we follow Jesus (John 13:34–35; Luke 6:27–36). God entrusted *to us* the message and ministry of reconciliation accomplished by Jesus (2 Corinthians 5:17–21).[3] The New Testament instructs us how to relate to one another (the twenty-one "one another" sayings) as God relates, for the integrity of his name and our social witness.

This relational vision of cosmic reality and especially of the body of Christ (God's family), gives significance to the appeal: "*Make every effort to live in peace with all people*" (Hebrews 12:14, *Shalom,* relational integrity). It is critical for personal, church, societal and cosmic health and wholeness. A "root of bitterness" (v. 15) can stem from the seed of *anger,* nurtured by unresolved conflict – *not* living at peace with the other. It not only "defiles" (poisons) the person concerned, but those within their relational reach, including their environment. "To be holy" (v. 14) is *a relational reality*, not a private morality – to get to heaven to "see the Lord" (v. 14). To be holy is to "set ourselves apart" to honour God, each other, ourselves and creation, in relational love and integrity. Then we "see the Lord", not only in heaven one day, but here and now, in the other, in ourselves, in nature – experiencing *Shalom* with all people and all things.

I know what you are thinking! Surely we cannot "live at peace

---

[3] Malachi (4:5–6) prophesied that the coming of Messiah would be accompanied by relational reconciliation and healing, turning the hearts of the fathers and mothers to their children, and vice versa, "or else I will strike the land with a curse", the economic-ecological impact of unresolved relationships.

with *all* people" *all* the time? Relational conflict is the norm.[4] What counts is whether we sincerely seek to resolve it. Some refuse reconciliatory efforts, rejecting any healing of relationships. We cannot be responsible for other people's responses or lack thereof. As long as we take responsibility for our part in the breakdown and "make every effort" at reconciliation and healing, we can leave the rest to God. In so doing we receive God's grace to forgive unconditionally, effectively preventing any anger or bitterness taking root within us and relational healing happens – at least on our side! We love our "enemy".

Understanding relational sickness and healing

Relational sickness is unresolved relational breakdown, which always affects both parties and others in their orbit. The fact that we have relational conflict and breakdown is not the issue – that will happen regularly because we are sinners. The issue is *unresolved* conflict, which festers and becomes infected with the poison of unforgiveness. If not addressed and healed, the relationship can become terminal, through permanent alienation, divorce, or even death via sickness, suicide and violence. We see the tragic results of this all around us.

The symptoms of relational sickness are seen relationally and personally. It starts "showing" in the body language of people: tearfulness, withdrawal, aggression, sickness, sadness. Different people manifest in different ways. When a person refuses to deal with an unresolved issue in a relationship, or is bitter and unforgiving, clearly there is relational sickness in their life. *The person has become relationally sick*, taking on the characteristics and consequences of the sick relationship. It becomes their way of living and identity. They are unable to conduct healthy relationships, constantly in conflict, withdrawal and break-up.

What are *the causes of relational sickness?* There are many *immediate and specific causes* of relational conflicts, like misunderstandings between people. They should be identified and resolved *effectively* or

---

[4]Note that this appeal was made to the Hebrew believers in the context of severe suffering, insults, persecutions and the confiscation of their property (Hebrews 10:32–34).

the integrity of the relationship is undermined and dis-ease sets in. These causes are mostly the superficial smoke from the smouldering embers of the *unhealed psycho-emotional brokenness* we bring into our relationships.[5]

Our sin and brokenness is *the deeper, long-term cause* of relational sickness. It not only contributes to our lack of relational skill – through learnt ways of survival, control and games play – but "hooks" the brokenness in the other person, causing the mutual brokenness to feed off each other. This is seen in unhealthy patterns of relating, regular conflict, lack of resolution and relational breakdown. Only *unconditional love*, that never leaves nor forsakes, can ultimately heal such brokenness in a person, and in a relationship. As Christians we are called to love unconditionally as God loves us.

We must take responsibility for our own *inner brokenness*: our spiritual and psycho-emotional healing and deliverance from demonisations. We cannot blame the other person, the relationship or God. *We can* own *our* stuff and forgive the other person, because God not only forgives us – and heals us – but he forgives them as well. There is *no sin or hurt* that any person can inflict upon us that is beyond God's forgiveness and healing. We are never a victim in a relationship if we turn to God as our source relationship.

Relational healing is the reconciliation and restoration of relationship(s), including the rehabilitation of our ways of relating. There is no clearer instruction on relational reconciliation and healing than Jesus' teaching in Matthew 5:21–26 and 18:15–35. Read these texts for the next section.

Jesus' teaching on relational reconciliation

The tragedy of the church of Jesus Christ and society in general, is that most people do not believe and practise Jesus' simple time-tested steps to resolve relational tension. We pay a destructive price for it,

---

[5]Differences in personality, worldview, race, gender or values are the "natural" causes of relational tension and conflict. The Bible recognises *only one cause* operating through the above: *our lower nature* – sin, selfishness, jealousy (1 Corinthians 3:1–4; Philippians 2:1–6; Ephesians 4:1–3, 25–32; James 4:1–2).

both in the church and in the world.[6] Jesus gives specific intervening steps if any "shadow" comes between two people, blurring "the light" of true *koinonia* ("fellowship", 1 John 1:5–10). By "shadow" I mean any tension, anger, hurt or offence which may arise. If left in the dark, it becomes sick and demonised; if brought to the light, it is healed and rehabilitated. Jesus gives *God's curative medicine for relational dis-ease*.[7]

The first step is one-on-one disclosure and confrontation, forgiveness and reconciliation. The person who *first* becomes aware of the shadow is obliged to go to the other to disclose and resolve it – no matter who or what caused it. Awareness means responsibility to go to the other without *telling anyone else*, to uphold relational integrity and personal dignity. It takes urgent priority, even over prayer and worship; it must be done before the sun sets (Ephesians 4:25–28). The one-on-one is to talk through the issue; disclose feelings and perceptions; own your part in it; forgive and/or ask for forgiveness, and resolve the issue by "winning" the other into reconciliation, restoration, healing and growth.

The key issue is disclosure and forgiveness, to "forgive from the heart" (Matthew 18:21–35). People find this difficult – Christians included – because it requires humility, vulnerability and faith in God. We struggle to confront and to disclose. We struggle to forgive when we are hurt due to our pride and misbeliefs: "To disclose and forgive is to be weak"; "If I forgive, they will take advantage of me"; "To forgive is to minimise or agree with their wrongdoing"; "Forgiveness won't allow me to get justice, to extract payment"; "They don't deserve forgiveness"; "They're not really sorry; they haven't apologised and changed". The other side is: "Oh, it is not a big deal"; "I do not want to make it an issue; I'll forget it"; "It did not hurt that much"; "Confronting won't help; it'll make it worse"; "It happened so long ago, why must I rake it up now?" However, psycho-emotional body language does not lie. Personal pain and sickness betrays unresolved issues, cover-ups, stiff-upper-lip suppression and/or superspiritual escapism.

---

[6] See 1 Corinthians 11:27–32: Christians suffer weakness, sickness and untimely death as part of God's discipline because of broken community – we live for ourselves and do not love one another by resolving relational sin and conflict.
[7] Here I summarise the steps – I recommend my full exposition in *Doing Reconciliation*, pp. 204–216.

Method 5: *Ministering healing to relationships*

Forgiveness is a decision not to escape reality, but to face it and put it under the blood of Jesus; to let it go by placing it in the hands of the Saviour and Judge of the universe. Forgiveness is an act of the will, no matter how we feel, *on the basis of faith in God* – what he has done for us in Christ, and that he is well able to take care of us. If God has forgiven us at such great cost to himself in Christ's death, we must forgive those who sin against us. If we do not forgive them, God will not forgive us (Matthew 6:12–15; Mark 11:25; Ephesians 4:32). We must forgive daily, as often as is required – more than four hundred and ninety times a day if necessary (Matthew 18:21–22). The decision to forgive disciplines our feelings into forgiveness. *Unforgiveness is a deadly "torturer",* damaging *us* far more than what we sustain through being sinned against.

The second step of mediation must be taken if the first step does not achieve its purpose. Only if either party believes the issue is not resolved *can they draw in two or three others ("witnesses") to help them reconcile*. This is *mediation* in conflict resolution. The mediators listen to both parties without partiality, helping them to

   a) understand each other and their respective issues;
   b) own their part in causing the tension, hurt or offence;
   c) facilitate the giving and receiving of forgiveness, and
   d) agree to a way forward in healing the relationship.

This second step can involve a series of such meetings, *with supportive individual counselling if necessary*, to come to a healthy resolution and restoration of the relationship, and of the people involved.

The third step of bringing it before the church (community) must be taken if, on the rare occasion, the second step fails to bring reconciliation and healing of relationship. To "tell it to the church" is to make it known to the governmental leaders (elders) of the church to which the people belong, for them to judge the unresolved issue. If "the church" is simply a house church, then they should all judge the matter.[8] This third step is no longer mediation, but *arbitration and judgment*. The elders hear the case from each party, including

---

[8] If one party does not belong to a church, then the offended party either has to release the person in unconditional forgiveness, or find an equivalent authority in the person's life – one whose ruling would be binding on them.

the mediators' report on attempts at reconciliation; then they make a judgment call as to who is responsible. They impose whatever corrective discipline is needed, putting in place a process of restoration and healing like counselling, accountability, community therapy and spiritual disciplines.

A fourth and final step of withdrawing fellowship (expulsion from community) can be taken if the person or parties responsible reject the judgment and discipline process of the elders (the church). In effect it means no community protection, leaving them to their brokenness; making them vulnerable to "attack" by evil and/or God's discipline. This step is due to the person's hardness of heart and must *only be taken as a last resort*, with fear and trembling.[9] In this case, the party "sinned against" has to let it go and forgive unconditionally.

"Preventative medicine" in relational health

Prevention is better than cure. Paul and others taught preventative relational health via twenty-one positive and seven negative "one another" instructions. They help us to "make every effort to keep the unity of the Spirit through the bond of *Shalom*" (Ephesians 4:1–3). How? We must "be completely humble and gentle … patient, bearing with *one another* in love" (v. 2). This is a command, not a convenience, nor a feeling. The Greek *allelon* ("one another") is a reciprocal pronoun, a two-way word involving both parties. One such saying is primary – mentioned twelve times – embodying and fulfilling all the others, namely Jesus' command to "love one another" ("as I have loved you", John 13:34–35).[10]

The seven negative instructions are not to judge, deprive, bite and devour, provoke and envy, lie to, slander, or grumble against one another. The twenty-one positive imperatives cover a range of attitudes and behaviour, from truly loving to greeting one another, accepting,

---

[9]See my cautions in this regard, *Doing Church,* pp. 213–216; *Doing Reconciliation,* pp. 214–216. There should be a "court of appeal" to broader leaders if the dissenting person appeals the arbitration. Ken Blue & John White, *Healing the Wounded: The Costly Love of Church Discipline* (Downer Grove: IVP, 1985) discuss Matthew 18 thoroughly, as *restoration of the wounded.*

[10]See John 15:12, 17; Romans 13:8; 1 Thessalonians 3:12; 4:9; 1 Peter 1:22; 1 John 3:11, 23; 4:7, 11, 12; 2 John 5.

welcoming, being hospitable to, serving, comforting, encouraging, honouring, preferring, edifying, admonishing, submitting to, living in harmony with, praying for, confessing our sins to, having the same care for, "being kind, tenderhearted and forgiving one another", and "bearing each other's burdens".[11] This is living the kingdom, the reign of Shalom. As Paul says: "Let the peace [Shalom] of Christ rule in your hearts, since as members of one body you were called to peace" (Colossians 3:15).

It is important to note that all these instructions are commands, imperatives. They call for obedient practice until they become habitual and instinctive. They are in fact part of our new nature in Christ. All these imperatives are preceded by the indicative (the facts) in the New Testament: *Because* of what God has done for us in Christ, behave and become accordingly. *Because* we *are* a new creation, *be* a new creation. We *have* Christ's new nature, so live it out – live like a new person in thought, attitude, word and deed. Then we increasingly become a new person after Christ's likeness as God's true image-bearer. *This implies that God has given us, by the Spirit, the inner resources and power to be and do what he requires of us.* Then we are transformed, personally and relationally, in a hidden, progressive and cumulative way. It is summarised in Paul's profound words: "Be imitators of God, *therefore,* as dearly loved children, and live a life of love, just as Christ loved us ..." (Ephesians 5:1–2).

Biblical and contemporary examples

Because I have discussed the biblical material on relational healing in more detail than the other dimensions of healing in the previous chapters, I will not give biblical and contemporary stories. I refer you to *Doing Reconciliation* (pp. 329–333), where I list eighteen biblical stories and passages with my questions, for use as case studies of relational reconciliation and healing.

---

[11] The *negatives* are: Romans 14:13; 1 Corinthians 7:5; Galatians 5:15, 26; Colossians 3:9; James 4:11; 5:9. The *positives* are: Romans 12:5, 8, 10, 16; 14:19; 15:5, 7, 14; 16:16; 1 Corinthians 11:33; 12:25; 16:20; Galatians 5:13; 6:2; Ephesians 4:2, 32; 5:21; Colossians 3:13, 16; 1 Thessalonians 4:18; 5:11; 1 Timothy 3:2; Hebrews 10:24; James 5:16; 1 Peter 3:8; 4:9; 5:5.

Part Three: Praxis

One biblical example that I missed in *Doing Reconciliation* is the relational rupture between the two great apostles, Paul and Barnabas (Acts 15:36–41). Paul refused to take John Mark with them on their second ministry trip because he had deserted the team on the first trip (Acts 13:5). He is the Mark who later wrote the Gospel. Barnabas, Mark's cousin (Colossians 4:10), insisted that he go with them. So sharp was their disagreement that Paul and Barnabas parted company and went their separate ways. It was obviously painful as they had been through so much together – they were like David and Jonathan. Barnabas had taken a risk in bringing Paul to Jerusalem to secure his acceptance by the apostles after his conversion (Acts 9:26–27). Years later he fetched Paul from Tarsus, integrating him into the Antioch church and leadership (Acts 11:25–26). Their relationship shifted from "Barnabas and Saul" (Acts 13:2, 7), to "Paul and Barnabas" and "Paul and his companions" as Paul took the lead under God's anointing (Acts 13:13, 43, 46).

This background highlights the seriousness of their disagreement. They did not "love one another" in this incident. They did not prefer, serve or submit to one another. They did not "maintain the unity of the Spirit in the bond of peace". Love and unity does not mean to agree, but to work out our differences agreeably *in community*. We can agree to disagree agreeably, and grow through it *together*. However, it is clear that Paul and Barnabas reconciled and healed their relationship. About six years after the incident, Paul speaks of Barnabas in warm and affirming terms (1 Corinthians 9:6). Paul also reconciled with John Mark. He talks of him, a few years later, as part of his team, "helpful to me in my ministry" (Colossians 4:10; Philemon 24; 2 Timothy 4:11). We do not know how they reconciled, but we do know that they resolved things to the point of working together again.

The fallout from unresolved tensions among leaders can result in the split and the death of a congregation. Such divisions are very painful, often second only to divorce, marriage being the most significant relationship we have on earth, outside of the Trinity.

There are millions of painful stories of oppression and abuse in *racial, economic and gender* relationships. I tell the story of South Africa in this regard – and my experience of it – in *Doing Reconciliation*. I lay out a biblical theology and praxis of reconciliation and healing in these key dimensions of personal and societal relationship.

A step-by-step method of relational healing

When ministering to a person, you often become aware of unresolved relational stuff, either by the Spirit's insight, by experience or the person telling you. Anger, resentment and bitterness are sure signs of unforgiveness. Unforgiveness is one of the most common blockages in receiving ministry and healing. On diagnosing relational brokenness and/or unforgiveness, whether in the interview stage or in the flow of ministry, take the following steps:

1. *Confront the person with it:* The first step is to get the person's attention, facing them with the relational sickness revealed by the symptoms or the Spirit. It is easier to address the relational sickness if the person is in touch with it. If they are not aware, or deny it, it becomes a sensitive and at times difficult spiritual battle. The point is to get the "diagnosis" into the open and to talk through the basics of what happened – enough to minister further.

2. *They must acknowledge and own it:* The person must own the relational sickness and their part in it – their relational brokenness and sin. Again, denial is not easily broken. You cannot minister further to them if they do not acknowledge the relational sickness and own their part in it.

3. *Confession, repentance and forgiveness:* Ask the person if they are willing to confess to God their part in it, *and* if they are willing to forgive the person or parties concerned. If they are not, end the time of ministry, explaining that they cannot go further with God unless they take this step. A later counselling session can possibly get them beyond their pride, denial and resistance. If they are willing to repent, lead them in a prayer of confession for their part in the relational brokenness. Speak God's cleansing and forgiveness over them. Help them verbalise forgiveness in God's name, as a decision in faith before God, towards the person or

parties involved in the relational alienation.

4. *Commitment to do whatever is necessary:* The logical consequence of confession, repentance and forgiveness is the willingness to do whatever is appropriate in seeking *Shalom* with the person or parties concerned. Sometimes no further action is required – if the person is dead. Even then, a letter to them, written before God, can bring great release and healing. In most cases, you need to guide the person in what they should do to make peace and seek relational healing with the other. Depending on the person and the relational sickness, you either take the next step *only after* they have done Step 4, or you can continue with Step 5.

5. *Ministering healing to related areas of pain:* There are few realities that cause such widespread havoc and damage in the whole person as relational malfunction. Emotional damage is a common immediate cause, and result of, relational sickness. There are also spiritual, psychological and physical disorders that cause, or are affected by, unforgiveness and relational sickness, which must be ministered to as per the previous chapters.

6. *Feedback and follow-up on required action for reconciliation:* In drawing things to a close, debrief the person on how they experienced the time of ministry. Reassure and bless them, but do not leave before getting agreement on a process of accountability and follow-up regarding their commitment to action (Step 4). Relational healing takes time. Probably a few sessions of counselling and ministry will be needed to do justice to the healing process.

Personal reflection, application and group discussion

1. How do you define "relationship"? Why are relationships so important in life?
2. Think about *your* most intimate and fulfilling experience of love and relationship. Then think about your most painful experience of a sick relationship. What elements were contributory factors in both experiences? What can you learn from them?
3. Read the text at the head of this chapter. Do you live at peace with all people, or at least make every effort to do so? Do you have any unresolved anger, a root of bitterness or unforgiveness? What are you going to do about it?
4. Give your own explanation of relational sickness, healing and health.
5. From a biblical viewpoint, why is preventative relational "medicine" so important? Do you practise it – all twenty-one "one another" sayings?
6. Do you agree with my understanding of Jesus' "curative" medicine (Matthew 5 and 18), and the steps I present in ministering relational healing?

19

Method 6:
Ministering healing to the dying and the dead

Since we have flesh and blood, Jesus too shared in our humanity so that by his death he might destroy the one who holds the power of death – that is, the devil – and free those who all their lives were held in slavery by their fear of death.
For just as each of us is destined to die once, and then to face God's judgment, so Christ was sacrificed once to take away our sins.
He will appear a second time, not to bear sins, but to bring salvation to those who eagerly wait for him.
– Hebrews 2:14–15; 9:27–28 RAP

"I am the Resurrection and the Life.
If you believe in me, you will live, even though you die.
*In fact, whoever lives and believes in me will **never** die.*
Do you believe this?"
– Jesus, John 11:25–26 RAP

Method 6: *Ministering healing to the dying and the dead*

As a pastor I have learnt about death by being at the death bed of some congregants and conducting many funerals. It is different when it touches you personally. Mortality and death became real to me in October 1993 when, at the age of thirty-eight, I was nearly killed in a car accident. It taught me that death can come in a moment; that I am destined to die; that I am basically dust and will return to dust. It also taught me that God is sovereign over death, saving me from death, giving me "a second chance" at life. I decided: *I must live well and love well to die well* – as I ought to have lived and loved from my conception.

Understanding death and life[1]

Understanding death helps us to face it in a healthy way – even more so knowing that Jesus has conquered death. Worldview – our basic assumptions about reality – determines how we see death and life. *Western materialists* place all reality in flesh: we are biological animals. They deny death (no life thereafter), resulting in the cult of comfort, affluence, technology and self-achievement. They either become *hedonists* ("eat, drink and be merry for tomorrow we die"), *altruists* ("leave a legacy – live on through your good works") or *pessimists* ("life is meaningless suffering"). Such are the atheists, agnostics, humanists: Death is the natural end to life, a return to the dust of nothingness.

Eastern and Southern religions and spiritualities (including Western New Agers) place reality in spirit: We are spirit beings. They accept death as entrance into life thereafter in various forms, depending on the belief or philosophy. It is a cyclical series of deaths and reincarnations for better *karma* (purification of spirit) toward *nirvana* (peace of complete detachment and emptiness); the immortal soul escaping from the prison of the body to another life; becoming an angel (to help humans); being absorbed into (G)god or the sea of universal consciousness; or death is sovereignly set by God as entrance into

---

[1] I give a broad-stroke theology of death. For further study see L. Coenen & W. Schmithals, "Death", *The New International Dictionary of Testament Theology*, vol. 1 (Exeter: Paternoster Press, 1975); Karl S.J. Rahner, *On the Theology of Death* (New York: Herder & Herder, 1961); George S.J. Maloney, *Death Where Is Your Sting?* (New York: Alba House, 1984); N.T. Wright, *The Resurrection of the Son of God*.

heaven or hell, depending on our good works and adherence to the religion. These beliefs result in either *legalism/asceticism* (discipline the body and serve humanity to earn blessing in the afterlife), *licentiousness* (do whatever you like in the body; it is the spirit that is "saved" in the afterlife), or *fatalism* ("It just happens"; "It is my *karma*"; "God is sovereign; I can do nothing").

There is a popular but faulty *Christian view of death*, influenced by some of these beliefs, especially Platonic philosophy and Gnostic thought: The spirit/soul is immortal and thus superior to the body and material world, which is temporary and inferior. Life is a brief sojourn into *the real life* beyond death (heaven), which releases us from our sinful body and its constraints – the evil world and its corruption. This view produces Christians who despise their bodies and avoid responsibility for this world, except "getting souls into heaven". Or they indulge themselves in a worldly way without conscience.

What is clear from all the above is that our view of (G)god and death and the afterlife affects how we live, our daily life choices. I will return to this later.

The biblical view of death is a Hebraic-Messianic *theology* of death, based on God's revelation, as opposed to a *philosophy or psychology* of death. The Old Testament has a developmental understanding of death. We all have an appointed time to die, when our breath returns to God and our body returns to the dust – as with the animals (Ecclesiastes 3:1–2, 19–21; 12:7). Human death is different because we are made in God's image, but it is still the end of life, as we go to *Sheol* ("the place of the dead", the grave). The link between sin and death developed: death is due to Adam's sin – and at times our own sin. Death is a great sadness, an enemy that *separates* us from the living, and even the fear of separation from God. The hope arose that "the righteous" who "live by his faith" in Yahweh (Habakkuk 2:4) will not suffer torment in death, but will rest in God's "house" (Psalm 23:6). When Messiah comes, he will defeat sin and sickness, *including death* (Isaiah 25:6–8). How? By *physical* resurrection (Isaiah 26:19) of *both* the righteous, for eternal life *and* the wicked, for eternal shame (Daniel 12:1–2).

The apostles understood and theologised death and eternal life in light of Jesus' death and resurrection. "Sin entered the world through one man [Adam], and death through sin, and in this way death came to all men, because all sinned" (Romans 5:12). Through one man, the Second Adam, sin and death have been overcome (1 Corinthians 15:21–22). Jesus died *our* death and rose from the grave to give eternal life to all who trust him. Paul says: "The wages of sin is death, but the gift of God is eternal life in Messiah Jesus our Lord" (Romans 6:23). Jesus is *the only human being* who went *through* death for us and came out the other side in bodily resurrection. Let me elaborate.

Jesus overcame death through resurrection

Eternal life (zoe aionios) is not a length of life, but *God's quality* of life, "the life of the ages". It is not disembodied life elsewhere, but *embodied life here on the new earth.* God breathed into Adam and Eve his eternal Spirit life. *That* life was dependent on relational trust in God. If they had *not* sinned, they would have grown in radiance, been alive today, filling the earth with *Shalom* paradise. (Some theologians disagree, saying death was a natural "pre-fall" creation.) Through their trusting obedience and loving service, heaven would have come to earth, God's will done on earth as it is in heaven. They would have known good and evil through "long obedience in the same direction",[2] not quick disobedience in the wrong direction through self-deception.

When Adam and Eve sinned, they did not die physically in an immediate sense, but wholistically in a progressive sense: alienated *spiritually, psychologically, relationally, ecologically* and *physically* – mortality and eventual death. God never intended or willed death; it was an intrusion in his creation. It is *not* natural for us to die – it is our enemy. We (our bodies) were designed for eternal life. Death originated with Lucifer's rebellion and his consequent *separation* from God's heavenly life and presence. He then tempted Adam and Eve

---

[2]Frederick Nietzsche's phrase in *Beyond Good and Evil,* trans. Helen Zimmern (London: 1907), Section 188, pp. 106–109; quoted in Eugene Peterson, *A Long Obedience in the Same Direction* (Downer Groves: IVP, 1980), p. 13. Nietzsche said: "The essential thing 'in heaven and earth' is … that there should be long obedience in the same direction; there thereby results, and has always resulted in the long run, something which has made life worth living."

to sin, setting up his kingdom of death on earth. "In Adam" we all die. He gave birth to "sinners" who live death in the whole of who they are, trusting in self, sin, evil, and whatever else is outside God's eternal kind of life. Those who have self, and thus Satan, as their god, in a sense already have hell on earth. Physical death in *this* state of wholistic death means continued alienation in eternity – the ultimate *fear and terror of death* by which Satan holds us in slavery.[3]

God's defeat of death and the devil in the death and resurrection of Jesus means that "in Christ" we who trust in him are made alive. The last Adam gives birth to "saints" with his *zoe aionios*. This *spiritual* resurrection ("born again") leads to progressive wholistic resurrection in trusting obedience and loving service: from psycho-emotional healing and demonic deliverance, to physical and relational healing and eventual bodily resurrection in consummated eternal life – having a transfigured body like Jesus' glorious body (Philippians 3:21).

Because Jesus defeated death in his physical resurrection, *all human beings will rise again bodily from the grave,* either "to live" or "to be condemned" (John 5:28–29). The righteous (believers) will rise first – at Jesus' Second Coming (1 Corinthians 15:22–23; Revelation 20:4–6; 1 Thessalonians 4:13–18). "God will bring *with Jesus* those who have died in Christ" (RAP) and their bodies will rise from the grave. We (our spirits) will rejoin, or be clothed with, our resurrected bodies in consummated eternal life, to rule with Christ forever – not in heaven, but on the renewed earth, as God originally intended with Adam and Eve. The rest of the dead (unbelievers) will rise at the end of the thousand-year (millennial) reign of Christ, to be judged in consummated "second death", which is "eternal fire prepared for the devil and his angels" (Revelation 20:11–15; Matthew 25:41). Human beings were never designed to go there. If they do, it will be *by default, by their choice of alienation from God.*

The question arises: *What happens when we die – between now and the resurrection of our bodies?* When we die, we separate from our bodies and continue to live in growing consciousness, with mind, emotions and will of all we knew on earth, and more. We continue either "with the

---

[3]See Ernest Becker's Pulitzer Prize-winning book, *The Denial of Death* (New York: Free Press, 1973), on how we avoid death, arguing that fear – the terror of death – is at the core of our societal ills and evils.

Lord" (heaven) or alienated from him (hell), awaiting the resurrection of our bodies. Theologians dispute the nature of this "intermediate state". Catholics and Orthodox believe in purgatory, a state of God's purifying fire of love between heaven and hell through which we grow into God's presence. Others believe we "sleep" in timelessness till the resurrection. Some believe God's irresistible love will eventually reconcile *all* human beings to his heavenly presence ("universal salvation"). However, it is clear that for believers "to be absent from the body (is) to be present with the Lord" (KJV) – that is "heaven" (Luke 16:22–31; 23:43; 2 Corinthians 5:1–10; Philippians 1:23).

To summarise the biblical vision of death and life: Death is not the end, but a ruptured transition to life-here-after, which is continued growth as a whole person, fully conscious of all things, in either eternal life or eternal death, alienated in shame and selfishness. Death has lost its sting in Jesus; the grave has lost its power (1 Corinthians 15:54–57). Christ's victory *over* death is our victory *through* death, reversing what Satan has done *in* death. Through death we are united with Jesus and all our loved ones "in the Lord" – and all God's family, "the spirits of righteous people made perfect" (Hebrews 12:22–24). This and other biblical texts (Revelation 4, 5, 7, 21; John 14:1ff) give us insight into heaven, the angels, and the "communion of the saints".[4] Heaven is *not* endless self-indulgence in all the pleasures this life had to offer. It is about *growth in ever-deepening joy, perfecting love and greater unity with God, others and his created world, through loving service*. In reality heaven is way beyond our wildest dreams and imagination (1 Corinthians 2:9).

This affects how we approach death, and how we live our present lives. We do not fear death, but face it with Jesus at our side. We do not grieve over loved ones who have died in Christ as those do who do not have the same hope (1 Thessalonians 4:13ff). Their grief is without hope – death *is* the enemy in a full and final sense. All the pseudo-

---

[4] The "communion of saints" refers to *all* God's born-again family in heaven *and* on earth, a communion transcending death by Christ and his Spirit. Catholics and Orthodox believe we relate to the dead by praying for and to them ("the saints"), asking them to intercede for us, feeling their support, doing good deeds and offering the "Divine Liturgy" for them. Protestant Evangelicals reject this, saying that Jesus is the only mediator/intercessor with God for us, but they have little *real sense* of "the communion".

spiritualities that offer esoteric salvation are but deceptive false hopes of a wonderful afterlife for those who reject Jesus as God's salvation. This vision motivates us to truly trust Jesus for our salvation, for our living *and* our dying. It motivates us to tell all others about *his* victory over death, to live and love well that we may die well; especially to love those close to us, telling them often that we love them. It motivates us to engage fully in this world, learning to rule over evil in all its forms through the power of God's love, in preparation to rule and reign with Christ *on* the new *earth* throughout the eternal ages.

Healing the dying

It should now be clear that healing can happen *before* death (of the spirit, emotions and demonisation, the body and relationships); *through* death (by entering God's presence, awaiting bodily resurrection), and *from* death (raising or resuscitating a dead person to life, as Jesus and the apostles occasionally did).

Healing of the dying is healing *through* death. It is preparing a person for death; helping them to face it, and go through it, by being with them in "the death process".[5] *The five stages of the death process are: denial, anger, bargaining, depression and acceptance.* They are not clear-cut stages; they overlap and yo-yo back and forth until the process comes to an end. Depending on various factors, it can be quick or take a long time. Personal faith in Jesus Christ does moderate the process, but does not transcend it completely as some suppose. Both the dying person and the family who grieve go through the death process. To understand and work with it is key. Listen empathetically (without judgment) as they go through the stages. The healing is in the listening and "being with", in the praying and caring, in the process itself, and in its ending.

To "heal the dying" is a rare privilege to tread on holy ground, even if it is only a brief encounter with a dying person. This, of course, assumes that the person does not die suddenly without warning or preparation. Biblically, one of the great blessings from God is long life and a good death, when we can bless our children and grandchildren,

---

[5]Pioneered by Elizabeth Kübler-Ross, *On Death and Dying* (New York: MacMillan, 1969); *Death: The Final Stage of Growth* (New Jersey: Prentice Hall, 1975).

having them with us as we breathe our last, ushered into God's presence by angels and loved ones who have gone before. The death of babies and children, the young and middle aged, is tragic. The fact that we do not consider the death (murder) of aborted babies truly tragic says so much about postmodern culture.[6] I cannot discuss the horror and guilt of this kind of death – and why people die young, violently, or ravaged by disease. We seem to have little or no control over the way people die; it is mostly a mystery.

However, we can pray and live for this great blessing. God's promise is: "Honour your parents that you may live a long and good life" (Deuteronomy 5:16 RAP), and thus die well. Abbot Christopher Jamison says: "The ability to die well is a seriously underrated skill in Western society."[7] It is because our death "is the most important moment of our entire earthly existence. That moment brings together and is conditioned by all previous choices. We are, at our death, the way we have chosen to live all through our life."[8] Dying *well* is an invaluable parting gift to those around us. Growing old is not easy, and dying slowly is worse. However, God gives us more grace and courage than we would ever realise – *the courage to let go graciously in greater trust of God.* That is what Jesus meant in saying to Peter: "When you are old you will stretch out your hands, and someone else will dress you and lead you where you do not want to go" (John 21:18–19). It is full circle back to being like a baby, vulnerable and dependent, dressed and led by family. In fact, the birthing of a baby is an apt description of death – a second birth.[9]

The opposite is keeping control, holding on "for dear life". Taking things into our own hands, like euthanasia or suicide, is the easy way out! We avoid pain and inconvenience to others at all costs; mainly due to fear and false pride. We have handed death and dying to retirement villages, anonymous others and the medical world. They

---

[6] Have you thought of the multiple millions of aborted and miscarried babies who grow to maturity in God's presence? God has given each a name. We will meet them some day. See George Maloney's sensitive discussion on "Suffer the Aborted to Come to Me" in *Death Where Is Your Sting?* pp. 77–91.
[7] In *Finding Sanctuary* (Minnesota: Liturgical Press, 2006), p. 158.
[8] George Maloney, p. 21.
[9] See Ronald Rolheiser's insightful use of this idea in his discussion on death and dying, in *Against an Infinite Horizon* (New York: Crossroads, 1995), pp. 106–122.

overmedicate and often wrongly keep us alive, prolonging the agony. Death and dying must be brought back to the family, where children and grandchildren can participate in the death process. A compelling Christian vision of death and eternal life will help in this regard. It certainly helps Christians to die well. It also helps unbelievers who are dying: Their ultimate healing lies in being gently led to faith in Jesus Christ.

Allow me to illustrate "the healing of the dying" by referring to my mother's death process. I will *italicise* the words indicating the stages – I am conscious that each story, person and process is unique. I had the awesome privilege of nursing her in the last weeks before she died. My sister and brother joined me towards the end. She died in her own bed in our arms, the way it ought to be. It was a holy experience – imprinted on my spirit forever – equal only to witnessing and participating in the birth of my two children. I subsequently did six teachings on "Dying Well" in honour of my mother.

The death process

I recall the *initial shock, numbness and disorientation*, both in her and in me, when we first heard the diagnosis of stomach cancer. It was too developed for her to undergo chemo or other therapy, the doctors said. *Denial* set in. Denial is a God-given mechanism to protect us from initial shock. But holding onto it can stop us from facing reality, making it difficult to distinguish between fact and fantasy. My mom responded: "It is not so bad, I'll be okay; I am not worried, Jesus will heal me!" Being a strong believer, she fought the cancer through healing prayer, diet, and other means – even fasting for 40 days on a "program" of beetroot, celery and carrot juice.

After the fast, I flew to Cape Town to be with her. Immediately I sensed, or saw, that she was dying. Breaking her *denial* was not easy. I had to help her to distinguish between faith and denial. She had shown great faith in God for her healing – that was not in question. "Mom, maybe you must face death and prepare for it, because you are dying – unless God does a miracle. He can do that anytime – even bring you back from death – but it is up to him. If he doesn't, he'll heal you *through* death – you'll be in God's presence and your body will rise again free from cancer and pain. So Mom, let's talk about death. Let's prepare for it, while continuing to trust God for a miracle. That's not a contradiction. It is not indulging in unbelief to face death – it takes real faith to do so."

This was not easy for her. She was initially *upset and angry*, but then saw the sense in what I was saying. The realisation that her fasting and prayer had not healed her *angered* her. She had to face the supposed prophecies some people gave her – through prayer, Scripture and "revelation" from God – that God would heal her. Evidently it was not happening, yet she believed God would perform a miracle, so how could she now contemplate dying? Her *disappointment* and *resentment* was evident. I pointed out that it was not about faith in fasting and prayer and prophecies, but faith in God – faith that goes beyond healing – at least healing in the way we want it to happen. "And Mom, what greater joy and healing is there than to 'push off to be with Jesus'?" I used her own phrase – my mom had her own unique language.

These conversations were sensitive and tense. I realise that she was *irritable and angry* from time to time during the seven-month struggle with cancer. I admit that I did not always understand and did not always respond well. Anger comes in many forms in the death process: "Why me?" "Why now?" "It is unfair!" The dying take out their anger on family, friends, caregivers, even God. Allowing them to vent, cry, talk, and listening lovingly, often without giving any answers, is a healing gift. On reflection I realise how unskilled I was in "healing" my dying mother. If I had it over again, I would have given her more time and attention, love and compassion.

Through the seven months I observed the phenomenon of *bargaining*. It seems to be an instinctive tactic of *desperation*. Times of anger and protest gave way to bargaining: "If you heal me, Lord, I will 'shout it out' to everyone" (a favourite Helga saying – it is on her gravestone!). "If I fast and pray for forty days, will you heal me? Or give me a few more years, as you did with King Hezekiah?" We begin to bargain when our backs are against the wall, when we realise that, in a real and final sense, we are at God's sovereign mercy. We set conditions, negotiate "deals", or placate God in various ways. We do not feel ready to die; we desperately want to live longer. People mean well, but they do not help us by saying, "Try this …"; "Do that …"; "God will heal you if …" If God *really* has spoken, it *really* will happen. Human sympathy clouds our hearing from God.

There was periodic *emotional meltdown* as weakness and physical wasting away became more evident. This is the *darkness of depression*, as you face reality squarely. I would see my mom *quiet, sad, heavy-hearted* – completely out of character for a talkative, extrovert optimist. At times she would just sit and cry. In those moments the only thing I could do was to hold her, pray for God to help her, and tell her how much I appreciated and loved her. Sometimes there was nothing to say – it would be trespassing on holy ground to say anything. Those moments taught me the power of touch, the mystery of embrace, the intimacy of simply "being with".

After her fast and our serious talks about facing death, she began to *accept* what was happening, yet was still open to God doing a miracle. That was the turning point. Four weeks later she died. She (and I) gave herself permission to journey towards death – with the sure hope of going home to the arms of the Father, and the future resurrection of her body. She said all her goodbyes. We talked about heaven, the passage through death and what it could possibly be like. I read Scriptures to her regularly. Hospice helped with morphine injections to control the pain. My sister and I washed and cared for her.

I witnessed grace in Mom's body as she slowly stopped eating, then stopped drinking, and then drifted in and out of consciousness and into a coma for three days before she died. She would respond with a slight hand-squeeze when I said, "Mom, Jesus is coming for you. Can you see him? Do you see his angels? Go to him." I could see she was moving away from us, entering the passage through death. "We release you, Mom. Go now and be with Jesus." Early in the morning, 23 December 2000, she breathed her last as we held her, praying and praising God. The room was filled with God's exhilarating presence. I understood what the psalmist meant: "Precious in the sight of the Lord is the death of his saints" (Psalm 116:15). We washed her body for the last time. I thought of another holy body that was tenderly washed by two old men in preparation for burial (John 19:38–42). An overriding sense of the dignity of the human person, of the sacredness of the human body, overwhelmed me, and remained with me. I kept saying to myself, "Thank you, Jesus, that this body will rise again."

Healing the dead

Healing the dead means raising a dead person to life: not as in the resurrection, but in the sense of resuscitation. Medical science practises resuscitation – they try to revive a person's heart when it stops beating. There is a difference between resuscitating a person who has just died and raising to life a person who has been dead for hours – four days, in the case of Lazarus (John 11:17). I am referring to raising a dead person to life in the name of the Lord as Elijah and Elisha, and Jesus and his apostles did; and as recorded periodically in church history.

The idea of resuscitation raises the phenomena of "near death experiences" and "out of body experiences". I must comment on this before I discuss how to heal the dead. Beginning in the 1960s and 1970s, near death experiences and out of body experiences have been clinically investigated and studied.[10] People who have been resuscitated from death – and some who were operated on – have commonly reported how they left their body and observed from above. Others have reported "travelling" through a dark tunnel to a light growing ever brighter and then, at some point, returning to their body. There is also the "spirit experience" of "astral travel", a kind of out of body experience not linked directly to death. Variations on these two kinds of experiences, all with similar or different feelings and levels of consciousness, have been reported.

Some medical scientists have concluded it points to life after death, while others say it is a psycho-physiological phenomenon in the person – a dissociative mechanism under extreme stress before their chemical brain finally closes down. All religions and New Age beliefs say it is consciousness or life after death. However, as Dr

---

[10]Dr Raymond Moody, *Life after Life* (Atlanta: Mocking Bird Books, 1975) and *Reflection on Life after Life* (New York: Bantam-Mocking Bird, 1977). Dr K. Osis & Dr E. Haraldson, *Deathbed Observations by Physicians and Nurses: A Cross-Cultural Survey* (New York: Parapsychology Foundations, 1962) and *At the Hour of Death* (New York: Avon Press, 1977).

Part Three: Praxis

Maurice Rawlings has convincingly shown, it is not all serene and rosy on the other side – as many believe. He gives detailed accounts of people who have been "to hell and back", similar to Jesus' story in Luke 16:19–31.[11] There are remarkable cases of people glimpsing heaven and returning to tell the story – giving us an almost tangible sense of what heaven is like.[12]

We learn about healing the dead – bringing a deceased person to life – from the biblical accounts, church history and contemporary cases. As I have discussed, our authority to heal the dead is Jesus' victory over death and his commission to "raise the dead" in his name (Matthew 10:7–8). This kind of healing is rare and particularly difficult for the Western mind. The key is clear prompting and leading from God and the exercise of his enabling gifts (faith). We must be careful not to claim things in God's name that do not happen, distressing the bereaved family by raising and dashing hopes. On the other hand, we must not be *so* cautious that we do not exercise faith and miss the grace of God. It is about attitude of mind, readiness of heart, listening to God, *and the way we go about it* – or we simply close our minds to any such crazy risk-taking.

Years ago I led a funeral when a man came up front without prior notice, saying he *had* to "do this" in obedience to God and love for his friend. He commanded the deceased to come to life in Jesus' name. I felt it was inappropriate, but I did not stop him. Nothing happened. I admired his chutzpah (more presumption than faith), but I felt for the family. Being strong believers, they were okay, saying "nothing ventured, nothing gained". In contrast, a pastor friend of mine felt led by God to raise to life a young man who had been tragically killed. He went to the mortuary without telling anyone except his wife. Taking a pair of clothes for the young man, he asked to be left alone with the body. After extensive prayer, rebuking death, commanding the man to come to life, nothing happened. Eventually he went home. I admire him for his faith-in-wise-action.

Younggi Cho, the Korean church leader, prayed *for hours* over his

---

[11]Maurice Rawlings, *Beyond Death's Door* (Nashville: Nelson, 1978), and *To Hell and Back: Life after Death – Startling New Evidence* (Nashville: Nelson, 1993).
[12]See Betty Malz's amazing story, *My Glimpse of Eternity* (New Jersey: Chosen Books, 1977).

Method 6: *Ministering healing to the dying and the dead*

son Samuel, after he had died from a drink laced with rat-poison – and he *did* come back to life. Angus Buchan, a farmer in South Africa, was called by his workers after lightning had struck fifty women to the ground, apparently killing one of them. They had covered her body with a blanket and would not go near it. He knelt down and prayed over her, then felt prompted to lift her up by the arms to stand her on her feet – and she stood. Whether she had been unconscious or dead, Angus does not know, but she was alive – he had obeyed God's prompting.[13]

How do we then heal the dead? We can summarise a few common practices or steps that we can use if the opportunity presents itself:[14]

1. There is always the *sense of tragedy*, the "premature" invasion of death as an enemy that triggers the miracle of resuscitation. The *desperate cry* for help from the grieving loved ones is part of it. It is as if a particular incident of death is *calling for intervention*. This includes the *mystery of timing* – there is a moment in which it *can* happen, or it passes.
2. There is always the *openness of the person* used in the healing. They are *moved with compassion* and/or motivated to confront death, often *on behalf of the bereaved*.
3. There is always a clearly implied *sense of God's leading*, promise, supernatural knowing, or infusion of faith that moves the healer into action.
4. There is always *sensitivity to the context*, atmosphere, mood of the people. This kind of healing, more than others, needs *a conducive environment of faith*. We have to create it as Jesus sometimes did – by driving out fear, hysterical emotion, unbelief and death itself. A few people of faith, or singing worship songs, can cause darkness and death to leave.
5. Then there is an *act of faith that releases the miracle*, raising the dead person to life. As with other kinds of healing, the acts of faith are *centred on touch* (body contact) and *the spoken word*

---
[13] Angus Buchan & Val Waldeck, *Faith Like Potatoes* (Greytown: Shalom Ministries, 1998), pp. 39–40.
[14] 1 Kings 17:17–24; 2 Kings 4:18–37; 13:21; Mark 5:21–43; Luke 7:11–17; John 11:1–57; Acts 9:36–42; 20:7–12.

(command). Death is verbally rebuked and life is called back into the person – they are commanded to awake or sit up. It can involve body-to-body contact; laying an item on the person (a stick or clothing that has been prayed over), or taking them by the hand and lifting them up. Either the person comes to life or they remain dead – we cannot manipulate it into being, no matter how much we shout or whatever we do. *God* does it, or it does not happen.

6. Lastly, there is the practical care and comfort when the person "comes around", like giving them a drink and reuniting them with their family. This aftercare includes the humble and honest witness of the event to Christ's glory – not the fanfare of modern Christian marketing that makes celebrities out of God's miracles and miracle workers.

Personal reflection, application and group discussion

1. What has been your understanding of death and the afterlife? Having read this chapter, what has changed for you? Why?
2. What is the significance of a *biblical, Christian view* of death and eternal life? What effect should it have on us, on our present lifestyle?
3. Do you believe that our death (the how and when) is pre-determined? Or do we have some "say" in it? Can we "die well"? How?
4. *Have you faced your own death at all?* How does it make you *feel* to think about dying? How would you like to die? Talk to God about it.
5. Have you had any direct personal experience of death in your family or with friends – attending to a dying person or being present at their death? Reflect on the experience and what you learnt from it, in light of what I have shared about healing the dying.
6. What is the difference between the resurrection of the dead and raising or resuscitating the dead?
7. Have you had any personal experience in attempting to raise someone from death? Or have you heard of a contemporary story of such a miracle? Reflect on the story to learn any principles and practices in terms of "healing the dead". Compare it with any of the biblical stories (footnote 14) and the practices that I summarised.

20

Discernment: Evaluating spiritual phenomena in healing

"Now about Spirit manifestations and spiritual phenomena, I do not want you to be ignorant."
— Paul, 1 Corinthians 12:1 RAP

"… the mature, who by constant use have trained themselves to distinguish good from evil."
— Hebrews 5:14

Understanding discernment

We are moving from the modern age of discovery to the age of discernment in postmodern culture. New technological developments happen daily with little ethical and spiritual discernment as to their real value and effect on our moral-societal-ecological fabric. There is an unprecedented openness to and hunger for "spirituality" and "psycho-spiritual experiences" in the West. Therefore, discernment is *one of the most needed gifts and skills today, to avoid the darkness of deception that is already upon the world* – and more so as evil counters God's Spirit-outpouring (renewal and revival around the world). The discerning are "the wise" that Daniel refers to (11:33; 12:3). Those who impart wisdom and direction give greater light as darkness increases.

"Discernment at its most basic level consists of recognising differences."[1] This applies to discernment in life, spiritual growth and direction, or counselling. I am discussing discernment *in healing ministry*. (See the gift of "discernments of spirits" in Chapter 11, with the biblical examples.) Without practising healing in Christ's name, discernment is a theory – it has no context in which to operate and grow. Being taught the theory of discernment *before* practice makes you overly cautious and critical – why some do not practise Spirit ministry. The charismatic Corinthians did the opposite: They practised Spirit manifestations as an end in itself – a self-indulgent party of spiritual phenomena – exercising little or no discernment, remaining ignorant and immature.

We need training in discernment in the context of ministry practice. When we engage in Spirit ministry, we quickly realise how little we know. It is often messy, unpredictable and mysterious.

- How do we make sense of people falling over, trembling, shaking, crying, feeling warm sensations and seeing visions?
- How do we know what God is doing in the manifestations that often accompany healing ministry?
- What is the exact nature of our experience of God or spirit?
- How do we distinguish good from evil – and from "neutral" – in these psycho-physiological manifestations?
- What are the biblical criteria for discernment?

Answering these questions will help us to move from ignorance to discernment of spiritual reality. The key is practice: *By reason of constant use we train our faculties to discern good and evil* (Hebrews 5:14). There is pressure on all fronts to reconcile good and evil into one, a monism called "love". Biblically they are forever separate: There is *real* ontological evil eternally opposed to a *real* good God.

So, *what is discernment in healing ministry?* Discernment is the Spirit's gift and cultivated ability to discern *God's presence and work*

---

[1]William Barry & William Connoly, *The Practice of Spiritual Direction* (San Francisco: HarperSanFrancisco, 1982), p. 102.

Part Three: Praxis

in a person's experience of ministry (positive aspect). Discernment is also evaluating spiritual manifestations to distinguish between spirits – knowing what motivates a particular experience or phenomenon: good (God), evil (Satan) or human (self or others).

Worldview and human nature

Discernment goes back to worldview and human nature. *Discernment of psycho-spiritual reality in ministry assumes a spiritual worldview and a wholistic view of human nature*, a highly complex unity. A rational-scientific worldview, with its material-analytical understanding of human nature gives no meaningful theory of personhood for psycho-spiritual discernment – it is about chemicals, material cause and effect, and psychological coping mechanisms.

I give a picture of worldview and human nature from a different angle to what I presented in Chapters 2 and 3. The following diagram[2] shows a *biblical view of the human person* as a basis for understanding and practising discernment in ministry. The diagram helps us to talk about our experience of reality – our encounter of God, evil and the natural material world.

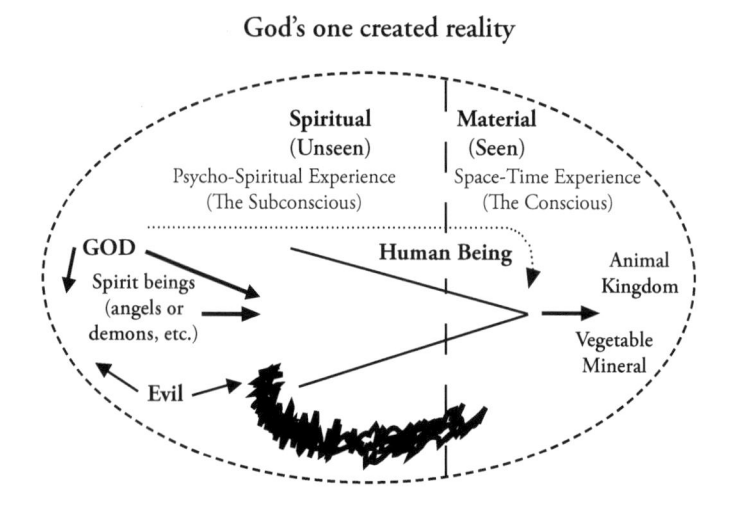

God's one created reality

Spiritual (Unseen) — Psycho-Spiritual Experience (The Subconscious)

Material (Seen) — Space-Time Experience (The Conscious)

GOD
Spirit beings (angels or demons, etc.)
Human Being
Animal Kingdom
Vegetable Mineral
Evil

---

[2] Adapted from Kelsey's basic diagrams, see *Discernment – A Study of Ecstasy and Evil* (New York: Paulist Press, 1978), p. 39; *Christo-Psychology* (London: Darton, Longman & Todd, 1982), pp. 32, 48; *Psychology, Medicine and Christian Healing*, pp. 246, 281.

There is one integrated reality. The dotted circle means God exists in and beyond his one created world, which has two dimensions: the spiritual and the material. The perforated line means the spiritual breaks into the physical world, which is the visible tip of the unseen iceberg. Likewise with human beings: the physical-conscious is the "tip" of the fathomless psycho-spiritual-subconscious.

God is spirit (John 4:24). He created spirit beings to live in the spiritual "heavenly" realm, interacting with the earthly realm as he assigns them. Human beings are uniquely created as embodied spirit beings *to live on earth in physical bodies*. This is *not* dualistic – that we are made of two parts, a superior spirit and inferior body. We are a dynamic, integrated unity, *uniquely straddling the two dimensions*: physically limited in time/space, but spiritually unlimited and opened-ended in our capacity to relate to (S)spirit, good or evil.

God "encounters" us in spiritual experience by his Holy Spirit, or via angelic messengers and even physical encounters (the dotted arrows). He seeks *willing* invitation and interaction for relational oneness in a shared (Trinitarian) life, to *progressively incarnate* himself in us with his Spirit and character, so that he comes *through our bodies* into the material world. We are his image-bearers, created to rule the earth on his behalf. The animal, vegetable and mineral kingdoms see us as God – we are God's primary instruments in the physical world. Our spiritual capacity is such that we can "be filled with all the fullness of God", as Paul prays (Ephesians 3:19 KJV). This will be fulfilled in the resurrection: our bodies will be *so* saturated with, and controlled by, God's Spirit, that we will transcend space-time limitations as God intended (Christ's resurrection body).

Evil entered God's creation through Lucifer's rebellion with his angels and spirits. He "encountered" human beings, deceiving them through their senses and appetites, separating them from God, enslaving their wills, darkening their minds, destroying their bodies and relationships. Satan interacts *indirectly* with the material world – his *primary means of access and control of planet earth is directly through human beings*. He seeks to incarnate himself progressively in people with his demonic spirits and evil character, to rule the earth *through them*, bringing "hell on earth", as he did with Hitler and the Nazis.

They become his image-bearers, filled with all the fullness of evil.

As human beings, we encounter *material reality* via our physical senses (conscious space-time experience). We encounter *spiritual reality* through our psycho-spiritual nature (subconscious experience or "twilight zone" between flesh and spirit). Words fail to describe, let alone understand, the psycho-spiritual complexity of human personality. We use words such as senses, emotions, thoughts, mind, memories, imagination, instincts, will, conscience, soul, spirit, heart to describe the "places" *through which* we experience spiritual encounter, and *from which* we respond, as seen in "outward" manifestations.

We cannot take a scalpel and dissect psycho-spiritual nature to see where the encounter is coming from, what is happening "in there". Only God knows the human being, the mysteries and motivations of the psyche (Jeremiah 17:9–10); only God's Word can penetrate and distinguish between soul and spirit, and discern the thoughts and intentions of the heart (Hebrews 4:12); only the Spirit, the "finger of God", can touch the deepest recesses of the human being in a redemptive and healing way. Spiritual encounter is complex because we are a dynamic body-spirit unity. It is mediated through, affected by, and can originate from, these various "places" within us. The question is: How do we discern what is of God, evil or ourselves in spiritual encounter?

Experience, encounter and discernment of phenomena

I have used the words "experience" and "encounter" carefully. All human *experience* of reality is about multidimensional *encounter*. Philosopher John E. Smith rescues "experience" from being dismissed as "subjective" (what happens "inside" us, especially "religious experience"), as opposed to the respected "objective" (what happens "outside" us, and can thus be "measured"). This contrast is a false dichotomy: "Experience ... [is] a product of the intersection of something encountered and a being capable of having the encounter, apprehending it, and feeling itself in the encounter, and capable of interpreting the results ... the labels 'subjective' and 'objective' vanish."[3]

---

[3] In *Experience and God* (New York: Oxford, 1968), p. 24, quoted in William Barry's discussion on the religious dimension of experience, in *Spiritual Direction*

Rationalism has questioned the legitimacy of human *experience*, resulting in our underdeveloped *affective* side. However, experience is *real*, not to be doubted by accusations of subjectivity, rather to be reflected on and evaluated by spiritual wisdom. We *experience God* in *spiritual encounter*: God's future kingdom breaks on us by the Holy Spirit – we "taste … the powers of the coming age" (Hebrews 6:4–5). The encounter is seen by the "signs" or manifestations of the kingdom, which are directly linked to faith and expectation. If we believe in God – that he *wants* to encounter us – and we ask and expect, it happens. If we do not believe, and we do not expect encounter, it mostly does not happen. Both the person receiving ministry *and* those ministering experience God encounter.

Our *life experience* includes *spiritual encounter* with evil. If we do not believe in personal evil – the devil and demons – we are blind to its encounter, deceived by its cunning. To be delivered from evil, we must believe in its existence by acknowledging its hold over us. We can open ourselves directly or indirectly to evil encounter in all the ways mentioned in Chapter 16 on demonisation.

All Spirit ministry in the name of Jesus is a spiritual experience of encounter *with God*. Evil does not normally intrude in such situations; rather, it is *manifested* as God's Spirit confronts its hold within us (sin, sickness, past hurt, demonisation) to drive it out, to heal us. The human element is central to the power encounter: it happens in our bodies – the battlefield of the "twilight zone". We respond or react accordingly, as seen in various outward phenomena. The absence of observable phenomena does not mean God is not encountering the person. Then we "fly blind" by Spirit intuition – we minister by faith and not by sight. However, the faintest outward manifestation and/or verbal feedback is helpful. It gets the juices flowing in working with God *and* the person to facilitate the power encounter. Ministry is a three-way encounter in discerning what God is doing, working with him to free the person.

How do we discern what God is doing in the psycho-physical manifestations of spiritual encounter? First, we must distinguish the Spirit

---

and the Encounter with God (New York: Paulist Press, 1992), pp. 24–41. See Kelsey's seminal work, *Encounter with God – A Theology of Christian Experience* (Minneapolis: Bethany, 1972).

encounter from *our* response, the manifestations. Second, we must evaluate the encounter itself – its source motivation, purpose and fruit – according to certain criteria, discussed below. We must avoid two extremes with regard to manifestations: identifying spiritual phenomena too readily with God's Spirit or the demonic, without discerning the human element (that leads to naïve endorsement of what happens); dismissing the phenomena as "emotionalism" or "deception", not discerning the Spirit's work, resulting in critical indifference and rejection.

The level of demonstrative or barely perceptible manifestations of the Spirit's encounter is determined by a mix of temperament, self-consciousness, environment, religious and cultural conditioning, desperation, pain, intensity of the Spirit's power and strength of evil's hold. The authenticity and effectiveness of the encounter should *never* be judged by the intensity of the human response, by the outward "shows of power" or lack thereof.

However, we can be *unresponsive to the Spirit* due to doubt, shyness, pride or fear. This can hinder or resist God's work in the ministry encounter. When a person senses something, I encourage them to cooperate and express what is happening, not to close up, withdraw, get scared, or become self-conscious. In so doing, we must *not* draw unnecessary attention to, or focus on, *the outward signs* or stimulate *them* to higher intensity. That is wrongful manipulation (like autosuggestion, crowd hype, mass hysteria/hypnosis), which is *the fourth element* that can motivate manifestations.[4] Spiritual encounter is an interactive and cooperative experience between the Spirit, the person and the minister(s). God rarely does it unilaterally without invitation and participation.

The point is, we experience God in the mysterious psycho-spiritual "complex" of who we are – broken and fragmented by sin and death. *Therefore we learn to evaluate outward phenomena without judging them too quickly or superficially.* Paul told the Corinthians to evaluate Spirit manifestations precisely because the human element through which they come could possibly be motivating them, or even the

---

[4]Besides God, evil, and personal psychological factors, whether conscious or unconscious. See John White, *When the Spirit Comes with Power* (London: Hodder & Stoughton, 1992), pp. 60–61.

intrusion of evil.[5] Every spiritual encounter is a mix needing at least some discernment and pastoring. We learn to discern good and evil and the human element *by practice, Spirit insight, honest feedback and conscious reflection.*

Biblical criteria for discernment

This discussion, and healing ministry itself, must be seen in *the context of God's kingdom power encounter in the Bible and church history*. Both are full of documented accounts of psycho-physical phenomena in power encounter.

The Toronto Blessing in the 1990s brought blessing and controversy in terms of the accompanying manifestations. Leaders went back to church history and the Bible "to see whether these things are so". The fresh outpouring of God's Spirit was similar to other refreshings, renewals, revivals and awakenings experienced throughout the centuries. They vary in intensity, length of time, purpose and fruit, but they *all* have an outburst of spiritual phenomena – a mixed bag of the good, human and evil, needing discernment and pastoring. Books have been written explaining these revival phenomena, both for[6] and against.[7]

The Bible records these phenomena. People responded – even re-

---

[5] Kelsey says: "Human beings are deeper and more complex than we ordinarily realise. Many things that appear demonic in us are actually rejected parts of ourselves. They have broken unceremoniously into our lives because we have refused to look at all of us and so have failed to work at integration and wholeness," *Discernment*, p. 81. Trying to "cast out" natural parts of the person that have been wounded, suppressed or are crying out for attention, can be damaging. Equally damaging is not driving out evil when it is present. I have seen bodily manifestations that are violent and strange, appearing demonic, but often they come from deep emotional wounding that needs compassionate healing (see footnote 4).

[6] Barry & Connoly (footnote 1); Dave Roberts, *The 'Toronto' Blessing* (Eastbourne: Kingsway, 1994); Dr Patrick Dixon, *Signs of Revival* (Eastbourne: Kingsway, 1994); William DeArteaga, *Quenching the Spirit: Examining Centuries of Opposition to the Moving of the Holy Spirit* (Florida: Creation House, 1992); Robert Burns, *Revivals: Their Laws and Leaders* (London: Hodder, 1909); Jonathan Edwards, *The Works of Jonathan Edwards*, vol. 1 (Edinburgh: Banner of Truth, 1979).

[7] D. Hunt & T. McMahon, *The Seduction of Christianity* (Oregon: Harvest House, 1985); John MacArthur, *Charismatic Chaos* (Grand Rapids: Zondervan, 1992); Peter Masters, *The Healing Epidemic* (London: Wakeman Trust, 1988). Most use Benjamin Warfield, *Counterfeit Miracles* (Edinburgh: Banner of Truth, 1972) as their source.

acted – to God's Spirit physically, emotionally, psychologically, not "spiritually and reverently". The Hebrews explained their experience of God in concrete terms: Mount Sinai shook and trembled under God's presence – like Jeremiah, who said, "all my bones tremble. I am like a drunken man ... overcome by wine, because of Yahweh and his holy words" (23:9). The Hebrew *rahapu* (tremble) means to flutter, shake, vibrate, like the flapping of a bird's wings – derived from *rahap*, used for God's Spirit "hovering" over the deep in Genesis 1:2. The Hebrew word *kabod* (glory) is from a root describing weight or substance that is heavy, making a person fall, as in 2 Chronicles 5:13–14.[8] Similar explanations apply to weeping (Nehemiah 8:9–10) and to overwhelming joy (Acts 2:13–18) in God's presence.

This is a sample of the many texts describing power encounter and consequent spiritual phenomena – similar to what happens in ministry encounters today. *What do we make of manifestations that are not substantiated by "chapter and verse" – extra-biblical experiences?* The fact that it is not in Scripture does not mean it is not of God. Extra-biblical stuff is okay; it is what directly transgresses Scripture that is *not* okay. Arguments from silence ("It is not in the Bible, so it is not true") and using the Bible to proof-text things, is seriously problematic. The biblical narrative is selective, not exhaustive. Certain doctrines are *derived* from Scripture, not systematically taught in Scripture, for example the doctrine of the Trinity, the foundation of Christian faith. The Bible teaches us to examine things by their fruit, not by their phenomenology.

In terms of biblical theology, Spirit manifestations are eschatological: the future kingdom breaks into the present by the Spirit. In that encounter we experience resurrection power in our bodies – a foretaste or "voltage surge" of the resurrection. No wonder our bodies and emotions react by trembling, shaking, falling, crying, and laughing! If *the full* resurrectional power of the Spirit came on us, our bodies would explode or be transfigured into glorified bodies, like Jesus' glorified body. These happenings produce *altered states of consciousness*, with the physiological characteristics attending such experiences.[9]

---

[8] See Gary Creig & Kevin Springer, *The Kingdom and the Power* (Ventura: Regal, 1993), pp. 435, 342.
[9] See them in Dr Patrick Dixon's helpful medical perspective in *Signs of Revival,* pp.

Discernment: *Evaluating spiritual phenomena in healing*

The danger is when we seek the altered state of consciousness as an end in itself. We get hooked on the repeated physiological phenomena (chemical release), wanting the intense reality of the first stimulation. But it wanes this side of the resurrection – the Spirit blows like the wind, coming and going. The result is the "routinization" of mystical experiences, perpetuating the outward form without the inner reality, a psychosomatic "technique of the Spirit", an empty religious ritual. The Desert Fathers and Eastern Church warned that mystical experiences are gifts to novices in the faith to "allure" them to God. The mature do not seek, want or need such "consolations". Although they experienced profound mystical "signs and wonders", they did not talk about them, downplaying and even ignoring them, seeking spiritual fathers/directors to discern them.[10]

Here are *other biblical principles and criteria for discernment*.

1. *What are the signs and wonders used for?* Deuteronomy 13 warns that signs and wonders (spiritual phenomena) do not determine nor legitimate the truth, or the person (prophet) through whom they come. If the encounter and manifestations lead the person away from pure worship of God, they are not of God. Signs and wonders can be done for self-glory, to deceive people into false beliefs, for personal power over others, and for financial gain.

2. *What is the content and intent of the phenomena?* Ezekiel 13 says prophetic phenomena can come from a person's spirit and imagination, motivated by their own sentiment and vested interests. They can also be "lying divinations" motivated by evil. How is that to be discerned? *Not* by the ecstatic phenomena accompanying the prophetic, but by *the content and intent as judged by other recognised and respected prophets.*

3. *What is the fruit that is produced?* This is the common and sure

---

258–279.

[10]Their experiences make modern Charismatics look tame! See Kyriacos Markides, pp. 78–93. George Maloney says "a good spiritual guide will direct a person of deep prayer away from any inordinate desire to 'possess' or collect mystical experiences as such. Such an attachment to the psychic phenomena … can spell the ruin of the budding mystic. Such spiritual sensuality can only lead to a sick self-centering that dehumanizes and prevents the flow of God's love toward others", *Discovering the Hidden Reality* (New York: Alba House, 2004), p. 178.

test of the motivating source and authenticity of spiritual phenomena. Fruit can be seen immediately, or it emerges over time, both in the person experiencing the phenomena, and in the ministering (prophetic) persons (Matthew 7:15–27). The fruit must be that *of the Holy Spirit* listed in Galatians 5:22, of the "wisdom that comes from above" listed in James 3:17. If the persons ministering the Spirit have these fruit, they are of God. If the phenomena result in healing, cleansing, transformation, joy, peace, intimacy with Jesus, obedience to his Word, it is of God. If it leaves the person more depressed, fearful, selfish, disobedient, divisive, carnal, it is the fruit of fallen nature (Galatians 5:19–21), and the "wisdom of the devil" (James 3:14–16).

4. *Does it glorify Christ?* What is motivated by God's Spirit glorifies Christ, confessing his Lordship (brings the person under Christ's rule). If the phenomena undermine Christ's Lordship (cursing him, glorifying another), they are not of God (1 Corinthians 12:1–3). We "test the spirits" by whether they affirm Jesus as God's Son come in the flesh (1 John 4:1–3). If the phenomena result in a denial of Christ's deity and incarnation, they are not of God.

5. *By the gift of the Spirit:* We can know whether certain manifestations are stimulated by God encounter or not, through the Holy Spirit's gift of distinguishing between spirits. This gift can operate via intuitive insight and/or experience in evaluating and judging. It operates with the Spirit's authority and clarity of "knowing", which is then proven to be correct. A track record of accuracy and wisdom builds, with increasing authority and clarity, which can be trusted.

There is a biblical criterion that some who are anti spiritual phenomena use from Paul in 1 Corinthians 14:12–40: that everything must be done "decently and in order to edify others". Whatever contradicts this purpose is not of God – spiritual phenomena included, they say. It is a misuse of Scripture. Paul assumes a church meeting with the purpose of group edification, such as a worship service or teaching meeting. These have their particular order. Spirit manifestations can "fit into" this orderly purpose to edify the body. *When we have min-*

istry meetings or *ministry times*, individuals are ministered to for the purpose of kingdom encounter and healing. The purpose and order is different – all sorts of spiritual phenomena take place. It can be a kind of "holy chaos" as the Spirit is freely poured out on those who *are there for that purpose* – to receive Spirit ministry.

There is a pastoral lesson to be learnt from Paul. If a person's manifestations "*de*-edify" others nearby – distracting or stopping them from receiving from God – we should adjust or tone the manifestations down by gentle intervention and instruction. "The spirits of the prophets are subject to the prophets" can be applied to the person's response to the Spirit manifestations: They *can* adjust or tone it down! We cannot say "God did it" or "God made me do it"! We are responsible.

Common phenomena and possible indications

To conclude this chapter, I list some Spirit manifestations that we began to tabulate in the early 1980s with John Wimber. They are drawn from ministry experience, not directly from Scripture. Some have *possible* indications as to what kind of healing *might be* happening, while others are unknown. You can learn from them and add to them *without* being dogmatic or making a theology out of them (which is our tendency!).

Spiritual phenomena on the person receiving Spirit ministry

1. Different *forms of tenderness and crying* are a common Spirit manifestation. Feeling tender, broken, soft crying, strong weeping or even deep bellowing and screaming all indicate different kinds of spiritual cleansing, emotional healing and, at times, demonic release. Various body postures go with it, from bowing the head, to crumbling to the floor, and curling up in a foetal position. There is a weeping that is neurotic, not of the Spirit, indicating self-pity.

2. Another common phenomenon is *fluttering of the eyelids, trembling of the hands* or *fluttering sensations*, often accompanied by a *glow or serenity* on the person's face. You see other expressions on the face: sadness, darkness, contortion, shiftiness of the eyes,

or a brazen stare, indicating guilt and shame, anger, grief or a demonic presence.

3. *Heat* in certain parts of the body being ministered to or heat generally in the body. People might perspire profusely. Some have *hot flushes, tingling or goose bumps* on the skin. These often indicate various physical healings. There is *a sensation of burning up* that can indicate a demonic presence being confronted and driven out.

4. *Cold* sensations on the skin or in parts of the body can also indicate healing, like applying a cold pack to an injury. There is a *different coldness* that can indicate a demonic presence. Once I felt the room temperature drop in a deliverance session.

5. *Sensations of power* in different forms and intensity: a power zone, air waves, electrical currents, surges, jerks in the body, often accompanied by heavy breathing, crying, groans, shouts, jumping, demonstrative body actions, even being lifted in the air. They can indicate God's liquid love or kinds of Spirit empowering.

6. There is also *trembling and shaking* of certain body parts, or the whole body, with varying intensity and movements, from mild to extreme and violent. These again may indicate pain or woundedness "trapped" in the body, now being released. Or there is resistance and reaction to God's power by a demonic presence.

7. The opposite is various forms of *stiffness, "stuckness", or contortions* in the body. People have reported their feet stuck to the ground, or they hold a fixed body position for hours. Different body parts can go stiff, clench, or contort – commonly the hands and fingers – indicating a power encounter of sorts (compulsive theft, lust and masturbation, violence, animal spirits).

8. There are different types of *bodily "heaviness", loss of balance and falling over*. I do not like the phrase "slain in the Spirit". I prefer "resting" or "being overwhelmed" by the Spirit. The phenomenon of loss of balance and falling over is common. It can indicate rest and refreshing in God's love or inner healing. But there is a way of falling that indicates a demonic reaction.

9. Different types of *peace, wooziness*, being *spaced out*, even a *trance-like state*. These may indicate reactions of stress, long-standing emotional pain, or the anaesthetic of the Spirit, as he operates and heals in deep ways, often with visions and revelatory experiences. Again, there is a type of sleepiness and spacing out that indicates a demonic evasive tactic.
10. Lastly, there are different kinds of *exhilaration, drunken joy and laughter*. As at Pentecost, there are degrees of *spontaneous* Spirit intoxication, laughter and jubilation. It can be profoundly healing: "A cheerful heart is good medicine" (Proverbs 17:22). Today people pay for laughter therapy with psychologists and gurus. There is a kind of laughter that is forced (attention-seeking); and a laughter that is jarring, jeering, scorning (demonic reaction).

The spiritual phenomena on the person(s) doing the ministry

These can be similar to the above, except that they are in service of the receiving person. If the manifestations on those ministering distract, manipulate, intimidate or dominate the recipient of ministry, they are out of order and must be corrected. The spirit of the prophet is subject to the prophet. These complement "How we hear God" in Chapter 12.

1. *Feelings of tenderness, tearfulness or weeping* are generally manifestations of God's compassion for the person – to be distinguished from crying that stems from sympathy, sentimentality or brokenness. It does not heal; if anything, it transfers our brokenness to the recipient, unless they resist it.
2. *Heat or cold or tingling in our hands* indicates an impartation of healing into the body, hence we "lay on hands". "Psychic healing" that operates by laying on "warm" hands is *not* benign as some suppose. The heat and healing come from another spirit. The psyche is merely an instrument, even if they think it is their own power.
3. *Sensations of power* can flow through us as we minister, from mild to strong, manifested in various ways: trembling hands, electric surges or power going out of our bodies. By practice you can feel if the power is being received or resisted by the recipient. We must

distinguish *God's* power from our own power – that of human personality and charisma, suggestion and persuasion, which does not heal, but over time enslaves those being ministered to.

4. *Various sensations on our skin* that indicate the Spirit is present and working, like goose bumps, a gentle breath, hot flush, cool breeze, and a fragrance.
5. *A sense of "disembodied" detachment or assertive engagement.* At times there is a sensation of standing outside yourself watching you do and say the impossible by the Spirit's prompting. Or there is a strong conviction and boldness that rises, causing you to say and do things in pure faith.

These two lists are selective, not exhaustive – least of all final. There are many other kinds of Spirit manifestations and phenomena on both the recipient(s) and the minster(s) that could be added. Each would have their corresponding indications of possible meaning and kinds of healing.

Personal reflection, application and group discussion

1. How do *you* relate to Spirit manifestations in general? What exposure have you had to them?
2. Have *you* experienced Spirit manifestations in your body? In receiving ministry and/or in doing ministry? Explain what happened, how you understand it, and what the manifestations have resulted in.
3. What has been your own experience and understanding of discernment related to the things of the Spirit? How have you defined discernment? Has your understanding changed in reading this chapter? How?
4. Why is discernment *so* important and *so greatly needed* in the church and world today?
5. Why, and how, are we unique when compared to both spirit beings and material creation – the animal, vegetable and mineral kingdoms? What implications does it have for understanding and practising discernment of spiritual phenomena?
6. Do you agree with my biblical criteria of discernment? Anything to add?
7. Practically, how do *you* exercise discernment in ministry? Explain.
8. What are *the dangers* we need to be aware of, both in experiencing and in ministering Spirit manifestations? And in discerning them?

21

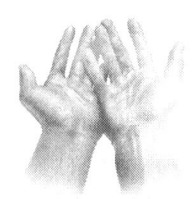

COMMISSION:
THE CHURCH'S HEALING
MINISTRY: "GO ..."

*"Go into all the world and preach the good news to all creation.
Whoever believes and is baptised will be saved,
but whoever does not believe will be condemned.
And these signs will accompany those who believe:
In my name they will drive out demons ...
they will place their hands on sick people,
and they will get well."*
– Jesus' Great Commission, Mark 16:15–18

The first time I experienced a "formal" impartation and commissioning for healing ministry was with John Wimber in 1982. It was in our third healing seminar. He called up those who wanted to be used by God to minister healing. At least half of the audience went forward, including me. He anointed our foreheads and hands with oil and said: "Receive the power! Go, drive out demons and heal the sick." The Spirit of God manifested in various ways.

After a while John asked all who were sick to stand – about a third responded. Then those he had anointed had to minister in twos and threes to those who stood for healing. Again, the Spirit of God broke out in all sorts of phenomena and healings. It was like a clinic or laboratory, where we experimented and practised the Spirit's gifts in safety, with many reported healings.

Whenever I have done this exercise after training times or in churches, it has had the same powerful effect. In doing so, I have noticed two things: it is mostly understood and received in individual terms, and spiritual warfare precedes and/or follows such powerful ministry times. Authentic community answers both these issues. In concluding this book, I want to comment on healing as a local church ministry and the spiritual warfare that accompanies healing ministry. I close with an impartation and commission to you, the reader, to go and minister the kingdom of God in the power of the Spirit.

Developing a healing ministry in the local church

Western individualism has undermined and destroyed community. We need to move from an individual mindset ("*I* do ministry") to a community mentality and responsibility ("*We* do ministry"). Most of us hear the great commission in individual terms, reinforcing our personal guilt for not "reaching the world". We are personally responsible, but it was addressed to the community of disciples – it was meant to be done *together* as the body of Jesus Christ.

Healing is done most effectively from within and through *God's local community* into the world around it. Mark's great commission implies a transfer of healing ministry in community: Those who believe are baptised; then *those believers* speak in tongues, drive out demons and heal the sick. Similarly Matthew says we must go and make apprentices of Jesus by baptising them into the Trinitarian God *and* teaching *them* to *obey all that Jesus commanded* (28:19–20). What is that? Jesus *commanded* them to preach the kingdom, heal the sick, raise the dead, cleanse the lepers and drive out demons, because freely they have received, so freely they must give (Matthew 10:7–8). It is truly tragic to see the powerlessness of the church. We have denied our calling to be a Spirit-healing church.

Part Three: Praxis

How do we, as a local church, heal the sick?

This has assumptions and implications: Are *you* committed to, and do you participate fully in a local church? Many local churches do not have a visible, coordinated and meaningful healing ministry. Consequently individual Charismatic Christians do their own thing. *Church leaders are responsible before God* to practise Spirit ministry; to model, train, transfer and multiply it in and through their congregations for the salvation of the world, in obedient fulfilment of the great commission.

I need to make two distinctions regarding a healing ministry in the local church. Between

1. A *disciplined practice* and a *gifted ministry*. Every follower of Jesus is called to practise laying on of hands in healing ministry as a matter of personal discipleship to Jesus. Not every believer develops faith and gifting to where healing is their recognised public ministry. The latter emerge as leaders in ministry, not to do the healing themselves, but to initiate and equip *the church* into the disciplined practice of healing.
2. The healing *dimension* and *intention*.[1] By nature the church is a healing community, thus everything the church does has or should have a healing dimension to it. Healing should be in the environment, felt and transmitted in all that the church does. But not all that the church does has a healing *intention*. Normally there is one, or maybe two ministries intentionally doing healing. *The leaders are responsible* to build the healing dimension *and* intention into the life of the church. How do they do that?

By taking the following steps – what we call "the Vineyard mantra", because it is so foundational. John Wimber repeated it wherever he went:[2]

- *Model* healing ministry intentionally and consistently so that the congregation can see it, how it is done, how God works. It creates an expectant environment and gives permission for

---
[1] Adapted from David Bosch in being a missional church, *Witness to the World,* pp. 199–201.
[2] See my discussion on this in *Doing Church,* pp. 197–200.

Spirit ministry to happen in church.
- *Educate* the congregation about healing ministry: Teach the Gospel stories; prescribe key books for reading; periodically invite *trusted* colleagues who are gifted in Spirit ministry, who represent your values.
- *Identify* those who show appetite for healing ministry, who willingly learn when it is practised. Initially throw the net wide by inviting all who are interested to participate in ministry. After a couple of months, some will emerge as enthusiastic and consistent learners, keen to practise ministry whenever they can. (See the "Qualifications" in Chapter 10).
- *Recruit* those you have identified, who "naturally" present themselves by faithful participation, as well as those whom God reveals, as he did to Jesus (Luke 6:12–16; John 17:2, 6, 9). To recruit is to invite them personally to commit to a planned process of training to achieve a particular vision.
- *Train* them via an intentional process, while educating the congregation and publicly practising healing ministry. To train is to equip them with ministry skills through show and tell – on-the-job coaching and other programs like seminars. The goal is to train a team to lead a healing ministry.
- *Deploy* them when ready to take responsibility for an ongoing healing ministry. It means commissioning (laying hands and anointing) them in a *program or structure* (with a leader) that serves the congregation and/or surrounding community in a healing ministry.[3]
- *Monitor* them by continuing to encourage, nurture and hold them accountable in both their personal practice and ministry program.
- *Get them to repeat the process* with others who are drawn into healing ministry by their practice – they model, identify, recruit, train and deploy. Thus it can grow into other types of healing ministries, and healing is multiplied in and through the church.

---

[3] They can be the authorised team responsible to do the ministry at Sunday meetings, mandated to draw others in to learn and practise ministry. There are many types of intentional healing ministries that emerge in and beyond the local church – like Living Waters, Healing Rooms, and various recovery groups.

Part Three: Praxis

Spiritual warfare in healing ministry

Healing ministry does not come without opposition from Satan. Any practice and multiplication of kingdom ministry will provoke reaction from evil, because sickness is the domain of Satan. He does not take kindly to us "plundering his house" (Matthew 12:28–29). We need to have an informed and responsible approach to spiritual warfare. Our greatest support, balance and protection is community. We are accountable to one another, disclose our struggles and temptations, and pray for each other. We also protect ourselves in spiritual warfare through personal vigilance and ongoing spiritual disciplines.

The devil attacks both community (the ministry program) and individually in our practice of healing, before, during and after Spirit ministry. *We need to be aware of how we are attacked,* putting on "the full armour of God so that [we] can take [our] stand against the devil's schemes" (Ephesians 6:11). We submit ourselves to God and resist the devil so that he flees from us (James 4:7).

The following lists are selective, merely giving an idea of how the devil attacks us.

How does Satan attack community – the healing team and ministry?

- Relational tensions and disagreements are by far the most common source of attack – they need to be resolved immediately and properly.
- Unmet expectations within the team and ministry – failed promises, seeking recognition, and leadership failure.
- Not responding to honest feedback and correction properly or not giving feedback and correction wisely and graciously.
- Accusations from dissatisfied or hurt people who were not healed. People and media outside the church can discredit the healing ministry. Blaming and disqualifying "the healer" and God is a common tactic of evil.
- Physical, emotional and spiritual attacks on team members and/or the leader.

What may happen before or on the way to do healing?

- Feeling disinterested, tired, irritated, frustrated or put out.
- Sudden depression or mood change, with feelings of worthlessness.
- Inner accusations of guilt and shame, doubt, inadequacy, and even fear.
- Tension or strife with people close to you – often your spouse or children.
- Specific incidents, circumstances, bodily attacks try to block you.

What may happen while you are ministering to the sick?

- Various kinds of inner and outer distractions and interruptions.
- No sense of anointing, faith – nothing happening – doing it mechanically!
- If dramatic things happen, a sudden injection of panic, fear, uncertainty.
- Confused doubts, unwholesome thoughts, condemning accusations.
- Inner feelings of discouragement, dismay, and/or defeat.
- A subtle temptation to overdo it; to push beyond your faith into presumption and manipulation; to be spectacular and heroic.
- Focus on the condition and not on the healing – especially if the condition is drastic – causing alarm, human sympathy, doubt and fear.

What may happen after you have engaged in Spirit ministry?

- Most common is exhaustion, self-doubt and depression.
- A sense of discouragement and failure – with inner accusations – especially if people were not healed, or if you made a "mistake".
- If it was a good experience, a sense of exhilaration can tempt our pride – the inner voice that says, "You are a prophet! God's man for the hour!"
- Indifference, mixed feelings, gnawing insecurity and uncertainty.

Not all of these happen all the time; some of them (and others I have not listed) happen some of the time. Being aware of them helps us to identify, resist and overcome them when they do happen. Lack of knowledge and awareness of the devil's tactics allows him to beat us up and destroy community, often with our unwitting cooperation (2 Corinthians 2:11). As Paul instructs, we need to put on God's full armour daily to resist and overcome Satan's attacks, especially when "the day of evil comes" (Ephesians 6:13–18).

Paul's list of armour is to *cultivate daily proactive attitudes and disciplines.* It is not reactive repetitions and confessions as some teach: "I claim the belt of truth; I put on the breastplate of righteousness; I wear the shoes …"

- *Truthfulness and integrity (v. 14)* – based on God's truth and truthfulness – as the seat or foundation of our existence.
- *Righteousness and good character (v. 14)* to protect our hearts – the source of our being and doing.
- *Constant readiness (v. 15)* to share the good news of Messiah's *Shalom* with people.
- *Strong faith in God (v. 16)* that shields us from Satan's attacks and overcomes them.
- *Assurance and understanding of salvation (v. 17)* to guard our minds from attack.
- *Knowledge and usage of God's Word (v. 17)* to resist temptation and defeat evil as Jesus did in the wilderness (Matthew 4:4, 7, 10).
- *Constant prayerfulness and vigilance (v. 18)* in all situations, with ongoing requests and interaction with God, including prayers for others.

These seven daily disciplines (cultivated characteristics) are the armour that protects us and overcomes the attacks of Satan, both in Spirit ministry and in general life. They proactively equip us to do ministry with growing power, precision and penetration, to plunder the kingdom of darkness.

The commission and charge

All that remains is to affirm Christ's commission and charge to the church – including you personally – and to pronounce a blessing or prayer of impartation over you, trusting that you will receive a fresh anointing for healing ministry.

The leaders and people who know you well, with whom you walk in learning to heal the sick and drive out demons, should lay hands on you. *They* are the ones who empower, recognise and release you, *not* to do your *own* ministry, but to continue *Christ's kingdom ministry*, which he entrusted to his church. You are accountable to God *through your community* for the continuance of Jesus' ministry in your church and in your world.

Therefore: "Go and preach the good news, drive out demons and heal the sick." You have heard that a thousand times! Let me rather RAP Paul's awesome charge to Timothy (2 Timothy 4:1–2), because we are all Timothys, learning to minister as Jesus ministered in the power of the Spirit.

Read and receive these words as addressed to you personally:

> *"In the presence of God and of Messiah Jesus, who will judge the living and the dead, and in view of his appearing and his kingdom, I give you this charge: Preach the Word, heal the sick, drive out demons. Be prepared to do this in season and out of season, with great patience and careful instruction."*

> *Father, in my own sinfulness, weakness and struggles,*
> *I pray for this person reading these words:*
> *Take what is of you in this book and plant it deep in their hearts.*
> *Assure them of your personal presence and unfailing love.*
> *Anoint them in the faithful usage of your spiritual gifts.*
> *Train them in the mysterious ways of your Holy Spirit.*
> *Transform them into your compassionate instrument of healing in your church, as authentic Trinitarian community, and in your world, as people for whom your Son died and rose again.*
> *Please do this Father, in the name of Jesus Christ. Amen.*

Part Three: Praxis

Personal reflection, application and group discussion

1. Why is healing ministry best done *in and through* local Christian community? Can we not do it anytime, anywhere, when we feel like it?
2. Do you belong to and participate in a local church? If not, why not? Does it have a healing ministry? How can you participate in it or help to develop it?
3. What has been your experience of spiritual warfare as it affects church and community, teams and ministry programs? Share an example.
4. What has been your personal experience of spiritual warfare in your own practice of ministry? Which of the attacks of Satan that I listed can you identify with? What others have you experienced that I have not mentioned?
5. How do you *recognise* Satan's attack in ministry? Practically, how do you deal with it and overcome it? How do you understand Paul's teaching to "put on the armour of God"? Do you agree with my interpretation of it?
6. Did you experience anything in reading my charge and impartation prayer? Have you ever had an "empowering for ministry" experience as I described at the opening of this chapter? What did it do for you?
7. List three, at most four, things this book has done for you – what God has said to you through it. What are you going to do about them?

Appendix 1: Understanding Gnosticism[1]

Introduction and definition

Gnosticism is a comprehensive belief system, a worldview that sees knowledge as key to salvation. Salvation is attaining higher levels of spirituality. Gnosticism is derived from the Greek *gnosis*, meaning knowledge (used in the New Testament). Gnosticism uses *gnosis* as a special, revelatory and secret kind of knowledge that initiates a person into a level of enlightenment ("salvation"), and thus into an elite group of "those who *really* know", those who are "spiritual".

Origin and influence

Gnosticism came from a mixture of Eastern mystery religions and Greek philosophy, used to re-interpret New Testament Christianity. It was incipiently present in the early church, refuted in John's Gospel, 1 John, Revelation 1–3, 1 and 2 Corinthians, Colossians, 1 and 2 Timothy and 2 Peter. The offer of personal spiritual experiences, as opposed to rational explanations, was Gnosticism's appeal. Secret rituals and intense experiences led to special knowledge that freed the person from problems and demons, making them more spiritual. It was a mix of beliefs – including Christian elements – becoming full-blown between 150 and 400 CE when the "Gnostic Gospels" were written – *The Gospel of Thomas, The Secret Teachings of John, The Gospel of Mary,* to mention a few. Dan Brown's novel *The Da Vinci Code* presents them as truth. Today Gnosticism is represented in the eclectic New Age beliefs and postmodernism, in a world traumatised by rapid change, tired of rational-materialism, and hungry for spiritual

---

[1] This is an adaptation of a paper I wrote years ago for our congregation on true biblical and false Gnostic spirituality. I have used Bible dictionaries, Derek Morphew, *Spiritual Spider Web* and Jeffrey Satinover, *Empty Self.*

experience. Throughout her history, the church has fought Gnosticism. It is no different today: Gnostic influence is like a widespread spiritual spiderweb in the contemporary church.

Basic beliefs

The heart of Gnosticism is a *dualistic view of reality*, the spiritual world versus the physical world. The former is inherently good (spirit) – the source of all things. The latter is inherently bad (physical body/material world) – it is a fallen expression of the spiritual. The spiritual is mediated to us via descending levels of emanations, spiritual beings and revelations, in order to enlighten the "spark" (our spirit) that is in us from God/the gods. The greater the revelations via more intense experiences and practices, the higher we ascend the ladder of spirituality. This naturally leads to pride and elitism. The dualism means that we are "saved" in our spirit, *not* in our body. Because of this we indulge and let our bodies go in license and licentiousness (we are saved in our spirit!), or we despise and reject our bodies in legalism and asceticism, to free the spirit in salvation and spirituality. See the diagram below.

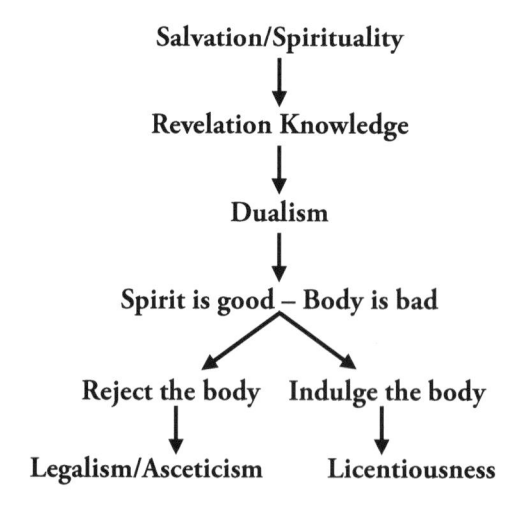

Salvation/Spirituality
↓
Revelation Knowledge
↓
Dualism
↓
Spirit is good – Body is bad
↙ ↘
Reject the body   **Indulge the body**
↓ ↓
Legalism/Asceticism   **Licentiousness**

Worldview confusion

Because the Gnostic worldview is *spiritual*, having elements that appear Christian, it appeals to some Christians. They do not realise that it is closer to a *magical worldview*, which believes that, by certain practices, we can experience and use spiritual powers for ourselves and others – we can manipulate and even control others through spiritual powers (1 Samuel 28:3–25; Acts 8:14–24). Biblically, we are *not* to consult, invoke or use spirits/angels. We are to consult and worship *only the God revealed in Jesus Christ*. We do so *through his Holy Spirit* – no other spirit. Some Christians practise religious rituals and spiritual disciplines to experience and use spiritual power (God and/or angels) for themselves and others. This is not Christianity; it is divination and witchcraft. We *never* "use" God for ourselves, nor manipulate or control people through God's power. We are *always and only* servants of God and his power.

False spirituality

With regard to Gnostic influence on Christian spirituality, Paul warned Timothy: "Turn away from godless chatter and the opposing ideas of what is falsely called knowledge (*gnosis*), which some have professed and in so doing have wandered from the faith" (1 Timothy 6:20). Gnosticism is preoccupied with revelation, distorting the truth of God's revelation. Those who are "truly spiritual" receive revelation (secret knowledge). This "hearing from God" makes them special, leading to spiritual pride, placing them above correction: "You do not agree with me because you do not understand: God hasn't revealed it to you yet. If you prayed enough and heard from God, *then* you would understand and agree with me." They take any disagreement or correction as personal rejection, which often results in projection: "You do not understand me because you're in the flesh" or "You're under a controlling spirit."

Scriptural misuse

As Peter says (2 Peter 3:15–16), some people misinterpret and misuse

Paul's (and John's) writings to teach forms of Gnostic thinking. Paul and John were Jews: they thought Hebraically, but wrote in Greek. *Their method of correcting Gnostic ideas is important*: They *directly* refuted errors fundamental to Christian faith – Gnostics denied the human incarnation of Christ and his physical resurrection – but they did *not* directly attack distortions to Christian truth that the Gnostics claimed for themselves. Rather, Paul and John used terminology that Gnostics used to reaffirm Christian truth, thus correcting error. Consequently some have misused this in support of Gnostic ideas. Here are some examples:

- *Secret wisdom and revelation:* In 1 Corinthians 1–2 Paul speaks of "revelation" and "secret wisdom" that has been "hidden". This got the Gnostics salivating. He uses it against them by saying the revelation and wisdom of God is Jesus Christ – not a spirit revealed to the initiated elite, but a man revealed to the ordinary everyone!
- *The spiritual versus the natural (and carnal):* In 1 Corinthians 2–4 Paul contrasts the "spiritual" person with the "natural" or "carnal". The spiritual are those who have received God's Spirit, not those who have great revelations. The natural live by worldly values and the carnal by their corrupted appetites – they are *not* those who are without revelation knowledge. Paul says in effect: "If you can't understand God's revelation, it is because of your pride, disunity and conflict." True spirituality is relational, not revelational.
- *Body and worldliness:* In 1 Corinthians 5–8 Paul deals with wrong views of sexuality, the body and worldliness. "Do not touch, do not eat, do not drink" type legalism leads to hidden immorality and even lawsuits against one another (see Colossians 3:13–23). Equally, "everything is permissible" leads to licentiousness. Both legalism and licence are false spiritualities. True spirituality is to honour our bodies and material creation by honouring God and one another with our bodies, as indwellings of God's Spirit.
- *Knowledge versus faith and love:* 1 Corinthians 8 contrasts knowledge with love. We are *not* saved by *gnosis*, which "puffs

Appendix 1: *Understanding Gnosticism*

up", makes proud, but by faith in Jesus Christ, which leads to love and service – true spirituality.

- *Super apostles versus true apostles:* 1 Corinthians 4 and 2 Corinthians 11 and 12 deal with Gnostic views of leadership. The real apostles are *not* those who have great revelations, are good orators, have title, position and power (called "super apostles"; Paul called them "false apostles"), but those who suffer for Christ's sake, laying down their lives for God's people and God's world (true spirituality).

- *Spirituality and manifestation gifts:* 1 Corinthians 11–14 corrects Gnostic excesses in worship and spiritual gifts. The spiritual are *not* those who have dramatic revelations, gifts and manifestations, nor those who use the gifts for personal power and glory. The spiritual are those who love and edify the body. ***All*** *revelations and manifestations are accountable to community discernment and correction,* because we "see in part, know in part".

- *The flesh versus the Spirit:* Paul's usage of "the flesh" has been misused to mean *our bodies* as sinful and worldly. "You are in the flesh, not in the Spirit, brother!" Legalism and asceticism supposedly help to "crucify the flesh" (punish the body). However, Paul uses "the flesh" to refer to an attitude of "the self" in rebellion – our fallen nature and corrupted appetites (Romans 5:5–8; Galatians 5:16–21). He also uses "flesh" to mean meat or body (not evil in itself), all people, or the frail and natural aspects of being human.

- *Spiritual realm versus earthly realm:* Paul's distinction of the unseen spiritual world and the seen physical world (2 Corinthians 4:16–18) is used to reinforce Gnostic dualism: the superior spiritual is eternal and the inferior material will "pass away". The Hebraic revelation is that God's material world was created "good" and "very good" (Genesis 1:4–31), and God will recreate the material world, "making everything new" (Revelation 21:5) after the resurrection of our bodies (Romans 8:19–23).

- *Fragmented versus wholistic human personality:* People use

1 Thessalonians 5:23 and Hebrews 4:12 to teach a tripartite understanding of the human person,[2] even dividing between soul and spirit, thoughts and intentions, defining each "part". This leads to a Gnostic fragmentation of human personality into superior and inferior "parts", autonomous "selves". Paul and Hebrews do not teach this. They use these Greek categories to insist on the Hebraic wholeness and complex unity of the human person, which only God's Word and Spirit can understand, penetrate and heal.

Other Gnostic tendencies

The following "symptoms" in themselves may not be Gnostic, but a few of them in the same person would point to Gnostic tendencies. The purpose of this list is to make us aware, not to use it in critical judgment against others. *It must not cause us to react against hearing from God, to doubt passionate prayer and spiritual warfare or to despise spiritual experiences and Spirit manifestations.*

- The obvious one: When a person despises and punishes their body through legalistic and ascetic practices in order to be more spiritual.
- Its opposite: The free indulgence of corrupted bodily appetites without conscience, believing that it doesn't matter because "God knows my heart".
- An air of superspirituality and elitism in constantly hearing from God for everything.
- Language and mentality that reveals a "stepladder" spirituality, ever wanting to attain "deeper" experiences or "higher" levels of revelation and holiness.
- A sense of secretiveness, mystique, intrigue, withdrawal – keeping their own counsel – implying, "If you really want to know, you can ask me."
- An unhealthy preoccupation and fascination with revelation,

---

[2] This is captured in a Gnostic slogan coined by E.W. Kenyon, popularised in Pentecostal/Charismatic circles via Kenneth Hagin and Kenneth Copeland: "I am a spirit being, I have a soul, and I live in my body." The biblical view is: "I am my body, soul and spirit, now and forever!"

angels, spiritual experiences and "words from the Lord".

- Forming a closed group of "like-minded" people, who engage in "deep spiritual warfare", revelatory experiences, intense practices and rituals. The giveaway is when they are no longer accountable to others – especially leadership – being exclusive and elitist, above correction.
- They create a sense of inferiority, guilt and self-doubt in others by their inferred superior spirituality, holiness or "hearing from God about everything".
- An implied judgment of others who do not understand or who disagree with the person's revelation, prophetic word or expressed spirituality.
- They judge, discredit and disqualify leaders who try to correct them, pointing to their "lack" of spiritual savvy, Spirit experiences and power.
- A critical or judgmental attitude based on measuring spirituality by outward criteria: how much we pray; how committed (intense) we are; how many spiritual experiences we have; how often we hear from God; how we dress; what we eat and drink, if we keep holy days and feasts.
- Using revelations, words, experiences and ministry to manipulate and control.
- The subjective, private and unaccountable nature of their experiences and revelations, and their inability to receive feedback, input or correction. The emotional defensiveness and aggression when confronted can point to past wounding and fear of rejection.
- Repeated dualisms in their talk, whether overt or implied, because "out of the abundance of the heart the mouth speaks". It reveals their division between:

Spiritual reality	Material reality
Spiritual realm (superior)	Earthly realm (inferior)
Heart (good, the Spirit, passion, truth, intuition)	Mind (questionable, bad, humanistic, rational, anti-Spirit)
Spirit (strong, holy, Spirit-control, of God)	"Flesh" (weak, physical, human control, sinful, worldly)
Spirit-led (free to do our own thing)	Leader-led (accountable and thus restricted and controlled)
Private (personal, unaccountable, subjective, in control)	Public (impersonal, objective, social construct, controlling)
Church (faith, the sacred, the spiritual, God's people)	Society (politics, the secular, worldly, "not my concern")

Appendix 2: Healing in the Old Testament

Genesis	1 Samuel	Psalms
20:17	6:3	6:2
	16:14–23	30:2
Exodus	25:6	32:3–5
4:6–7		34:19–20
15:26	**1 Kings**	38:3, 7
21:18–19	13:4–6	41:4
23:25	17:17–24	55:18
		103:1–5
Leviticus	**2 Kings**	107:17–20
13:1–46	2:19–22	147:3
14:1–32	4:8–37	
15:1–33	5:1–14	**Proverbs**
16:29–30	13:21	3:8
	20:1–11	4:22
Numbers		12:18
12:1–15	**2 Chronicles**	13:17
16:41–50	7:14	15:4, 30
21:4–9	20:9	16:24
	28:15	
Deuteronomy	30:20	**Ecclesiastes**
7:15	32:24–26	3:3
32:39		
	Job	**Isaiah**
Joshua	5:18	6:10
5:8		19:22

Isaiah cont.	30:12–17	Hosea
30:26	33:6	5:13
32:3–4	46:11	6:1
33:24	51:8–9	7:1
35:5–6		11:3
38:1–8, 16	**Lamentations**	14:4
53:5	2:13	
57:18–19		**Nahum**
58:6–8	**Ezekiel**	3:19
61:1	30:21	
	34:4, 16	**Zechariah**
Jeremiah	47:12	11:16
3:22		
8:15, 22	**Daniel**	**Malachi**
14:19	4:34, 36	4:2
17:14		

Appendix 3: The Healing Ministry of Jesus: Overview

Key			
A	Drove out demons	F	Preaching of Jesus
B	Word spoken	G	The person's faith
C	Touched by Jesus	H	Jesus moved by compassion
D	Prayer of another	I	The person touches Jesus
E	Faith of another	J	Teaching of Jesus

Appendices

	Description	Matthew	Mark	Luke	John	A	B	C	D	E	F	G	H	I	J
												Key page 333			
1	Man with unclean spirit		1:23	4:33		X	X								
2	Peter's mother-in-law	8:14	1:30	4:38			X	X	X						
3	Multitudes	8:16	1:32	4:40			X	X		X					
4	Many demons		1:34			X					X				
5	Leper	8:2	1:40	5:12			X	X				X	X		
6	Man with palsy	9:2	2:3	5:18			X			X					
7	Man with withered hand	12:10	3:1	6:6			X					X			
8	Multitudes	12:15	3:10			X									
9	Gadarenes demoniac	8:28	5:1	8:26		X	X								
10	Jairus' daughter	9:18	5:22	8:41			X	X		X					
11	Woman with issue of blood	9:20	5:25	8:43								X		X	
12	A few sick people	13:58	6:5					X							
13	Multitudes	14:34	6:55							X				X	
14	Syrophoenician's daughter	15:22	7:24						X	X					
15	Deaf and dumb man		7:32				X	X	X						
16	Blind man		8:22				X	X	X						
17	Child with evil spirit	17:14	9:14	9:38			X	X		X	X				

Appendix 3: *The healing ministry of Jesus: Overview*

	Description	Matthew	Mark	Luke	John	A	B	C	D	E	F	G	H	I	J
18	Blind Bartimaeus	20:30	10:46	18:35			X	X				X	X		
19	Centurion's servant	8:5		7:2					X	X					
20	Two blind men	9:27				X						X			
21	Dumb demoniac	9:32				X									
22	Blind and dumb demoniac	12:22		11:14		X									
23	Multitudes	4:23		6:17							X				X
24	Multitudes	9:35									X				X
25	Multitudes	11:7		7:21							X				X
26	Multitudes	14:14		9:11	6:2						X		X		
27	Great multitudes	15:30													X
28	Great multitudes	19:2													
29	Blind and lame in temple	21:14													
30	Widow's son			7:11		X	X								
31	Mary Magdalene and others			8:2									X		
32	Woman bound by Satan			13:10			X	X							
33	Man with dropsy			14:1			X	X							
34	Ten lepers			17:10		X						X			

Appendices

	Description	Matthew	Mark	Luke	John	A	B	C	D	E	F	G	H	I	J
35	Malchus' ear			22:50			X								
36	Multitudes			5:15											
37	Various persons			13:32		X									
38	Nobleman's son				4:46		X			X					
39	Impotent man				5:2		X								
40	Man born blind				9:1		X	X				X			
41	Lazarus				11:1		X								

Appendix 4: The book of Acts: Signs and wonders and the results

1. Speaking gifts – these occur four times (three in which the church grows)

Example	Result
Tongues – 2:4	3 000 added – 2:41
Tongues – 10:44	Baptised believers – 10:47
Prophecy (?) – 13:1	Church plants, 13 and 14.
Tongues/Prophecy – 19:1–7	Conversion of John the Baptist's disciples – 19:7

2. Visions – there are four recorded instances

Example	Result
Cornelius – 10:1	Baptised believers – 10:47
Peter – 10:9	Led to conversion of Cornelius
Paul, Macedonia man – 16:8	European churches
Paul – 18:9	Church at Corinth

3. Power Encounter – one is recorded between Paul and Elymas 13:4ff. Result – the Proconsul believed

4. Dead raised – two resuscitations are recorded

Example	Result
Dorcas – 9:36	Many believed – 9:42
Eutychus – 20:9	Great relief

Appendices

5. Miracles (Specific) – these occurred six times	
Example	Result
Ananias/Sapphira – 5:1–11	Fear – 5:12
Spirit caught up Philip – 8:39	Appeared and preached elsewhere
Paul blinded – 9:1–9a	His conversion
Blindness of Elymas – 13:11	Proconsul believed – 13:12
Paul stoned/raised – 14:19–23	Disciples – 14:21
Viper bites Paul – 28:3–10	Church established – not recorded in Acts but recorded in church history
6. Healings (Specific) – seven are recorded	
Example	Result
Lame man – 3:1	5 000 men – 4:4
Sick and unclean spirits – 5:16	Healed – 5:16
Paul's blindness healed – 9:1–9a	His baptism
Aeneas' paralysis healed by Peter – 9:32–35	All Lydda and Sharon turned to the Lord – 9:35
Lame man – Lystra – 14:8	Disciples – 14:21
Demon expelled – 16:6	Brethren – 16:40
Publius' father – fever/dysentery – 28:3–10	All sick on island healed – church started according to church history
7. Laying on of hands – this occurs five times	
Example	Result
Seven chosen – 6:6	Signs and wonders/Stephen – 6:8
Samaria/Receive Spirit – 8:17	Signs/Philip – 8:6; Simon brought in – 8:24
Ananias to Paul – 9:17	Paul healed and filled with the Spirit
Church to Paul and Barnabas – 13:1–3	Sent out, empowered to do church planting
Paul on Ephesian believers – 19:6	Received the Holy Spirit

Appendix 4: *The book of Acts: Signs and wonders and the results*

8. Sense phenomena – this occurs three times	
Example	**Result**
Sound like wind/tongues like fire – 2:4	3 000 converts – 2:41
Gate opens for Peter – 12:8f	Peter set free
Earthquake, fetters unfastened, doors opened – 16:25ff	Jailer converted – 16:34

9. Signs and wonders – these occur nine times, and are the most frequent. Luke refers to them (2:22) and records that they are the things which Jesus did while he was with the disciples. These would include healing, expelling demons, miracles with nature and food, raising the dead, being transported from one place to another.

Example	Result
By disciples – 2:43	Daily adding to church – 2:47
Power of God shown in mighty works – 4:33	(No reference to consequent church growth)
Hands of apostles – 5:12	Multitudes added – 5:14
Stephen – 6:8	Persecution, scattering of believers (evangelism) – 8:4
Philip – 8:6–7	Samaria church – 8:12
Hand of Lord with them 11:20–21 cf. 13:11	Great number believed and turned to the Lord – 11:21
Full of Spirit – 11:24–25 cf. Stephen – 6:8	Lord added to the church – 11:24
Paul and Barnabas – 14:1–7	Believers – 14:4, 20
Extraordinary miracles/teaching at Ephesus – 19:11	All churches in book of Revelation started during these two years

10. Angelic visitation – three are recorded.	
Example	**Result**
Philip – 8:26	Baptised eunuch – 8:38
Peter – 12:7–9	Released from prison
Paul – 27:23–26	People saved from drowning

Appendices

11. Signs/wonders and preaching and church growth

Signs and wonders	Preaching	Church growth
2:4–12	2:14–36	2:41, Jerusalem church plant
3:1–10	3:11–26; 4:2	4:4, Jerusalem church growth
5:12, 15–16	5:20–21, 42	5:14, 16, growth beyond Jerusalem
6:5–6, 8	6:7, 10, 7:2ff	6:7, more growth – among priests
8:6–7, 13	8:4–6	8:8, 12, Samaria church plant
8:26–30	8:35	8:38, Ethiopian eunuch believes
10:3–7, 9–20, 44	10:34–43	10:47, Gentiles believe
11:21	11:20	11:21, Antioch church planted
11:24–25	11:25–26	11:24b, Antioch church growth
13:1–3, 6–12	13:5, 16f	13:44, 48–49, the Gentile mission
14:3	14:1, 3	14:4, 21–22, Iconium church plant
14:8–18	14:7, 15	14:21–22, Lystra, Derbe church plants
16:16–18, 25–26	16:29–32	16:34, 40, Philippi church plant
18:1, Corinth cf. 1 Cor 2:4–5	18:4–5, 11	18:8–10, 18, Corinth church plant
19:11–12	19:8–9	19:10, Ephesus and Asian plants

Bibliography

Alblas, J.T. *A Different Breed* (E-Publication, Cape Town: VIP, 2006).
Augsburger, David. *Caring Enough to Confront: How to Understand and Express Your Deepest Feelings towards Others* (Ventura: Regal Books, 1983).
Backus, William. *Telling Yourself the Truth: The Principles of Misbelief Therapy* (Minneapolis: Bethany House Publishers, 1985); *Telling the Truth to Troubled People: A Manual for Christian Counselors* (Minneapolis: Bethany House Publishers, 1985).
Barclay, William. *And He Had Compassion* (Edinburgh: The Saint Andrew Press, 1975).
Barker, Joel. *Future Edge: Discovering the New Paradigms of Success* (New York: William Morrow and Company, Inc., 1992).
Barry, William. *Spiritual Direction and the Encounter with God* (New York: Paulist Press, 1992).
Barry, William & Connoly, William. *The Practice of Spiritual Direction* (San Francisco: HarperSanFrancisco, 1982).
Basham, Don. *A Manual for Spiritual Warfare: Questions and Answers on Christian Exorcism* (Pennsylvania: Manna Books, 1974).
Bateson, Gregory. *Steps to an Ecology of Mind* (Chicago: University of Chicago Press, 2000).
Baxter, Sidlow. *Divine Healing of the Body* (Grand Rapids: Zondervan, 1979).
Beattie, Melody. *Codependent No More: How to Stop Controlling Others and Start Caring for Yourself* (San Francisco: Harper & Row, 1987).
Becker, Ernest. *The Denial of Death* (New York: Free Press, 1973).
Berger, Peter & Luckmann, Thomas. *The Social Construction of Reality: A Treatise in the Sociology of Knowledge* (Garden City: Doubleday, 1966).
Berkouwer, G.C. *Studies in Dogmatics – Man: The Image of God* (Grand Rapids: Eerdmans, 1962).
Berne, Eric. *Games People Play* (New York: Grove Press, 1964).
Best, Gary. *Naturally Supernatural: Joining God in His Work* (Cape Town: Vineyard International Publishing, 2005).
Best, Gary & Davids, Peter. *Implications of the Kingdom* (Cape Town: Vineyard Bible Institute, 2000).
Blamires, Harry. *The Christian Mind: How Should a Christian Think?* (London: SPCK, 1963).
Bloch, Marc. *The Royal Touch* (New York: Dorset Press, 1989).
Blue, Ken. *Authority to Heal* (Downers Grove: IVP, 1987).
Blue, Ken & White, John. *Healing the Wounded: The Costly Love of Church Discipline* (Downers Grove: IVP, 1985).
Bly, Robert. *The Sibling Society* (London: Hamish Hamilton, 1996).

Borg, Marcus. *Jesus: A New Vision* (San Francisco: Harper, 1991).
Bosch, David. *A Spirituality of the Road* (Scottdale: Herald Press, 1979); *Witness to the World* (Atlanta: John Knox Press, 1980); *Transforming Missions: Paradigm Shifts in Theology of Mission* (New York: Orbis Books, 1991).
Bosworth, F.F. *Christ the Healer*, 9th ed. (Old Tappan: Fleming Revel Company, 2000).
Bradshaw, John. *Healing the Shame That Binds You* (Deerfield Beach: Health Communications Inc., 1988).
Brother Lawrence, *Practicing the Presence* (Albany: Books for the Ages, Ages Software, 1996).
Brown, Colin. *Philosophy and the Christian Faith* (Downers Grove: IVP, 1968); *Miracles and the Critical Mind* (Grand Rapids: Eerdmans, 1984).
Brown, Colin (ed.). "Heal", "Might", "Authority", "Throne", "Miracle", "Wonder", "Sign", in *The New International Dictionary of New Testament Theology*, vol. 2 (Exeter: Paternoster Press, 1978).
Brown, Michael. "Israel's Divine Healer", *Studies in Old Testament Biblical Theology* (Grand Rapids: Zondervan, 1995).
Brueggemann, Walter. *Living Toward a Vision: Biblical Reflections on Shalom* (New York: United Church Press, 1976); *The Land – Place as Gift, Promise, and Challenge in Biblical Faith* (Minneapolis: Fortress Press, 2002).
Buchan, Angus & Waldeck, Val. *Faith Like Potatoes* (Greytown: Shalom Ministries, 1998).
Burns, Robert. *Revivals: Their Laws and Leaders* (London: Hodder, 1909).
Calvin, John. *Institutes of the Christian Religion.* Trans. Henry Beveridge (Christian Classics Ethereal Library, 1998).
Chandler, Russell. *Understanding the New Age* (Dallas: Word Inc., 1988).
Coenen, L. & Schmithals, W. "Death", *The New International Dictionary of Testament Theology*, vol. 1 (Exeter: Paternoster Press, 1975).
Copeland, Gloria. *God's Will for Your Healing* (Forth Worth: Kenneth Copeland Publications, 1972).
Crabb, Larry. *Connecting: A Radical New Vision* (London: Word Publishing, 1997).
Creig, Gary & Springer, Kevin. *The Kingdom and the Power* (Ventura: Regal, 1993).
Darling, Frank. *Christian Healing in the Middle Ages and Beyond* (Boulder: Vista Productions, 1990).
DeArteaga, William. *Quenching the Spirit: Examining Centuries of Opposition to the Moving of the Holy Spirit* (Florida: Creation House, 1992).
Deere, Jack. *Surprised by the Power of the Spirit* (Eastbourne: Kingsway, 1993).
De Vinck, Christopher (ed.). *Nouwen Then: Personal Reflections on Henri* (Grand Rapids: Zondervan, 1999).

Dixon, Patrick. *Signs of Revival* (Eastbourne: Kingsway, 1994).
Drane, John. *What Is the New Age Saying to the Church?* (Great Britain: Marshall Pickering, 1991).
Edwards, Jonathan. *The Works of Jonathan Edwards,* vol. 1 (Edinburgh: Banner of Truth, 1979).
Endicott, Mike. *Healing at the Well* (Great Britain: Terra Nova Publications, 2000); *The Passion to Heal* (Great Britain: Terra Nova Publications, 2003); *Christian Healing* (Great Britain: Terra Nova Publications, 2004).
Erwin, Howard. *These Are not Drunken As Ye Suppose* (New Jersey: Plainfield, 1968).
Fee, Gordon. The First Epistle to the Corinthians, *The New International Commentary on the New Testament* (Grand Rapids: Eerdmans, 1987); *God's Empowering Presence: The Holy Spirit in the Letters of Paul* (Peabody: Hendrickson Publishers, 1994).
Fiddes, Paul. *The Creative Suffering of God* (Oxford: Clarendon Press, 1988); *Participating in God: A Pastoral Doctrine of the Trinity* (London: Darton, Longman & Todd, 2000).
Foster, David. *Sexual Healing: God's Plan for the Sanctification of Broken Lives* (Hermitage: Mastering Life Ministries, 1998).
Frankl, Viktor. *Man's Search for Meaning: An Introduction to Logotherapy* (London: Hodder & Stoughton, 1964).
Friesen, James G. *Uncovering the Mystery of MPD* (Oregon: Wipf and Stock Publishers, 1997).
Frost, Evelyn. *Christian Healing: A Consideration of the Place of Spiritual Healing in the Church of Today in the Light of the Doctrine and Practice of the Ante-Nicene Church* (London: A.R. Mowbray, 1940).
Gillet, Archimandrite Leviticus. *The Jesus Prayer* (New York: St Vladimir's Seminary Press, 1987).
Goleman, Daniel. *Emotional Intelligence: Why It Can Matter More Than IQ* (London: Bloomsbury Publishing, 1995).
Gordon, A.J. *The Ministry of Healing* (Harrisburg: Christian Publications, 1882).
Green, Michael. *I Believe in Satan's Downfall* (Grand Rapids: Eerdmans, 1981).
Grunland, Stephan & Lambrides, Daniel. *Healing Relationship: A Christian's Manual for Lay Counseling* (Pennsylvania: Christian Publications, 1984).
Hagin, Kenneth. *Healing Belongs to Us* (Tulsa: Kenneth E. Hagin Evangelistic Association, 1977).
Harrel, David. *All Things Are Possible* (Bloomington: Indiana University Press, 1975).
Harris, Russ. *Christ-Centered Therapy: Empowering the Self* (New York: The Haworth Press, 2002).

Harris, Thomas. *I'm OK – You're OK* (New York: Avon Books, 1967).
Hart, Archibald. *Healing Life's Hidden Addictions* (Ann Arbor: Servant Publications, 1990).
Hiebert, Paul. "The Flaw of the Excluded Middle". *Missiology: An International Review,* American Society of Missiology, vol. X, no. 1, January 1982.
Horrobin, Peter. *Healing Through Deliverance, vol. 1. The Biblical Basis* (Tonbridge: Sovereign Word, 1994); *Healing Through Deliverance, vol. 2. The Practical Ministry* (Tonbridge: Sovereign Word, 1995).
Hughes, Philip. The Second Epistle to the Corinthians, *The New International Commentary on the New Testament* (Grand Rapids: Eerdmans, 1962).
Hunt, Dave & McMahon, T.A. *The Seduction of Christianity* (Oregon: Harvest House, 1985).
Jackson, Bill. *The Quest for the Radical Middle: A History of the Vineyard* (Cape Town: VIP, 1999).
Jamison, Christopher. *Finding Sanctuary* (Minnesota: Liturgical Press, 2006).
Janse van Rensburg, Johan. *The Paradigm Shift: An Introduction to Postmodern Thought and Its Implications for Theology* (Pretoria: Van Schaik, 2000).
Jenkins, Philip. *The Next Christendom: The Coming of Global Christianity* (New York: Oxford University Press, 2002).
Josephus. *The Works of Josephus: Complete and Unabridged.* Trans. William Whiston (Peabody: Hendrickson Publishers, 1987).
Keating, Thomas, Pennington, Basil & Clark, Thomas. *Finding Grace at the Center* (Massachusetts: St Bede Publications, 1978).
Keener, Craig. *Gift and Giver: The Holy Spirit Today* (Grand Rapids: Baker Academic, 2001).
Kelsey, Morton. *Encounter with God – A Theology of Christian Experience* (Minneapolis: Bethany, 1972); *Healing and Christianity* (San Francisco: Harper & Row, 1973); *The Christian and the Supernatural* (Minneapolis: Augsburg, 1976); *Discernment – A Study of Ecstasy and Evil* (New York: Paulist Press, 1978); *Inward Adventure* (Minneapolis: Augsburg, 1980); *Christo-Psychology* (London: Darton, Longman & Todd, 1982); *Psychology, Medicine and Christian Healing* (San Francisco: Harper & Row, 1988).
Kissel, Barry. *Walking on Water: Rediscovering the Supernatural in the Life of the Church* (London: Hodder & Stoughton, 1986); *The King Is Among Us: Learning to Minister in the Power of the Holy Spirit* (London: Hodder & Stoughton, 1992).
König, Adrio. *The Eclipse of Christ in Eschatology – Towards a Christ-Centered Approach* (Grand Rapids: Eerdmans, 1989).
Koyama, Kosuke. *No Handle on the Cross* (Maryknoll: Orbis, 1977).
Kraft, Charles. *Christianity with Power: Your Worldview and Your Experience*

of the Supernatural (Ann Arbor: Servant Publications, 1989).

Kübler-Ross, Elizabeth. *On Death and Dying* (New York: MacMillan, 1969); *Death: The Final Stage of Growth* (New Jersey: Prentice Hall, 1975).

Kuhn, Thomas. *The Structure of Scientific Revolutions* (Chicago: University of Chicago Press, 1970).

Ladd, G.E. *The Presence of the Future* (Grand Rapids: Eerdmans, 1974).

Lane, William. The Gospel of Mark, *The New London Commentary Series* (London: Marshall, Morgan and Scott, 1974).

Lederle, Henry. *Treasures Old and New: Interpretations of "Spirit-Baptism" in the Charismatic Renewal Movement* (Peabody: Hendrickson, 1988).

Leman, Kevin & Carlson, Randy. *Unlocking the Secrets of your Childhood Memories* (Nashville: Thomas Nelson Publishers, 1989).

Leuner, H. "Guided Affected Imagery", *American Journal of Psychotherapy*, 1969, 23.

Lewis, C.S. *The Problem of Pain* (London: Fontana Books, 1957); *Miracles: A Preliminary Study* (New York: Macmillan Publishing, 1977).

Linn, Dennis & Matthew. *Healing of Memories: Prayer and Confession Steps to Inner Healing* (New York: Paulist Press, 1974); *Healing Life's Hurts: Healing Memories through Five Stages of Forgiveness* (New York: Paulist Press, 1978).[1]

Livesey, Roy. *Understanding Alternative Medicine: Holistic Health in the New Age* (Chichester: New Wine Press, 1985).

MacArthur, John Jr. *Charismatic Chaos* (Grand Rapids: Zondervan, 1992).

MacMurray, John. *The Self as Agent* (London: Faber & Faber, 1957).

MacNutt, Francis. *Healing* (Notre Dame: Ave Maria, 1974); *Power to Heal* (Notre Dame: Ave Maria, 1977); *Deliverance from Evil Spirits: A Practical Manual* (Grand Rapids: Chosen Books, 1995); *The Nearly Perfect Crime: How the Church Almost Killed the Ministry of Healing* (Grand Rapids: Chosen, 2005).

Maddox, Morris. *The Christian Healing Ministry* (London: SPCK, 1981).

Maloney, George. *Death Where Is Your Sting?* (New York: Alba House, 1984); *Discovering the Hidden Reality – A Journey into Christian Mystical Prayer* (New York: Alba House, 2004).

Malz, Betty. *My Glimpse of Eternity* (New Jersey: Chosen Books, 1977).

Mangalwadi, Vishal. *In Search of Self: Beyond the New Age* (London: Spire, 1992).

Markides, Kyriacos. *The Mountain of Silence: A Search for Orthodox Spirituality* (New York: Image Books, 2001).

Marshall, Howard. *Luke, Historian and Theologian* (Exeter: Paternoster Press, 1970); The Acts of the Apostles, *New Testament Guides* (Sheffield:

---

[1] The Linn brothers have written many books on most forms/dimensions of healing. I have merely listed two of their earlier well-known books.

Academic Press, 1997)

Marshall, Paul, Griffioen, Sander & Mouw, Richard (eds.). *Stained Glass: Worldviews and Social Science* (Lanham: University Press of America, 1989).

Masters, Peter. *The Healing Epidemic* (London: Wakeman Trust, 1988).

May, Gerald. *Addiction and Grace: Love and Spirituality in the Healing of Addictions* (San Francisco: HarperSanFrancisco, 1988).

McDonnel, Killian & Montague, George. *Christian Initiation and Baptism in the Holy Spirit: Evidence from the First Eight Centuries*, 2nd ed. (Collegeville: Liturgical Press, 1994).

Montgomery, John Warwick (ed.). *Demon Possession* (Minneapolis: Bethany House Publishers, 1976).

Moody, Raymond. *Life after Life* (Atlanta: Mocking Bird Books, 1975); *Reflection on Life after Life* (New York: Bantam-Mocking Bird, 1977).

Morphew, Derek. *Breakthrough – Discovering the Kingdom* (Cape Town: VIP, 1991); *The Spiritual Spider Web* (E-Publication, Cape Town: VIP, 2003).

Morris, Leon. The Gospel According to John, *New London Commentaries* (London: Marshall, Morgan and Scott, 1971).

Nathan, Rich & Wilson, Ken. *Empowered Evangelicals: Bringing Together the Best of the Evangelical & Charismatic Worlds* (Columbus: Vineyard Church of Columbus, 1995).

Naugle, David. *Worldview: The History of a Concept* (Grand Rapids: Eerdmans, 2002).

Nietzsche, Frederick. *Beyond Good and Evil*, trans. Helen Zimmern (London, 1907).

Nouwen, Henri. *The Wounded Healer* (New York: Image Books, 1979); *In the Name of Jesus: Reflections on Christian Leadership* (New York: Crossroad, 1989).

Oden, Thomas C. *The Rebirth of Orthodoxy: Signs of New Life in Christianity* (San Francisco: Harper, 2003).

Ornish, Dean. *Love and Survival: How Good Relationship Can Bring You Health and Well-Being* (London: Vermillion, 1998).

Osborn, T.L. *Healing the Sick* (Tulsa: OSFO Foundation, 1959).

Osis, K. & Haraldson, E. *Deathbed Observations by Physicians and Nurses: A Cross-Cultural Survey* (New York: Parapsychology Foundations, 1962); *At the Hour of Death* (New York: Avon Press, 1977).

Padovani, Martin. *Healing Wounded Emotions: Overcoming Life's Hurts* (Mumbai: St Paul Press, 1987).

Palmer, Parker. *Leading from Within: Reflections on Spirituality and Leadership* (Washington D.C.: Servant Leadership School, 1992).

Payne, Leanne. *The Broken Image* (Wheaton: Crossway Books, 1981); *The*

Healing Presence (Wheaton: Crossway Books, 1989); *Restoring the Christian Soul: Overcoming Barriers to Completion in Christ through Healing Prayer* (Grand Rapids: Baker Books, 1991); *Real Presence* (Grand Rapids: Baker Books, 1995).

Peterson, Eugene. *A Long Obedience in the Same Direction* (Downer Groves: IVP, 1980); *Answering God: The Psalms as Tools for Prayer* (San Francisco: HarperSanFrancisco, 1989); *Eat This Book: A Conversation in the Art of Spiritual Reading* (Grand Rapids: Eerdmans, 2006).

Pfeifer, Samuel. *Healing at Any Price? The Hidden Dangers of Alternative Medicine* (Milton Keyes: Word Publishing, 1988).

Philips, Vera & Robertson, Edwin. *The Wounded Healer: J.B. Philips* (London: Triangle SPCK, 1984).

Prince, Derek. *Faith to Live by* (Fort Lauderdale: Derek Prince Publications, 1977); *Blessing to Curse: You Can Choose!* (New Jersey: Chosen Books, 1990); *They Shall Expel Demons* (Tamil Nadu: Rhema Books, 1998); *Derek Prince on Experiencing God's Power* (Pennsylvania: Whitaker House, 1998).[2]

Pytches, Mary. *A Healing Fellowship* (London: Hodder & Stoughton, 1988).

Rahner, Karl S.J. *On the Theology of Death* (New York: Herder & Herder, 1961).

Ratzinger, Joseph. *Jesus of Nazareth* (New York: Doubleday, 2007).

Rawlings, Maurice. *Beyond Death's Door* (Nashville: Nelson, 1978); *To Hell and Back: Life after Death – Startling New Evidence* (Nashville: Nelson, 1993).

Richards, John. *But Deliver Us from Evil: An Introduction to the Demonic in Pastoral Care* (New York: Seabury Press, 1974).

Roberts, Dave. *The 'Toronto' Blessing* (Eastbourne: Kingsway, 1994).

Roberts, Oral. *If You Need Healing, Do These Things!* (Tulsa: Healing Waters Inc, 1952).

Rolheiser, Ronald. *Against an Infinite Horizon* (New York: Crossroads, 1995).

Sandford, John & Paula. *The Transformation of the Inner Man* (Tulsa: Victory House, 1982); *Healing the Wounded Spirit* (Tulsa: Victory House, 1985).

Sanford, Agnes. *The Healing Power of the Bible* (New York: Trumpet Books, 1969).

Satinover, Jeffrey. *The Empty Self: C.G. Jung and the Gnostic Transformation of Modern Identity* (Westport: Hamewith Books, 1996).

Scanlan, Michael. *Inner Healing* (New York: Paulist Press, 1974).

Scanlan, Michael & Cirner, Randall. *Deliverance from Evil Spirits: A Weapon for Spiritual Warfare* (Ann Arbor: Servant Books, 1980).

---

[2]This is a compendium of Derek's shorter books on the Holy Spirit, healing, rejection, fasting, and spiritual warfare.

Schaeffer, Francis. *How Then Shall We Live?* (Old Tappen: Revell, 1976).
Seamands, David. *The Healing of Memories* (Wheaton: Victor Books, 1985).
Simpson, A.B. *The Gospel of Healing* (New York: Christian Alliance Publishing, 1915).
Sire, James. *The Universe Next Door: A Basic Worldview Catalog* (Downers Grove: IVP, 1976).
Smith, Edward. *Healing Life's Hurts through Theophostic Prayer* (Ann Arbor: Vine Books, 2002).
Smith, John. E. *Experience and God* (New York: Oxford, 1968).
Springer, Kevin (ed.). *Power Encounters Among Christians in the Western World* (San Francisco: Harper & Row, 1988).
Stapleton, R.C. *The Gift of Inner Healing* (Waco: Word Books, 1976).
Stendahl, Krister. *Paul among Jews and Gentiles and Other Essays* (Philadelphia: Fortress Press, 1976).
Stibbe, Mark. *Prophetic Evangelism: When God Speaks to Those Who Don't Know Him* (London: Authentic Media, 2004).
Tapscott, B. *Inner Healing through Healing of Memories* (Houston: Tapscott, 1975).
Trocmé, André. *Jesus and the Non-violent Revolution* (Scottdale: Herald Press, 1973).
Tucker, Gareth & Flagg, David. *A Question of Healing: Reflections of a Doctor and a Priest* (London: Fount Paperbacks, 1995).
Twelftree, Graham H. *Jesus the Miracle Worker: A Historical and Theological Study* (Downers Grove: IVP, 1999).
Van Huyssteen, Wenzel. *Theology and the Justification of Faith: Constructing Theories in Systematic Theology* (Grand Rapids: Eerdmans, 1989).
Venter, Alexander. *Doing Church: Building from the Bottom up,* (Cape Town: VIP, 2000); *Doing Reconciliation: Racism, Reconciliation and Transformation in Church and World* (Cape Town: VIP, 2004).
Von Balthasar, Hans Urs. *Prayer* (New York: Paulist Press, 1967).
Walsh, Brian & Middleton, Richard. *The Transforming Vision: Shaping a Christian Worldview* (Downers Grove: IVP, 1984).
Warfield, Benjamin. *Counterfeit Miracles* (Edinburgh: Banner of Truth, 1972).
White, John. *When the Spirit Comes with Power: Signs and Wonders among God's People* (London: Hodder & Stoughton, 1988).
Willard, Dallas. *The Spirit of the Disciplines: Understanding How God Changes Lives* (San Francisco: Harper, 1988); *In Search of Guidance: Developing a Conversational Relationship with God* (San Francisco: Harper, 1993).
Wimber, John. *Living with Uncertainty: My Bout with Inoperable Cancer* (Anaheim: Vineyard Ministries International, 1996); *Signs and Wonders and Church Growth, Parts 1 & 2* (Anaheim: VMI, 1984); *Healing vol. 4: Models and Methodology* (Yorba Linda: VCF, 1982).

Wimber, John with Springer, Kevin. *Power Evangelism: Signs and Wonders Today* (San Francisco: Harper & Row, 1986); *Power Healing* (London: Hodder & Stoughton, 1986).

Wright, Henry W. *A More Excellent Way: Be in Health* (Thomaston: Pleasant Valley Publications, 1999).

Wright, N.T. *Bringing the Church to the World: Renewing the Church to Confront the Paganism Entrenched in Western Culture* (Minneapolis: Bethany House, 1992); *The New Testament and the People of God* (Minneapolis: Fortress Press, 1992); *Jesus and the Victory of God* (Minneapolis: Fortress Press, 1996); *The Challenge of Jesus* (London: SPCK, 2000); *The Resurrection of the Son of God* (London: SPCK, 2003).

Yancey, Philip & Brand, Paul. *The Gift of Pain* (Grand Rapids: Eerdmans, 1993).

Yoder, John Howard. *The Politics of Jesus – Behold the Man! Our Victorious Lamb*, 2nd ed. (Grand Rapids: Eerdmans, 1994).

Endorsements for *Doing Healing*:

Careful and sound kingdom theology, great storytelling about real, verified healings and life combine to make this a major textbook on healing. I suspect it will become a standard work in many places, for theological formulation and practical training.

– **Derek Morphew**, Director, Vineyard Biblical Institute

If you are looking for a comprehensive treatment of the ministry of healing, you will not find a better book than Venter's Doing Healing. *Our church has been involved in praying for the sick for over two decades. Yet even with this experience, I found an extraordinary amount of fresh, helpful material in Venter's book. Written in an extremely winsome style, Venter thoughtfully examines how we can all partner with Jesus to bring healing to our broken world. Whether you are a veteran in the ministry of healing, or just beginning to explore this subject,* Doing Healing *is a deep reservoir from which we all can draw wisdom. I'm grateful for this wonderful addition to the literature on healing ministry.*

– **Rich Nathan**, Senior Pastor, Columbus Vineyard, teacher and author

Alexander Venter's book on healing, Doing Healing, *is a masterpiece, one which I shall carry in our three different Schools of Healing and Impartation. I love the way he teaches through stories, but doesn't allow the storytelling process to reduce the content to pure testimonies only. There are powerful insights from biblical studies and theology. That is one reason I think it should be considered a masterpiece. Since I too was most strongly influenced by John Wimber and Francis MacNutt's books and writings, it is a great privilege to endorse this* Doing Healing. *Whoever is interested in the ministry of healing should make sure they own this book. I shall include it on our students' required reading for our Global School of Supernatural Ministry at our headquarters. I shall encourage all my personal interns to read it as soon as it is available.*

– **Randy Clark**, Founder of Global Awakening and Apostolic Overseer of the Apostolic Network of Global Awakening, a network of pastors and itinerate ministers

I know many Christians who, for all practical purposes, have given up on healing. Healing, for many people, is attached to "Charismatic" Christianity. So much weird stuff has happened in the name of "Charismatic" Christianity

that reasonable people have deduced that there is no sensible way to pursue healing through the power of the Spirit as an aspect of the kingdom of God. Thankfully, Alexander Venter's life, thoughtfulness and practice combine to form a bright light which illumines a way forward – a way that honours God, respects people, is non-manipulative, non-superstitious and wholistic in its approach. I hope Doing Healing *revives the healing faith of millions of Christians and thousands of churches.*

– **Todd Hunter**, Former Director, Vineyard Churches USA, President, *Three is Enough Groups*, Church Planter, *Anglican Mission in the Americas: West Coast*

For over twenty years Alexander Venter has been a dear friend, colleague and teacher in Christian ministry. I have heard him on numerous occasions boldly proclaim the availability of the kingdom of God and minister powerfully to those who are sick and wounded. I have constantly been struck by the clarity of his preaching and the effectiveness of his ministry. When it comes to the healing ministry of Jesus Christ, he is both a thoughtful theologian and a committed practitioner. Anyone with a desire to share in Christ's healing ministry will find this book a treasure house of biblical insight, practical wisdom and warm encouragement. I commend it warmly to both individuals and groups who want to embark on a serious study of this essential ministry of the local congregation.

– **Trevor Hudson**, Methodist minister, author, conference speaker and retreat leader

I have found Doing Healing *invaluable in the training of my students and in my own ministry of healing. As the distillation of Alexander's years of work in this field, it is a gift to the church. It is a rare combination of teaching (theology and right thinking are essential to the author), personal companionship (Alexander journeys with the reader by his honest self-revelation), invitation to intimacy (Christ's invitation to closer relationship is core to understanding healing) and wise coaching (Alexander's writing comes from years of lived experience and impartation to others). My understanding of healing was sharpened and deepened, my hunger to taste God renewed, and my desire to embody the Spirit's healing presence strengthened and confirmed.*

– **Vic Graham**, Pastoral Theologian, College of the Transfiguration, Grahamstown, South Africa

I have been teaching on the themes of the kingdom of God, spiritual gifts, healing and deliverance for over twenty years and have always thought of writing a book to provide students with a succinct overview of these biblical themes combined with practical application. Now I don't have to write it. Alexander Venter has given us that one book that will show people how to continue the ministry of Jesus. Doing Healing *is very good scholarship, very thorough and very practical. It is a must-have for all church bookstores and should be required reading for all those hoping to enter into the power aspects of Jesus' ministry.*

– **Bill Jackson**, Academic Dean & Professor, Trinity Learning Community and Teaching Pastor, Inland Vineyard, Corona, California

Anyone who dares to embrace the healing ministry of Jesus will battle doubt and discouragement – both within and without. Alexander's book is a tremendous gift to help us to understand our call to healing, to live in its reality and to freely give it away. It is filled with wisdom, experience and faith and I know that I will literally wear out my copy!

– **Gary Best**, National Team Leader, Vineyard Churches, Canada

Readers may differ on some points, but Venter's kingdom approach happily avoids the extremes of antisupernaturalism and 'claiming' all healings. Venter writes with moving compassion and humble transparency, and I have learned from its examples and its spirit some principles valuable for ministry.

– **Craig Keener**, Professor, Eastern Seminary, USA; Biblical Scholar